D1548560

The End of the Pacific War

THE END OF THE

PACIFIC WAR

Reappraisals

EDITED BY

Tsuyoshi Hasegawa

Stanford University Press, Stanford, California, 2007

Stanford University Press
Stanford, California
© 2007 by the Board of Trustees of the
Leland Stanford Junior University

Library of Congress Cataloging-in-Publication Data

The end of the Pacific war : reappraisals / edited by Tsuyoshi Hasegawa.
    p. cm. — (Stanford nuclear age series)
  Includes bibliographical references and index.
  ISBN-13: 978-0-8047-5427-9 (cloth : alk. paper)
  1. World War, 1939–1945—Armistices. 2. World War, 1939–1945—
Japan. 3. World War, 1939–1945—Soviet Union. 4. World War, 1939–
1945—United States. I. Hasegawa, Tsuyoshi.

D813.J3E64 2007
940.53'52—dc22   2006028407

Printed in the United States of America
on acid-free, archival-quality paper.

Typeset in 10/12.5 Times Roman

For ROBERT J. P. BUTOW, *whose book published more than half a century ago has greatly benefited us all*

The Stanford
Nuclear Age Series

Conceived by scientists, delivered by the military, and adopted by policymakers, nuclear weapons emerged from the ashes of Hiroshima and Nagasaki to dominate our time. The politics, diplomacy, economy, and culture of the Cold War nurtured the nuclear arms race and, in turn, have been altered by it. "We have had the bomb on our minds since 1945," E. L. Doctorow observes. "It was first our weaponry and then our diplomacy, and now it's our economy. How can we suppose that something so monstrously powerful would not, after forty years, compose our identity? The great golem we have made against our enemies is our culture, our bomb culture—its logic, its faith, its vision."

The pervasive, transformative potential of nuclear weapons was foreseen by their creators. When Secretary of War Henry L. Stimson assembled a committee in May 1945 to discuss postwar atomic energy planning, he spoke of the atomic bomb as a "revolutionary change in the relations of man to the universe." Believing that it could mean "the doom of civilization," he warned President Truman that this weapon "has placed a certain moral responsibility upon us which we cannot shirk without very serious responsibility for any disaster to civilization."

In the decades since World War II that responsibility has weighed heavily on American civilization. Whether or not we have met it is a matter of heated debate. But that we must meet it, and, moreover, that we must also prepare the next generation of leaders to meet it as well, is beyond question.

Today, over half a century into the nuclear age the pervasive impact of the nuclear arms race has stimulated a fundamental reevaluation of the role of nuclear armaments and strategic policies. But mainstream scholarly work in strategic studies has tended to focus on questions related to the developments, the deployment, and the diplomacy of nuclear arsenals. Such an exclusively managerial focus cannot probe the universal revolutionary changes about which Stimson spoke, and the need to address these changes is urgent. If the academic community is to contribute imaginatively and helpfully to the increasingly complex problems of the nuclear age, then the base of scholarship and pedagogy in the national security–arms control field must be broadened. It is this goal that the Stanford Nuclear Age Series is intended to support, with paperback reissues of important out-of-print works and original publication of new scholarship in the humanities and social sciences.

Martin J. Sherwin
General Editor

Contents

Maps and Table

Maps

Table

Acknowledgments

Many institutions and individuals have contributed to producing this volume. Above all, I would like to thank the Center for Cold War Studies at the University of California at Santa Barbara for supporting the initial conference in 2001 and extending continuing support for producing this volume. We received generous financial support from the University of California Institute for Global Conflict and Cooperation (IGCC), the University of California Pacific Rim Program, the Interdisciplinary Humanities Center, the Department of History, and Global and International Studies Program at UC Santa Barbara. I especially thank David Marshall, dean of humanities and fine arts at UC Santa Barbara, who extended general financial support for the conference and has been a steadfast supporter of the Center for Cold War Studies.

I also thank the late Boris Slavinsky, Martin Sherwin, Tom Maddux, Roger Dingman, James Hershberg, Fredrik Logevall, and Vladislav Zubok, who participated in the initial conference. In particular, Fredrik Logevall, who, as co-director of the Center for Cold War Studies at UC Santa Barbara, before he moved to Cornell University, was the inspiration for this project.

But most of all, I would like to thank all the contributors for their patience, understanding, and the civility with which they have treated the editor, despite constant delays and requests for revisions.

The unsung heroes of this project are the late John Coleman, who died of cancer two years after he superbly organized this conference, and Debra Nash, who managed the shoe-string budget, always with a cheerful smile.

Finally, I would like to thank Muriel Bell, Kirsten Oster, Peter Dreyer, and John Feneron of Stanford University Press for their patience and their confidence in the volume.

T.H.

Contributors

BARTON J. BERNSTEIN is professor of history at Stanford University, specializing in modern U.S. history, with emphases on international relations, crises and decision making, nuclear history, and some issues in science, technology, and medicine. His numerous publications on the atomic bomb issue are listed in the Select Bibliography.

RICHARD B. FRANK is an independent scholar. His major publications are *Guadalcanal* (1990), which won the General Wallace C. Greene Jr. Award from the Marine Corps Historical Foundation, and *Downfall: The End of the Imperial Japanese Empire* (1999), which won the Harry S. Truman Book Award. He recently contributed to PBS and BBC programs on the end of the Pacific War.

TSUYOSHI HASEGAWA is professor in the Department of History and the co-director of the Center for Cold War Studies at the University of California at Santa Barbara. Born in Tokyo in the year the Pacific War began, he received his B.A. in international relations at Tokyo University and his M.A. in Soviet Area Studies and Ph.D. in history at the University of Washington. He taught at the State University of New York at Oswego and at the Slavic Research Center of Hokkaidō University before he moved to the University of California at Santa Barbara in 1990. Specializing both in the Russian Revolution and in Russo-Japanese Relations, he has written *The February Revolution: Petrograd 1917* (1981); *Daily Life of Petrograd During the Russian Revolution* (1989; in Japanese); *The Northern Territories Dispute and Russo-Japanese Relations*, 2 vols. (1998), which received the Ohira Masayoshi Memorial Prize for 1999, its revised Japanese version (2000), *Racing the Enemy: Stalin, Truman, and the Surrender of Japan* (2005), which received the Robert Ferrell Book Prize from the Society of Historians of American Foreign Relations in 2006, and its revised translation into Japanese: *Antō: Sutarin, Toruman to Nihon no kōfuku* (2006), which received the 7th Yomiuri-Yoshino Sakuzō Prize in 2006.

SUMIO HATANO is professor in the Graduate School of Humanities and Social Sciences at the University of Tsukuba, Japan. He received his M.A. degree and his doctorate in law and political sciences from Keiō University. He served as assistant professor in the War History Department at the Japanese Institute for Defense Studies [Bōei Kenkyūjo Senshishitsu] in Tokyo before coming to Tsukuba as associate professor in 1988. His book *The Pacific War and Japan's Asian Policy* (1996; in Japanese) won the Yoshida Shigeru Memorial Prize in 1997. He also wrote *The History of Anglo-Japanese Relations, 1600–2000*, vol. 3 (co-authored, 2003) and *Postwar Japan's Policy Toward Southeast Asia* (2005; in Japanese).

DAVID HOLLOWAY is Raymond A. Spruance Professor of International History, professor of political science, and Senior Fellow at the Institute for International Studies at Stanford University. Born in Dublin, Ireland, and having received his undergraduate degree (in modern languages and literature) and his Ph.D. (in social and political sciences) from Cambridge University, he taught at the universities of Lancaster and Edinburgh before joining the Political Science Department at Stanford University in 1986, where he has served as chair and co-chair of the International Relations Program, co-director of the Center for International Security and Arms Control, associate dean in the School of Humanities and Science, and director of the Stanford Institute for International Studies. His book *Stalin and the Bomb: The Soviet Union and Atomic Energy, 1939–1956* (1994) was chosen by the *New York Times Book Review* as one of the eleven best books of 1994 and won the Vucinich and Shulman prizes of the American Association for the Advancement of Slavic Studies. Holloway also wrote *The Soviet Union and the Arms Race* (1983) and co-authored (with Sidney Drell and Philip Farley) *The Reagan Strategic Defense Initiative: Technical, Political and Arms Control Assessment* (1984). He has contributed to the *New York Review of Books*, the *Bulletin of the Atomic Scientists, Foreign Affairs*, and various scholarly journals. His current research focuses on the history of nuclear weapons.

The End of the Pacific War

Introduction

TSUYOSHI HASEGAWA

Over sixty years after the end of the Pacific War, we have still not come to terms with its consequences. In the United States, as the storm of controversy over the *Enola Gay* exhibit at the Smithsonian's National Air and Space Museum in 1995 vividly reminded us, the debate on the U.S. decision to drop the atomic bomb still touches a raw nerve in Americans. At the sixtieth anniversary of the Hiroshima and Nagasaki nuclear bombings, the debate was more muted than that at the fiftieth, but it is hardly settled. As David M. Kennedy pointed out in an article in a special anniversary issue of *Time* magazine, the dropping of the bombs still raises a nagging moral issue of where the United States crossed the moral threshold.[1] The Hiroshima and Nagasaki bombings clearly divide American and Japanese public opinion. While many Americans believe that they led directly to Japan's decision to surrender, a majority of Japanese feel a sense of victimization. Despite the sixty-year defense alliance in the postwar period between the United States and Japan, memories of Pearl Harbor and Hiroshima-Nagasaki have bubbled up to remind us that the United States and Japan have not really come to terms with the legacy of the Pacific War.

If memories of the Pacific War serve as a subterranean psychological barrier between the Americans and the Japanese, they have directly pitted Japan against the Soviet Union and now Russia for the past sixty years. The "Northern Territories" dispute, which directly resulted from the Soviet occupation of the Kuril Islands at the end of the Pacific War, still prevents the two countries from concluding a peace treaty.

And in Japan's Asian neighbors, memories of war are still a contentious issue. Prime Minister Koizumi Jun'ichirō's repeated visits to the Yasukuni

Shrine, where Class-A war criminals are buried, and Japanese government–approved history textbooks that minimize Japan's past transgressions of colonialism and aggression, have provoked a storm of protests in China and South Korea. These recent events provide a vivid reminder that the memory of the Pacific War still remains a divisive contemporary issue among Asian nations.[2]

President George W. Bush's trip to Europe for the sixtieth anniversary of the VE Day in Moscow in May 2005 touched off a contentious debate between Americans and Russians about the meaning of the Yalta Agreement. Although this debate was concerned with the consequences of the Yalta conference on European borders, the Yalta Conference also dealt with Far Eastern matters. But, strangely, these issues were not raised at the sixtieth anniversary of the end of the Pacific War. In fact, while representatives of sixty-six nations, including Germany, gathered in Moscow to commemorate the sixtieth anniversary of VE Day, there was no comparable gathering for the sixtieth anniversary of the end of the Pacific War. It is inconceivable that the countries that fought the Pacific War could gather in Beijing, Seoul, Moscow, or Washington with Japan's representatives present. The Pacific War is still hotly contested terrain in Asia.

It is therefore worthwhile to revisit the issues of how the Pacific War ended and help to place the contemporary debate in a new light. Needless to say, how the Pacific War ended is merely one issue in the long list of questions concerning Japan's war in Asia and in the Pacific, but it is an important one, which touches on crucial aspects of the contemporary debate about the subject.

The American debate on the end of the Pacific War has almost exclusively focused on the U.S. decision to drop the bomb. Broadly speaking, there are three different schools of thought, the orthodox, the revisionist, and the neo-orthodox, which have passionately debated President Harry S. Truman's motives for dropping the bombs. Since Barton Bernstein discusses this issue more fully in Chapter 1, while using a somewhat different set of categories, it suffices here to characterize these three schools in a crudely schematic matter. The orthodox historians contend that Truman's decision to drop the atomic bombs on Hiroshima and Nagasaki was necessary and justified, because doing so directly and immediately prompted Japan's decision to surrender, thus saving millions of American and Japanese lives. The revisionists challenge this view, arguing that dropping the atomic bombs was unnecessary and unjustified, since Japan had already been thoroughly defeated, and the United States used the bombs, not to defeat Japan, but to intimidate the Soviet Union. The neo-orthodox historians argue that although the bomb was primarily used to defeat Japan and provided a powerful cause for Japan's decision to surrender, the Soviet factor played a secondary role.[3]

The debate is somewhat parochial, however, and focuses almost exclusively on the American side of the story. The American discussion is concerned with the reasons for the Truman administration's decision to drop the bomb, but it has not fully explored the effects of the bombs on Japan's decision makers. Historians who participate in this debate have assiduously mined the American archives, but it cannot be said that they have searched Japanese materials with the same diligence to assess the impact of the atomic bombs on Japan's decision. Until early 2005, the best authoritative monograph in any language on the subject was Robert Butow's *Japan's Decision to Surrender*, which was published more than a half century ago.[4] One of the two most important goals of the present volume is to shift the focus from the American side of the story to the Japanese side, examining how the atomic bomb and the Soviet entry into the war influenced Japan's decision to surrender.

Since Butow's book, until early 2005, there had been only three other serious works on Japan's decision to surrender, an article by Sadao Asada in the *Pacific Historical Review* 67, no. 4 (1998) and two books, Leon Sigal's *Fighting to a Finish: The Politics of War Termination in the United States and Japan, 1945* (1988) and Richard Frank's *Downfall: The End of the Imperial Japanese Empire* (1999).[5] Sigal's book is largely based on the translated interrogations and statements that Butow used. Asada is the first historian to have utilized a wide array of newly available Japanese sources to examine the impact of the atomic bombs on Japan's decision to surrender. Frank is the first American historian since Butow to have attempted to use important Japanese sources, especially some monographs in the multi-volume series on the Pacific War edited by Japan's Defense Institute. His incorporation of Japanese sources, in addition to his mastery of American archives, especially Magic and Ultra intercepts, has resulted in his thoughtful interpretation, especially on the significance of Japan's last-ditch defense strategy called Ketsu Gō. Asada's article and Frank's book are landmark achievements, which argued for the defense of the orthodox interpretation on the basis of new Japanese sources. Two of the authors of this volume, Sumio Hatano and Tsuyoshi Hasegawa, critically evaluate their interpretations.

Since the chapters in this volume by Frank, Hatano, and myself deal with the detailed political process by which the Japanese government came to accept surrender, it is necessary here to describe the Japanese decision-making mechanism briefly for the uninitiated. The emperor sat at the pinnacle of power, but he served mainly as a figurehead and was not involved in actual decision making, leaving all decisions to the cabinet, although a recent biography of Hirohito by Herbert Bix argues that the emperor was more actively involved in various decisions.[6] As Bernstein argues in Chapter 1, the issue of imperial power and the role of the Shōwa emperor is a subject of debate.

In the final days of the war, decision making became concentrated in the

Supreme War Council, or Supreme Council for the Direction of the War (Saikō senso shidō kōseiin kaigi), consisting of the six key political and military leaders: the prime minister (Suzuki Kantarō), the foreign minister (Tōgō Shigenori), the army minister (Anami Korechika), the navy minister (Yonai Mitsumasa), the army chief of staff (Umezu Yoshijirō), and the navy chief of staff (Toyoda Soemu). Decisions by the Supreme War Council required unanimity and the approval of the cabinet. Thus the military virtually enjoyed veto power. An army minister's resignation, for instance, was sufficient to cause the cabinet to collapse. Also important was the complete control that the military enjoyed over matters related to military command, which was formally the exclusive prerogative of the emperor alone, beyond the reach of the cabinet.

The peculiarity of Japan's decision to surrender consisted of a departure from the traditional decision-making process. Both the Supreme War Council and the cabinet found themselves in a stalemate, a condition that under normal circumstances would have meant the collapse of the cabinet. But in the unprecedented crisis caused by the atomic bombings of Hiroshima and Nagasaki and the Soviet entry into the war, two imperial conferences were held, at which, breaking with tradition, the emperor twice made the final decision to terminate the war.

A few words are necessary to explain the concept of the Japanese national polity centered on the imperial system, called the *kokutai*, preservation of which became the highest priority of Japan's policymakers at that time. This nebulous concept was never precisely defined until, facing the crisis brought on by the atomic bombing of Hiroshima and the Soviet entry into the war, Japanese policymakers were confronted with the issue of formulating concrete surrender terms. Tōgō and the foreign ministry consciously attempted to define the terms as the preservation of Japan's unbroken lineage of the imperial house, but during the intense debate on August 9 to 10, this concept expanded to include "the emperor's status in the constitution" and eventually "the emperor's prerogatives as the sovereign ruler." This definition and its relation to the unconditional surrender demanded by the Potsdam Proclamation were the most important issues that delayed Japan's surrender.[7]

The second major goal of this volume is to bring the Soviet Union to center stage in the drama of ending the war. If historians have failed fully to examine the effect of the atomic bomb on Japan's decision to surrender, the question of how the Soviet Union influenced Japan's decision has received even less attention. As long as the Communist Party of the Soviet Union exercised its dictatorial power, Soviet archives were inaccessible to foreign scholars, and what Soviet historians wrote about the Pacific War fell into the category of propaganda rather than genuine scholarship. The result of this sorry state led non-Soviet historians to treat the Soviet role in the ending of the Pacific War as virtually a sideshow. But since the last days of the Soviet period, and especially after the collapse of the Soviet Union, new documents have been published, and access to Soviet archives has become possible to a limited extent. Making use of these materials and the hitherto inaccessible foreign ministry archives and naval archives, Boris Slavinsky published a series of monographs that challenged the traditional orthodox interpretation by stressing how Stalin's geostrategic interests drove Soviet policy.[8]

The availability of new sources, both in Japan and Russia, allows historians to reexamine the ending of the Pacific War in an international context, not merely from the narrow American perspective. It was out of acute awareness of this need that the Center for Cold War Studies at the University of California at Santa Barbara convened a workshop to reexamine the ending of the Pacific War by inviting a small of group of specialists in March 2001. This two-day workshop was remarkable, not merely for the intensity of the discussion of the issues that were examined in view of new evidence, but also for the civility of discourse among specialists with often sharply different points of view, a rare form of discourse in light of past discussions dealing with the atomic bombings of Hiroshima and Nagasaki.

With the agreement of the participants, we decided to produce a collective volume. Hatano and Asada Sadao, though unable to participate in the workshop, readily agreed to contribute to the volume (although the latter eventually did not do so). Unfortunately, Boris Slavinsky, an important participant in the conference, will not be able to see its final outcome in print, because he passed away in April 2003. I myself have contributed Chapter 6 on the Soviet role in ending the war in his stead.

In Chapter 1, Barton J. Bernstein places the debate on the role of the atomic bomb in ending the Pacific War in historiographical context and broadens the historiographical angles to look at the treatment of how and why Japan surrendered. His introductory chapter in examining the publications in the atomic bomb debate since the death of the Shōwa emperor can be viewed in some ways as a sequel to his seminal article "The Struggle over History: Defining the Hiroshima Narrative," published in 1995.

The three chapters that follow Chapter 1 deal with the central question: whether the atomic bombings of Hiroshima and Nagasaki or the Soviet entry into the war against Japan had a more decisive impact on Japan's decision to surrender. In Chapter 2, on the basis of his meticulous analysis of Japan's Ketsu Gō strategy, the military's plan for a last-ditch defense of the homeland, Richard Frank argues that the Americans had no alternative but to use the atomic bomb. Frank also contends that the atomic bomb, not Soviet entry into the war, had the decisive impact on the emperor's decision to terminate the war, and that to the extent that the emperor was the only legitimate authority able to impose that decision on the military, this was the most crucial factor in ending the war.

Chapter 3 by Sumio Hatano, on the other hand, takes the view that while the atomic bomb had a decisive impact on the civilian decision makers, the Soviet entry into the war was more decisive in the army's decision to accept surrender. An important feature of his article is the careful reconstruction of the process, on the basis of new sources, by which the Japanese policymakers reached the decision to accept surrender.

In Chapter 4, I challenge the view represented by Asada and Frank and argue that although neither the atomic bombings nor the Soviet entry into the war alone provided the knock-out punch, the Soviet entry was a more decisive factor in Japan's decision to surrender.

Originally, Sadao Asada had agreed to contribute a chapter in the form of a revised version of his *Pacific Historical Review* article, but he decided to withdraw it at the last moment. Since the intention was to represent a wide spectrum of views, I regret Asada's decision to withdraw. Interested readers may, however, consult his original article in the November 1988 issue of the *Pacific Historical Review.*

Holloway's Chapter 5 and my Chapter 6 both examine the Soviet factor in ending the Pacific War, a hitherto understudied subject in the literature. Holloway presents Moscow's motivations in participating in the war in a longer and broader perspective than I do, going back to the historical Russo-Japanese rivalry and to the end of Soviet operations in the Kurils immediately after the war. I focus more narrowly on interactions between the Soviet Union and other powers during the period from the conclusion of the Soviet-Japanese Neutrality Pact in 1941 to the Soviet entry into the war, arguing that geostrategic gains in line with Soviet strategy were Stalin's main objective.

Finally, Bernstein's Chapter 7 sums up and places the chapters of this volume in a broader historiographical context. The volume also includes a brief bibliographical note on Russian and Japanese sources and a selective bibliography of published sources in English, Russian, and Japanese used in the present volume (and also in Asada's article), which, we hope, represents the most recent bibliographical work on the end of the Pacific War.

This volume, by design, does not attempt to present a unified view. Among the contributors, Frank, Hatano, and I disagree (as does Asada) on which factor—the atomic bombings or the Soviet entry into the war against Japan—played a more decisive role in Japan's decision to surrender. These disagreements stem from different emphases on certain sources and different interpretations. Holloway and I disagree on a number of important points, including the date of the Soviet attack on the Japanese forces in Manchuria set prior to the Potsdam Conference, the role of the Potsdam Proclamation, and Stalin's assessment of the atomic bomb in determining Japan's decision to surrender. We interpret the same sources in different ways and arrive at different conclusions where crucial sources do not exist.

Although we have not reached any consensus on many issues, we hope that this volume will serve as the starting point of new scholarly debate on the ending of the Pacific War, and that the new issues raised here will be further addressed as new evidence becomes available. Finally, we hope that the collegiality, respect, and spirit of cooperation among the contributors in producing this volume, which sometimes involved sharing research materials and critical reading of chapters, will set an example of scholarly discourse on this often contentious issue.

Note on Spelling, Transliteration, Names

For Japanese words, we have adhered to the Hepburn transliteration system, with slight modifications. For instance, we write *shinbun* instead of *shimbun*, and Matumoto Shun'ichi rather than Matsumoto Shunichi. We also use macrons to indicate elongated vowels (except in the case of Tokyo and where the original sources quoted do not use macrons). Japanese surnames precede given names with respect to Japanese sources: hence, for example, we write Suzuki Kantarō, not Kantarō Suzuki. But if a Japanese author's publication is in English, we have reversed the order, and placed the surname last. For instance, Tōgō Shigenori's memoirs in Japanese are cited as Tōgō Shigenori, *Jidai no ichimen*, but the English translation is cited as Shigenori Togo, *The Cause of Japan*.

For Russian words, except for well-known names such as Yalta, we have used the Library of Congress transliteration system: hence, for example, Vasilevskii, not Vasilevsky. Soft signs are omitted in the text, but shown in the notes.

r

Introducing the Interpretive Problems of Japan's 1945 Surrender

A Historiographical Essay on Recent Literature in the West

BARTON J. BERNSTEIN

> Significant changes in the postwar world would have resulted even from a shift in the date of surrender by two weeks one way or the other—before the atom bombs and the Soviet entrance into the war or after the Russian armies had penetrated further into the Far East and Japan had been more irreparably destroyed.
>
> —Edwin Reischauer, foreword to Robert J. C. Butow, *Japan's Decision to Surrender* (1954)

The Japanese government's mid-August 1945 surrender constitutes an unusual case in warfare.[1] A large industrial nation with a still-powerful military, despite some then-serious weaknesses in training and equipment, surrendered without the enemy having landed in its homeland. Normally, a major industrial nation's strategic surrender in the modern world has required an enemy invasion, dramatic battles within the beleaguered nation, and substantial casualties for the army defending its homeland before that nation's central government, if still operating, has decided to surrender.[2]

In such cases, as in others, surrender has required more than a nation's being near defeat. Indeed, there could be a great gap in time between a nation being near defeat, with ultimate victory impossible in the war, and that nation's government taking the painful action of actually surrendering. Surrender could be a terrible blow to the leadership, who would usually feel humiliated and might fear repudiation at home, as well as harsh treatment by the victors in the aftermath. Governmental surrender has required, essentially, a *political* act of giving up, based on, among other considerations, assessments of the military situation and the costs of continuing, of the enemy's surrender terms and its postwar intentions, and of the social and economic conditions in the beleaguered homeland. Those various factors could easily be assessed differently by various members of the government, reading the evidence through differing prisms of interest and desire and of background and culture.

Often nations do not surrender when, in the judgment of presumably objective third parties at that time or later, defeat is clear and that nation's surrender seemingly inevitable. For some or even most leaders in the losing nation, the situation during the war may often look quite different, because perceptions can be shaped by an amalgam of peculiar hopes, unrealistic fears, and often related personal and organizational-bureaucratic concerns. Such leaders may still retain hopes of snatching victory from the jaws of total defeat, or at least of securing better terms, by greatly increasing the cost to the more powerful nation, perhaps in a last bloody battle.

Some outside observers, especially in the aftermath of war, would view such hopes as incorrect and therefore irrational. But some latter-day observers, though decidedly fewer, might conclude that the losing nation's leaders' hopes for better surrender terms, even if ultimately incorrect, were actually a rational assessment of possibilities. Post-surrender studies, having both the advantage and the liability of knowing when the surrender occurred and normally the terms on which the war ultimately ended, must struggle to reconstruct the process of a nation's *moving toward* surrender and how matters looked to the defeated nation's leaders themselves as key decisions were made in that process. Such historical reconstruction is not easy, and it is made more difficult, as in the Japanese case, when the number of contemporaneous documents from the defeated government is small, and postwar testimony by the defeated leaders is often heavily used to explain wartime action.

At the time of the first atomic bombing on August 6, 1945, Japan was still seeking to deal with the Soviet Union, ostensibly to have it serve as an intermediary in peace negotiations with the United States. The relevant Japanese diplomatic and military messages, secretly intercepted and decrypted at the time by the United States, provided substantial evidence of these Japanese efforts and also of Japanese military plans for conducting the war. The primarily diplomatic messages, after decryption and translation, were later declassified by the United States as "Magic" or "Ultra" intercepts, with these two terms often used loosely and interchangeably.

Early non-government analysts in the postwar West did not have access to these secretly declassified messages, but some were summarized in various postwar memoirs and in official American compilations. Many more messages became available in the archives in the 1970s and 1980s, with an additional burst of files opened in the 1990s.

After the war, scholars would disagree on what Japan's government was actually seeking to accomplish by its 1945 wartime approaches to the Soviet Union, and whether Japan's leaders before the Hiroshima bombing had agreed upon reasonable peace terms to end the war. There would, however, be unanimity among scholars that Moscow had not agreed to such Soviet-Japanese negotiations and was basically stringing things out. But there would be some disagreement on why the Soviets acted as they did, and what Joseph Stalin's actions might show about his larger purposes in the war and for the postwar world, and whether, and, if so, when, the atomic bomb propelled Stalin to move up his schedule for Soviet intervention in the war against Japan.

Resolving the interpretive issues of Soviet entry into the war and Stalin's purposes, and the relationship of the A-bomb to Stalin's policies, is not essential to explaining Japan's surrender. But these issues are important in addressing questions about "atomic diplomacy" (that is, the relationship of the A-bomb to U.S.-Soviet diplomacy, including alleged American nuclear threats), the origins of the Cold War, and the role of Far Eastern policy in wartime and postwar U.S.-Soviet relations. Such questions easily slide into related matters about various missed opportunities—to end the Asian/Pacific war earlier, to avoid the Cold War, or to keep the USSR out of Manchuria.

In the near-aftermath of Japan's surrender, and over the later years, partly because of the unusual nature of the circumstances at the time of Japan's surrender, as well as because of the use of the A-bombs and what may figuratively be termed the last-minute entry of the USSR into the Pacific/Asian war, analysts would ask, and probe, why Japan had surrendered in mid-August 1945. Sometimes they would also ask, partly because of Japan's summer 1945 approach to the USSR, whether Japan would have surrendered before the American-scheduled November invasion if there had been no atomic bombing and no Soviet entry, or even without only one of those two events. If with only one of these events, which would have been decisive, or might the answer be either?

Put otherwise, would the strangling naval blockade and the deadly conventional bombing, without both the A-bombing and Soviet intervention, have been sufficient to produce a pre-November 1945 surrender and obviate the invasion? If so, would the naval blockade or the conventional bombing have made the crucial difference, and how could "crucial difference" be assessed in such an analysis? In the process of analysis, should only the Japanese situation of summer 1945 be examined, or should analysts go back to 1944 or possibly further back to consider the comparative effects of naval warfare versus air power on Japan's economy and government? To these many questions about what occurred, why that occurred, and what might have otherwise occurred, the answers would range broadly. The difficulties of interpretation, at least partly because of problems with sources and the heavy use of counterfactual arguments, would be substantial.

In adding to those interpretive difficulties, some analysts would ask, quite properly, why the Japanese government did not surrender even before August 1945 and thus before the atomic bombing and Soviet entry. Could the entire top level of the Japanese government be seen as the cause and therefore blamed, or only the so-called diehard militarists and not the so-called peace group for continuing the war? Was there, in fact, such a sharp division between these two groups in the Japanese government, and, if so, when and why did it emerge? Were the so-called military diehards, for example, propelled to take tough positions partly because they felt pressured by lower-level officers and others in the military, who might otherwise go out of control, threaten their superiors, and even move to a coup? That set of questions about the so-called diehards and pressures from below in the military is especially crucial in seeking to understand the key role of General Anami Korechika, the army minister, who chose not to support the coup of August 14/15 and thus helped to stifle it.

Significantly, how could Emperor Hirohito's behavior be interpreted, especially in the spring and summer of 1945? Was he eager for peace but fearful of trying to act to achieve a surrender before the key events of the atomic bombing and Soviet entry in early August? Or was he, somewhat like the so-called diehard militarists, pushing for another dramatic battle, until the painful events of early August changed matters? A related question: Could he have successfully pushed earlier for a conditional surrender on reasonable terms, and would the Japanese government, and especially the military leaders, have agreed? If so, would military forces in Japan's homeland and abroad have accepted such a decision, or might the military (especially the army) have rebelled and continued the war anyway?

When the Supreme Council for the Direction of the War (the Supreme War Council), also known as the Big Six, and then the cabinet acceded on the 10th and on the 14th to Hirohito's pleas, there are important questions about why these men agreed to endorse the emperor's position. Were they substantially agreeing with him because they accepted his reasoning? If so, how important was the particular context—especially of Soviet entry and the atomic bombing? Most interpreters emphasize aspects of that context, and frequently seek to parse out the question of which—the atomic bombing or Soviet entry—had greater weight. But, perhaps surprisingly, few analysts, if any, seek closely to examine the questions of how much the recalcitrant members acceded to Hirohito's stated position on surrender *mostly* because of their respect for and loyalty to Hirohito and the emperorship, and not because of his expressed reasoning.

Many of the questions about the causes and motives for Japan's August surrender, and the roles of key actors in Japan, are obviously unique in detail. But frequently they are generally familiar in structure to historians and other interpreters, because such questions are like those asked over the years about crucial decisions in other times and situations by nations to go to war or to surrender. Historians and other analysts, including social scientists and post-event journalists, writing about such issues, continue to disagree, often in spirited fashion, even on such seemingly distant events as the American Revolution, the Napoleonic wars, or World War I. For such complicated events, the evidence is seldom if ever unalloyed on major issues, and careful investigators, looking at multiple factors in immediate and underlying causes, can easily disagree on what is crucial, what is important, and what is comparatively marginal or even less important. In relying often upon criteria that are not made adequately explicit for the privileging of evidence and the establishment of chains of causation, interpreters construct their own explanation of the major events, frequently using a narrative form to define what is crucial, who is key, how the top decision makers interacted, what they believed, and how their motivations operated and sometimes changed under unfolding events.

Teasing out the interpreters' criteria for evidence, and determining their causal explanations, is often difficult, partly because the narrative form frequently used by historians, even when they mix it with more didactic prose, can often leave ambiguity and also conceal ambivalence and uncertainty. Adding to the difficulties, historians and other interpreters, unlike analytical philosophers in the Anglo-American tradition, often use language without razor-sharp precision, thereby leaving ambiguity and creating perils for later analysts, who may sometimes bring unduly high standards for precision in seeking to construe others' interpretations.

Undoubtedly the fact of the atomic bombings, because of the horror evoked by these powerful weapons, sometimes gave the questions about Japan's surrender decision added importance and introduced value commitments in the postwar years in providing interpretations. Frequently, questions about the surrender involve substantial regret about "might-have-been" alternatives that would have avoided the atomic bombings. To some in the West, as elsewhere, there are also related questions about whether American terms allowing a Japanese constitutional monarchy, if offered in June or July 1945 or in the early August days before Hiroshima, might have obviated Soviet entry into the Pacific/Asian war and produced different power relations in parts of postwar Asia. If so, as some would argue, had American policy failed by not having made such an offer? Sometimes a different question would be asked of whether a Potsdam Proclamation or something like it in late July also signed by the

Soviet Union, and thus constituting a de facto Soviet declaration of war, might have hastened the surrender by a few weeks, possibly obviating the atomic bombing and perhaps actual armed Soviet entry into the war.

Plausible counterfactuals, though sometimes implicit, are often an important part of the dialogue and analyses about such major events as the outbreak or ending of wars. Japan's surrender, for various reasons including especially the use of atomic bombs by the United States, has often evoked counterfactual analysis in an effort to understand what happened and what might reasonably instead have occurred.[3]

Much of that counterfactual analysis dates back to two mid-1946 reports by the presidentially authorized U.S. Strategic Bombing Survey (USSBS) and to a 1950 article in the *Atlantic Monthly* by the *New York Times* military analyst Hanson Baldwin, and then his 1950 book *Great Mistakes of the War*, and received further support from the historian Robert Butow's important 1954 volume *Japan's Decision to Surrender*, which helped define many of the questions and answers for decades. Despite differing interpretations, the USSBS reports and Baldwin's study, as well as Butow's somewhat ambivalent book, indicated to many readers that the atomic bombings had been unnecessary and thus, by implication or assertion, that the war could have been ended at a reasonable time by other means.[4]

The meaning of "reasonable time" could beg questions, though usually it meant definitely *or* probably—that phrasing is, itself, indicative of a significant range of judgment—before the scheduled November 1 invasion. For those understandably inspired to wish that the atomic bombings had not occurred, there was frequently an assumption—sometimes unstated—that Japanese lives could have been saved had the A-bombs not been used. But that judgment was often based upon unexplored assumptions: notably, that the A-bombs killed more people, and that in comparison, fewer residents in Japan would have died in the continuing fire-bombings of Japanese cities before the surrender if the war had dragged on. Adding to the complexity were the related assumptions, also normally unstated and unexplored, that (1) the number of the fire-bombed killed in Japan and (2) the number of Asians on the mainland dying in battle, as well as (3) those other residents on the Asian mainland and (4) in Japan dying of malnutrition, as well as (5) Allied POWs dying in camps, and (6) Americans and non-Asian Allies dying in battle would not in toto exceed in number the Japanese (and Koreans in Japan) killed in the two atomic bombings.

No one has ever succeeded in quantifying the likely dead in each of these categories persuasively and systematically and offering a carefully put together comparison, even based, as it would have to be, on various soft numbers and loose extrapolations, to provide a set of acceptable conclusions. So many numbers are so soft, partly because extant data are not firm and the extrapolations "iffy," that any such effort would undoubtedly be very vulnerable to error, while also possibly seeming ghoulish.[5]

Yet a very rough calculation *suggests*—given the soft data, no stronger verb than "suggests" is acceptable—that a late August surrender, if achieved without the atomic bombings but with continued conventional bombings and the blockade, as well as the struggle on the Asian mainland and massive problems of malnutrition, might well have saved lives overall. In contrast, it seems quite likely that a very late October surrender, without the atomic bombings but with the conventional bombings and the blockade, as well as the struggle on the Asian mainland and massive problems of malnutrition, would have cost more lives, even if only Asian and not American and Soviet lives are counted. It is in the wide calendar range from about early September through about mid-October that the greatest uncertainty lies in calculating comparative numbers for using the A-bombs versus not doing so in a prolonged war in which many deaths for military forces and civilians by other means would have occurred. It seems likely, however, in view of American military plans excluding any significant American ground campaign in the August–October 1945 period before the November invasion, that the number of Asians killed in the atomic bombings significantly exceeded the number of Americans who would have died in combat, or in combat *and* from noncombat injury, in the hypothetical mid-August-to-late-October period, which is the two-and-a-half-month period *before* the Olympic invasion.

In conclusion, in looking overall at mid-August through late October for Asians and various Allied (non-Asian) forces, for both noncombatants and combatants, such an admittedly loose set of calculations—involving various comparisons—helps to provide some perspective on possible "might have beens." It is important to stress that this essay does not depend, logically or evidentially, in its general analysis on this brief and somewhat speculative counterfactual discussion of comparative deaths with or without the two atomic bombings.[6]

Some critical interpreters and lay readers, even if accepting such a counterfactual enterprise, would often disagree, however, on what was a reasonable time. It is a conception that could depend in part on how they assess the value of different lives—noncombatant and combatant, Japanese, other Asian, and various Allied, including, of course, American lives. And some would flatly reject the implications of the U.S. Strategic Bombing Survey, Baldwin, and Butow and insist that the A-bombs were clearly necessary. The precise criteria for "necessary," like much in the dialogue on why Japan surrendered and whether the surrender might have occurred without the use of nuclear weapons, would sometimes be less than rigorous in phrasing, and thus there would be some troubling ambiguities.

Popular Understanding and the Published Literature

After the war's end in 1945, and for about the next twenty years, few Americans focused on the dissident postwar contentions by about a handful of top U.S. wartime generals and admirals about the atomic bombing of Japan. Among these postwar dissenters, most notably, were Generals Douglas MacArthur and Henry Arnold, and Admirals William Leahy, Ernest King, and Chester Nimitz. They variously stated or implied that the Pacific War could have been ended in a reasonable time without either the atomic bombing or an invasion of Japan's home islands—and often thus, by implication, without Soviet entry into the war.[7]

Nor was much attention paid in the West or in Japan to dissident postwar comments sometimes uttered by other important former American diplomatic and military officials, notably by former Under Secretary of State Joseph Grew, that an American offer of modified surrender terms allowing a figurehead emperor in the postwar Japanese system might well have avoided the atomic bombing and the invasion, while producing the desired surrender before early August 1945. Such *post*-surrender counterfactual analyses, emerging significantly from former high-ranking Americans, would often help inspire academic and journalistic analysts, and even lead to their using such postwar counterfactual claims by former high-ranking officials as evidence—sometimes as substantial evidence—that the war might well have ended without the A-bomb and Soviet entry.[8]

Grew, along with the Bombing Survey, Baldwin, Butow, and various Japanese memoirists, also helped ratify the dominant interpretive framework for many Western-based studies' analysis of Emperor Hirohito, which assumed that he had been a passive figure in most of the war and that the emperor's role in practice had been mostly that of a symbolic figurehead in Japan's prewar and wartime governmental structure.[9] In the West, this powerful interpretive framework generally endured, almost undented, until about the mid 1990s, notwithstanding some minor challenges in the early 1970s and then in the late 1980s.

On the Japanese side, in the 1980s, mostly on the political left, and significantly growing in Japan in the 1990s, after the Shōwa emperor's 1989 death, that view came under substantial attack. The problem of how to interpret Emperor Hirohito's role is now often a sharply contested issue in Japan and in the West among scholars. Sometimes that question is an important key for interpreters in explaining Japan's surrender and why Japan did not surrender earlier, and also under what plausible conditions, if any, the war might or might not have continued after mid-August 1945.

Far more than issues about the emperor, the questions of why, and how, the A-bomb was used on Japan have spawned a large and mostly Western literature. For many years, for various reasons, these A-bomb questions, perhaps surprisingly, did not usually spill over for A-bomb-focused authors into looking closely, in real depth, at Japan's wartime policy and thus at how and why Japan surrendered in August 1945. Japanese policy was greatly slighted in Western A-bomb-focused studies.

Generally, and probably surprisingly, there was also a rather separate and different literature on why and how Japan surrendered. That literature usually did little with the issues of America's wartime A-bomb policy, while focusing heavily on Japan and its 1945 policies and actions on the path to surrender. The end-of-the-war studies normally did not probe into American A-bomb policies and purposes, discuss in any depth the decision to use the bomb, or closely consider pre-Hiroshima, high-level American thinking about the bomb, its likely effects, and its role in the war and in the postwar world.

For historians in particular, the crossing of academic boundaries in depth between A-bomb issues and end-of-the-war/surrender issues, which were often defined by knowledge in depth of a particular nation-state and its policy and culture as the focused unit of study, could be both intellectually difficult and professionally perilous. Even many journalists and popular historians, though normally using looser standards than academics for evidence and frequently not worrying about language difficulties, were rather wary of seeking to work in depth in the same study on both large areas of interpretive problems— America's A-bomb policy and Japan's end-of-the war policy.

By about the mid 1990s, however, the situation somewhat changed for the better. A number of A-bomb scholars started devoting more attention than had most earlier A-bomb-focused works to Japanese wartime policy in 1945. In turn, those primarily studying Japan and the end of the war also came, at least on some occasions, to look more closely at America's A-bomb policy. Yet, into late 2005, aside from Leon Sigal's *Fighting to a Finish: The Politics of War Termination in the United States and Japan, 1945* (1988) and Tsuyoshi Hasegawa's *Racing the Enemy: Stalin, Truman, and the Surrender of Japan* (2005)—and each is only a partial exception—no academic scholar in the West, or in Japan,[10] has focused in a substantial publication almost equally and in considerable depth on both (1) America's A-bomb policy and (2) Japan's end-of-the-war policy. For most serious authors, the task of truly merging these two areas of inquiry by working in depth—partly because of language problems and bulky sources—remains formidable, even daunting.

The problems can become even more severe if a decision is made by the scholar that an analysis of relevant American A-bomb policy, contrary to a number of interpreters, must start well before 1945 and Truman's presidency. Going back to Roosevelt and 1941–45, or even possibly to 1939–45, and looking at the thinking about the power and targeting of the A-bomb, and studying the shift in conventional bombing to area bombing and often to hitting noncombatant populations, adds to the formidable difficulties of research. Conceivably, a full understanding of Japan's end-of-the-war policy, some analysts might argue, should also begin in depth before 1945 to understand power relations within the Japanese government, the role of Hirohito, his relationship to key advisers and others, and Japanese governmental attitudes toward the Soviet Union and the United States and hopes about the likely shape of the postwar Asian world.

The two literatures—A-bomb studies and end-of-the-war studies—are also different in other ways. Before the late 1980s, many Western end-of the-Pacific/Asian War studies, unlike the A-bomb articles and books, were not explicitly presented by their authors as part of an ongoing scholarly dialogue among rival interpreters. Whereas the A-bomb literature since about the mid 1960s has often been spirited and sometimes even rancorous, and there is frequently a deep engagement in the published text and notes with competing A-bomb interpretations, the end-of-the-war studies published in the West were usually written with little open acknowledgment of rival positions. Even the notes frequently avoided direct, systematic confrontation and an explanation of interpretive differences. In the West, the exceptions, until about the late 1980s, were rather occasional. With greater emphasis on open dispute against competing interpretations, this pattern slowly changed in about the late 1980s, and the difference is often apparent in the 1989–2005 period.

There has been a new vigor in recent scholarship involving the role of the emperor, the competing weights of different strategies in ending the war, how close Japan was to surrender before the Hiroshima bombing, the nature of the wartime Japanese government and its policies, and the importance of the A-bomb versus Soviet entry into the war in propelling surrender. Most of the more detailed Western studies published in 1989–2005 address the arguments of rival analysts. More than occasionally, the interpretive disagreements are not openly framed as part of a vigorous dialogue, but they are at least privately conceived by the authors that way—and can and should be so read by other scholars.

The literature published in the West on Japan's surrender—and usually this is substantially an American-produced literature, supplemented by some British and Japanese studies—merits close critical examination, because it raises many interesting questions. To date, unlike with the A-bomb scholarship,[11] there is no published historiographical analysis of that end-of-the-Japanese-war literature, including a critical assessment of the arguments, uses of evidence, and development of interpretive themes. Ideally, this literature should be examined since its beginnings in 1945–46, but that would involve close study of over sixty-five books, articles, and government reports. Such an analysis would likely run to hundreds of pages of text, not counting notes, making it more like a book than a chapter in one. The aim of this essay is certainly more modest: to study the significant literature on the subject in the West between 1989 and 2005, dipping back briefly into the earlier period, especially with regard to A-bomb "revisionism," for background in understanding the 1989–2005 publications.

In order to examine closely and often in depth the main publications in the seventeen-year period, 1989–2005, this essay has been organized to move, usually but not always precisely chronologically, through the relevant pieces of literature, analyzing at least briefly each significant article or book on the subject. Such intentional didacticism has the great advantage of taking seriously each of the major publications on Japanese policy, and thus permitting an explanation and assessment of each study's own conceptions and analyses. The normal alternative approach, usually followed in historiographical essays, but intentionally not in this one, is to organize the essay significantly by a few analytical categories and then to discuss the pieces of literature within that useful but also rather restrictive framework. Doing that, however, would not allow the critic to explain substantially, and the reader to understand in suitable depth, how the literature has developed, and often the strong and weak points of particular articles and books.

The remainder of this essay begins with a discussion of "A-bomb revisionism," focusing mostly on three U.S. historians, Gar Alperovitz, Martin J. Sherwin, and Barton J. Bernstein, before moving on to consider two leading mid-1990s, U.S. anti-revisionists, Robert J. Maddox and Robert P. Newman, and then briefly discussing the mid-1990s criticism of the Strategic Bombing Survey's often-cited counterfactual contentions that the atomic bombing was probably unnecessary to end the war. Having dealt with some issues of bombing, the essay then examines the case of Robert Pape, an American political scientist who in the 1990s denied the importance of both conventional bombing and the atomic bombing in producing Japan's surrender, and then turns to Lawrence Freedman and Saki Dockrill, two British historians who analyze the roles of the atomic bombing and Soviet entry in producing Japan's surrender. Shifting focus somewhat, the essay then looks at two British authors, Edward Behr and Stephen Large, and a Japanese historian, Irokawa Daikichi, who in the 1989–95 period analyzed the role of Hirohito, before the chapter moves on to consider the differing views of the Harvard-trained historian Herbert Bix and the military historian Edward Drea. The last two segments, short of the conclusion, deal with the efforts of the political scientist Forrest Morgan in 2003 to explain Japan's surrender partly within a context of strategic culture, and then-American-based historian Yukiko Koshiro's 2004 essay disputing most earlier work on high-level Japanese interest before Hiroshima in Soviet entry in the war.

The A-bomb Revisionists: The Bomb, the USSR, and *Sometimes* Japan

A useful study of the literature must begin in part by discussing, even if only briefly, some terms or categories that periodically appear in analyses—notably, A-bomb revisionism and Cold War revisionism. Such terms, like categories for most schools of historical interpretation, are less than precise and often employed in somewhat different ways by different writers.

Yet despite more than a little fuzziness around the edges, and sometimes near the core, A-bomb revisionism can be usefully defined to include those who emphasize: (1) that anti-Soviet motives played a primary role or at least some role (some say a "bonus") in the American decision to use the bomb on Japan; and (2) that the bomb was definitely or very probably unnecessary to end the war before the November invasion. Such A-bomb revisionism usually assumes that the atomic bombing should be judged as morally undesirable, and this may be a defining aspect for some uses of the term A-bomb "revisionist" and an accompanying (but not defining) term for others. A-bomb revisionists usually conclude that the bomb's use, if not also earlier wartime American A-bomb policy, played an important role in producing or propelling the Cold War. Thus A-bomb revisionists are normally Cold War revisionists.

But the reverse is not true. Not all Cold War revisionists are A-bomb revisionists, and more than a handful of Cold War revisionists are probably not. Defined most basically, Cold War revisionism concludes that the United States was substantially or primarily responsible for the Cold War. Such revisionists normally conclude that plausibly different American policies—involving opening the second front in Europe earlier, providing postwar economic aid to the Soviet Union, acceding without protest or pressure to Soviet dominance in eastern Europe, and providing substantial reparations to the USSR from West Germany—might well have avoided the Cold War. Not all Cold War revisionists, however, view the American A-bomb decision as significantly motivated by anti-Soviet purposes, and mostly on that basis, a number of Cold War revisionists do not consider themselves A-bomb revisionists, even though some self-designated A-bomb revisionists argue that anti-Soviet purposes were present but not controlling in the A-bomb decision.

In America, and in the West in general, A-bomb revisionism only gained dramatic visibility in about summer 1965, amid the expanding Vietnam War, with the publication by Gar Alperovitz, a former William Appleman Williams student, then aged 29, of *Atomic Diplomacy: Hiroshima and Potsdam*. That influential book was heavily documented and clearly intelligent, though deeply flawed both in conception and in its use of evidence. It was energetically argued, and seemed persuasive to many, helping to change judgments in academia and often particularly among American historians. The volume was especially influential among younger members of the history profession, who were more inclined to challenge older orthodoxies about American policy, partly because they were upset by the developing Vietnam War and often began to explain American foreign policy in frameworks that uncovered unpleasant motives for U.S. policy.

Alperovitz's book gained considerable attention in the American media, appearing propitiously near the twentieth anniversary of Hiroshima and Nagasaki. His bold volume sharply challenged conventional thinking about the use of the A-bomb and about the origins of the Cold War, and thus contributed significantly to both Cold War revisionism and A-bomb revisionism. Alperovitz's chief stated concerns in his forceful study were to show that the A-bomb had greatly influenced American policy before Hiroshima, that President Harry S. Truman's A-bomb-related policy had helped produce the Cold War, and that Truman had reversed what Alperovitz deemed to have been FDR's late-wartime policy of accommodation in dealing with the Soviet Union.

Alperovitz argued that most top American military leaders before Hiroshima believed that the A-bomb was unnecessary to end the Pacific War. Despite some slight hedges, he concluded that Truman and his top advisers (notably Secretary of State James F. Byrnes and Secretary of War Henry L. Stimson) had used the bomb on Japan primarily to gain leverage on the USSR—what Alperovitz termed "atomic diplomacy." Despite some slight hedging, Alperovitz's strong implication, and the underlying framework of the book, was that the bomb had been unnecessary, and that Truman and his top civilian advisers had understood that before Hiroshima. These conclusions raised the hackles of some scholars, most often older men, in both the United States and Britain in the 1960s and 1970s. Alperovitz had challenged the stated American motives for using nuclear weapons as expressed after Hiroshima by Truman, Stimson, Byrnes, and other wartime American policymakers, who contended that the A-bombs had been dropped to end the war speedily and save U.S. lives by making an invasion unnecessary. In Japan, in contrast, Alperovitz's interpretation, building on the British physicist's P. M. S. Blackett's popular 1940s book (the American title is *Fear, War, and the Bomb*) helped confirm feelings among scholars, who were often on the political left, that the atomic bombing had been unnecessary and was causally connected to anti-Soviet policy and thus to the origins of the Cold War.

Alperovitz's array of evidence, the structure of parts of his analysis, and the tone and phrasing of his writing indicated that he believed that the atomic bombing had been unnecessary, and that Japan would have soon surrendered without the nuclear attacks. For supporting evidence, he even trustingly quoted the U.S. Strategic Bombing Survey's mid-1946 conclusion that the bomb "in all probability" had been unnecessary to produce a pre-November 1945 surrender.[12]

But the questions of why Japan actually surrendered, and how close Japan was to surrender in the pre-Hiroshima days, did not receive sustained attention from Alperovitz. He probably devoted fewer than seven pages of his 1965 text to actual pre-Hiroshima events and policy in Japan, as opposed to what American leaders had allegedly thought about Japan before Hiroshima. He offered basically no research in the kinds of sources, translated into English, of postwar interrogations with wartime Japanese officials that Butow had used in the early 1950s and that were available in the National Archives. *Atomic Diplomacy*, despite assumptions and implications—and some hedged assertions—that the atomic bombing was unnecessary, was primarily a book about Truman's A-bomb policy and the origins of the Cold War—in short, about U.S.-Soviet relations.

Some critics in the West focused on Alperovitz's conceptual framework, his uses of evidence on A-bomb and Cold War issues, his conclusion that American leaders had primarily used the A-bomb on Japan for anti-Soviet purposes, and his contention that the atomic bombing had been unnecessary. Perhaps surprisingly, some of his most demanding critics—notably the historians Gabriel Kolko, who had a Harvard doctorate, Martin J. Sherwin, who had a UCLA doctorate, and Barton J. Bernstein, a Harvard doctorate—were, like Alperovitz himself, on the American political left. Like Alperovitz, they were also Cold War revisionists and all born in the early or mid 1930s. These critics were not defenders of the atomic bombing or of America's early Cold War policy, and they contended on various evidential and conceptual grounds that Alperovitz had deeply erred in his presentation of A-bomb and Cold War history.

Alperovitz's important book did not generally evoke a sharp dialogue and vigorous research on Japanese policy itself among A-bomb writers, including most of his Western critics. Perhaps partly because of language problems and despite the availability of some translated sources on Japan's policy, A-bomb interpreters were not spurred to investigate closely the important questions of how near Japan was to surrender in 1945 before the atomic bombing, of whether Soviet entry into the Pacific/Asian War without the atomic bombings would probably have produced a speedy Japanese surrender, and of whether the crumbling Japanese economy, without the atomic bombing and Soviet entry, might well have forced Japan's surrender before the scheduled November 1945 invasion. The A-bomb interpreters were generally concerned with the A-bomb "decision" and the connection of the A-bomb's use to the origins of the Cold War and to related Soviet-American relations. Investigating Japanese policy in depth did not initially attract A-bomb interpreters, though the issue of Japan's mid-1945 policy gained somewhat more attention from A-bomb interpreters starting about a decade after Alperovitz's *Atomic Diplomacy*.

The reason for the repeated use of quotation marks around "decision" is because some critics challenged what seemed to be Alperovitz's guiding assumption in most of his book text (though not his preface): that Truman and others had engaged in carefully weighed and calculated considerations—what is called a "robust" decision. Bernstein, and sometimes Sherwin,[13] framed the process as closer to being the implementation of inherited assumptions. Thus, there was technically a decision in that there was a volitional act (using the bomb), but it was *not* the product of a robust process.

A-bomb revisionists could, and did, openly disagree about whether anti-Soviet motives in using the bomb had been primary, secondary, or just supplementary. Frequently, A-bomb revisionists, by tone or argument, also contended that alternative policies to the atomic bombing could have *probably* or *definitely* ended the war before, and thus without, the November invasion. Obviously, there was a great gap—one in which many people in late 1945 could have died—between "definitely" and "probably." That gap in interpretation helped separate Alperovitz ("definitely") and Bernstein ("probably"), with Sherwin generally seeming to move closer over time to Alperovitz's position. The "probably" position also potentially opened the way to anti-revisionism, or at least helped invite a further assault on Alperovitz's position.

In the 1970s, aided by Butow's substantial research, and after an initial essay on the A-bomb that paid remarkably little attention to Japanese policy, Bernstein spent some time studying the Tokyo tribunal transcripts and U.S. files on postwar interrogations of Japanese officials. Having deepened his Japan-related research, and being assisted by some specially translated sources, Bernstein concluded in various 1970s lectures, and in later publications, that it was quite possible, though less than definite, that both use of the A-bomb and an invasion could have been avoided and a Japanese surrender achieved before November 1945 if the United States had awaited the impact of Soviet entry, continued its blockade and heavy bombing of Japan, and modified its unconditional-surrender policy to allow a constitutional monarchy. On the basis of such research, he also contended that the Nagasaki bomb was very probably unnecessary, perhaps speeding the peace by a few hours or days.[14]

After more research in translated Japanese sources, Bernstein focused in a journal article on the crucial but little-studied August 10–14/15 period in the United States and Japan on the ending of the war. This was the critical time from Japan's offer of a conditional surrender on August 10, through Truman's decision on the 10th not to use a third atomic bomb on Japan and Washington's intentionally ambiguous response on the 11th, to Japan's August 14/15 decision at the behest of the emperor to accept the American terms. Bernstein's analysis of this brief period, focusing significantly for that limited time on both Japanese and American decision making, emphasized how close Japan came to continuing the war because of the ambiguous American response on allowing an emperor system.[15]

Bernstein's study of that crucial period in August, and also of high-level American thinking about employing tactical nuclear warfare against Japan in October–November 1945, helped him conclude that American leaders had not expected that one or two atomic bombings would speedily end the war. In his analysis, top-level U.S. leaders had some hope but no real expectations of a speedy surrender and were surprised, on the 10th, by Japan's offer of a surrender, albeit a conditional surrender.

In 1985, Alperovitz reissued *Atomic Diplomacy*, adding to it an intelligent, energetically presented, but rather flawed 60-page introduction rebutting some critics (including Sherwin and Bernstein), discussing new evidence, arguing that the atomic bombing had been unnecessary, and stressing, among other matters, that Japan was close to surrender even before the atomic bombing on August 6 and Soviet entry on August 8. Significantly, while emphasizing some evidence available to him in 1965 of Japan's midsummer 1945 "peace-feelers," Alperovitz in 1985 also used some declassified Truman Library files on the subject.[16] Thus, his 1985 revision, like a few others' works in the 1970s, may have helped somewhat to move the focus of A-bomb scholarship toward looking at Japan itself and Japanese policy in mid 1945.

Drawing selectively on the available evidence about "peace feelers," Alperovitz emphasized that the Japanese messages, in his judgment, showed that the *major* impediment to Japan's surrender in June–July 1945, and certainly before the August atomic bombing, was the American insistence on Japan's unconditional surrender. Such an interpretation was possibly correct. But, unfortunately, Alperovitz, in discussing unconditional surrender, acted as if that requirement troubled Japanese leaders *only* because they wanted continuation of an emperor system, and that Japan's government would have surrendered before the atomic bombing if the United States had made clear that the emperor system could be continued.[17]

The then-declassified Japanese message traffic, buttressed by other 1945 sources, made clear, Bernstein argued in 1995, that the Japanese government in June–July and even in early August 1945, before the atomic bombing, was deeply divided on surrender terms, and that the issues were substantially greater than just continuation of an emperor system. One might plausibly argue, as had Butow, that America's yielding on that one issue of the emperor system might have produced a July surrender and thus obviated the atomic bombing, but such an interpretation was not clearly indicated by the decrypted diplomatic cables of summer 1945 between Foreign Minister Tōgō Shigenori and Japanese ambassador Satō Naotake.

It seems certainly a strained interpretation to conclude, as Alperovitz asserted in his 1985 introduction, in a passage that he italicized to stress its importance: "*It is very clear that well before atomic weapons were used, both the Japanese and U.S. governments had arrived at the same understanding of acceptable terms of surrender.*"[18] In his frequently wide-ranging, often impressive, large 1995 volume, *The Decision to Use the Atomic Bomb and the Architecture of an American Myth*, Alperovitz sought to provide more evidence for this key argument including some Japanese material, but his basic interpretive framework, and the similar selective use of the Tōgō-Satō cables, did not significantly change. His 1995 book, which had a first printing in the United States of 50,000 hardback copies, followed by a paperback reprint and a generally well-received Japanese edition, and became the basis for at least one American TV documentary, had vulnerabilities very similar to those of his 1985 revision.[19]

Although they deeply influenced the dialogue on the necessity for the atomic bombing and on American motives in using the atomic bomb on Japan, Alperovitz's publications in 1965–95 and those of Sherwin and Bernstein in the 1970s, 1980s, and 1990s had less of an impact, until about the mid 1990s, on the writings of Western scholars who focused primarily on Japanese policy and Japan's decision to surrender. The two streams of scholarship—A-bomb studies with some judgments about Japan's surrender, and end-of-the-Pacific/Asian War studies—usually did not deeply and explicitly intersect until about the mid 1990s.

Even then, the shift was partial, certainly not monumental. At that point, the A-bomb scholarship, and especially Bernstein's and Alperovitz's differing conclusions about the role of Soviet entry in ending the war, and whether the atomic bombing had been necessary to produce an August surrender, began to attract the attention of some scholars writing on Japan's policy and behavior leading to the 1945 surrender. Notably, that A-bomb scholarship and the end-of-the war scholarship also further ignited interest in the related but separate questions of: (1) whether Soviet entry, without the atomic bombing, could have speedily ended the war in about mid-August 1945 or at least before the November invasion; and (2) whether Soviet entry or the atomic bombing had been more significant in producing Japan's mid-August surrender. That A-bomb scholarship also raised the question of whether an American pre-Hiroshima guarantee of a constitutional monarchy would have helped, amid the brutal war and perhaps with Soviet entry, to speed Japan's surrender, thus probably making a November invasion unnecessary.

The Anti-Revisionist Assault: The Bombs Were Necessary (and Morally Justifiable) for Japan's Timely Surrender

In the early 1990s, the approaching fiftieth anniversary of Hiroshima and Nagasaki and of Japan's surrender had helped bring a number of American scholars and journalists to questions about the dramatic events of ending the Pacific/Asian War in 1945. To the surprise of some longtime A-bomb scholars, the A-bomb interpretive controversy, which had not been very heated in recent years and had sometimes involved published differences mostly between friendly A-bomb "revisionists," took on new fervor and sometimes became venomous by about the mid 1990s with the entry of some new analysts. That apparent mean-spiritedness, marking much of the new dispute, was probably triggered partly by the 1994–95 controversy over the Smithsonian Institution's National Air and Space Museum presentation of the *Enola Gay* exhibit, which had even led to the firing of the museum's director.

In 1995, the historian Robert J. Maddox of Pennsylvania State University and Robert P. Newman, a communications professor who had recently retired from the University of Pittsburgh, issued spirited, separate volumes assailing what they variously defined as A-bomb revisionist arguments. Like the A-bomb revisionists, both Maddox and Newman focused mostly on American policy. But rather like some of the 1990s A-bomb revisionist work, Maddox and Newman also looked into Japanese policy and used some of the American-based, English-language archival sources to interpret Japanese policy.[20]

Maddox cites most of the American archival collections (aside from the Strategic Bombing Survey file materials) on Japanese policy in the bibliography of his 1995 book *Weapons for Victory: The Hiroshima Decision Fifty Years Later*, but judging from his notes, he seems to have drawn only sparingly from these Japanese-policy sources in his interpretation of events.[21] In his own 1995 volume, *Truman and the Hiroshima Cult*, Newman, while not providing a bibliography of archival materials, apparently cast a somewhat deeper and wider research net than had Maddox in the English-language Japanese materials. Each of these authors was sharply anti-Alperovitz in interpretation.

Both Newman and the spiritedly anti–Cold War revisionist Maddox, who had pummeled Cold War revisionists since his early 1970s writings, sometimes operated virtually as litigators on what had recently become, after a nearly two-decade hiatus, a feverishly contested set of issues about the atomic bombings. The technique of "prosecution" that they used against revisionist interpreters had really begun on A-bomb issues a generation before, in about the mid 1960s in the Gar Alperovitz–Herbert Feis exchanges, and then generally disappeared, despite published differences among A-bomb revisionists.[22]

Notwithstanding differences in phrasing and emphasis, as well as in the depth and quality of research, Maddox and Newman contended in their 1995 books that both atomic bombings had been necessary and justifiable, that pre-Hiroshima Japan had not been close to surrender in August, that the atomic bombings had speedily ended the war and obviated the invasion, and that soft American peace terms in June–July, with provision for a Japanese constitutional monarchy, would not have ended the war before November without the atomic bombings. Despite their limited research, the works by Maddox and Newman helped spur anti-revisionism on the A-bomb and contributed to the expanding focus in the A-bomb literature to deal with Japanese policy in summer 1945. But other than Newman's thoughtful indictment of the Strategic Bombing Survey's conclusion that the A-bombing had probably been unnecessary, the two men's books probably had very limited influence on the larger end-of-the war literature by Japan specialists focusing heavily on Japanese policy.

Of the World War II generation, Newman himself, as he privately explained in the 1990s, had not initially been greatly hostile to A-bomb revisionism. His earlier research on the general period, including writing a book on the China expert Owen Lattimore, who was pilloried in the early Cold War by venomous McCarthyites, and some related research by Newman on pro-McCarthyite former Japan experts close to Under Secretary Grew, had apparently helped change Newman's views. For him, as he recently recalled, the crucial research event pushing him into anti-revisionism was working on the Strategic Bombing Survey's archival records (on microfilm), and concluding that, in his judgment, the key Bombing Survey reports on A-bomb matters had "fudged" the conclusions. Though he became a forceful supporter of Truman's 1945 atomic bombing policy, Newman was also a strong foe of some later Truman administration's positions in foreign affairs and nuclear-weapons and defense matters.[23]

Newman was sharply intelligent. He shrewdly spotted others' overstatements and often angrily focused on his opponents, virtually pouncing on them. Vigorously disputing some A-bomb revisionists' charges, Newman was undoubtedly correct that Truman's main purpose in using the A-bomb on Japan was to end the war speedily and without risking American battle casualties, but curiously Newman nearly entirely ignored the issue of anti-Soviet motives on the part of American leaders in using the A-bomb. He ardently defended the Roosevelt-Truman pre-Hiroshima unconditional-surrender position, though noting, as had other writers earlier, that the Potsdam Proclamation of July 26, while speaking of unconditional surrender, had really indicated conditions including some promises for a postwar Japan.[24]

The crux of Newman's work was that Japan was not near surrender before the Hiroshima bombing. He moved too effortlessly from that reasonable conclusion to disregard Butow's 1954 arresting contention that an Allied declaration in June–July 1945 allowing a constitutional Japanese monarchy might have produced Japan's surrender before early August, thus obviating the atomic bombings and Soviet entry. Newman, a stalwart Stimson supporter, also omitted Stimson's similar 1948 statement that America might have dangerously prolonged the war by not providing a pre-Hiroshima declaration allowing a Japanese constitutional monarchy. In arguing rather strenuously that the Nagasaki bombing was necessary, Newman minimized the impact of Soviet entry on Japanese decision makers and ultimately rested his argument on the questionable contention that Hirohito could not have persuaded the Japanese militarists to accept a surrender with a single condition had the second bomb not been used. That speculation is not unreasonable, but it generally lacks directly corroborative evidence. In casting his ardent defense of Truman's use of the A-bombs on Japan, Newman was normally wary of using words like "possibly," "probably," and "maybe," or phrases like "the evidence implies" and "the evidence suggests." Like a forceful debater, he usually preferred assertive decisiveness, and energetic firmness, turning what could have been a calm, focused, probing dialogue into a harsh dispute with a clear winner and thus, presumably, clear losers.[25]

In studying the end of the war and justifying the use of the atomic bombs, neither Newman nor Maddox looked closely at the impact of Soviet entry and its influence in August 1945 on Japanese decision making. Nor did either of them seem to know in any depth the relevant recent literature in English, especially the work by Herbert Bix and Stephen Large on Hirohito and Japanese policy. In many ways, the two 1995 books by Maddox and Newman seemed underresearched and overargued, especially when dealing with explanations and assessments of Japanese policy.

Some of Newman's and Maddox's major arguments about the necessity for both A-bombs rested on implicit counterfactual assumptions: surrender would not otherwise have occurred within a few weeks, or possibly even within about two and a half months, even after Soviet entry into the war and Allied permission for a Japanese constitutional monarchy. Newman believed that a few weeks' delay would have been too much, and that certainly two-and-a-half months would have been dangerously late, because many non-Japanese would have died in the interim, so any delay beyond mid-August (the actual date) of Japan's surrender was morally unacceptable.[26]

The volumes by Maddox and Newman probably did not attract significant attention among professional historians, but a 1995 article by Maddox in *American Heritage* summarizing his position, a strongly supportive review essay by the Yale historian Donald Kagan in *Commentary,* and a spirited op-ed exchange between Newman and Alperovitz in the *Washington Post* probably helped win public attention for the anti-revisionists' work and their conclusions.[27] Yet whether Maddox and Newman altered the views of many American historians and laypeople, or simply confirmed pro-A-bomb believers in their pro-A-bombing conclusions, is hard to gauge.[28]

It seems likely, though it is less than systematically established, that the books by Newman and Maddox were primarily useful in providing evidence for those who had already reached pro-A-bomb-use conclusions. Influence upon college students is more difficult to determine, though sales figures may provide some indirect leverage on that issue. Newman's more thoughtful book reportedly only sold under about 500 hardback copies by 2004, and Maddox's apparently about 3,000 in hardback before going into paperback in 2004.[29]

Maddox and Newman, like Alperovitz and Bernstein in the 1990s, had done more work investigating Japanese policy than had A-bomb revisionists and most non- or anti-revisionists on the A-bomb when writing in the 1960s and early 1970s. Yet it would be too much to claim that the once divided streams of end-of-the-war studies and A-bomb studies had fully, or even substantially on most occasions, come together in the mid 1990s. The overlap in focus, however, was certainly greater by the mid 1990s than in earlier decades. That growing but still not large general overlap, while usually less than desirable, was represented by the publication in the mid 1990s of at least a handful of studies from both pro- and anti-A-bomb interpreters, who did seriously, but seldom greatly, look into Japanese policy and examine Japanese decision making.

The Critical Examination of the U.S. Bombing Survey Counterfactual(s)— Focusing Sharply on Some Virtually Official History

The U.S. Strategic Bombing Survey, authorized by President Roosevelt in World War II, had received the added task in mid-August 1945 from President Truman to study the war against Japan. In mid 1946, after about nine months of work, which included only a few months in Japan on the part of its members, the Survey asserted, in a passage crafted by its vice-chairman, the 39-year-old Paul Nitze, two important conclusions: that (1) "in all probability" before November 1945 and (2) "certainly" before the end of that year, Japan would have surrendered unconditionally even if there had been no invasion or planned invasion, no atomic bombing, and no Soviet intervention in the war.[30] Those influential contentions, which Nitze, a former Wall Street financier, claimed publicly were based on "all" the evidence, became virtually a form of official history. They were often used by historians including the interpretive antagonists Herbert Feis and Gar Alperovitz, and did not come under sustained, research-based criticism in publications until mid 1995. Because of the frequent importance of those assumptions in the scholarship, and often in the related journalistic studies, for nearly forty years up to the mid 1990s, their reassessment merits separate consideration.

In 1995, as part of their A-bomb studies, two very different American scholars—the staunchly pro-use-of-the-A-bomb writer Robert Newman and the moderate A-bomb revisionist Bernstein—separately published critical analyses of the Bombing Survey's 1946 contentions. Both Newman and Bernstein, working through the Survey's unpublished records, which had been largely open since about the early 1970s and later microfilmed, concluded that Nitze, the architect of the two arresting propositions, had failed to mention important contrary evidence in his published analyses. Nitze had, indeed, pushed well beyond the available evidence gathered by the Survey. In particular, both Newman and Bernstein, in examining the Survey's postwar interrogation transcripts of high-ranking Japanese officials, concluded that the evidence for the so-called "pre-November" claim was weak and that significant counterevidence had gone unacknowledged in the Survey's reports.[31]

Contrary to the conclusions in the Bombing Survey's two major 1946 reports, for example, Prince Konoe Fumimaro had stated in his postwar interrogation with the Survey that the war would probably have gone on *throughout 1945* if the atomic bomb had not been dropped on Japan. In his own postwar interrogation, Premier Suzuki had also indicated that the atomic bombing made an important difference in ending the war, and only after some coaxing by Survey questioners had Privy Seal Kido Kōichi given them testimony suggesting that the atomic bomb had been unnecessary.

Both Newman and Bernstein contended that Nitze had overargued his case and that Nitze had believed that the scheduled mid-August bombing of Japanese railroads, with the likely resulting food shortages, would very probably (Nitze said, "in all probability") have produced Japan's surrender before the November invasion. In Newman's harsh judgment, Nitze had misused the interview sources with Japanese leaders, thereby totally invalidating his contention that a pre-November surrender would "in all probability" have been achieved without the atomic bomb.

Bernstein, while finding that Nitze's "in all probability" contention was too firm, sought briefly to examine the likely impact of the bombing of railroads, of the damaging of the already burdened Japanese internal transportation network, and of looming food shortages in Japan. Bernstein concluded that Nitze had been far too optimistic about a pre-November surrender, without the A-bombing, Soviet entrance into the war, or modified surrender terms allowing an emperor-as-figurehead system. But Bernstein contended, as he had in other work, that Soviet entry, the continuing conventional warfare, and allowance of an emperor system might well have ended the war before November without an invasion.

Such analysis underscored that the choices for the Truman administration in 1945 were not simply the A-bomb versus invasion, or even the A-bomb and invasion. There were other strategies, both diplomatic and military, that the administration—had it desired—might have chosen instead of the atomic bombing. It was important to realize that the administration had felt no desire to avoid using the A-bomb and thus did not seek ways by early August to end the war without the atomic bombing.

Unlike Newman, Bernstein also sought to address Nitze's pre-1946 counterfactual assertion that a Japanese surrender "certainly" would have occurred without the A-bombing, Soviet entry, or an actual or planned invasion. Bernstein concluded that "certainly" was an exaggerated judgment, but that a Japanese surrender, under such conditions, would have been quite likely before the end of 1945. It was, he concluded, "far more likely than not."

In the process of addressing various interesting propositions, based substantially on long-available postwar interrogation testimony with former Japanese officials, Bernstein had sought to determine the relative influence of the bomb and Soviet entry on Japan's surrender in the context of the general American siege strategy (heavy conventional bombing and blockade) and what might have occurred if only the A-bomb or only Soviet entry had occurred along with that siege strategy. Looking at the A-bomb and Soviet entry in the context of the siege strategy, he concluded that the A-bomb had a greater impact, but also contended that Soviet entry, without the bomb, might reasonably have produced a pre-November surrender.

Bernstein's admittedly speculative analysis—about a past that never occurred without either the A-bombing or Soviet entry—did emphasize the impact of both the strangling naval blockade and conventional bombing on Japan's plight. His analysis also loosely implied, but failed to stress, that much of the postwar interview testimony by high-ranking Japanese officials might have been tainted by their desire to protect the emperor and to portray him as more peace-seeking than warranted. Whether or not Bernstein properly assessed that testimony in such a context remains an unaddressed question in the literature. Unlike his 1970s analysis, Bernstein's 1995 portrayal of Hirohito somewhat departed from Butow's genial version, but stopped considerably short of the journalist Edward Behr's harsh 1989 portrait.

Robert Pape's "Why Japan Surrendered"— the Distorting of History

Historians, journalists, and writers of popular history have generally dominated end-of-the-Japanese-war studies in the West. Social scientists have only occasionally worked in any depth in this field, and up to the early 1990s, only two or three had done so. But in 1993, before the A-bomb controversy became very heated, Robert Pape, a 33-year-old political scientist then teaching at the U.S. Air Force's Air University, addressed the difficult question "Why Japan Surrendered" in the prestigious, Harvard-based journal of security studies, *International Security*. Pape's 48-page essay was part of his larger University of Chicago doctoral project, culminating in his important 1996 book *Bombing to Win: Air Power and Coercion in War*, which apparently helped Pape receive a faculty appointment at the University of Chicago. The book focuses mostly on five cases of bombing: Germany and Japan in World War II, the Korean and Vietnam wars, and Iraq in 1991.[32] Pape's analysis of Japan's surrender—in his 1996 book, and little changed from his 1993 essay—is of primary concern here.

Pape was generally uninterested in A-bomb revisionism and in recent anti-revisionist challengers who asserted that the atomic bombings had been necessary to produce Japan's mid-August surrender.[33] Pape, who apparently did not know Japanese, chose not to use any archival sources—not even the American-based, English-language materials on postwar interrogations of Japanese wartime officials—for his own study of American bombing and Japan's surrender. Those rich interrogation materials, located in the National Archives at College Park, Maryland, were also mostly available on microfilm and could be obtained, if desired, through interlibrary loan from various major research libraries. Instead of consulting these sources, Pape normally just trustingly used other authors' summaries and the published quotations in the secondary literature, frequently drawn from primary-source materials. Pape does not explain why he chose this strategy, though it was not unusual in political science work (and especially American scholarship) on international relations. He was certainly not unusual—but probably rather typical—in his research strategy as a political scientist of comfortably assuming that the necessary archival facts had been uncovered and accurately and adequately reported in the secondary literature.

In his 1993–96 publications, Pape contended that the main interpreters had explained Japan's surrender—incorrectly, in his stated judgment—in terms of Japanese civilians' vulnerability to attack and injury. In asserting that "civilian vulnerability" was the main argument of previous interpreters, Pape failed to note that about half of his cited authors had been unclear on just why the atomic bombing, with its massive deadly results, had in their judgment helped produce Japan's surrender. Thus, contrary to Pape, putting such interpreters in the "civilian vulnerability" group was highly questionable.[34]

"The principal implication of [the main] arguments," Pape contended, "is that had American air power not driven up the costs and risks to civilians, Japan would not have surrendered prior to invasion of the home islands." In contrast, Pape declared that the appropriate explanation was not air power but the naval sea activity, and Japan's *military* vulnerability, not civilian vulnerability. By military vulnerability, he meant the feared inability to withstand the anticipated invasion of the home islands.[35]

In pursuing much of that strained argument for military vulnerability, Pape never explained why there had to be a choice between civilian and military vulnerability, and why a suitable and indeed judicious analysis could not instead also include both kinds of vulnerability. Aside from that fundamental weakness in framing interpretive issues and thus in erecting this questionable basic conceptual approach to the case study of Japan's surrender, his analysis had other severe problems—in reasoning, evidence, and research. That may seem harsh, but it is not an unreasonable judgment on deeply flawed work. At some points, moreover, Pape even seemed to contradict himself, or at least to undercut his own argument.

Part of his essay and book chapter, in seeking to deal with the problem he had framed of civilian versus military vulnerability, focused on whether assaults other than bombing had produced Japan's military vulnerability. As a result, part of his essay—using the kind of data that the Strategic Bombing Survey's mid-1940s reports had often tucked away—correctly emphasized that the American naval action had drastically cut crucial imports, thus reducing Japanese military production. That meant, Pape stressed, that Japan's capacity to defend itself against invasion was impaired.[36]

But Pape wanted to go much further: to establish that the sea blockade—not conventional bombing or atomic bombing, or a combination of those two types of bombing with the navy's sea action and the air force's mining of waterways—had produced Japan's surrender by creating military vulnerability. As a self-styled vigorous critic of various claims about strategic bombing's great effects, he was unwilling to acknowledge the psychological impact on Japanese leaders of the devastation that strategic bombing, including the A-bomb, had wrought—the many deaths in cities and the destruction of numerous factories. He was often even more reluctant to deal adequately with the psychological impact of the atomic bombing on some key Japanese leaders.

Pape chose, curiously, to acknowledge and then to minimize the then-available evidence that the emperor had apparently decided to intervene on behalf of surrender *in part because of the first atomic bombing* of Japan, which Pape himself acknowledged the emperor had interpreted in terms of *both* civilian and military vulnerability. Until the news of the atomic bombing, as Pape presumably knew, Hirohito had not chosen to intervene directly with cabinet members and the Big Six on behalf of imminent surrender.[37]

Pape tried to minimize the importance of the emperor's intervention at the special imperial meeting in the early morning of August 10 in calling for Japan's surrender. Yet Pape's very own words undercut that argument. Without the emperor's intervention on the 10th, Pape admitted that, among other possibilities, "Surrender might have come days later as the import of the disasters in Manchuria [Soviet entry] and *at Nagasaki* [the second A-bomb] had time to sink in, or not until weeks later when invasion appeared imminent, or *not at all*" (emphases added).[38] "[O]r not at all" certainly did not fit Pape's overall argument. Indeed, "not at all" demolished his central argument.

Pape also minimized the threat to Japanese leaders and to the Japanese nation of the continued American conventional bombing by contending, in a peculiarly strained argument, that the "'hostage' [i.e., apparently Japanese cities of over 100,000] was already dead." Significantly exaggerating the number of Japanese rendered homeless by nearly double-counting them, he unwisely minimized the crucial fact that millions of Japanese still lived in large and medium-sized cities in early August 1945.[39]

Because he had done so little research, and had never examined the records of postwar interrogations with Japanese officials, he did not have to deal with the evidence in those materials that would have further undercut his analysis on "military vulnerability." For example, ex-Premier Suzuki claimed in a postwar interview that some top Japanese military leaders realized after the first atomic bombing that the likelihood of an American invasion was greatly reduced, and that it was much more likely that the United States would rely upon bombing—both conventional and nuclear—to destroy Japan's homeland.[40] Some Japanese leaders evidently thought the invasion might never occur, and that the United States would just keep bombing Japan until Japan surrendered.

Pape concluded that Japan would "likely have surrendered before [the November] invasion . . . and at roughly the same time [as it did] in August"

1945, even if the United States had never conventionally bombed cities or used the atomic bomb. In contrast, Soviet entry, he argued, played an important role in producing Japan's surrender, because the inability of the Japanese to repel the Soviet invasion of Manchuria indicated the nation's military vulnerability, and "by analogy . . . the home army was unlikely to perform as well against the Americans as had been expected." Pape provided very limited evidence that any top Japanese military or civilian official drew that particular conclusion about the weakness of the home army from the demonstrated weakness of Japan's Kwantung Army, and no evidence that top civilian leaders had done so. He failed to go back to the archival sources on the two pieces of evidence he used involving Japanese military leaders, and thus he did not know that the Japanese vice chief of the army's general staff (Kawabe Torashirō), contrary to Pape, had actually said that he was unsure whether the A-bomb or Soviet entry had been more important in producing Japan's surrender.[41]

Adding to Pape's difficulties, he gravely misunderstood the subtle matter of the nature of the American response on August 11 to Japan's offer to surrender with only the single condition of allowing a form of emperor system with prerogatives. Pape concluded, incorrectly, that the United States did not budge on this matter. But, in fact, a subtle reading of the evidence, or even an accurate reading of a 1958 political scientist (Paul Kecskemeti) cited by Pape, would recognize that the United States, in a calculatedly ambiguous message, offered the *implication* of a significant concession on the emperor system but not the explicit promise of one. Put accurately, the United States budged somewhat but not fully. The lack of full budging did create severe problems in Japan.[42]

Thus, in important events that Pape *entirely overlooked* in his text, the Japanese government on August 12–14, after the ambiguous American reply, again divided sharply on the question of surrender—until Emperor Hirohito once more intervened, and called for acceptance of the newly stated American terms. In Hirohito's statement, as reconstructed by a later analyst, the emperor stressed that the nation was being turned into "ashes," thus denoting the American bombing (probably both conventional and atomic) of Japan. Disregarding such evidence, as Pape did, greatly undermined important parts of his argument about the centrality of "military vulnerability."[43]

Pape's emphasis on U.S. naval activity and the blockade is undoubtedly a valuable corrective in helping to understand the Japanese context in early August 1945, before the atomic bombing and Soviet entry into the war. And his emphasis on the Soviet entry is also valuable in reminding some analysts that it did play an important role in helping to produce Japan's surrender in mid-August 1945. But, in overarguing a weak case from severely limited evidence, while often not dealing with contrary evidence, Pape's essay and chapter seemed to go too far, to undercut portions of his own contentions, and to seek, unsuccessfully, to deny the impact of the A-bomb and of conventional strategic bombing in helping significantly to produce Japan's surrender. It was a surrender that, without the conventional and atomic bombing and without the suggestive American reply of the 11th on the imperial institution, might have been dangerously delayed for some time.

Most historians and other analysts, aside from some social scientists and a few revisionists, have treated Pape's interpretation of Japan's surrender as largely irrelevant and as substantially underinformed.[44] His work on why Japan surrendered did not help close the normally rather wide gap between historians, on the one side, and political scientists and security analysts, on the other; however, it helped underscore the width of this gap for most attentive scholars (who usually were historians) closely studying and seeking to understand the end of the Pacific/Asian war.

Bringing Together Strategic Studies and History: The A-Bombing and Soviet Entry on the Surrender

Pape in his 1996 book chapter on Japan's surrender had not dealt with the relevant work of the eminent, internationally recognized British scholar in strategic studies, Lawrence Freedman (now Sir Lawrence), including notably the essay he co-authored with the slightly younger Saki Dockrill in 1994, entitled "Hiroshima: A Strategy of Shock." Born and initially educated in Japan, Dockrill earned various degrees in the United Kingdom and then took a position as a lecturer in Freedman's war studies program at King's College, London, where she is now a professor. Their joint 1994 essay obviously appeared after Pape's 1993 article, and possibly too late for Pape easily to take it into account before the 1996 publication of his book.[45]

While doing his degree under the distinguished military historian Michael Howard (later Sir Michael) at Oxford, Freedman had initially published a small article in 1978 on the Hiroshima bombing in the first volume of the *Journal of Strategic Studies*. Freedman did not use American archival sources for this essay, but relied upon published materials, and he thus missed some important themes. Focusing mostly on American thinking on the use of the bomb, he largely dismissed A-bomb revisionist interpretations about the primacy of anti-Soviet American motives in the use of the bomb. He contended that American use had stressed the "strategy of shock" to produce Japan's surrender. Though not distinguishing as would Pape years later, Freedman in 1978 apparently meant substantially what Pape would later term "civilian vulnerability." The bomb, Freedman argued, was used so that its "terrible and spectacular . . . quality . . . might have an immediate impact on the Japanese ruling group."[46]

Following Butow's still-dominant 1954 book to some extent, Freedman was reluctant to emphasize the bomb over Soviet entry in producing Japan's mid-August surrender. "It was this [Soviet entry], as much as the bomb," Freedman wrote, "that led the cabinet to take the unprecedented step of calling upon the Emperor to make the decision to surrender." Freedman only devoted about half a page to Japanese decision making, had not worked through any of the archival sources on that subject, and was not primarily interested in why Japan surrendered. But, using Butow, the general answer seemed reasonably obvious to Freedman—Soviet entry *and* the A-bomb together.[47]

In his generally acclaimed, wide-ranging 1981 volume *The Evolution of Nuclear Strategy*, however, Freedman seems to retreat from his 1978 interpretation of Japan's surrender. Treating the issue of Japan's surrender in an elliptical manner in only a few lines, he seems to take his stand in 1981 with the major strategist Sir Basil Liddell Hart. Summarizing with approval and partly quoting Liddell Hart's *Revolution in Warfare* (1946), Freedman wrote, "The speed with which the use of the bomb was followed by Japan's surrender meant that [in Liddell Hart's words] 'its decisive effect can hardly be disputed.'"[48] The implication seemed to be that the bomb, and it alone, was decisive in the August 1945 context. Thus, presumably, Soviet entry was at most minor, certainly not essential.

Until Freedman's 1994 essay written with Dockrill, who could read Japanese sources fluently, Freedman did not focus at any length on how and why Japan surrendered. About ten pages, approximately half of their article, was devoted to these issues; the other half was basically a slight reworking of the analysis in Freedman's 1978 essay.

Admitting that it was hard to disentangle the impact of Soviet entry versus that of the bomb on Japan's surrender, the Freedman and Dockrill article initially inclined to stress somewhat the greater role of the atomic bombing.[49] As their essay unfolded, however, their argument for the primacy of the bomb's role grew stronger and their emphasis on the influence of Soviet entry usually declined. They neither denied the usefulness of Soviet entry, however, nor argued explicitly that Soviet entry was unimportant.

They concluded that Hirohito on the 8th, after the Hiroshima bombing and before Soviet entry, had virtually committed himself to a surrender. Quoting from Foreign Minister Tōgō Shigenori, they wrote that Hirohito stated, "Japan could no longer afford to talk about the conditions of her surrender terms. She must aim for a speedy resolution of the war."[50] The Freedman-Dockrill essay did not deal with a basic issue: Was Hirohito committing himself to *any* surrender terms, or did he mean surrender with the single condition of preserving some form of the emperor system?

After Soviet entry, according to Freedman and Dockrill, who apparently relied heavily on Kido's diary, Hirohito told his Privy Seal, "now that the Soviets have entered the war with Japan, there was urgent need to resolve the problem of a ceasefire." Unfortunately, Freedman and Dockrill did not address the important question: On what terms, and did a cease-fire mean surrender?[51]

Freedman and Dockrill contended that Japan's army leaders had already anticipated Soviet entry into the war, and therefore presumably that they were not shocked by the Soviet action. In contrast, the atomic bomb, according to Freedman and Dockrill, "took Japan's leaders completely by surprise." The co-authors stressed that Japanese military leaders, after briefly understating the significance of the bomb, soon heard the alarming assessment by General Anami, relying on an American prisoner's claims, that the United States had 100 A-bombs, that it could drop three a day, and that "the next target might well be Tokyo." Emphasizing their conclusion, Freedman and Dockrill contended that the impact of Soviet entry into the war was "*indirect*," presumably because it occurred in Manchuria, whereas the atomic bombing's impact was direct—on the home islands. Thus, by their analysis, the A-bomb, as they believed American leaders intended, provided the necessary "shock" to produce Japan's surrender.[52]

Their essay went one step further—it sought briefly to justify the atomic bombing on moral grounds. Japan, they contended, would probably have used the bomb if it had developed the weapon in time. Therefore, according to Freedman and Dockrill, America's use of the weapon (especially because the injurious radiation effects were not generally anticipated) was justifiable.[53]

The two authors, like many, did not address the troubling problem of the second atomic bombing? Was it necessary? Did it crucially influence Japanese decision making in the next few days? That was a curious omission, and not easy to explain, if only because of the two authors' argument about "shock."

Unlike Freedman's 1978 article, the two co-authors in 1994 briefly indicated there was a "likelihood" of "an early Japanese surrender," without the atomic bombing and by using "realistic alternatives." But "*how* early," they stated, "remains moot." They loosely implied that anti-Soviet motives might have been present in influencing the American A-bomb decision, but they minimized such motives and stressed, directly contrary to Alperovitz, "that the primary motive for the atomic bombing remained the defeat of Japan."[54]

Their 1994 essay's approximately ten-page segment on Japanese decision making skips over various events, briefly makes favorable assumptions about Emperor Hirohito, and does not focus sharply on him, his purposes, policies, and desires.[55] The essay seems uninfluenced by the emerging critical scholarship in the West or in Japan on Hirohito and on why, and when, he moved into the so-called peace camp. In defense, the two co-authors might well have contended, very reasonably, that they were only writing a short essay, not a deep, broad-ranging analysis of Japan's surrender.

The Freedman-Dockrill essay is significant for a number of reasons. It provided what was, in effect, a partial rebuttal of Pape's analysis, after the latter's 1993 article and before his book, although their 1994 essay, which was undoubtedly in press before Pape's article appeared, does not cite it. The Freedman-Dockrill essay sought seriously to combine history and strategic studies, and it was written by two scholars—one English, the other Japanese— partly embedded in the international strategic studies community. Their article was also the first analytical essay in English on Japan's surrender even partly by a Japanese-educated scholar and the first scholarly essay in English on the subject written even partly by a woman. If considered in such cultural terms, their essay indicated the broadening by the 1990s of international history and of strategic studies across both multinational and gender lines.

But there is little likelihood that scholars interested in the relationship between an author's gender and the style and argument of written work would have been able to determine Dockrill's gender from this collaborative enterprise with a senior scholar, Freedman, who had supervised her doctoral work. Nor, contrary to most Japanese historians writing in Japan, did she treat the Japanese as A-bomb victims or appear to regret the atomic bombing.

The Freedman-Dockrill essay was seldom cited by later analysts, but it obviously heavily influenced a similarly entitled article by the bilingual Japanese scholar, Dōshisha University professor Asada Sadao, published in English in 1998, justifying the atomic bombing and emphasizing the role of the bomb in producing the surrender. Unlike Freedman and Dockrill, however, Asada did suggest regret about the atomic bombing and sometimes dwelled on what he stressed as the key role of a peace-seeking Emperor Hirohito. His essay, understandably, relied more substantially on Freedman and Dockrill for their view of American A-bomb policy, and on their general understanding of the bomb as a "shock" in Japan, but not substantially on their interpretation of Hirohito.[56] Asada's essay, unlike the Freedman-Dockrill article, would often be used as a key "authority" in anti-revisionist studies on the A-bomb.

Reexamining Emperor Hirohito's Role and Power: Behr, Large, and Irokawa

Independently of A-bomb revisionism and anti-revisionism in the West, some on the political left in Japan, even before Hirohito's 1989 death, had been critical of him for complicity in World War II.[57] But such contentions in Japan seldom found an audience beyond portions of the left in that nation. In Britain and in the United States, such themes had generally received no serious hearing since David Bergamini's discredited 1971 book on Hirohito, perhaps partly because Bergamini had produced such a harsh, unpersuasive treatment of the issues.[58] Up to the late 1980s, the postwar Japanese-American rapprochement had undoubtedly created suspicion in the United States, and perhaps in Britain, of hostile interpretations of Hirohito's wartime role.

In mid 1989, in a volume prepared before Hirohito's death but published after it, the British journalist and television writer and producer Edward Behr issued a study, *Hirohito: Behind the Myth*, challenging the prevailing view of Hirohito. Not knowing Japanese, Behr, a former *Newsweek* bureau chief, had relied upon translators for access to Japanese materials, and also on the Japanese historian Inoue Kiyoshi, an early critic of Hirohito. Behr apparently chose to disregard and perhaps to be unconcerned by the fact that Inoue's analysis of Hirohito, somewhat reminiscent of Bergamini's 1971 work, had been pummeled in the West.[59]

According to Behr's 1989 rendering, as in Bergamini's 1971 treatment, the image of the wartime emperor had been "sanitized" in the Cold War to protect Hirohito. On that, Behr was undoubtedly correct and shrewdly so. But the pressing issues were: What had Hirohito actually done? With respect to what events had he been protected? What was the significance of that protection?

To Behr, Hirohito had frequently known in advance—and sometimes even been significantly involved in the decision-making leading to much of Japan's aggression: the Manchurian Incident of 1931, the Marco Polo Bridge Incident of 1937, and the movement of Japanese forces into Indochina in 1940–41. Too often, unfortunately, Behr turned speculation and slivers of information into certainty, and sometimes ignored—or at least did not mention—contrary evidence.

In rendering a conception of an activist, involved, knowledgeable Hirohito in the years before Pearl Harbor and during World War II, Behr had interestingly redefined the dialogue on the so-called 1941/1945 question: Why did not Hirohito intervene to prevent Pearl Harbor if he could intervene in 1945 to end the war? One part of Behr's important answer was blunt: Hirohito did not want to do so in 1941.

But the other part of Behr's treatment of this problem was sometimes more subtle. Alternately empathetic and harsh, Behr portrayed an emperor in summer 1945 who sometimes found his will paralyzed as he contemplated surrender, and whose generals often deceived him by indicating that the Americans would depose him and probably destroy the emperor system. Behr implied that Hirohito, had he been more decisive, could have guided his government to surrender on reasonable terms in June–July 1945 and thereby have avoided the atomic bombing.[60]

In a rather loose sketching of the chronology of events, Behr implied—contrary to Bernstein and Sherwin, and much closer to Newman and Maddox in their 1995 works—that the second atomic bombing (the Nagasaki bomb) might well have played an important role in the emperor's decision, revealed to the imperial conference on the 10th, to surrender. Behr certainly implied that the first A-bomb and Soviet entry had been essential in propelling the emperor to push on August 10 at the special imperial meeting, for surrender with the single condition of maintenance of an emperor system.[61]

Critics of Behr's study did not usually focus on the end-of-the-war events but rather on Behr's dissenting interpretation of Hirohito and on Behr's related charges that Hirohito was, in effect, a war criminal. The eminent American Japanologist John Dower, though noting many of Behr's errors in the use of sources and calling it "a flawed work," was nevertheless pleased that the question of Hirohito's ethical responsibility for the war, jointly with other Japanese leaders, was being critically reexamined, and that a portrait of an often active, engaged emperor was being presented in place of the earlier picture of a figurehead emperor unable, before summer 1945, to affect policy.[62]

In contrast to Dower's rather mixed review of Behr, the Cambridge University historian Stephen Large, then working on a biography of Hirohito, pummeled Behr for errors and suggested that Behr had often fundamentally misunderstood Hirohito, the emperor system, and the operation of the Japanese government under the Meiji constitution. Large went so far as to endorse instead a recent volume, *Hirohito and His Times*, by Toshiaki Kawahara, a pro-Hirohito observer of the imperial system. That volume, helping to cement the postwar American-Japanese rapprochement despite the alliance's economic strains, was a superficial account, full of anecdotes, genial in its treatment of matters, and conceived apparently to solidify Hirohito's image as a man of decency, compassion, and honor.[63]

In 1991, in a useful review-essay, Large noted the recently available evidence that Hirohito in 1946, in looking back on 1944–45, said he had sanctioned Japanese efforts in the battles in the Philippines in the quest for *a decisive battle* to push the United States to provide better peace terms for Japan. For Large, trustingly and uncritically accepting Hirohito's 1946 admission, there was no question but that the emperor in seeking such a battle had done so "in desperation."[64] To Large, there was no reason to focus sharply on Hirohito's admission about a decisive battle, and to ask more questions about the emperor's wartime judgment and his purposes. To other, less friendly Western interpreters of the emperor, however, this self-acknowledged quest by Hirohito for a decisive battle would soon help open the way for critical, and even hostile, assessments of the emperor and his 1945 involvement in Japan's war effort.

In his own useful 1992 book *Emperor Hirohito and Showa Japan: A Political Biography*, Large, building on his earlier work, staked out an interpretive ground far from Behr and rather close to the older picture of a figurehead emperor. Despite a few critical comments lamenting that Hirohito did not try to prevent the Japanese government's decision for war in 1941, Large, like Butow in 1954 and Dockrill in 1992, thought that Hirohito would very probably have been unsuccessful in seeking to head off war before the Pearl Harbor attack.[65]

Stephen Large's Hirohito, while possessed of somewhat more agency than Butow's emperor, seems rather similar to Butow's. Large, like Butow, found Hirohito occasionally seeking to use "his influence to end the fighting through a negotiated settlement."[66] Large's 1992 description and analysis of Japan's summer 1945 movement toward surrender does not differ markedly in substance from Butow's 1954 treatment of those events.

But whereas Butow had briefly speculated that a July 1945 guarantee of an emperor-as-figurehead system would probably have ended the war before the atomic bombings, Large, perhaps because he was writing a biography of Hirohito and not a study of Japan's end-of-the-war policy, chose not to speculate on this interesting matter. Nor did Large's narrative allow even a close reader to reach any judgment on its author's weighing of the comparative influence of the atomic bombing and Soviet entry on the emperor's August 9/10 decision for surrender.

Significantly, Large condemned the atomic bombing as "morally unjustifiable, and at that point in the war, militarily unnecessary."[67] But unfortunately, he did not move to discuss how, and under what circumstances, he believed the war would otherwise have ended. Such an omission, in view of his strongly stated judgment on the A-bomb, was both peculiar and disappointing.

Large's book, like most earlier and later studies of Hirohito, whether pro or con on the Shōwa emperor, did not address the question of what would have happened if Hirohito had not intervened on August 10 to break the stalemate in the Japanese government by proposing a one-condition surrender, and if he had decided on the 14th that America's ambiguous reply to Japan's proposal for a single-condition surrender was unacceptable. Would not the war have gone on to a third atomic bombing and continued heavy conventional bombing of Japanese cities, with the strangling blockade and possibly even the use of gas against Japanese soldiers and chemical warfare against rice crops? How much longer, if Hirohito had insisted on a clear Allied guarantee of permitting an imperial system, might the war have continued? Might there have been an upheaval in Japan, as some in the pro-peace forces there may have earlier feared?

Large's book came out in the West the year after the prominent Japanese social historian Irokawa Daikichi published his anti-Hirohito volume in Japan, which was translated and published in the United States in 1995 as *The Age of Hirohito: In Search of Modern Japan,* with an admiring foreword by Columbia University's Carol Gluck, a major American interpreter of modern Japan. Irokawa's book differed greatly from Large's analysis and came rather close to Behr's perspective on Hirohito. To Irokawa, who was on the Japanese left and had been a political activist, Hirohito was far more than a figurehead emperor or a legally constrained constitutional monarch who had to accede to Japanese military aggression.[68]

To Irokawa, Hirohito might have been able to prevent Japan's aggression against Asians on the mainland and the Japanese government's movement into World War II. According to Ikowara, Hirohito had frequently been attentive to military matters, gave advice on military strategy, and was possibly a war criminal. Had Hirohito so willed, he could have ended the war earlier, Irokawa contended, thereby saving over a million Japanese lives and many other Asian lives. Part of Irokawa's analysis relied on an interpretation of the Meiji consti-tution, in which the emperor, in Irokawa's view, could control the military.[69]

Irokawa's book was rather briefly (if not skimpily) documented, and in many ways it was basically a set of loosely connected essays, written from a politically left perspective, on Hirohito and his age. It was a volume in which the distinguished author uneasily sought to link social history (history of the masses) and the imperial history of the Japanese state. At times, Irokawa seemed dismayed that Hirohito had received such widespread support from the Japanese masses during the war, as well as in its aftermath, and Irokawa wrestled uneasily with this interpretive problem of why an undemocratic lead-er who led Japan astray and helped cost Japan so many lives should be popu-lar. Irokawa was too honest to deny the popular support for Hirohito, and far enough on the left that he regretted such support, which offended Irokawa's democratic commitments and sensibilities.[70]

Irokawa's general interpretation of the prewar and wartime Hirohito was arresting and unsettling. The book offered a perspective that left-leaning Japanese historians were generally more willing to put in writing after the em-peror's death, which greatly liberated them. Moreover, the availability of new sources—including, notably, the emperor's 1946 monologue (his long-secret discussions of wartime and prewar policy)—provided important new materials to help buttress their critical reinterpretation of Hirohito.

For example, Irokawa, quoting Hirohito's 1946 recollections in his monologue about 1943 events, stressed that the emperor, when the war turned sour for Japan in 1943, said to the army chief of staff, "Can't you give the American forces a walloping [elsewhere]?" And in mid 1945, as Japan was suffering a painful defeat on Okinawa, Hirohito, according to his postwar recollection in the monologue, was advising his military leaders to attack elsewhere to produce "a heavy blow against England and America" in the Far East. Such advice—bellicose, fiercely nationalist, and certainly not peace-inclined—was far from the older Western image of the gentle, passive or figurehead monarch who had not roused himself to engage in military and diplomatic policy until mid 1945, and then to push only for peace.[71]

Irokawa's interpretation of the emperor, in addition to receiving support in the limited reviews in the Asian studies field in the United States and Britain in 1996–97, also won plaudits from a reviewer in the *New York Times*. Irokawa's book did not receive wide attention in the West beyond Japan specialists, but the volume did contribute to the emerging intellectual movement in the post–Cold War period in the West that interpreted Hirohito more harshly, found him somewhat to blame for World War II in Asia, and contended that he could and should have acted earlier to end it. This was a position, despite differences in emphasis, that such Western-based major historians of Japan as Carol Gluck of Columbia and John Dower of MIT, among others, were generally endorsing in the mid 1990s and sometimes earlier.[72]

Indirectly contributing to those issues, Irokawa's quotations from Hirohito's 1946 monologue did provide some limited information—not commented on by major Western reviewers of *The Age of Hirohito*—on the emperor's and his government's motivation in moving for Japan's surrender in mid-August 1945. "Faced with this [Soviet entry into the war on the 8th]," the emperor stated in 1946 in his then-secret monologue, "we felt that there was no alternative but unconditional surrender." Hirohito continued in his 1946 monologue, looking back on August 1945, to add: "The air raids increased in intensity daily. The atomic bomb made its appearance on August 6. The people were in desperate straits. The Soviet Union commenced fighting in Manchuria. Thus we were forced into a situation in which we had to accept the themes of the Potsdam Declaration."[73]

This explanation, by linking conventional and atomic bombing and Soviet entry in a brief narrative, failed to distinguish the comparative weights of these three separate factors. In effect, Hirohito, in this retelling, had treated all three factors as nearly equal. But it might be a mistake to rely too heavily on his loose formulation stated in 1946 of why Japan had surrendered in August 1945 to conclude, necessarily, that all three factors had operated almost equally for Hirohito and for top members of Japan's government in August 1945.

Hirohito's 1946 statement probably cannot really support such careful parsing, and it should presumably be treated as suggestive, and certainly not definitive, in disclosing his August 1945 motivation. Not surprisingly, future interpreters in the West relied neither on this statement nor on Irokawa in seeking to explain why and how Japan surrendered.

A Challenge from the Left to the Belief in Missed Opportunities: Bix and the Emperor

In Japan, after Hirohito's death in January 1989, a substantial critical literature, including Irokawa's book, had begun to emerge reassessing the emperor's role in the movement to war in the 1930s, in the decision to attack Pearl Harbor in 1941, and sometimes in ending the war in 1945. In that new literature, Hirohito was not treated as a figurehead, or simply as a weak constitutional monarch, but, rather, as someone who exercised authority, supported the war, and could often have acted otherwise to avoid the war or end it earlier.[74] That new interpretation of Hirohito—though suggested in more extreme form in the west by Bergamini in 1971 and by Behr in 1989, and by some on the Japanese left before Hirohoto's death—often benefited from the availability, beginning in 1990, of the emperor's "monologue," upon which Irokawa had sometimes relied.

The monologue text, actually the emperor's dictated statements taken down in March–April 1946 at a series of then-secret sessions, was discovered in 1989 and first published in Japanese in December 1990. The exact purpose of those 1946 meetings of the emperor and the reasons for his making the monologue text would remain in some dispute, though most interpreters assumed that Hirohito had done so in preparation for the Tokyo war-crime trials and possibly to resist calls for his abdication. Whether or not in early 1946 he still feared an indictment, or being called to testify, or whether he was simply taking the precaution of preparing a defense, even if deemed probably unnecessary, and also protecting himself from calls for abdication, remains unclear.[75]

Generally, in using the monologue, often to show that the old version of Hirohito as weak and passive is a dubious interpretation, historians in the West have not adequately addressed a puzzling matter: Why did Hirohito provide so much evidence in his 1946 statements that he had strongly supported the war at critical junctures and had been significantly engaged in discussions of military strategy? One speculative answer might be that he did not like his emerging image as a passive figurehead and sought in 1946 to project that of an informed, aggressively involved wartime emperor. Yet the more he contended in the 1946 monologue that he had been active and engaged, the more likely that the monologue could be used against him in a war-criminal trial or a belated American effort to push him to abdicate because of his war involvement.

Building substantially on the new Japanese dissident literature, Herbert Bix, an American historian of Japan, argued in an important 1995 essay that Hirohito's slowness in moving toward surrender in summer 1945 had delayed the end of the war and cost many Japanese lives.[76] Bix was intentionally challenging the competing view, which had long dominated most Western literature on the atomic bombing and on Japan's end-of-the-war decisions. For Bix, the Strategic Bombing Survey, Under Secretary of State Joseph Grew, and Butow's *Japan's Decision to Surrender*, as well as many others, had fundamentally misunderstood Hirohito. They had erroneously seen him as virtually powerless, and had therefore incorrectly insulated him from any causal role, and thus blame, for the prolonged Pacific/Asian War. In stressing this position, Bix was close to the analysis in a 1989 Japanese book by Nakamura Masanori, translated by Bix and others under the title *The Japanese Monarchy: Ambassador Joseph Grew and the Making of the "Symbol Emperor System," 1939–1991* (1992).

Bix had long been a critic of Hirohito and of the emperor system. In the early 1980s or somewhat earlier, and certainly well before Hirohito's death in 1989, Bix had started reassessing Japan's emperor system. Unlike many analysts in the West, who had viewed the prewar and wartime emperor as a figurehead, Bix had argued that there was an "emperor-system fascism," with an often powerful emperor involved in a larger capitalist system that could be characterized as fascist. Bix's early 1980s work had focused less on the emperor himself and far more on Japan's political-economic system, and in 1991, Bix had warned against focusing on decision making and not stressing the larger context.[77] Yet, in contrast, Bix's own later 1990s writings, including his 1995 essay "Japan's Delayed Surrender: A Reinterpretation," tended to dwell on Hirohito and not to stress an analysis of the larger political-economic system.

Bix's general view of the emperor was expressed in his 1992 article "The Showa Emperor's 'Monologue' and the Problem of War Responsibility": Hirohito "was both a supra-constitutional monarch and an active generalissimo" who often endorsed Japanese aggressive policy. In Bix's 1995 analysis, Hirohito shifted away from the quest for a decisive victory—only belatedly— when the Okinawa campaign went so badly. After that, Hirohito "accepted the need for an early but not an immediate peace." To Bix, Hirohito had delayed unwisely.[78]

Bix, a Harvard-trained historian, was himself on the American political left, and his 1995 interpretation also fit much of the thinking on Japan's left.

Departing from many A-bomb revisionist arguments that there had been a missed opportunity to end the war before August 1945 if the United States had allowed maintenance of the emperor-as-figurehead system, Bix claimed that such revisionist contentions, along with those by Grew and Butow, among others, basically misunderstood the emperor system. Bix argued that the desires by Suzuki, Tōgō, Kido, and other so-called "moderates" in wanting an Allied guarantee preserving "the [emperor's] prerogatives to rule the state" were not a plea for retaining a very limited constitutional monarchy, but, rather, far more than that.[79] In Bix's view, they were seeking to protect a system in which the emperor had considerable power and had used it for pro-war purposes.

No single one of Bix's 1990s articles, unsettling though they were, provided sufficient evidence to establish his important central contentions about Hirohito's power and the nature of the wartime monarchy. Still operating with rather limited evidence that failed to establish part of his core argument, Bix published a very significant book on Hirohito in 2000 that had considerable impact. Entitled *Hirohito and the Making of Modern Japan*, running 770 pages with notes, it partly knitted together revised versions of some of his 1990s essays and also dealt in some depth, and at considerable length, with the earlier life of Hirohito. Bix, who had moved to Japan to teach at Hitotsubashi University in Tokyo, rooted much of his extended argument in the development of the prewar monarchy under Hirohito.[80]

Bix won the Pulitzer Prize for this volume, but some critics found much of his argument strained and the evidence sometimes less than adequate. They were also justifiably annoyed that he did not deal explicitly with recent rival interpretations by Stephen Large, Edward Drea, Asada Sadao, and others. Perhaps that was a strategy Bix and his editor devised partly for commercial reasons: to produce an important, readable book partly in order to gain a good-sized audience outside academia, and therefore not to do, as historians in journal and monographic literature often do, and argue explicitly with other analysts while even identifying them by name. Such argumentation, which is important in the academy and frequently the focus of seminars and history-association meetings, often reaches beyond the tolerance of a lay audience, unless the issues are part of their own deeply felt concerns.[81]

Even those troubled by some of Bix's strategies and who may reject his general framework are now compelled to ask again, as have some Japanese critics of Hirohito, why the emperor did not move earlier in 1945 to end the war—well before the atomic bombings and Soviet entry? Was the emperor, as many believed, being cautious and seeking to avoid a coup? Or had Hirohito, as Bix harshly contended, supported the war for too long and failed to appreciate that Japan was badly losing it? Did Hirohito, as Bix also maintained and as

Irokawa had suggested, placed his own person and the emperor system above the welfare of his citizens?

In a volume entitled *Hirohito and War* (1998), Peter Wetzler, a Berkeley-trained historian of Japan, offered a more moderate interpretation of the emperor. While mostly focusing on the prewar Hirohito, Wetzler directly but very briefly—probably too briefly for our purposes—addressed Bix's depiction of the wartime emperor. Wetzler offered a carefully modulated view, one almost midway between the positions of Large and Bix, though inclining a bit closer to Bix's. "Depending on the forces around him [the emperor]," in Wetzler's view, "sought peace or made war, referring always to the constitution but preoccupied mainly with assuring the position and continued existence of the imperial house in Japan." Hirohito could exploit and even shape opportunities, and had more authority than an English monarch, but, contrary to Bix's version, Wetzler's Hirohito was not the person "more than anyone else [in the Japanese government] who delayed Japan's surrender."[82] Unfortunately, Wetzler did not deal systematically and in detail with Bix's argument about Hirohito and the 1945 road to surrender, because Wetzler was primarily interested in the period up to about Pearl Harbor.

To most scholars, Bix's work had the quality of undercutting many A-bomb revisionists' arguments that the use of the bomb had been unnecessary to end the war, that Japan was already on the verge of surrender in early August, and that softer surrender terms allowing a limited constitutional monarchy would have ended the war without the A-bomb and well before the November invasion. In his 1995 essay, Bix concluded that such an Allied offer would probably not have been accepted *before* the atomic bombing and Soviet entry unless Japanese leaders had believed that the *kokutai* (the polity with the emperor) was threatened from within.[83]

In his 1995 essay and in his 2000 book, Bix tellingly quoted from Premier Suzuki, who shortly after the Potsdam Proclamation of July 26 had treated that Allied statement as evidence of the enemy's weakening resolve and thus, in Suzuki's view, mandating Japan's not yielding. "[C]ircumstances have arisen," Suzuki privately contended, that forced the Allied powers to talk of unconditional surrender, because they were actually eager "to end the war." He went on to counsel: "[I]f we hold firm, then they will yield before we do." The Potsdam Proclamation, he asserted, was no reason for Japan to stop fighting.[84]

Bix's book usefully underscored important differences between America and Japan in left-oriented scholarship focusing on the end of the Japanese war. In Japan, much of that scholarship blames the Japanese leadership for prolonging the war, and holds the emperor significantly responsible for the extended bloodshed. Had the war not been prolonged into August, as that scholarship stresses, there obviously would have been no atomic bombing of Hiroshima and Nagasaki. That line of analysis is not designed to justify the atomic bombings, but, for some readers, it can constitute, nevertheless, justification as well as explanation. For many American A-bomb revisionists, however, Japan was near surrender in July, allowing an imperial system would probably or definitely have ended the war before early August, and the American use of A-bombs on Japan was therefore unnecessary and even immoral.

Repeating part of his 1995 analysis, Bix dealt in his 2000 book with why Japan moved to surrender. "The evidence," he wrote, "suggests that the first atomic bomb and the Soviet declaration of war made Hirohito, Kido, and other members of the court group feel that continuation of the war would lead precisely to that destruction [of the *kokutai*]. They knew that the people were war-weary and despondent and that popular hostility toward the military and the government was increasing rapidly, along with popular criticism of the emperor himself."[85]

Significantly, Bix's analysis departed from Irokawa's interpretation. Irokawa, basically a social historian, had not emphasized such deep uneasiness among Japan's leadership about the social order unraveling, and he rather lamented the widespread popular support for Hirohito among the Japanese masses.

Bix usefully focused, though rather briefly, on the efforts in the imperial system and among others in the government of "the younger generation of bureaucrats" who aided their superiors and pushed for peace. These underlings included Privy Seal Kido's secretary (Matuidaira Yasumasa), Suzuki's secretary (Sakomizu Hisatsune), Kase Toshikazu, and Rear Admiral Takagi Sōkichi. Bix also noted—but surprisingly did little with—the evidence that representatives of Japan's leading business interests by early August 1945 wanted acceptance of the Potsdam Proclamation, because it would end the war and allow Japan to have nonmilitary industries and engage in international trade.[86]

Differing greatly with the Strategic Bombing Survey's mid-1946 *Japan's Struggle to End the War*, with Robert Butow's 1954 book, and with most previous major Western interpretations of the end of the war, Bix argued that "an almost paranoiac fear" of revolution, triggered by the bomb and Soviet entry, propelled the Japanese government to surrender. In Bix's view, the fear was not simply of a collapse of the nation's social order, but, rather that the "people would react violently against their leaders." According to Bix, Japan's government leaders, including especially the emperor, were unpained by the death of their countrymen in the conventional and the atomic bombings of Japan's cities. For Bix, the top Japanese leaders, and especially Hirohito, did not care about the Japanese people. These men did worry deeply, however, about the polity with its emperor system.[87]

Emphasizing the impact of the A-bomb *and* Soviet entry on the decision to surrender, Bix also suggested that those two sets of events were useful pretexts for Japan's government to act to end the war. He quoted, as would Asada in part a few years later, Navy Minister Yonai Mitsumasa's words on August 12 to Admiral Takagi Sōkichi: "[T]he atomic bombs and the Soviet entry into the war are, in a sense, gifts from the gods. This way we don't have to say that we quit the war because of domestic circumstances [fear of upheaval]."[88]

Tellingly, Bix thought that neither America's decision in July not to guarantee an emperor system nor America's decision in July not to have Stalin sign the Potsdam Proclamation could explain Japan's failure to surrender. By inference, according to some interpreters who closely read his work, Bix seemed to mean that neither a July guarantee of the emperor nor Stalin's signing the July proclamation, or even these two acts taken together, would have produced Japan's surrender before early August and the time of the atomic bombing.[89]

Though Bix did not explicitly deal with the question of whether only one of the crucial events of early August 1945—the atomic bombing or the Soviet entry—would have been sufficient to produce the mid-August surrender, that question would linger for other analysts. What did *seem* initially clear to many readers, however, is that Bix's study, with its animus toward the emperor and its view that the Japanese government had been far from surrender before the atomic bombing and Soviet entry, gave little succor to those A-bomb revisionists who thought that Japan was quite close to surrender before the atomic bombing of August 6 and therefore that the atomic bombing had been unnecessary. Yet, curiously, what seemed clear to most readers turned out to be contrary to Bix's own later explanation.

Bix's emphasis on fear of a social upheaval on the part of Hirohito and the Supreme War Council suggested a line of analysis that Bix did not pursue in his book or essays: that even without the atomic bombing and Soviet entry, continued conventional bombing—which might, moreover, be expected to increase—might eventually have produced similar fears of a popular upheaval.

Reviewing Bix's study in the *Washington Post*'s *Book World*, the A-bomb revisionist Gar Alperovitz claimed to find support for his own conclusion that the atomic bombing had been unnecessary. In Alperovitz's rendering, Bix's book proved that Hirohito and other Japanese leaders long feared Soviet entry into the war, and therefore, Alperovitz argued, in reaching beyond Bix's explicit statements, an American effort to depend on Soviet entry, and not the A-bomb, would have very probably produced the desired surrender, especially if the United States in the Potsdam Proclamation had allowed continuation of an emperor system. Alperovitz's contentions—which seemed to push Bix's own arguments to unstated implications and to dismiss Bix's explicit judgments—angered some readers, including, notably, Richard Frank, a strong anti-revisionist on the A-bomb, who had recently issued his own book-length interpretation emphasizing the importance and justifying the necessity of the atomic bombing in forcing Japan's mid-August surrender.[90]

Bix's explicit argument was apparently rich enough in unstated implications that, perhaps surprisingly, both Alperovitz and Frank could find support for their competing conclusions, leaving some uncommitted third parties uncertain about who was correctly interpreting Bix. Perhaps surprisingly, when I queried him about this in 2004, Bix responded that he regarded Alperovitz's interpretation of his book as accurate, and Frank's view as incorrect.[91]

Bix's volume, like Alperovitz's, sold well in the United States and in translation in Japan. Through 2004, the American edition of *Hirohito* reportedly sold at least 50,000 hardback copies, and at least 25,000 more in paperback. In Japan, where the study was divided into two parts, the first volume (stopping in the late 1930s) sold about 50,000 copies in hardback, with about 25,000 for volume II, which included the 1940s war and the "Delayed Surrender" sections. The book also did well in paperback in Japan, and soon went into Chinese-language editions and in 2006 into a Korean-language edition.[92]

In Japan, Bix's interpretation of the emperor was not very new. But in America, and presumably in Britain, his challenging book, aided by a number of reviews in newspapers and in general intellectual journals, introduced attentive readers to a comparatively new scholarly view of Hirohito. Irokawa's slender volume, despite similarities in interpretation, had not reached many American or British readers.

Blaming Hirohito and the Supreme War Council partly for the atomic bombing because they had delayed ending the war promised to expand the focus of end-of-the-Japanese war studies in other ways. Bix's analysis also implied the need for such studies to go beyond the examination of government decision making and the problems with Japan's military to analyze both the desires of important business interests and the threat of upheaval at home unless the government ended the war. The implications, rooted partly in Bix's Marxist view of Japanese society, indicated the possibility in such studies of linking an analysis of Japanese decision making and of Japanese social history in a framework partly informed by political economy.

Significantly, Bix's work, like John Dower's important recent work, usefully emphasized how much the earlier conception of Emperor Hirohito was rooted in the Cold War reconstruction of history and was designed to justify retaining him on the throne in the postwar period. To many who had focused on the A-bomb issues and made certain casual assumptions about what might be termed "the innocent, figurehead wartime emperor," this new conception of the wartime Hirohito and the postwar Japanese polity added an important dimension to the complexity of World War II history and to understanding Japanese decision making, the roads for Japan to war and to surrender, and the postwar rewriting of Japan's wartime history.

"Chasing a Decisive Victory": Edward Drea's Hirohito

Between Bix's 1995 essay and his 2000 book, the American military historian Edward Drea, who had long served as an official historian for the army before moving to the Defense Department, issued his own interpretation of Hirohito and the ending of the war. Entitled "Chasing a Decisive Victory," Drea's 1998 study was part of a thoughtful collection of military-oriented essays, *In the Service of the Emperor*. Believing that the A-bomb had been necessary to end the war, Drea presented a discussion critical of Hirohito, focusing on what Drea believed had been the emperor's quest for a decisive battle that would allow Japan to negotiate a favorable settlement ending the war.[93]

Drea was often at odds with Bix, though not dealing with Bix head-on by name. Whereas Bix was harshly critical of Hirohito and saw him as far more than a constitutional monarch, Drea, though not sympathetic to Hirohito, viewed the emperor as a constitutional monarch often restricted by his own beliefs, by the counsel of his advisers, and by the limits of his office. Portrayed by Drea as timid and bookish, but attentive to military matters, Hirohito in Drea's rendering was a deeply flawed man and leader but not malevolent. Drea's Hirohito unfortunately pursued the "chimera of the decisive battle, be it on land or sea." Drea stressed that this was the quest not only of Hirohito but also of the Japanese imperial court, the high-level bureaucracy, and the military, but that the aim shifted over time, especially for Hirohito, from seeking a true victory to a decisive battle that would preserve the *kokutai*.[94]

Speaking specifically of the period up to about the Okinawa defeat in late June 1945, but apparently referring generally at least to the period up to the Hiroshima bombing on August 6 and Soviet entry into the war on August 8, Drea wrote, "When Hirohito and the peace faction or any other Japanese who mattered talked about ending the war, they meant by a negotiated settlement, not a capitulation and certainly not an unconditional surrender."[95]

By the time of the Japanese defeat on Okinawa in June 1945, Drea argued, anyone attentive to the evidence should have understood that Japan was defeated and that only surrender remained as a viable option. In Drea's interpretation, Hirohito rationally understood the merit of that conclusion, but "he could not rid himself of the irrational notion that a single battlefield victory would somehow allow Japan to negotiate its way out of a losing war." According to Drea, that had been Hirohito's quest from about late 1942, even as bleak reports came back on the course of the war.[96]

Asking why Hirohito did not act in June 1945 to end the war, Drea, more critical than Butow, answered that Hirohito was "a timid and conservative monarch" who would not give up on the military's hopes for a decisive victory or the diplomatic quest to keep the USSR neutral. Furthermore, according to Drea, the fear of a military coup—not Bix's left-wing revolution, but, rather, in Drea's analysis, a right-wing assault—"haunted Hirohito to the end."[97]

Unlike Bix, Drea did not hold Hirohito chiefly responsible for the prolonged war, and Drea stressed that the emperor's top military men—both navy and army leaders—had often misled him about Japan's military activities. Operating not in dishonesty but in self-deception, they claimed, according to Drea, that actual defeats had been victories. Whatever the general merits of that analysis for 1943 and 1944, it does not seem to fit the evidence, as suggested by Drea himself, for the period of the Okinawa defeat in June 1945 and afterward. Yet, because Drea, unlike Bix, saw the emperor as usually constrained by the constitutional rules of a limited monarchy, Drea was unwilling, unlike Bix, to single out the emperor for blame in the prolonged war.

By about July 24, according to Drea, Hirohito had finally given up on the quest for the decisive battle. But he still aimed for a settlement that preserved the *kokutai,* with the imperial system and the symbols—including the three prized regalia—of that system.[98]

Drea chose not to focus in depth on the impact of the A-bomb and Soviet entry in producing Hirohito's decision to intervene on August 10 to plead for a surrender with the single condition of a guarantee of the imperial system. At that meeting, as Drea stressed, Hirohito pointed out that the army's hope for a decisive battle against the invading American forces might well mean the destruction of the Japanese people. "If this [mass destruction] comes to pass," Hirohito said, according to one cabinet member's summary, quoted by Drea, "we will be unable to pass on to our progeny the country called Japan that we received from our imperial ancestors."[99]

Drea briefly emphasized Hirohito's fears that an invasion, with the likely destruction of the symbols and substance of the imperial system, would mean the end of the *kokutai.* In an arresting conclusion, only partly anchored in his earlier pages, Drea wrote at the end of his 1998 essay:

Only the immediate danger to *kokutai* jolted him [Hirohito] from his passive role and forced him to action. Perhaps more than fire raids, atomic bombs, the Soviet entry into the war against Japan, and the specter of the invasion, it was the threat to his imperial ancestors, and therefore the survival of the imperial institution itself, that provided the steel otherwise [previously] missing from Hirohito's regal backbone.[100]

Drea argued that Hirohito's action was not narrowly self-serving but motivated on behalf of the symbols and substance of the imperial system and of the Japanese state. In contrast, Bix seemed unwilling to believe that any monarch, constitutionally limited or not, would take such symbols seriously. To Bix, apparently, that was virtually irrational. To Drea, however, it was part of the Japanese national tradition.

On balance, judged more by its tone and structure than by its formal argument, Drea's essay seemed to see both the A-bomb and the Soviet entry as essential in producing Japan's surrender of mid-August 1945. But for readers desiring a systematic consideration of the key issues so deeply rooted in much of the literature on Japan's end-of-the-war policies and surrender, Drea's argument can seem tantalizingly elusive. In fairness to him, however, he would undoubtedly and reasonably say that he was not seeking to join issue directly with much of that literature, but, rather, to understand Emperor Hirohito in terms of his own limitations and strengths in the emperor's long-term but ultimately failed quest for a decisive military engagement.

Though treating Bix indirectly, Drea was more forceful in criticizing some of the Japanese authors on whom Bix had sometimes relied. Yamada Akira's book on the Shōwa emperor's wartime leadership, according to Drea, "was frankly a polemic indictment of the emperor's wartime leadership based on Yamada's extensive, if selective, work in the Japanese archives." Drea likened Yamada's work to that of Inoue Kiyoshi, on whom the journalist Edward Behr had relied for his 1989 biography of Hirohito. Drea also somewhat questioned the accuracy of what he called Yoshida Yutaka's "insightful account" of how wartime Japanese history had been misconstructed after the war. Yoshida contended that the history had been willfully and cleverly rewritten and that the emperor's role had been deceitfully sanitized. Bix endorsed this view, but Drea avoided taking an unambiguous position on this important matter of how, and why, wartime history had been rewritten after World War II, what interests that "new" history served, and whether it was involved in larger Cold War purposes.[101]

Drea's thoughtful work, outside the small arena of military historians and end-of-the war analysts, apparently attracted little attention in the United States or Britain. His book, published by the University of Nebraska press, reportedly sold just over 1,000 copies in hardback before going into a small-market paperback edition, and it apparently received only a handful of reviews (aside from brief notes) in the main Asian studies and history journals.[102]

The Separation of Scholarly Communities: Forrest Morgan and Strategic Culture Versus History

Even by 2003, the interpretations by Asada Sadao, Edward Drea, and Richard Frank, among others, had apparently not generally penetrated into the very small American and Western political science, policy studies, and strategic studies communities dealing with why and how Japan surrendered. Yet Asada, Drea, and Frank had published their important studies by 1999—four years earlier. In 2003, unintentionally underscoring the isolation of the strategic studies community and much of the related political science and policy studies community from recent history writings, Forrest Morgan, a retired American air force officer at RAND, published a book-length analysis, *Compellence and the Strategic Culture of Imperial Japan*, which included a lengthy chapter on Japan's surrender, but disregarded most of the recent history literature on the subject.[103]

Like Pape, Morgan had been on the faculty at the U.S. Air Force's Air University. Morgan had done his graduate dissertation work at the University of Maryland in College Park with the future Nobel laureate in economics Thomas Schelling, a father of deterrence/coercion theory (he coined the word "compellence"), who had migrated from Harvard, and with the political scientist George Quester, who also worked on these issues. To historians, the University of Maryland's proximity to the National Archives in College Park, Maryland, had great advantages because of easy access to rich archival materials, but to Morgan, as a policy studies scholar, that was apparently irrelevant in defining and doing his research. Like Pape, Morgan eschewed directly consulting archival materials and apparently never looked at the relevant files that were within two miles of the university.

Morgan, who used no Japanese-language sources or unpublished American or Japanese archival materials, seemed generally unaware of most of the recent history literature, aside from Bix's work. In *Compellence*'s surrender chapter, Morgan draws upon Bix in endnotes, but his text mostly disregards Bix's interpretation of the emperor, and it seems as if Morgan's references to Bix's book may have been added belatedly. As a political scientist, Morgan is far more attentive to the political scientist Leon Sigal's 1988 book on the end of the Pacific War, on which he sometimes leans, and to the mid-1990s work of the political scientist Robert Pape, with whom Morgan sometimes significantly disagrees.[104]

Ultimately, after working through his three case studies on Japan, Morgan was eager to provide policy conclusions on "Crafting More Effective Security Strategies." Thus, in presenting his revised doctoral thesis, he subtitled his book *Implications for Coercive Diplomacy in the Twenty-First Century*. To some historians, such policy purposes may seem impure and likely, automatically, to sully the doing of history. But a more reasonable standard would be to judge how well the analyst concerned with policy does in studying the history, in understanding the complexity of events, and in dealing with the substantial historical literature not simply by drawing on it for its "facts" but in thoughtfully responding in terms of its interpretations. Slicing into complicated historical events for policy-related purposes can be both reasonable and risky. It is often very tempting for the policy-oriented analyst to use the historical literature entirely, or mostly, for its "facts" and not to grapple with that literature's interpretations.

In his *Compellence* book, Morgan offered a bulky conceptual apparatus, involving fifteen hypotheses about Japanese strategic culture, to present an analysis that varied between the insightful, the obvious, and the dubious. In many ways, much of Morgan's actual argument on the surrender—stripped of the political science categories that were so important to him and to his scholarly and policy subfields—reads like warmed-over Butow, though rendered in more recondite terms and with far less attention to sources and details. Emphasizing this great reliance on Butow's book, Morgan's surrender chapter cites Butow in nearly half of its notes.[105]

Put briefly, to summarize Morgan's sometimes complicated analysis, he contends that the often-used strategic studies categories of cost/benefit motivation and of balance of interests (the asymmetrical commitment to purposes by competing nations) cannot adequately explain Japan's surrender nor why it took so long. According to Morgan, if these two sets of analytical categories are employed, the surrender should probably have occurred earlier than mid-August 1945, because (1) the cost (injury to Japan) far exceeded likely benefits to Japan of continuing the war, and (2) in view of the strength of Allied motives for forcing Japan's surrender, Japan should not have wasted time trying to involve the USSR as an intermediary in peace negotiations.[106]

To explain the delay in Japan's surrender, Morgan emphasizes the need to examine the internal dynamics of the Japanese government. In doing so, he focuses upon what he calls the "strategic culture," by which he means core values and symbols. His aim is to combine some cultural anthropology with political science to emphasize the importance of culture. Despite the multiple meanings ascribed to "culture," he seems not to have understood that many historians, with a less formal analytical apparatus, had sought to do something resembling this over the years when looking deeply into the Japanese government.

Understanding the strategic culture, Morgan maintains, often means emphasizing it in order to supplement, not displace, the other two sets of analytical categories. Unfortunately, segments of Morgan's chapter sometimes ramble beyond his ostensible purposes, and as a result pieces of his argument, despite his hopes for rigor and clarity, can seem murky.

Unlike Pape, Morgan concludes that "the threat of imminent Allied invasion had no coercive effect on Japan's military leaders." They wanted a decisive battle on their nation's home islands.[107] Ultimately, Morgan argues, Emperor Hirohito's efforts, and primarily his interventions in the two imperial conferences on August 10 and 14, made the crucial difference in producing Japan's surrender. The atomic bomb and Soviet entry made the critical difference, "jar[ring] Japanese leaders out of their torpor [to] bring about an unconditional surrender."[108]

In Morgan's analysis, the first atomic bombing "so grieved" Hirohito that he agreed, upon the efforts of Privy Seal Kido and others in the peace faction, to intervene in policy to push for surrender with a single condition—maintenance of the imperial system. Soviet entry into the war further propelled the peace group to act. Soviet entry, Morgan says, "contributed to [the situation] that persuaded the [Japanese] military rank and file to accept the emperor's command" that all should agree to Japan's surrender. Morgan stresses that all wanted a conditional surrender, with united agreement on the need to protect the "core" value—an imperial system. But when the Truman government refused to provide such terms, according to Morgan, "the emperor sacrificed *kokutai* [the imperial system] for the only value that he, as father of the Japanese national family, held more dear—the survival of his people."[109]

Morgan implies that others in the Japanese government, out of respect and loyalty, deferred to the emperor on this matter. But Morgan does not adequately deal with the dispute within the Japanese government in the few days before the emperor's second intervention on the meaning of the ambiguous American reply of August 11 on surrender terms. Nor does Morgan seem to have understood the nature of the actual American reply, which implied, but did not guarantee, allowing an imperial system. Hirohito was not clearly and intentionally sacrificing *kokutai*. He was taking a calculated risk, predicated on various judgments, about what America was stating and what it was intending. There is a great difference between making a clear sacrifice and taking a risk.[110]

Speaking most often to political scientists and strategic studies scholars, and generally ignoring historians, Morgan emphasizes, as though making a comparatively new point, that the Japanese government was not a unitary rational actor and must not be so treated in analyses dealing with the surrender.[111] Indeed, it is unclear whether any serious Western historian writing in depth on Japan's decision to surrender had accepted and used an implicit *unitary* rational-actor framework in studying Japan's government. All the major literature, dating back to the Strategic Bombing Survey in mid 1946, had stressed differences within Japan's government about whether and when to surrender, and about possible terms for ending the war. Whereas Pape often simplifies the historical writing, Morgan often simply disregards whatever in that corpus does not fit the points he wishes to make.

Morgan does usefully note that Pape's peculiar argument that Japan surrendered because of military vulnerability is flawed and dubious.[112] Morgan stresses instead Hirohito's distress at the mass killing of Japanese citizens, and the emperor's fear that the carnage would continue unless Japan surrendered. That view of Hirohito, to repeat, was markedly at odds with Bix's interpretation, but Morgan in his text on the surrender chooses not to dwell on their differences.

At best, in dealing with Bix in 2003, Morgan engages in a kind of flanking assault, in what many readers might easily overlook in *Compellence*'s surrender chapter, because the skirmish occurred mostly in a single endnote, in which Morgan draws substantially upon Bix's quotation from Hirohito in the emperor's 1946 monologue to try to show that Bix misinterpreted the *wartime* Hirohito. According to Morgan, Bix is wrong to contend that the emperor lacked concern for the Japanese people during the war and thus errs in saying that the emperor did not propose surrender in order to spare them.

Here, in Morgan's effort to refute Bix, is the key quotation—used by Morgan from Bix's book—of Hirohito's postwar words in the emperor's 1946 monologue explaining his 1945 decision for surrender: "The main motive behind my decision [to urge surrender] at that time [in 1945] was that if we . . . did not act, the Japanese race would perish and I would be unable to protect my loyal subjects."[113]

These words seem clear in meaning and in significance. But are they *reliable*, uttered as they were in 1946 on Hirohito's 1945 motives? Can Hirohito's words in 1946 be trusted to explain his wartime behavior? Or might he have been dissembling in 1946 for various reasons, including his possible desire to rewrite his recent past, and conceivably even to protect himself from prosecution as a war criminal or related embarrassment? Morgan does not squarely face these key issues and offers only some rather oblique evidence on this matter.

Bix, in many ways mistrusting Hirohito's postwar words, sometimes treats Hirohito's postwar claims in the emperor's 1946 monologue as the "manufacture of historical memory." In view of the centrality of Hirohito's concerns in part of Morgan's analysis, it is surprising—some might say, disappointing—that Morgan does not dwell on his differences with Bix and explain in depth, with more than two pieces of somewhat ambiguous evidence in his surrender chapter and a longer endnote in his concluding chapter, why his image of a benign Hirohito is more appropriate than Bix's harsh view of the emperor.[114]

On the question of whether only the atomic bombing or Soviet entry would have produced Japan's mid-August surrender, Morgan's implicit answer is that both were necessary. He is not really interested in such analysis, so it is probably not surprising that he does not explicitly deal with the related question of whether the Nagasaki bombing was necessary.

Like Pape's, Morgan's work is probably unlikely to influence Western writing on the end of the Pacific/Asian War to any great extent, and even less the literature on that subject in Japan. The end-of-the-Japanese-war field in the West is still primarily an arena, and sometimes a dialogue, involving historians, other academic specialists on Japan, writers of popular history, and journalists. The historians and other specialists, aside from those focusing mostly on A-bomb issues, are generally people who know and use the Japanese language in their studies and who pay some attention to A-bomb scholarship but none to strategic studies writings.

Morgan's book and his interpretive framework may have some, albeit limited, impact in political science and on the strategic and policy studies communities. Those sometimes interlocking communities may find it useful to be reminded of the need to reassess compellence theory within the context of particular cultures. The notion that compellence operates differently on different cultures is hardly new, but to many in political science and in policy studies and security studies, who are often indifferent to cultural and biographical variations when seeking to understand particular nation-state behavior, this may prove a valuable point.

To historians and area studies scholars, however, there is no need to stress what they normally understand: culture matters. Therefore conceptions of rationality, honor, loyalty, and obligation, as well as judgments about the appropriate responses to concessions, threats, and force, can vary significantly in different cultures.

Yukiko Koshiro: A Bold Challenge

Between 1989 and 2004, as earlier, there was a large area of agreement in much of the literature on the end of the Pacific/Asian War, even when there was strong controversy on particular issues. It would be too much to claim that there was a dominant paradigm, but despite some exceptions, among the historians who published on the subject, there was generally what might be called a reigning interpretive *strategy* of approach, of focus, and frequently of questions. That strategy had largely originated with the U.S. Strategic Bombing Survey's two mid-1946 reports and was crystallized in Butow's *Japan's Decision to Surrender*. Together, these studies helped shape much of the later discourse of those who focused, especially in the West, on why and how Japan surrendered.

Like the Bombing Survey and Butow's book, much of the recent literature in the West focusing on Japan's end-of-the-war policy, other than the biographies of Hirohito, looks closely, and sometimes very closely, at military and diplomatic issues within a narrow framework. Many of the end-of-the war studies, heavily informed by Butow's careful approach, even when disagreeing with his assumptions about sources and his conclusions about Hirohito, provide rather close-grained analyses of Japanese decision making.

The important question of the roles of Soviet entry and the A-bomb in producing the mid-August surrender, and whether both, only one, or neither were significant, is frequently treated centrally by the writers of these studies. Most, when dealing with 1945 Japanese-Soviet relations up to August 8, focus on the details of those relations and stress various Japanese leaders' hopes, but without richly placing the negotiations in the larger analytical context of Japan's foreign policy in 1939–45. Many analysts treat Japanese efforts in the 1945 efforts at negotiations with the USSR as a grave mistake, even a puzzling mistake. How, more than a few writers basically ask, could Japan have been so naive as to expect help from the Soviet Union?

What might be termed this reigning strategy of approach, of focus, and often of questions was challenged briefly in 2001 in part of Yukiko Koshiro's review-essay "Japan's World and World War II," and then sharply in 2004 in her long article "Eurasian Empire: Japan's End Game in World War II" in the *American Historical Review*. Koshiro, a 1992 Columbia University Ph.D. and a native-born Japanese scholar then teaching in the United States, had published an earlier prize-winning book on race perceptions in the U.S. occupation of Okinawa. Her experience of being raised in Japan but educated at the graduate level in the United States in Japanese history indicates, like Saki Dockrill's biography, the progressive internationalization of the field of Japanese studies and Japanese history and the inclusion of women in this activity.[115]

Exploiting some previously unused or little-used Japanese sources and often making excessive claims, Koshiro's forceful 2004 essay boldly offered a new interpretive framework and a stunning line of analysis of Japan's end-of-the-war policy: Japan delayed its surrender in mid 1945, after Germany's in May, because Japanese policymakers continued to investigate how and when to surrender so that there would be a Soviet presence in postwar Asia, offsetting American power and thereby allowing more opportunity for Japan to revive in the postwar period. Koshiro further contends in places in her essay that Japanese leaders purposely delayed surrender because they were actually waiting for the entry into the war of the Soviet Union, which would establish a postwar counterweight to the United States in Asia.[116]

Koshiro's essay is often overargued and loosely constructed. In developing her central themes, she is sometimes ambiguous or murky. At times, she seems to speak of a policy of using the Soviet Union as a counterweight as having been "adopted" by Japan in 1945, but sometimes she describes a Japanese policy still in flux, while leaning toward an emphasis on the USSR as a future counterweight to American power. The gap is wide between claiming that there was (1) an *actual policy* and claiming that (2) a set of ideas was being *seriously considered*. Ultimately, Koshiro claims what seems less than credible: Japan was purposely delaying its surrender until the Soviet Union could enter the war.[117]

In 1945, many Japanese leaders had been expecting Soviet intervention, she asserts. Japan's delayed surrender is not explained in terms of diehard militarists versus a peace group but rather by Japan's developing, and even trying parts of, a shrewd Soviet policy. She also implies that the much-disputed issue of the *comparative* influence of the A-bomb versus Soviet entry is not fruitful in understanding the basic course of events in Japan's 1945 policy. In disposing of such traditional formulations, she was undoubtedly too hasty—and arguing far too much.[118]

Unintentionally underscoring the evidential problems in her study, Koshiro is often vague about exactly whom she means when discussing Japanese officials. Such key figures as Privy Seal Kido, Army Minister Anami, Army Chief of Staff Umezu, and Navy Chief of Staff Toyoda, as well as Emperor Hirohito, are largely or entirely missing. In addition, Foreign Minister Tōgō's role in her framework is generally unclear, and Premier Suzuki's role seems uncertain.[119]

Koshiro almost entirely but purposely disregards the English-language scholarship on the issues. She emphasizes her sharp disagreement with Butow's 1954 book, and with Akira Iriye's 1980s lament about the failure of Japan to surrender well before August 1945, but she does not engage the substantial English-language literature on high-level Japanese thinking about how and why to deal with the Soviet Union in summer 1945.[120]

Koshiro's essay entirely omits the substantial evidence that as late as August 9/10, before Hirohito's early morning intervention at the imperial conference, Japan's top military leaders were talking about a last battle. There is no evidence that they welcomed Soviet entry into the war, or that anyone else at that crucial imperial meeting did so. Nor, significantly, is there any evidence that anyone at that meeting discussed the issues of American versus Soviet influence in postwar Asia. Koshiro apparently chose not to confront these problems, involving both evidence and interpretation.

Despite various weaknesses of her article, Koshiro, who in 2006 returned to Japan to teach there, has usefully enlarged the focus of end-of-the-war studies by proposing that Japan's negotiations with the Soviet Union in 1944–45 were serious, not naive, efforts to broaden power relations in Asia and to help shape postwar international arrangements there. By reminding readers of Japan's earlier participation in the 1940 Tripartite Pact with Germany and Italy and in the 1941 Neutrality Pact with the Soviet Union, and of Japan's various pre–Pearl Harbor ventures to try to combine these alliances to constitute a counterweight to Anglo-American influence in Asia, Koshiro has, in effect, emphasized the useful interpretive framework of competing imperialisms in Asia. Thus, end-of-war issues are to be understood in that broad context, she suggests.

In treating Japanese foreign policy as rational and shrewdly calculating, and as being conceived in 1945 in a world seen in terms of competing imperialisms where the United States was also viewed as imperialistic, Koshiro has tilted the interpretive framework politically leftward and away from what she views as an earlier misguided focus. That earlier framework, she implies, was rooted in a naiveté about the United States and Japan. For Japan, she stresses, the politics of war in 1945 reflected a strong concern about the postwar period and postwar large-power rivalry in Asia.

Koshiro's provocative essay, despite significant weaknesses on central points, constitutes a useful challenge to reexamine Japan's 1945 pre-surrender diplomacy and to consider a broader framework of interpretation. Ultimately, the challenge, however, is not to jettison an emphasis on decision making, but to do that decision-making analysis well, while also taking seriously Japan's late-wartime diplomacy and its leaders' thinking then about the shape of the postwar period in Asia and Japan's place in it.

The politics of war for pre-surrender Japan, as well as for the United States and the Soviet Union, involved serious thinking about the shape of the postwar world. Theories of competing imperialism are useful theoretical guides to examine often neglected questions, but there is a need to move deeply into the broad arena of archival evidence in Japan, as well as in the United States and the Soviet Union, to move from speculative theory to grounded interpretation.

Conclusions

The various contributors to the present volume—Richard Frank, Hatano Sumio, and Tsuyoshi Hasegawa on Japanese policy, and both Hasegawa and David Holloway on Soviet policy—generally conceived their essays without any interest in the work of Pape, Morgan, and Koshiro.[121] For those in this volume writing on Japanese policy and the ending of the war, the analyses by Pape, Morgan, and Koshiro have not seemed especially useful, even if, as in the case of Hasegawa, the writer found grounds for some moderate agreement with Pape on the importance of Soviet entry into the war. For those in the volume interested in Soviet policy, Koshiro's essay has marked liabilities, partly because she intentionally neglects Soviet policy in what she presents as *only* an analysis of Japanese policy.

This volume's three contributors on Japanese policy, all aware of the significant literature on the subject since about 1989, were usually in dialogue, whether implicit or explicit, with that literature. Often that meant being in dialogue with one another and sometimes exchanging drafts and sharing research materials.

Though the essays by Frank, Hatano, and Hasegawa focus heavily on Japanese policy, the categories of A-bomb revisionist and anti-revisionist are useful, though fragmentary lenses, for reading their work. Hasegawa falls into the revisionist camp, and Frank strongly into the anti-revisionist camp. Hatano, on the basis of his essay in this volume, does not easily fit into this categorization, though he clearly is much closer to anti-revisionism or non-revisionism.

For Hasegawa, Soviet entry in the war was far more important than the atomic bombing, though he concludes that it was also essential to produce a mid-August surrender, but he challenges the need for the second A-bomb. For Frank, the A-bomb was far more important in producing the Tokyo government's surrender, though he notes the importance of Soviet entry in the Japanese central government's securing of the compliance of military forces in outlying areas. For Hatano, the atomic bombing and Soviet entry were equally important in producing Japan's surrender.

The revisionist and anti- or non-revisionist categories are not especially useful in helping to interpret the competing interpretations by Holloway and Hasegawa of Soviet policy. Most notably, the interpretive differences are suggested by Holloway's conception that Stalin was involved in "jockeying for a position," while Hasegawa sees a substantial Soviet versus U.S. race for power and influence. Those interpretive differences are intimately connected with the two authors' competing views of whether Stalin became deeply concerned before or after Hiroshima about the A-bomb's use on Japan and whether, before Hiroshima, he expected the bomb to end the war speedily. For Hasegawa, Stalin, even before the bomb's use, viewed it as a decisive weapon. For Holloway, unlike Hasegawa, the great concern for Stalin about the bomb followed its use on Hiroshima.

The issues of the bomb's influence on Stalin spill over into issues not forcefully addressed in this volume about the relationship of the atomic bombing of Japan, the injury to American-Soviet relations, and the origins of the Cold War. Ironically, what had been near the core of A-bomb revisionism in the mid 1960s, and often near the core of anti-A-bomb revisionism in that decade, has—at least in the present volume—ceased to receive vigorous, focused attention, because the dialogue has both broadened and somewhat shifted. As a result, Hasegawa, in his mid-2005 volume, contends—albeit briefly—that the atomic bombing did not signify the beginning of the Cold War and he implies that the Cold War developed later. In his own important book on Stalin and the bomb, and in his essay in this volume, Holloway comes to similar conclusions, though for different reasons.[122]

Ketsu Gō

Japanese Political and Military Strategy in 1945

RICHARD B. FRANK

With few exceptions, Americans in 1945 believed fervently that the use of atomic weapons at Hiroshima and Nagasaki ended the Pacific War and saved countless lives. That conviction dominated national discourse for approximately two decades. Since that time, various scholars and writers have mounted multiple challenges to what one critic labeled the "patriotic orthodoxy."[1] These critiques contain more diverse strains than some defenders of the "orthodoxy" acknowledge. But the challenges share a common foundation of three basic premises. First, that Japan's strategic position in the summer of 1945 was catastrophic. Second, that its leaders recognized their hopeless situation and were seeking to surrender. Finally, that access to decoded Japanese diplomatic communications armed American leaders with the knowledge that the Japanese knew they were defeated and were seeking to surrender. Thus, argue an array of critics, American leaders comprehended that neither the atomic bomb nor perhaps even an invasion of the Japanese home islands was necessary to end the war. Accordingly, they charge that American leaders inflicted needless nuclear devastation on Japan in pursuit of some other goal: to justify the enormous expenditure of funds; to satisfy perverse intellectual curiosity; to perpetuate the Manhattan Project as a bureaucratic empire; or to intimidate Moscow.[2]

But the harsh reality is that the key Japanese leaders in the summer of 1945 did not view their situation as hopeless. Nor were they simply staggering on with the war in a fanatical trance, oblivious of their actual plight. On the contrary, a coherent and thoughtfully conceived military and political strategy called Ketsu Gō (Decisive Operation) impelled them. Understanding both the particulars of Ketsu Gō and the investment of Japanese leaders in this strategy is key to grasping, not only why the war continued, but also the most important facet of how and when it ended. Likewise, American decision making cannot be comprehended correctly without knowledge of the influence of radio intelligence revelations about Ketsu Gō and U.S. strategic thinking that recognized that the surrender of a Japanese government did not guarantee the capitulation of Japan's armed forces. Moreover, radio intelligence also unmasks a crisis in the path to peace Japanese leaders sought to obscure, which sheds light on the role of Soviet intervention in producing an end to the war.

Grand Strategy: American

President Franklin Roosevelt publicly articulated the national political goal of the United States at the Casablanca Conference in January 1943 as the unconditional surrender of the Axis powers. As it evolved over the next two years, unconditional surrender was not simply slogan about victory but a policy about peace. It provided the legal authority for the extensive plans to renovate the internal structures of the Axis nations.[3]

The American military strategy forged by the Joint Chiefs of Staff (JCS) in the spring of 1945 to secure that national political goal was an unstable compromise of two conflicting visions. The U.S. Navy, led by Fleet Admiral Ernest King, had studied war with Japan since 1906. From these decades of analysis, naval officers distilled a number of principles about defeating Japan. None of these axioms was more deeply ingrained than the conviction that an invasion of the Japanese home islands represented absolute folly. Naval planners calculated that Japan would muster larger ground forces for defense than the United States could ever deploy across the Pacific, and that Japan's terrain would negate American advantages of firepower and mobility. At the nub, naval leaders placed casualties as the ultimate internal threat to securing American war aims. Thus, they advocated ending the war by a campaign of blockade and bombardment, including intense aerial bombardment by sea- and land-based aircraft.[4] The U.S. Army, led by General of the Army George C. Marshall, had never invested the same intellectual capital in examining a conflict with Japan. It had, however, explored the prospect of war with Japan in the late 1930s and concluded that invasion might be necessary. Thus, when the army turned its attention to the problem of ending hostilities with Japan in 1944, it swiftly adopted a strategy of invasion of the home islands. This choice reflected the bedrock army conviction that time was the critical challenge to achieving American war aims.

The JCS merged these two conflicting views into a strategic plan in May

1945. The Chiefs authorized the continuation and intensification of the strategy of blockade and bombardment until November 1, 1945. At that point, the United States would launch a two-phase invasion of the Japanese homeland under the overall code name Operation Downfall. The first step, Operation Olympic, involved the seizure of approximately the southern third of Kyūshū, the southernmost main Japanese home island, by the Sixth Army, starting on November 1, 1945. Olympic would obtain air and naval bases to support a second phase, Operation Coronet, tentatively set for March 1, 1946, involving two armies to secure the Tokyo-Yokohama region.

As the JCS pointed out in the policy paper they adopted to support this strategy, the overall Allied war aim remained unconditional surrender. This would provide the legal authority to execute the far-ranging political changes in Japan designed to assure that it never again posed a threat to peace. As the JCS acknowledged, however, in some two thousand years, no Japanese government had ever surrendered to a foreign power. Moreover, throughout the entire course of the Pacific War, no Japanese unit had ever surrendered. Thus, the JCS cautioned that there was no guarantee that the surrender of the Japanese government could be obtained, or that even if a Japanese government capitulated, the Japanese armed forces would comply with that surrender. Therefore, an invasion was vital, because it was most likely to compel the surrender of the Japanese government. Moreover, an invasion would best position the United States to deal with the situation if there was no surrender or the Japanese armed forces refused to comply with the surrender of a Japanese government.[5] Thus, the JCS recognized that the ultimate dire situation the United States faced was not Operation Downfall, the two-phase initial invasion, but the absence of an organized capitulation of Japan's armed forces. In the latter case, the United States would face the prospect of defeating in detail four to five million Japanese men under arms in the home islands, on the Asian continent, and across the Pacific Ocean. This made even the potential casualties in Downfall only a down payment on the ultimate cost of the complete defeat of Japan.

U.S. President Harry S. Truman reviewed the invasion strategy in June 1945. He authorized Olympic, the invasion of Kyūshū, but withheld sanction for Coronet. American naval and ground commanders drafted detailed plans for the invasion of Kyūshū. These aimed at securing key terrain that would provide sites for a massive complex of airbases and a set of naval bases. The initial landings aimed at two locations on the southeastern coast of Kyūshū and one on the southwestern coast. There was a contingency plan for a fourth landing along the southern tip of Kyūshū. All of these plans assumed a significant American superiority in ground and air forces at the time of the landings.

Grand Strategy: Japanese

New Year's Day 1945 found Japanese military and naval leaders sober but resolute. Their entrenched attitudes toward their American adversaries had remained constant since the summer of 1941; only their goals had altered. These men had plunged Japan into war with only a rough draft as to how it would end. None of them believed Japan could physically conquer the United States, and no Japanese leader questioned the ability of the United States to produce vast quantities of matériel. But they calculated that America would be compelled to divert much of it to Europe to counter Germany and Italy. The bedrock belief shared by almost all Imperial Army officers and many Imperial Navy officers, however, was that Americans, lacking the racial purity and spiritual stamina of the Japanese populace, possessed only brittle morale. A lengthy war with increasing losses would sap American will to see the war through and force American political leaders to negotiate an end to the conflict on terms favorable to Japan. Initially, those terms would include Japanese control of resource areas in Southeast Asia and a bristling defense perimeter to protect them. By 1945, Japanese militarists viewed the attainable terms as at least the preservation of the homeland, with a political order in which their position remained dominant. They also hoped that Japan might still retain important gains on the Asian continent.[6]

A series of victories during the opening six months of the war seemed emphatically to confirm the perceptions of Japanese leaders, particularly concerning American morale. But during 1942, the United States checked Japan's advances and then launched a counterattack almost a year earlier than the Japanese had anticipated. From early 1943, Japan sustained an almost unbroken series of reverses, yet Japanese officers retained confidence in their basic attrition strategy. Buttressing this belief was the delusion that Japanese island garrisons and their sea and air supporting units were inflicting vastly greater casualties on U.S. forces than was actually the case. These hugely inflated loss figures provided the foundation for the conviction that even the American victories were steadily leeching away U.S. morale.[7]

Commonly skewing retrospective assessments of Japan's situation are the type of "War in the Pacific" maps that depict a line representing Japan's greatest advance bulging halfway across the ocean and then a line nearly rubbing Japan's shores representing its situation in the summer of 1945. Senior leaders at Imperial General Headquarters in Tokyo understood that Japan had lost its navy and with it control of the western Pacific right up to its shores. But the imperial realm still included huge territories with vast resources and hundreds of millions of vassals on the Asian continent and to the south—areas on those

"War in the Pacific" maps that American eyes often ignore. These territories also represented potential bargaining chips—some to keep as a profit from Japan's gamble on war and others to trade away to secure those gains or, in the final accounting, at least preserve the old order in the homeland. If Japan's air power was much diminished, there remained thousands of planes and a bountiful supply of young men prepared to crash them into enemy ships. Above all, there was still a formidable army, backed by a stalwart civilian population, and the priceless asset of Japan's home soil—arranged by Providence to negate all the advantages of an attacker dependent upon machines rather than men.

Officers at Imperial Headquarters coupled a reassuring assessment of the current strategic picture with an acute appreciation of future U.S. intentions. Americans lacked the patience for a protracted strategy of blockade and bombardment; they therefore surely would seek to end the war quickly by an invasion of homeland.[8] That aim presented opportunity. If the initial assault could be repulsed, or even if its cost could just be made prohibitive, Japan might yet extricate itself from the war with honor. Thus, with this goal in mind, the emperor sanctioned a new strategic directive, published on January 20, that candidly declared that the homeland itself would be the arena for "final decisive battle" of the war.[9]

Preparations for the defense of the homeland itself demanded new commands, plans, and forces. The "Joint Army-Navy Air Agreement" of February 6 resolved the acrimonious issue of command of aviation units. This provided that all homeland air units (except training and air defense components) would be concentrated to protect the "national defense sphere," primarily with suicide attacks to smash an invasion force. The agreement eschewed unity of command under a single army or navy officer in favor of a cooperative arrangement.[10]

With sole jurisdiction over major ground units, the Imperial Army executed its own new homeland defense scheme. This plan basically created two theater commands. The First General Army (roughly equivalent to a U.S. army group), with headquarters in Tokyo, took responsibility for most of central and northern Honshū. The Second General Army, with headquarters at Hiroshima, exercised jurisdiction over forces on western Honshū, Shikoku, and Kyūshū. Under each general army were several area armies (effectively the equivalent of a U.S. army). Imperial General Headquarters separately entrusted the defense of Hokkaidō, the northernmost home island, to the Fifth Area Army.

There were only twelve field divisions in all of Japan on New Year's Day 1945. With so few field units available, Imperial General Headquarters embarked on a huge program of homeland reinforcement. From Manchuria came four divisions (two armored and two infantry). But by far and away the major

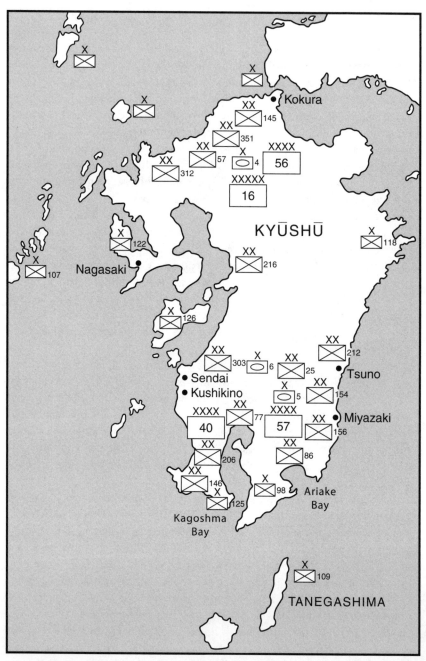

Ketsu Gō and Kyūshū

Ketsu Gō Mobilization

	General Army Headquarters	Army Headquarters	Coastal Divisions[a]	Counterattack Divisions[b]	Independent Mixed Brigades	Tank Brigades
Phase One:			13		1	
Phase Two:	2	8		8		6
Phase Three:			9	7	14	
TOTAL:	2	8	22	15	15	6

[a] The coastal combat division was a static unit designed to grapple in close-quarter fighting with a landing force a short distance inland from the water's edge.

[b] The counterattack division was a mobile unit, effectively a reduced-strength field division, organized to march rapidly from inland positions and deliver punishing blows against a beachhead.

increase in strength sprang from a February 26 order for a gigantic, three-phase mobilization program to create new legions, as shown in the table.

At the end of the mobilization, the forces available to defend the homeland would number sixty divisions (thirty-six field and counterattack, twenty-two coastal combat, and two armored divisions) and thirty-four brigades (twenty-seven infantry and seven tank). Counting the necessary logistic and administrative infrastructure, the mobilization would add 1.5 million men to the home defense commands. The aggregate strength of the homeland armies would total 2,903,000 men, 292,000 horses, and 27,500 motor vehicles.[11]

On April 8, frenzied staff officers in Tokyo completed a sprawling master defense plan for the impending struggle for the homeland and contiguous areas, dubbed Ketsu Gō. This plan envisioned that the American invaders would be confronted and crushed in one of seven key areas, with emphasis on Ketsu Number Three (the Kantō-Tokyo Area) and Ketsu Number Six (Kyūshū). Preparations would extend in three phases, from April to October, but forces on Kyūshū would achieve emergency readiness by early June.[12]

Three features marked the Ketsu-Gō plan. First, operations aimed not at destroying the enemy either at the water's edge (the tactics prior to mid 1944) or far inland (the tactics from mid 1944 to Ketsu Gō). The Japanese realized the folly of immediate beach defense in the face of massive American pre-landing bombardments, but they also grasped that their adversary could never be dislodged if permitted to consolidate its positions after a landing. Therefore, Ketsu Gō aimed to destroy the beachhead, the perimeter established by the invader a few days after the landing, anchored on the coast, but stretching only a few miles inland.

The second distinctive feature of Ketsu-Gō was the comprehensive devotion to *tokkō* (special attack or suicide) tactics, not only the now routine air and sea suicide attacks, but also suicide attacks onshore. The incorporation of the civilian population into the defense scheme represented the third highly singular feature of Ketsu Gō. Under the "National Resistance Program," commanders would be able to summon all able-bodied civilians, regardless of gender, to combat.[13]

The Imperial Army successfully accomplished the first and second phases of the massive mobilization. During this same interval and extending for some time thereafter, a series of orders and publications, such as the National Resistance Manual, elaborated a comprehensive scheme of final defense of the homeland.[14] The inexorable progress of American forces on Okinawa in May, however, triggered a series of urgent measures that shuffled more (and better) units to Kyūshū.[15] This supreme effort utterly exhausted equipment resources for units not deployed to Kyūshū. Imperial General Headquarters could only hope that future production would make good the deficiencies by October.

Ketsu Gō on Kyūshū

The Japanese did not rely upon espionage or code breaking to reach their prescient assessment that the Americans would target Kyūshū, and specifically southern Kyūshū, for their initial invasion. Rather, they simply deduced their antagonists' intentions from the elementary clues of American operational techniques and obvious goals. American superiority in combat power during the Pacific War rested upon overwhelming air and sea power, not ground forces. It followed that U.S. plans to invade Japan must encompass the ability to bolster American ground units with masses of planes and ships. While carrier-based aviation permitted almost unlimited scope in picking an invasion site, it represented just a fraction of available American air power. If the United States employed ground-based air units, the invasion site must fall within aircraft range, particularly of fighter planes, of the nearest bases.

In January 1945, the Japanese shrewdly perceived that the most advanced U.S. air bases in the middle of the year would be on Iwō Jima and Okinawa. Okinawa provided the capacity to support several thousand aircraft. Iwō Jima did not. Thus, an arc representing American fighter plane range from Okinawa foretold the likely American landing areas. Kyūshū and parts of Shikoku fell within that arc. Compared to Shikoku, the southern ranges of Kyūshū around Miyazaki, Shibushi Bay, and the Satsuma Peninsula were the most obvious targets, with plentiful airfield sites and naval bases forming easy stepping-stones for an invasion of the Kantō (Tokyo) plain.

According to a U.S. terrain analysis, southern Kyūshū "is a complex jumble of small lowlands and low but rugged uplands." It harbors three long narrow plains extending three to ten miles east to west by twenty to thirty miles north-south. These plains possessed military significance both as real or potential airfield sites and as natural avenues of movement, although terracing and a paucity of roads made them unfriendly to vehicles. Two of these plains abut the southeastern coast of Kyūshū; one lies north of Miyazaki and a second unfurls from the headland of Ariake Bay past Miyakonojō. A third plain lies along the southwest coast near Kushikino.[16]

The mission of defending Kyūshū fell to Field Marshal Hata Shunroku's Second General Army, which established its headquarters on April 18 at Hiroshima on western Honshū. Immediately under the Second General Army were two area armies. The Sixteenth Area Army defended Kyūshū, while the Fifteenth Area Army guarded Shikoku and western Honshū. In their initial estimate of the situation, the staff of the Second General Army surmised that the United States would seek to end the war quickly after Okinawa by a direct thrust into southern Kyūshū.[17]

The Sixteenth Area Army commander and staff on Kyūshū generally agreed with the Second General Army that the Americans would most likely target Miyazaki, Shibushi (Ariake) Bay, and the Satsuma Peninsula in southern Kyūshū for their potential as air or naval bases.[18] Japanese staff officers had extracted a number of lessons about American techniques from prior campaigns that shaped their calculations. In summary, these teachings were that large forces would land simultaneously along broad fronts, close to ultimate objectives. The Americans would assign high priority to the capture and use of airfields very early in the operation. They also would prefer areas where they could exploit their superiority in heavy equipment. Relatively small emphasis would be placed upon surprise, as opposed to other considerations, and they would not avoid strong defenses provided their other requirements were met.[19]

Based upon these criteria, and judgments as to the scale of American efforts, up to April 1945, the Japanese deemed the Shibushi Bay front to be the most threatened region. Accordingly, they deployed the only field division on the island there. From about the middle of April 1945, however, the broad Miyazaki beaches looked more likely to attract a U.S. assault, estimated at six to eight divisions. By July, judgments again shifted. It appeared that the onset of the typhoon season would dictate further delay in the date of the landings, but this in turn meant that the scale of the U.S. attack would burgeon to fifteen to sixteen divisions. The Sixteenth Area Army believed such a massive assault would strike several areas and include a landing in southwestern or southern Kyūshū along the Satsuma Peninsula to seize the protected anchorage of Kagoshima Bay. Thus, the Sixteenth Area Army became convinced that

Shibushi, Miyazaki, and the Satsuma Peninsula were all likely American targets.[20]

Although only one field division garrisoned Kyūshū in January 1945, over the next five months, the Imperial Army flooded the island with reinforcements, which brought the defenders on Kyūshū to fourteen field divisions, three tank brigades, and eight independent mixed (infantry) brigades. The aggregate forces numbered some 900,000 men. In the words of Major General Sanada Jōichirō, the deputy chief of staff of the Second General Army, Field Marshal Hata and his staff believed that the struggle for Kyūshū would be "the last chance to change the war situation in our favor." When the enemy landed, they intended to reinforce Kyūshū with three to five divisions from the Fifteenth Area Army and the First General Army, but this was neither sufficient to deal with multiple landing sites nor certain, since these units would have to traverse long distances under bombing and bombardment. Obviously, it would be far better to have crack counterattack units immediately to hand. So in May and again in June, the Second General Army beseeched Imperial General Headquarters to dispatch at least four divisions (two armored and two infantry) of the Thirty-sixth Army, the most powerful and efficient in the homeland, to Kyūshū. This request confirms that Hata and his staff anticipated concurrent American amphibious assaults. Furthermore, the expected severing of communication lines by American aircraft added urgency to the need for an early decision. Imperial General Headquarters effectively rejected this plea with silence. Tokyo did shift additional air power to Kyūshū, but resisted what might well have been an irretrievable gamble by sending the heart and soul of effective Tokyo defenses there, where they might be stranded by destruction of communications.[21] The actual disposition of the Sixteenth Area Army reflects the acuity of Japanese assessments of American intentions.

In northern Kyūshū, the Fifty-sixth Army comprised four divisions, one independent mixed brigade, and one tank brigade. The strategic importance of this region necessitated this cautionary deployment, even though no American attack was expected there. Elements of this army would be sent south to confront an invasion.

In southeastern Kyūshū, the Fifty-seventh Army had five infantry divisions, two independent mixed brigades, the 4th Antiaircraft Division, two tank brigades, and a host of other units. These forces deployed particularly around Miyazaki and Shibushi Bay, the anticipated American landing points on southeastern Kyūshū.[22] In southwestern Kyūshū, the Fortieth Army had four divisions, one independent mixed brigade, and one tank regiment to defend the alternative American landing site at the southern tip of Kyūshū and on the targeted southwestern coast.

In addition to the three field armies, several other commands on Kyūshū answered to the Sixteenth Area Army. The Kurume and Kumamoto Division Districts, originally administrative commands, assumed tactical control of three independent mixed brigades and the 216th Division. Also under the Sixteenth Area Army were the 107th Independent Mixed Brigade in the Gotō Islands and the Tsushima Fortress. Of these various units, the 216th Division was earmarked for counterattack against any invasion, and the other units represented a reservoir of twenty-six additional infantry battalions (the equivalent of the number of riflemen in nearly three more infantry divisions) potentially available for use against an invasion.

Feeble naval but formidable air forces backed this ground battle array. The Imperial Navy's surface naval forces amounted to a handful of cruisers, destroyers, and submarines. Many of these actually served to convey small, short-range suicide weapons close to their launching points. But Imperial General Headquarters decided to devote all of Japan's air power to Ketsu Gō. That meant converting thousands of training aircraft into suicide planes. By a drastic policy of declining combat and dispersing and hiding planes, the Japanese swelled their combat aircraft inventory in 1945. These they divided into pre-designated kamikazes and planes initially intended for conventional operations. The leader of the Imperial Army air units told American officials after the war, however, that he had intended eventually to commit all Imperial Army aircraft to suicide attacks. It is doubtful the Imperial Navy would have failed to match this commitment. By midsummer, the Japanese fielded over ten thousand aircraft to confront the invasion, about half already earmarked for kamikaze attacks. The great bulk of these planes defended Kyūshū.[23]

Overall, the Imperial Army faced severe logistical shortfalls for the Ketsu Operation, notably in ammunition and weapon supplies. These acute shortages placed a premium on selecting priorities in distributing available equipment and ammunition. From the outset, Imperial General Headquarters effectively staked its fortunes on Kyūshū.[24] Moreover, Imperial General Headquarters prudently aimed to pack Kyūshū with ample supplies and arms well before a landing and discounted the prospect of substantial replenishment after an invasion. As a result of these priorities, the general equipment situation on Kyūshū was adequate based on a match of authorized to actual equipment levels—it was sumptuous compared to other regions, save perhaps Tokyo.[25]

Preparations for Internal Defense and Resistance

Since experience on Saipan, American planners incorporated the prospect of facing a "fanatically hostile population" into their situation estimates for an invasion of Japan. Two subsequent events fortified this expectation. There had been about 38,280 Japanese civilians, including government officials, businessmen, farmers and their families, and civilian employees of the Japanese armed forces, in the Philippines, and "except for the extremely aged and the very young, almost all of these Japanese civilians came to serve the armed forces in one way or another." There is no explicit breakdown of losses among these civilians, but almost exactly two-thirds of the 381,550 Japanese in the Philippines (not counting Leyte) died.[26] It was much worse on Okinawa, where at least 35,000 and perhaps many as 100,000 to 150,000 civilians may have perished.[27]

In March 1945, Imperial General Headquarters moved to make this American nightmare a reality and to establish a seamless fusion of the military, the government, and the people. On March 24, Imperial General Headquarters directed the formation of Area Special Policing Units to be placed under the area commanders. These organizations would represent the practical mergers of the governmental and civilian spheres. Every village or town would form its own platoon or company of Area Special Policing units from the local inhabitants, who would be aggregated into formations of about 300. These contingents would provide a pool of auxiliary combat or combat support units, as was soon illustrated by their direct attachment to operational units, usually in coastal areas. The members were scheduled for call-up in May, June, and July, for periods of three to four days each, for rudimentary but morale-boosting instruction.[28]

On March 27, Public Law Number 30 mobilized all citizens in the coastal areas to perform fortification, transportation, construction, or other work to assist the decisive battle strategy. This followed upon the decision by the cabinet on March 18, the Decisive Battle Educational Measures Guidelines, which suspended all school classes, except grades one to six, from April 1, 1945, to March 31, 1946. All of these students—and their teachers—would be mobilized for the production of food, military supplies, air raid work, and other tasks to facilitate the decisive battle.

On March 23, the cabinet ordered the formation of the Patriotic Citizens (or Volunteer) Fighting Corps across the whole nation. This corps constituted a mechanism to induct the whole body of citizens and enable military authorities to summon them upon invasion. The entire public, in effect, became subject to call-up under the "Volunteer Enlistment Law." This applied to all men aged 15 to 60 and all women aged 17 to 40. They were organized into units called the Volunteer Fighting Units and subject to military discipline and control through the local area commands. The scale of these organizations was formidable: a tabular representation of these units in Kumamoto prefecture on Kyūshū, for example, gives a breakdown by subjurisdiction and notes that the figures represented all the citizens in the age groups, a total of over a million people.[29]

What this sea of civilians lacked, besides training, were arms and even uniforms. A mobilized high school girl like Kasai Yukiko found herself issued an awl and told: "Even killing just one American soldier will do. You must prepare to use the awls for self-defense. You must aim at the enemy's abdomen." Many civilians found themselves drilling with sharpened staves or spears. Japan lacked the cloth to put those civilians now mobilized as combatants into uniform—one senior general spoke of his hope of providing them with patches on their civilian clothes. This lack of distinguishing identification would undoubtedly have made it impossible at normal combat range for a soldier or marine to identify which civilians represented the Japanese armed forces and which did not, a sure prescription for vast numbers of deaths. At least one U.S. Fifth Air Force intelligence officer took the Japanese at their publicly broadcast word of total mobilization and declared: "the entire population of Japan is a proper Military Target . . . THERE ARE NO CIVILIANS IN JAPAN."[30]

The significance of these plans cannot be exaggerated. This mobilization aspired to create from the mass of the population a huge pool of untrained men and women who would be married to tactical units, where they would perform direct combat support and ultimately combat jobs. This would literally add tens of millions to the strength of the ground combat units, albeit of little formal combat power for lack of training and equipment. It would also guarantee huge civilian casualties and make a reality the disturbing American nightmare of a "fanatically hostile population." By mustering millions of erstwhile civilians into the area swept by bombs, artillery, and small arms fire, Japan's military masters willfully consigned hundreds of thousands of their countrymen to their deaths. Moreover, by deliberately obliterating any distinctions between combatants and noncombatants, they would compel American soldiers and marines to treat virtually all Japanese as combatants, or fail to do so at their peril.

Ketsu Gō Versus Operation Olympic

American officers subjected the massive amphibious assault on Kyūshū that never occurred to several postwar assessments. The staff of the Fifth Amphibious Corps contributed the most comprehensive survey. This study, while allowing that the struggle would have been "costly," overall tended to deprecate Japanese prospects. The compilers of this report, however, acknowledged that they had secured copies of very few enemy plans and orders, that demobilization had disorganized and dispersed Japanese units, and that they confronted many conflicts in the testimony of Japanese officers. This analysis likewise was skewed by the fact that the Japanese units facing the Fifth Amphibious Corps were the weakest Imperial Army detachments on Kyūshū.[31]

Even with the far better perspective offered by the much more comprehensive Japanese material, the assessment of the Fifth Amphibious Corps study that Ketsu Gō could not defeat Operation Olympic still appears sound. In essence, American firepower and material superiority were simply too overwhelming. While the exact costs of the struggle envisaged on Kyūshū can never be known with certainty, a reasonable and very conservative approximation can be ventured. The Japanese would probably have committed at least a half million combatants and sustained at least 200,000 to 250,000 killed. Probably another 380,000 Japanese fatalities would have occurred among the erstwhile civilian population, overwhelmingly among those press-ganged into militias. A fair speculation as to American losses, based upon a troop list of about 681,000, the lower planning ratio for losses proposed by the JCS planners in April 1945, and a campaign lasting no more than ninety days, would yield projected casualties of 132,385, including 25,741 killed and missing. To these would be added naval casualties ranging from 7,228 to 12,942 killed, and 16,809 to 30,098 wounded. This brings combined U.S. land and sea losses to the range of 149,194 to 162,483, of whom between 32,969 and 38,683 would be killed.[32]

But the real significance of Ketsu Gō versus Operation Olympic cannot be measured in hypothetical victory or defeat or hypothetical human costs. The Japanese comprehended astutely that they need not repulse Olympic to achieve their overarching political objective of reaching the pain threshold in terms of casualties that would induce American policymakers to parlay for terms to the taste of the Japanese militarists. Moreover, they correctly perceived that this threshold would be constituted not just by the raw number of losses in Olympic, but also the *implications* those casualties carried. The Japanese did not have to reach the ultimate American pain threshold in the battle against Olympic. They only needed to convince U.S. policymakers and the American public that the bloodletting on Kyūshū foretold an unbearable cost to root out all the Japanese defenders in the home islands—and perhaps those warriors spread across Asia and the Pacific.

The American tolerance for casualties to secure unconditional surrender was never tested in reality, so it cannot be certified, but there are several benchmarks by which it may be judged. First, with total battle deaths for the war at 290,907, each additional 29,900 dead increased the war's cost by 10 percent. Moreover, and perhaps more telling, the highest death total for any one month of the war, 20,325 in March 1945, could easily have been exceeded in the first thirty days of Olympic.[33] Because battle casualties fell in great disproportion on combat as opposed to support troops, battle casualties ashore of only 92,500—a number well within Japanese capabilities—would have doubled the losses for the entire war among the assault divisions.[34] This carried dire implications for combat effectiveness and morale. Any soldier or marine infantryman slated for Olympic who believed the atomic bomb saved him from death or wounds had solid grounds for this belief. The other men earmarked for Olympic, whatever their jobs, would have become unwilling participants in a gigantic and deadly game of kamikaze roulette where chance determined who lived and who died.

There is at least one contemporary suggestion of what a key policymaker deemed unacceptable: General Marshall recoiled sharply at estimates from General Douglas MacArthur's headquarters of casualties exceeding 100,000 for Olympic. Indeed, Marshall's message inviting MacArthur to disavow such projections explicitly cited President Truman's sensitivity to casualties, plainly a matter with heavy political freight.[35] By these measures, if Ketsu Gō against an unaltered Operation Olympic produced casualties in the 140,000 to 160,000 range, the implications for the ultimate cost of obtaining unconditional surrender may well have been enough to secure Japanese political objectives—or at least Japanese leaders possessed a sound basis to believe this. Alternatively, and perhaps more likely, losses in that range in Olympic might have driven American strategy back to blockade and bombardment aimed at starving out Japan, at a cost of millions of deaths, mostly civilians.

Japanese field commanders possessed a sound grasp of Ketsu Gō's purely military prospects. After an inspection trip in June, Major General Sanada Jōichirō remarked to Field Marshal Hata, the commander of the Second General Army: "The morale of all front-line forces, from army and division commanders on down, is excellent. In view of their advantages of ample equipment, naval strategy and favorable terrain, I believe that the first wave of enemy troops could surely be pushed back into the sea. If the enemy attempts a second and a third landing, however, it is highly doubtful that he can be completely repulsed." Hata replied: "You are probably correct. As long as we lack powerful general second and third line reserves, we cannot be certain of repulsing a second and third enemy landing."[36] But the key opinions on Ketsu Gō were those in Tokyo, where political implications were preeminent. According to a postwar statement, Major General Amano Masakazu, chief of the Operations Section, Imperial General Headquarters, assessed the outlook for Ketsu Gō as follows: "We were absolutely sure of victory. It was the first and the only battle in which the main strength of the air, land and sea forces were to be joined. The geographical advantages of the homeland were to be utilized to the highest degree, the enemy was to be crushed, and we were confident that the battle would prove to be the turning point in political maneuvering."[37]

Likewise the chief of the intelligence section, Lieutenant General Arisue Seizō, explained to his American interrogators: "If we could defeat the enemy in Kyushu or inflict tremendous losses, forcing him to realize the strong fighting spirit of the Japanese Army and people, it would be possible, we hoped, to bring about the termination of hostilities on comparatively favorable terms."[38]

The most critical attitude of all was that of Army Minister Anami, and the evidence on his views is overwhelming. According to his close subordinate, Lieutenant General Yoshizumi Masao, Anami embraced the conviction that there were "considerable chances of victory in the decisive battle in the homeland." Indeed, Yoshizumi related that army officers universally believed in Japan's victory in the "first decisive battle" (i.e., against the first landing attempt). Anami's military secretary, Colonel Hayashi Saburō, flatly reported that the army minister "believed that the initial landing of the American invasion forces could be repulsed." Moreover, Anami thought that if Japan inflicted heavy damage in Ketsu Gō, it might be able to continue the fight, or at least come to a peace other than unconditional surrender. Even in extremis, he continued to believe that Japan should either insist on something other than unconditional surrender or continue the war, reflecting his confidence in the political rewards Japan stood to accrue from Ketsu Gō to the very end.[39] What a realistic assessment shows of Ketsu Gō as the Japanese saw it is that the belief that Japan could yet salvage something from its war other than unconditional surrender was grounded in solid fact.

Validation

Quite apart from the illumination of retrospective assessments, powerful contemporary validation for Ketsu Gō emerges from the reaction of U.S. leaders once radio intelligence compromised the Japanese plan. American intelligence originally calculated that on November 1, 1945, the scheduled date of Operation Olympic, the Japanese would protect Kyūshū with only six field divisions, and that just three of these would defend the southern Kyūshū target area. The Japanese were expected ultimately to deploy eight to ten field divisions, with a total of 350,000 troops, against Olympic. The Imperial Army and Imperial Navy would have available only 2,500 to 3,000 planes to support these troops.[40]

From July 9 and continuing well into August, radio intelligence (codenamed Ultra or Magic) unmasked the massive buildup of Japanese forces in the homeland in general and the even more disturbing evidence of a huge bolstering of Kyūshū, centered in the proposed landing areas. By war's end, intelligence had identified thirteen of the fourteen field divisions (nine in the southern half of the island) and five of the eleven brigades on Kyūshū. The final revised estimate of August 20 credited the Japanese with all fourteen field divisions and 625,000 troops on Kyūshū.[41]

And the picture was equally as dark with regard to Japanese air power, although differences existed between various intelligence centers. By the surrender date, the newly created Joint Army-Navy Committee on the Japanese Air Forces estimated Japanese air strength in the homeland at 5,911.[42] The intelligence center for the Commander in Chief Pacific Fleet (CINCPAC) calculated by August 13 that the Japanese had 10,290 aircraft available for homeland defense.[43] The actual total was about 10,700.[44]

As this collage of alarming intelligence accumulated, it was passed to civilian and uniformed leaders. In this context, it is now clear that the routine daily delivery to President Truman and other top policymakers included both the "Magic" Diplomatic Summary covering diplomatic dispatches and the "Magic" Far East Summary, which presented the evidence on the Japanese buildup in the homeland, including particularly Kyūshū.[45]

The evidence of Japanese preparations on Kyūshū first triggered an emphasis on its political significance. In an assessment prepared by naval intelligence but disseminated to all senior policymakers on July 27 in the top secret "Magic Far East Summary":

An analysis of Japan's situation, as revealed through Ultra sources, suggests her unwillingness to surrender stems primarily from the failure of her otherwise capable and all-powerful Army leaders to perceive that the defenses they are so assiduously fashioning actually are utterly inadequate. . . . until the Japanese leaders realize that an invasion cannot be repelled, there is little likelihood that they will accept any peace terms satisfactory to the Allies.[46]

If Washington-based naval officers deemed the Japanese buildup "utterly inadequate" to confront the invasion on July 27 (before the full extent of the buildup was recognized), they soon changed their tune to harmonize with the dirge of their peers overseas. By July 29, Major General Charles A. Willoughby, General MacArthur's intelligence chief, declared that further unchecked increase of Japanese strength on Kyūshū threatened "to grow to [the] point where we attack on a ratio of one (1) to one (1) which is not the recipe for victory."[47] Ultra disclosures served to reinforce CINCPAC in the view Admiral Chester Nimitz expressed as early as May 25 in an "Eyes Only" message to Admiral King that Olympic was unwise. ("Eyes Only" means the text of the message is a highly personal communication between two commanders. It is not to be read by anyone else, save perhaps by the discreet signals personnel who perform the initial coding and final decoding of the message.) On June 4, a weekly intelligence summary at CINCPAC noted that the Japanese were "definitely anticipating [an] invasion of Kyūshū," with top priority given the southern part of the island. By June 18, the same weekly summary recorded that the Japanese had drafted a priority list for defensive installations, with north and south Kyūshū and the Tokyo plain in the top positions. The calendar barely showed July when a CINCPAC estimate declared flatly that Kyūshū "has been receiving the enemy's most concentrated attention in troop reinforcement and build-up of defenses against invasion."[48] Nimitz clearly implied that he remained very pessimistic about the prospects for an invasion of Kyūshū in an August 3 message to King concerning the proposed transfer of one of his key subordinates, Rear Admiral Forrest Sherman. Nimitz insisted that Sherman must remain at CINCPAC Headquarters until completion of planning for Olympic, but said that he could then be released, because Olympic "might drag [on] indefinitely."[49]

Senior staff officers of the Joint Chiefs of Staff in Washington shared Willoughby's and Nimitz's doubts about Olympic. "There is every indication that the Japanese have been giving the highest priority to the defense of Kyushu and particularly to southern Kyushu," noted the Joint Intelligence Committee (JIC) in an early August report. They rated southern Kyūshū, followed by Shikoku, northern Kyūshū, and the Kantō plain, as the focus of Japanese attention. Fully anticipating the destruction of their communication lines, the Japanese were toiling relentlessly to "concentrate the greatest part of the forces to be used for the defense of these vital areas in close proximity to the most threatened points of probable Allied assault." By the JIC recapitulation, from early 1945, Japanese ground strength on Kyūshū had swelled from about 150,000 troops, 75 percent on the north end of the island, to about 545,000 men, 60 percent in the southern part of the island. The report emphasized the massive buildup of Japanese air strength, particularly kamikazes. Fifty special bases for suicide planes had been identified on Kyūshū, Shikoku, and Honshū west of 133 degrees longitude (i.e., within range of Olympic). Deployment of conventional combat planes also showed tactical emphasis on Kyūshū-Shikoku.

The JIC also highlighted a buildup on Shikoku from no active divisions at the start of the year to four active and one depot divisions, with support troops totaling about 150,000 men. The air deployment that covered Kyūshū also substantially covered Shikoku. While the Japanese clearly appeared to believe the initial assault would come in the south, they had not neglected the Kantō (Tokyo) plain. There, strength had burgeoned from four active and three depot divisions (with other troops totaling 300,000 men) to a total of nine active divisions (one armored), three depot divisions, and other troops, totaling 560,000. Aircraft and suicide craft deployment there, however, notably trailed that in Kyūshū.[50]

The day the first atomic bomb was dropped on Hiroshima, August 6, the Joint War Plans Committee of the Joint Chiefs of Staff in Washington forwarded a report "Alternatives to 'Olympic' " to the Joint Staff Planners, a body just below the Joint Chiefs themselves. Noting the alarming fresh intelligence estimates of Japanese preparations on Kyūshū, the committee observed that: "The possible effect upon Olympic operations of this build-up and concentration is such that it is considered commanders in the field should review their estimates of the situation, reexamine objectives in Japan as possible alternates to Olympic, and prepare plans for operations against such alternate objectives." An attached draft message to MacArthur and Nimitz observed that while the dramatic increase in Japanese strength did not yet require a change of the directive, it did compel focus on the prospects for Olympic and mandate that commanders formulate "alternate plans and submit timely recommendations." It advised that "[o]perations against extreme northern Honshū, against the Sendai area [Sendai on Honshū, not Sendai on Kyūshū], and directly against the Kantō Plain are now under intensive study [in Washington]."[51] The Joint Staff Planners formally reviewed these reports on August 8, two days after Hiroshima and one day before Nagasaki. Probably because of this timing, the minutes of their meeting show that the Planners temporized. They "took note of . . . the fact that the Joint War Plans Committee is preparing studies on alternate objectives with a view to presentation to the Joint Chiefs of Staff."[52]

But General Marshall had already acted. On August 7, Washington time, he sent the following dispatch to MacArthur:

Intelligence reports on Jap dispositions which have been presented to me and which I understand have been sent to your Staff are that the Japanese have undertaken a large buildup both of divisions and of air forces in Kyushu and Southern Honshu. The air buildup is reported as including a large component of suicide planes which the intelligence estimate here considers are readily available for employment only in the vicinity of their present bases. Concurrently with the reported reinforcement of Kyushu, the Japanese are reported to have reduced forces north of the Tokyo plain to a point where the defensive capabilities in Northern Honshu and Hokkaido appear to be extraordinarily weak viewed from the standpoint of the Japanese General Staff. The question has arisen in my mind as to whether the Japanese may not be including some deception in the sources from which our intelligence is being drawn.

In order to assist in discussions likely to arise here on the meaning of reported dispositions in Japan proper and possible alternate objectives to Olympic, such as Tokyo, Sendai [northern Honshu], Ominato [extreme northern Honshu], I would appreciate your personal estimate of the Japanese intentions and capabilities as related to your current directive and available resources.

Marshall provided a copy of this message to Admiral William Leahy, Truman's chief of staff.[53]

"I am certain," MacArthur intoned, in the expeditious "personal estimate" of August 9, "that the Japanese air potential reported to you as accumulating to counter our Olympic operation is greatly exaggerated." While he allowed the possibility of some increases on Kyūshū, he deprecated "the heavy strengths reported to you in southern Kyushu." MacArthur insisted that Allied tactical air power, in addition to the B-29 force, would "quickly seek out and destroy" Japanese air potential and "practically immobilize" and "greatly weaken" Japanese ground forces in southern Kyūshū.

"In my opinion," MacArthur declared, "there should not be the slightest thought of changing the Olympic operation." The purpose of Olympic, he stressed, was to obtain air bases to cover a strike into "the industrial heart of Japan." Olympic was "sound and will be successful." After criticizing the proposed alternatives, MacArthur ended with a peroration that selectively recalled history and played up to Marshall's own admitted doubts that perhaps the Japanese had cleverly managed to hoodwink Ultra: "Throughout the Southwest Pacific Area campaigns, as we have neared an operation intelligence has invariably pointed to greatly increased enemy forces. Without exception, this buildup has been found to be erroneous. In this particular case, the destruction that is going on in Japan would seem to indicate that it is very probable that the enemy is resorting to deception."

MacArthur's conclusion contained an extraordinarily brazen lie about past history in his theater, where his intelligence officers consistently underestimated, not overestimated, Japanese strength.[54] But behind this lie was something else. Marshall had observed to Secretary of War Stimson in December 1944 that MacArthur was "so prone to exaggerate and so influenced by his own desires that it is difficult to trust his judgment."[55] The inescapable conclusion is that MacArthur's resort to falsehood now was motivated by his personal interest in commanding the greatest amphibious assault in history.

After receipt of MacArthur's self-serving estimate late on August 9 (Washington time), Admiral King moved to intervene decisively in the controversy over Olympic. He gathered both Marshall's original query and MacArthur's reply into a package, and sent both "Eyes Only" to Nimitz, asking CINCPAC for "your comments" and requesting that a copy of these be sent to MacArthur. King did not set a deadline for Nimitz's response.

King clearly aimed to bring on an explosive interservice confrontation over Olympic, and probably the whole invasion strategy. On April 30, he had informed his colleagues on the Joint Chiefs of Staff that he had only agreed to permit orders to be issued for an invasion so that the necessary preparations could be put in train to maintain that option. He had also warned that the Joint Chiefs would be revisiting this issue in August or September. Now, precisely as he had predicted, this had come to pass.[56]

Nimitz had advised King that he no longer supported an invasion of Japan in an "Eyes Only" communication on May 25, so no army officer was aware of this fact. King now forced Nimitz either to avow support for Olympic (which could safely be ruled out, given the intelligence developments since May 25) or to break the interservice consensus behind Olympic in particular and the invasion strategy in general. It was obvious that if Nimitz withdrew his endorsement of Olympic, he would create a major confrontation with the army institutionally, as well as personally between MacArthur and himself. By the time Nimitz received King's order, however, a second atomic bomb had been dropped, and the Soviet Union had entered the war against Japan. Moreover, very shortly thereafter, evidence appeared for the first time that Japan might seriously be contemplating suing for peace. Indeed, the next major message from King to Nimitz, only some thirteen hours after the order for Nimitz to declare his position on Olympic, began "This is a peace warning." Nimitz understandably hesitated to see whether events would deliver him from the onerous duty of igniting what was certain to be a firestorm over American strategy to end the war.[57]

While Nimitz temporized, Marshall received a situation estimate from Major General Clayton Bissell, his chief intelligence officer, on August 12. Bissell projected that "large, well disciplined, well armed, undefeated Japanese ground forces have a capacity to offer stubborn fanatic resistance to Allied ground operations in the homeland and may inflict heavy Allied casualties." Bissell further calculated that the "[a]tomic bombs will not have a decisive effect in the next 30 days."[58] The following day, August 13, Major General John E. Hull, the assistant chief of staff for operations at the War Department, telephoned Colonel L. E. Seeman of the Manhattan Project at the express direction of General Marshall. Hull explained that the chief of staff believed that the two atomic bombs had "had a tremendous effect on the Japanese as far as capitulation is concerned," but Marshall doubted that further atomic bombing would influence any Japanese decision to end the war. Therefore, Marshall commissioned Hull to examine an alternative strategy to reserve all additional atomic weapon production and then deploy them in direct support (i.e., "tactical" support) of the invasion "rather than [on] industry, morale, psychology, etc." The upshot of this conference was an estimate that seven bombs probably would be ready for use by October 31.[59]

Thus, in the last weeks of the war American leaders faced the prospect that Ketsu Gō had made Olympic not unnecessary but unthinkable. They were embroiled in the opening moves of a massive confrontation between the army and navy over the whole invasion strategy. Moreover, it is inconceivable that in the summer of 1945, any American president would have failed to use nuclear weapons in the face of this evidence.

Ketsu Gō and Ending the War

While it is not feasible to conduct a detailed examination of all aspects of Japanese decision making in August 1945, no understanding of this process is possible without placing the Ketsu Gō strategy in its central and pivotal position. As Robert Butow explained more than fifty years ago, only eight men held the ultimate power to decide Japan's fate. This select body comprised the members of an inner cabinet styled the Supreme Council for the Direction of the War (known in shorthand as the Big Six): Prime Minister Suzuki Kantarō, Foreign Minister Tōgō Shigenori, Army Minister Anami Korechika, Navy Minister Yonai Mitsumasa, Chief of the Imperial Army General Staff Umezu Yoshijirō, and Chief of the Imperial Navy General Staff Toyoda Soemu. The other two individuals who exercised real power were the emperor and his principal adviser, Lord Keeper of the Privy Seal Marquis Kido Kōichi.[60]

The Big Six were the ultimate authority within the legal government of Japan. But they were nearly paralyzed on the issue of terminating the war by a procedural rule that required the complete unanimity among them to make a decision. This rule conferred an effective veto on any single member of the Big Six. The four serving officers of the Imperial Army or Navy among the Big Six allowed ample redundancy, ensuring that the militarists had to concur in any government policy.[61] The available record shows that the Big Six never on their own volition agreed to end the war on any terms the United States and its allies could or should have accepted. As late as the morning of August 9, 1945, after years of military defeat, months of blockade and increasingly devastating bombardment by air and sea, two atomic bombs, and Soviet intervention, the Big Six refused to capitulate unless the Allies met four terms. These were not simply a guarantee of the preservation of the imperial institution, and perhaps the incumbent emperor, but also that the Allies agree to three further conditions: Japan's repatriation of its own armed forces; Japan to have sole jurisdiction over "so-called" war crimes trials, and no occupation of the homeland.[62] These terms aimed to assure the continuance of the old order in Japan and the possibility of future military resurgence.

Only the intervention of Emperor Hirohito broke the deadlock among the Big Six, a fact that underscores the fundamental point that the end of hostilities by Japan in 1945 required two steps. First, a legitimate authority had to decide that Japan should yield to the Allied terms for capitulation. Second, the Japanese armed forces had to comply with that decision. The cabinet of Prime Minister Suzuki, the legal government of Japan, never agreed on its own to surrender on terms that would have been acceptable to the Allies. No one can now know whether this cabinet ever would have reached agreement on such terms. More fundamentally, no one can now know whether the Suzuki government would even have survived. The reaction of Imperial General Headquarters to Soviet intervention, following the atomic bombs, was to draft a plan to declare martial law and, if necessary, dispense with any semblance of authority outside Imperial General Headquarters itself.[63] Furthermore, while the cabal of officers who orchestrated the coup d'état on the night of August 14–15 failed, had they enjoyed more time to spread the contagion of revolt and assassinate anyone who stood in their path, they might have succeeded, with incalculable consequences.

The legitimate authority that decreed that Japan had to accept the allied terms for capitulation was the emperor. The contemporary evidence and the emperor's own voice in his 1946 memoir *Shōwa tennō dokuhakuroku* demolish the postwar myth that Hirohito eagerly sought surrender throughout 1945 and thus could have been mobilized to end the war by American diplomacy. He remained in fact a vigorous advocate of Ketsu Gō until he was confronted with the prospect of final defeat on Okinawa. He later admitted that his instinctive choice of an alternate strategy then was for Japan to launch a new offensive in China! Only after the Imperial Army rejected this proposal did he look to diplomacy as a way to extricate Japan from its predicament.[64] Even then, he looked to Soviet mediation to avoid anything like unconditional surrender. Neither the contemporary documentation nor *Shōwa Tennō dokuhakuroku* suggests he ever contemplated terms to end the war less favorable for Japan than the concepts Kido drafted in early June, which resembled the Treaty of Versailles, not unconditional surrender.[65] Tellingly, Suzuki's disastrous *mokusatsu* rejection of the Potsdam Declaration passed without criticism from the emperor. Nor did his principal adviser, Kido, object initially to the original proposal of the Suzuki cabinet on August 9 to submit an offer of surrender subject to four conditions congenial to Army Minister Anami and the other military leaders that would have been wholly unacceptable to the Allies. Since Kido was the man most intimately aware of the emperor's mind-set, this episode is further compelling evidence of the emperor's actual thinking.[66] As Tsuyoshi Hasegawa persuasively demonstrates in *Racing the Enemy*, almost to the very end, Hirohito sought, not simply to preserve the imperial institution and his seat on the throne, but to retain actual substantive power.[67]

Why did Hirohito finally intervene to halt the war? When he first announced his decision in the early morning hours of August 10, he said that he had "given serious thought to the situation prevailing at home and abroad." That he made any allusion to Japan's internal situation is significant. There is a great deal of direct and indirect evidence demonstrating that fear (perhaps exaggerated) of domestic upheaval that would topple the throne gave key leaders such as former Prime Minister Konoe, Navy Minister Yonai, and ultimately Kido and Hirohito powerful impetus to end the war. This collapse of domestic morale arose from the general trajectory of the war, but the naval blockade and the sheer terror and destructiveness of the bombing made it much more acute in the summer of 1945—and the atomic bomb threatened a quantum leap in the spread of unrest. Beyond the collapse of national morale, Hirohito explicitly cited the inadequate preparations to resist an invasion. This point has been consistently underplayed by historians, but it is, in reality, extremely important. Here Hirohito directly confronted and discounted the fundamental rationale offered by his senior generals and admirals for continuing the war. His reference to the situation abroad is vague as to whether he meant Japan's lack of allies, its host of enemies, or perhaps both. He did not specifically refer to the Soviet intervention, even in the context of why he had lost faith in Ketsu Gō.[68] This was the most critical decision of his reign, and perhaps by any Japanese emperor in two thousand years. In my view, the notion that he was really motivated by Soviet intervention but completely failed to mention it is incredible.

As to the members of the Big Six, in the first imperial conference on August 10, no less an authority than General Umezu, chief of staff of the Imperial Army, told Hirohito that Soviet intervention made no difference as to the execution of Ketsu Gō.[69] Moreover, at that moment, neither the Kwantung Army in Manchuria nor anyone in Tokyo grasped the full extent of Soviet intervention or its success.[70] Thus, there is no basis for believing that the military facts of Soviet intervention, or the crushing of the Kwantung Army by the Red Army in the following days, played any role in the emperor's decision on August 10. Indeed, Imperial General Headquarters had already written off Manchuria, and the only strategic goal of the Kwantung Army was to hold out in a redoubt comprising the southeastern corner of Manchuria.[71]

Why did Umezu state that Soviet intervention made no difference to Ketsu Gō? Whatever the precise state of Japanese intelligence on Soviet forces on August 10—and it was sorely defective—the Japanese did correctly comprehend one key factor. While the USSR potentially or actually could field massive ground and tactical air forces in the Far East, it lacked naval forces to move and support large bodies of soldiers and airmen. Moscow's situation paralleled that of Hitler in the summer of 1940, when the English Channel negated the capacity of the German Army to subdue the United Kingdom. The

Soviet scheme to seize Hokkaidō hinged on the ability of the Soviet Navy to shuttle forces over in increments of a regiment or two at a time. (A Soviet rifle regiment comprised about 2,500–3,000 men, with light weapons.)[72] Moreover, the Soviet Navy lacked the specialized landing vessels to move significant quantities of tanks and heavy equipment. What it could and did do in August 1945 was lift units of essentially light infantry to seize positions in Korea and the Kuril Islands northeast of Hokkaidō.[73] The ability of the USSR to provide effective air cover for an actual landing on Hokkaidō was untested. Even a relatively small number of kamikazes could have inflicted devastating losses on the sparse Soviet sealift. In hindsight, it is reasonable to project Soviet success in seizing Hokkaidō, particularly as its defenses were then oriented toward a U.S. attack from the east, not a Soviet incursion through what was effectively the western back door. But the discounting of Soviet intervention in terms of Ketsu Gō was not mere wishful thinking.

There are two ironic aspects of the emperor's argument that Japan was ill prepared to confront an invasion. The first is that Hirohito explicitly cited the defenses of Tokyo as an example of the inadequate preparations. It was true that Tokyo lagged significantly behind Kyūshū in overall preparedness. But this reflected the explicit choice of Imperial General Headquarters to accord priority to Kyūshū, for the excellent reason that it, not Tokyo, would sustain the first invasion attempt. Here it might be argued that the military leaders' decision to concentrate on Kyūshū first, though strategically sound, proved at this moment to be a political disaster. The second is that at literally the same moment when Hirohito dismissed Japan's defensive preparations as inadequate, those same defensive preparations were propelling American leaders to a massive confrontation over the plan to invade Kyūshū.

The emperor did cite both the Soviet intervention and the enemy's "scientific power" (the emerging euphemism for nuclear weapons) when he met early on August 14 with Japan's most senior military officers and reaffirmed his determination to end the war. This appears to be the only contemporary instance where Hirohito expressly identified Soviet intervention as a reason for his decision up to August 15, and even then, he coupled it with the atomic bomb.[74] At an imperial conference later that same morning, August 14, the emperor reiterated his decision to end the war, whose continuance, he declared, would reduce the nation to "ashes" (a reference to atomic or conventional weaponry or both) and kill tens or hundreds of thousands.[75] Finally, in the imperial rescript on ending the war, Hirohito characterized the military situation as developing "not necessarily to Japan's advantage, while the general trends of the world have all turned against her interest." This tortured circumlocution was Army Minister Anami's posthumous reaffirmation of his faith in Ketsu Gō.[76]

These phrases also left Soviet intervention (and perhaps Germany's defeat) as at best veiled references. But Hirohito went on to speak explicitly on one point: the enemy's employment of a "new and most cruel bomb, the power of which to do damage is indeed incalculable, taking the toll of many innocent lives."[77] Just a week after the surrender ceremony in September, Hirohito wrote a letter to the crown prince providing his analysis of Japan's defeat. The emperor castigated "our people" for their dismissive attitudes toward the United States and Britain and for extolling spirit over "science." This extraordinary private communication, which would not see the light of day for decades, makes no reference to the USSR.[78]

The most direct and compelling commentary on the factor that moved the Big Six was provided Suzuki in December 1945, elaborating on a thought he had articulated on August 13:

The Supreme War Council, up to the time of the atomic bomb was dropped, did not believe that Japan could be beaten by air attack alone. They also believed that the United States would land and not attempt to bomb Japan out of the war. On the other hand there were many prominent people who did believe that the United States could win the war by just bombing alone. However the Supreme War Council, not believing that, had proceeded with the one plan of fighting a decisive battle at the landing point and was making every possible preparation to meet such a landing. They proceed with that plan until the Atomic Bomb was dropped, after which they believed the United States would no longer attempt to land when it had such a superior weapon—that the United States need not land when it had such a weapon; so at that point they decided that it would be best to sue for peace.[79]

Thus, by any reasonable standard, the atomic bombs were essential to obtain the emperor's intervention as the essential first step to ending the war. In the eyes of the Big Six, the bombs also negated the Ketsu Gō strategy, which was the fundamental reason for the top military leaders to insist that they could still obtain something better than unconditional surrender for their country. Without the decision by a legitimate authority that Japan must capitulate on allied terms, the question of the compliance of Japan's armed forces with surrender would not even have arisen.

Soviet Intervention and the Second Crisis of the Surrender

To give primacy to the atomic bombs as the key factor in motivating Hirohito's crucial intervention and undermining Ketsu Gō, however, is not to deny a role for Soviet intervention. No less than American officials, Japanese leaders questioned whether the emperor's soldiers and sailors would obey an order to surrender. Not only did events prove these doubts well founded, but code breaking too captured a disturbing portrait of the volatile situation for the United States. Code breaking also shed light on these events when Hirohito and his supporters sought to keep them in the dark, since they cast doubt on his aura of authority, which was essential to preserve his position.

On August 11, the day following the emperor's first pronouncement of his decision that Japan must capitulate, Foreign Minister Tōgō radioed news of the government's surrender proposal to his overseas ministers, noting that he had not yet "received the agreement of the Army and Navy on [the surrender offer]."[80] Underscoring Tōgō's caution was a message from Imperial General Headquarters to overseas commanders the same day that instructed them to continue to prosecute the war "to preserve the Fatherland as well as complete annihilation of the fanatic enemy and not to be affected by the numerous reports on the progress of the war."[81] Both these messages were intercepted and decoded.

At approximately the same time as Tōgō's dispatch, the vice chief of the Imperial General Staff, Lieutenant General Kawabe Torashirō, recorded in his diary that another very senior officer in Imperial General Headquarters had imparted his doubts that the overseas commanders would comply with the government's decision. Kawabe noted in his diary that he agreed.[82] This information would not be known for years, but the fact that the number two figure on the operational side of the Imperial Army doubted the obedience of senior officers in overseas commands to a surrender order speaks volumes about the uncertainties still existing, despite the emperor's intervention.

The initial official transmission of emperor's decision to overseas commanders provoked defiance, not compliance. On August 11, Field Marshal Terauchi Hisaichi, the commander of the Southern Army (which directed units in Burma, Indochina, present-day Indonesia, the Philippines, and the South Pacific), declared: "The plans of the Southern Army have changed in no way whatever. Each Army . . . will go ahead to strengthen war preparations more and more." The same day the vice chief of the Imperial General Staff insisted in another intercepted message: "The Imperial Army and Navy shall by no means return the sword to the scabbard."[83] Even following the emperor's broadcast on August 15, the China Expeditionary Army commander, General Okamura Yasuji, exclaimed: "Such a disgrace as the surrender of several million troops without fighting is not paralleled in the world's military history, and it is absolutely impossible to submit to unconditional surrender of the million picked troops, in perfectly healthy shape, to the Chunking forces of defeated China."[84]

Trepidation in Tokyo that overseas commanders were spurning the emperor's order to surrender could not be ignored—or readily admitted. This defiance did not only threaten Hirohito's prestige, and hence his future value to the occupying powers, it also threatened the imperial institution. If Japan's overseas armies disregarded an emperor's order, the imperial institution would have failed in the most crucial initial role the Allies were anxious for it to perform. Moreover, there remained the possibility that such flagrant disobedience might prove contagious even within the homeland, where ambivalence over the previously unthinkable surrender coursed through the minds of many soldiers and sailors. Although the major coup d'état on the night of August 14–15 was suppressed, a revolt erupted at Atsugi airfield near Tokyo that underscored the precariousness of the situation.[85]

Faced with this serious danger, Hirohito responded by offering to issue a special imperial rescript to the officers and men of his armed forces and by dispatching imperial princes to personally convey his will to overseas commanders. Although drafted earlier, the separate "Rescript to Soldiers and Sailors" throughout the armed forces at home and abroad was not issued until August 17. This message declared, in pertinent part:

Now that the Soviet Union has entered the war against us, to continue . . . under the present conditions at home and aboard would only recklessly incur even more damage to ourselves and result in endangering the very foundation's of the empire's existence. Therefore, even though enormous fighting spirit still exists in the Imperial Navy and Army, I am going to make peace with the United States, Britain, and the Soviet Union, as well as with Chunking, in order to maintain our glorious national polity.[86]

Did this message, not the more famous broadcast on August 15, reveal the "real reason" why Japanese leaders surrendered?[87] There are multiple reasons why this message tells us little of the first crisis in the surrender process—the requirement that some legitimate authority decide Japan must surrender—but a lot about the second crisis—the peril that there would be no organized capitulation of Japan's armies overseas. First, the rescript issued on August 17 was explicitly targeted to deal with the incipient mutiny of overseas commanders who controlled approximately a quarter to a third of all the empire's warriors. The emperor had managed to obtain the surrender of the government and the obedience of the senior commanders in Tokyo to that command by his intervention and actions between August 10 and 15. If Soviet intervention had actually been paramount in his thinking or his arguments in this period, the record fails to reflect that. From August 11, however, the blunt challenges to his order to surrender from his overseas commanders posed threats to both his authority and his fate. The emphasis on Soviet intervention over the atomic bombs reflected the best practical argument Hirohito could advance to support his demand that the overseas commanders obey his order. The might of Soviet ground and air forces posed a real and powerful threat to the overseas commands in Manchuria and China, unlike their effect on the homeland. Furthermore, the overseas commanders lacked any firsthand knowledge of the power of the atomic bombs. Likewise, overseas commanders were unlikely to be impressed with the atomic bombing of cities, because the large urban areas in their regions housed few Japanese nationals and bombing them posed no threat to domestic morale in the homeland. (It must be noted in passing that the August 17 rescript again refers to the domestic situation, implying that fear of internal strife loomed as important in the emperor's calculations.) Thus, the August 17 rescript reflects, not the "real reason" for the emperor's intervention and order to the government to surrender between August 10 and 15, but his attempt to present the most compelling argument for his recalcitrant military lieutenants overseas to obey the surrender order and save Hirohito and the imperial institution.

Louis Allen gives a riveting account of how the question of compliance of the Southern Area Army played out in this drama. Alerted on August 10 that Japan's surrender might be forthcoming, on August 13, Field Marshal Terauchi conferred with his staff on what was treated as the open question of whether his command would comply with a surrender order. The Southern Area Army, like the China Expeditionary Army, was already preparing to continue the war with all communication with the homeland severed. The meeting reached no decision. The day after the emperor's public radio broadcast on August 15, the most senior officers in the Southern Area Army again assembled to examine their response. Two of the most senior generals openly debated whether they actually knew the emperor's real intentions, despite the broadcast. Terauchi, however, appeared to lean to the view that they did and must comply. The following day, August 17 (the day of the rescript), the imperial envoy, Prince Kan'in, appeared and confirmed the emperor's will to surrender. Yet, despite all of these indications that the Southern Area Army would comply and the indisputable evidence of the emperor's will, its leaders still stalled until August 23, *after* it was absolutely clear that all the other commands would obey, before meeting directly with local British leaders to arrange the actual surrender.[88]

It may well be that one particular intercepted message during this period and the ultimate compliance of the overseas commands with the surrender played a major role in the emperor's fate. On August 15, the navy minister in Tokyo sent a dispatch to all commands seeking to establish the bona fides of the surrender order. In that message, he "respectfully submit[ted] a report on events which led to the Empire's acceptance of the Potsdam Declaration." The navy minister described expressly how the deadlock within the government had been broken by the emperor's personal intervention.[89] This revelation, from an absolutely impeccable source, showed that the emperor could be useful to occupation authorities—provided, of course, that the overseas commanders obeyed the surrender. When the overseas commanders fell into line, this provided powerful evidence supporting the advocates for retention of Hirohito during the occupation.[90]

The end of the Pacific War is and will continue to be fertile soil for speculation about the paths that history did not take. Any realistic attempt to explore this subject, however, must grapple with the facts of 1945, not the wishes of later years. That the war ended with the capitulation of the Japanese government and the universal compliance of Japan's armed forces with that surrender does not mean that this outcome was inevitable. Indeed, events provide an alarming demonstration of just how contingent it was. Japan's leaders were not blind fanatics, staggering onward in a trance, oblivious to their nation's plight. Nor could they bring themselves to confront an end to the war that involved an end to the old order prior to Hiroshima. American leaders confronted military realities in the summer of 1945 that confounded any optimism about how and when the war would end. Moreover, radio intelligence gave them ample knowledge of just how far from any acceptable end to the war Japan remained. Failure or refusal to confront these realities leads, not simply to paths history did not take, but to paths history could not have taken.

The Atomic Bomb and Soviet Entry into the War

Of Equal Importance

SUMIO HATANO

The Soviet Entry into the War

Although each factor was of a different nature, both the atomic bombs and Soviet entry into the war contributed to creating the *gaiastu* (external pressure) that finally forced Japanese leaders to move beyond "indetermination." The atomic bombs caught Japan completely by surprise, whereas the Soviet entry was not totally unexpected. Indeed, well before Japan found itself stunned by the former, some preparations for the latter had already begun on the assumption that it was quite possible. As early as May 30, 1945, Imperial General Headquarters issued *Tai-So sakusen junbi* (Preparation for Operations Against the Soviet Union) and *Man-Sen hōmen tai-So sakusen keikaku* (Operation Plan Against the Soviet Union in the Korean-Manchurian Theater), anticipating that the Soviet Union might enter the war in August or September. The Kwantung Army in Manchuria followed on July 5 with its own plan for operations against the Soviet Union, which presumed that the army would be ready for such an operation by the end of September, although the Army General Staff in fact anticipated the expected Soviet entry to occur at some point in August or in September.[1]

In early August, the army's Bureau of Military Affairs initiated a review of external diplomatic and domestic measures in anticipation of eventual Soviet entry into the war. It was widely assumed that the Soviet Union would join the conflict only after presenting Japan with an ultimatum, rather than "without any prior warning." Having issued the ultimatum, the study speculated, the Soviet Union would then enter the war "independently," not as a member of the Allied Powers. In the ultimatum, the USSR would unlikely specify conditions for peace with the United States and Britain and might be expected to "positively reciprocate for past favors." In concrete terms, it was assumed that Moscow would demand the full withdrawal of Japanese military forces from the Asian mainland (with the exception of the Korean Peninsula). How Japan should respond to such an ultimatum—accept it, continue the war, or seek a Soviet-brokered cessation of hostilities—would depend entirely upon "the extent and conditions of the empire's war power at that point," the study concluded.[2] This report thus suggests the deep extent to which the Japanese leadership continued to cling to the hopeful view that the Soviet Union could be separated from the United States and Britain. And yet the eventual Soviet entry on August 9 swiftly crushed this speculation. The Soviet Union acceded to the Potsdam Proclamation once it entered the war, without any prior presentation of an ultimatum to Japan. It was obvious to all that there had never been any real likelihood of the USSR taking an "independent" position in regard to the Allied Powers. The army's Bureau of Military Affairs, however, still adhered to the unrealized premise of separating the Soviet Union and the Allied Powers, even on the very day of the Soviet entry. Consider the following draft "proposal" in regard to measures to be taken henceforth in the direction of the war, which was to be introduced at the Supreme War Council:

NATIONAL POLICY

The empire shall proceed to terminate the war with the Soviet Union as early as possible, and continue to wage war against the United States, Great Britain, and China, while securing Soviet neutrality.

We might expect that, under unavoidable circumstances, we shall take immediate and resolute actions to end the Great East Asian War.

We shall, however, continue to wage the war, literally staking our fate on it, if a change in the *kokutai* [national polity] might be anticipated.

PROSPECTUS

1. The empire shall, immediately and firstly, carry out defensive operations against the Soviet Union and endeavor to at least secure the southern part of the Manchurian-Korean border.

2. We shall not declare war on the Soviet Union.

3. We shall continue diplomatic negotiations with the Soviet Union and, as changing circumstances may permit, end the war against the Soviet Union. At this time, under unavoidable circumstances, we shall take immediate and resolute action to end the Great East Asian War through Soviet mediation.

4. Under no circumstance shall we abandon the *kokutai* [national polity] of the empire.

5. As far as domestic measures are concerned, we shall strengthen our arrangements further and press forward in waging this war for preservation of the national polity, with the nation completely united.[3]

This draft was never actually submitted to the Supreme War Council. Nonetheless, it clearly demonstrates what the Bureau of Military Affairs, the most adamant advocate of continuing the war, had in mind during the final stage of the conflict. First, it did not see a decisive battle on the home islands as the only option left; rather, it was very eager to keep an alternative alive, that is, the possibility of peace with the United States and Britain through Soviet mediation. In a nutshell, it was a policy of refraining from declaring war on the Soviet Union and exploring the possibility of peace through Soviet mediation, while nonetheless proceeding with defensive operations.[4] Although the Bureau of Military Affairs was not in a position to know about Prince Konoe Fumimaro's planned mission to Moscow, it is quite remarkable that only after the Soviet entry into the war did it consider the option of peace through Soviet intervention, which had already been adopted in secret at a mid-May meeting of the so-called Big Six (Prime Minister Suzuki Kantarō, Foreign Minister Tōgō Shigenori, Army Minister Anami Korechika, Chief of the Army General Staff Umezu Yoshijirō, Navy Minister Yonai Mitsumasa, and Chief of the Navy General Staff Toyoda Soemu).

Second, along with the presumption that the war would end with Japan's Korean colonial territory intact, this proposal regarded preservation of the emperor system as the sole and ultimate condition for terminating the war. Whereas the Big Six and the cabinet, meeting on August 9, had discussed three conditions in addition to the preservation of the emperor system, the Bureau of Military Affairs saw this as the sole criterion. The so-called "four-conditions dispute," therefore, must have astonished its personnel. In reference to the "four-conditions dispute" that erupted during the Big Six meeting on the morning of August 9, some junior officers in the Bureau of Military Affairs asserted: "[T]he meeting is now falling into a mood of appeasement and studying conditions for peace, instead of discussing whether we should seek negotiation or not in the first place. How hopelessly weak-kneed they are!"[5]

The fact that this proposal could not go beyond the staff level of the Army Ministry makes it clear that the army as a whole did not accept it.[6] And yet this fact does not reduce the significance of the shift triggered by the Soviet entry. Clearly, there was increasing room in the Bureau of Military Affairs for consideration of peaceful options in achieving an end to the fighting, even before the supposed homeland battle, with the sole condition of preserving of the emperor system. Furthermore, this shift seen in the Bureau of Military Affairs likely had little to do with the atomic bombing of Hiroshima, since it took some time before the division's staff finally came to realize the impact of that attack.

The "Four-Conditions" Dispute

At around 1:00 A.M. on August 7, 1945, President Harry S. Truman's state-ment exalting the power of the atomic bomb arrived at the radio station of the Dōmei News Agency in Kawagoe. It was immediately relayed to the Foreign Affairs, Army, and Navy ministries, the General Staff, and the Imperial Court, but information about the utter destruction of Hiroshima had already reached them. Informed at dawn, Deputy Chief of Staff Kawabe Torashirō, who al-ready knew about "a bomb harnessing atomic fission energy" promptly sensed that Hiroshima's annihilation must have been caused by an atomic weapon.[7] Meanwhile, at around noon that day, Lord Keeper of the Privy Seal Kido Kō-ichi received a report that "the United States used an atomic bomb against the city of Hiroshima yesterday morning, inflicting enormous causalities of about 130,000."[8] Soon the army launched an investigation by dispatching an envoy (Arisue Seizō, chief of the Information Bureau in the General Staff) along with engineers of the Army Aviation Bureau and Dr. Nishina Yoshio in the evening of August 7.

At the cabinet meeting on August 7, Foreign Minister Tōgō pointed out, without waiting for the formal report of the envoy, that "atomic bombs may trigger revolutionary changes in the war," and that more such bombs might be dropped on other cities. On the morning of August 8, he submitted his as-sessment to the throne, urging the early termination of the war. The Hiroshima catastrophe having already been widely reported in detail, the emperor came to the conclusion that the "arrival of that sort of new weapon now makes it im-possible to continue the war." He ordered the foreign minister to "exert every effort to terminate the war without delay" and to inform Prime Minister Suzuki accordingly.[9] Suzuki, meanwhile, found the atomic bomb a "very suitable ex-cuse" for commencement of "peace parleys." In response to the requests of the emperor and Foreign Minister Tōgō, he hastily started preparing for a Big Six meeting, but it failed to be convened on August 8.[10] What finally brought it about was the Soviet entry into the war.

At around 4:00 A.M. on August 9, news of the Soviet invasion arrived at the Dōmei News Agency and the Radio Office of the Foreign Ministry through a broadcast from Moscow. It came almost five hours after Ambassador Satō Naotake received the declaration of war in Moscow, but before the urgent tele-gram had arrived in Tokyo. Deputy Foreign Minister Matsumoto Shun'ichi, Chief of Treaty Bureau Andō Yoshirō, and Chief of the Political Affairs Bureau Shibusawa Shin'ichi promptly gathered at Tōgō's house for consultation. The men quickly agreed to accept the terms of the Potsdam Proclamation on the condition of preserving the emperor's position.[11] This policy was based on the conviction that it was "best to signal our intention to accept the Potsdam Proclamation unilaterally [to the Allied Powers]." In other words, there was a determination not to negotiate a surrender. With this in mind, Tōgō visited Suzuki's house.

Cabinet Secretary Sakomizu Hisatsune, who had his ear to the ground through the Dōmei News Agency regarding the Soviet entry, was by then already at Suzuki's house. Sakomizu put forward three plans: cabinet resignation, acceptance of the Potsdam Proclamation, or continuation of the war. Suzuki's first choice was acceptance of the Potsdam Proclamation. In Suzuki's own words, "the Soviet entry into the war meant the collapse of peace negotiations through Soviet mediation, the most important policy of the cabinet." In order to take responsibility for this failure and aid the emperor, he explained later, he had resolved to terminate the war by himself instead of following the regular procedure, that is, cabinet resignation.[12]

Suzuki immediately went to the Imperial Palace and expressed his intentions to the emperor through Kido. Before 10:00 A.M., the emperor had already asked Kido to "thoroughly consult with the prime minister, because I think it is necessary to conclude the study on how to remedy the war situation as early as possible." Kido met Suzuki at the palace and "urged him to terminate the war under the terms of the Potsdam Proclamation."[13] Suzuki finally decided to accept the Potsdam Proclamation, and ordered Sakomizu again to convene an urgent session of the Big Six.[14]

In this way, the Big Six meeting was eventually convened, starting at 10:30 A.M. Prime Minister Suzuki remarked: "We have been hit hard by the atomic bombing of Hiroshima. Now we have the Soviet entry into the war. It has become almost impossible to continue the war any longer. We seem to have no other choice but to accept the Potsdam Proclamation." After a weighty pause for a moment, Navy Minister Yonai broke the silence by saying: "I wonder if we should unconditionally accept the Proclamation, or if we should take the initiative of putting forward conditions. If we are to propose conditions, what sort of conditions should we come up with?" They should consider four points, he suggested: (1) the emperor system, (2) the disarmament of the Japanese Armed Forces, (3) the issue of war criminals, and (4) postwar military occupation. After explaining the background, Foreign Minister Tōgō said that he considered it appropriate to accept the Potsdam Proclamation, while only expressing reservations about "the safety of the imperial family." Yonai seconded Tōgō's position.

On the other hand, Army Minister Anami, Chief of the Army General Staff Umezu, and Chief of the Navy General Staff Toyoda all insisted on the need to add three more conditions: (1) the Japanese would disarm themselves voluntarily, (2) the Japanese would punish war criminals themselves, and (3) military occupation of the homeland should be avoided. Should that prove impossible, the size of the occupying force and the deployment area should be minimized. Tōgō responded: "We need to be ready to accept a breakdown in the negotiations if we dare press for these conditions. Could we still have a good chance of winning even after the negotiations are broken off?" Umezu and Anami, however, did not agree with the idea of further reducing the conditions of surrender. Instead, they pinned their hopes on a presumed "single and decisive blow" against the Allies, asserting: "[E]ven though the odds of ultimately winning are against us, we can still put up a last-ditch fight."[15]

Chief of the Navy General Staff Toyoda found himself in a difficult position in this dispute. According to Toyoda, he, Anami, and Umezu were not entirely united. While Anami and Umezu clung to the issues of war criminals and the occupation, Toyoda insisted that it was the question of disarmament on which they should seek compromise in advance of peace negotiations.[16] Anami and Umezu were in agreement with this position, but the Toyoda "did not support or oppose" the points regarding war criminals and the occupation. Although he "totally agreed with the navy minister on the terms of peace at that time," Toyoda's support for Anami was motivated merely by his desire not to isolate the army. In any case, the issue was not immediately resolved and had to be put aside until the afternoon session of the cabinet meeting. During this confrontation, the news of the atomic bombing at Nagasaki interrupted the meeting, but it did not significantly alter the course of discussion.

The extraordinary session of the cabinet, which started at 2:30, witnessed lively debate over Tōgō's report on developments regarding the Soviet entry, on the Konoe mission, and on the atomic bomb, and then on Anami's report on the military situation. "With the atomic bomb and the Soviet entry into the war, we now have few chances of winning if those factors are taken at face value," said Anami, "but there must be some hope in the midst of our fighting for the honor of the Yamato race. Disarmament is out of the question, in particular, disarmament of our forces outside Japan." Yonai, in contrast, intervened by expressing his doubts. "I cannot help but question if we should continue to wage the war simply in light of the current domestic situation, rather than the atomic bomb and the Soviet entry. . . . We have no chance of winning, judging from both physical and psychological conditions," Yonai lamented. Solicited by Yonai, Toyoda, Agriculture Minister Ishiguro Tadaatsu, Transportation Minister Kohiyama Naoto, and Internal Minister Abe Genki all presented similarly somber outlooks. While admitting the erosion of public trust in the military and an increase in public antipathy toward it, Anami was still adamant in his beliefs. "All in all, a hundred million Japanese will surely rise up indignantly when the time of the homeland battle comes."[17]

The cabinet meeting recessed from 5:30 to 6:30 P.M., and then the discussion turned more directly to the question of how to respond to the Potsdam Proclamation. Suzuki started by reporting: "There was a general consensus in the Big Six meeting [held that morning] that we cannot help but accept the proclamation." Then Tōgō followed by presenting his views about "the four conditions." He suggested that the problems of the occupation and war criminals might not be categorical and absolute, and that the disarmament problem could be worked out during the peace agreement negotiations. However, there should clearly be no concession on the fate of the emperor. Anami argued against Tōgō, saying: "[Y]ou are wrong to think that what the foreign minister now explained reflects the mood of the meeting. The majority's opinion is that, first of all, we should try to communicate the four conditions to the United States and Britain through Sweden and Switzerland. We should seek peace if those conditions are accepted, or continue the war if they are not." In Anami's words, "[W]e can defend the national polity [*kokutai*] only with that set of four conditions."[18]

In this way, the cabinet meeting remained in hopeless stalemate until past 10:00 P.M. With some impatience, Education Minister Ōta Kōzō insisted that "the cabinet should resign to take responsibility." Prime Minister Suzuki rejected this proposal, however, saying: "I had expected a day like this to come eventually. Unfortunately, a chance for diplomacy through the Soviet Union was missed. I will resign only after I fulfill my responsibility." As Sakomizu observed, "If the army minister had been a dedicated advocate of continuing the war, he would have given thought to the possibility that he could force a cabinet collapse and then form a military-led cabinet."[19]

In fact, this was exactly what Deputy Chief of Army Staff Kawabe had in mind. He suggested to his boss, Umezu, that they should place the nation under martial law, replace the cabinet, and "the military will take over." Umezu's response, according to Kawabe, "seemed not to be against it, even though, typical of his nature, he did not make his opinion clear." Then he called on Army Minister Anami and was "much encouraged" when he knew of Anami's support for continuation of the war. In fact, however, Anami was not willing to force the cabinet to collapse by resigning and letting "the military take over political power."[20]

The Decision of August 10 and Its Background

In the meantime, word soon reached the palace, various senior statesmen, the Foreign Ministry, and the military that the four conditions had been the focal point of discussion at the Big Six meeting, and that the meeting was expanding the discussion circle concerning acceptance of the Potsdam Proclamation.

While the Big Six and other cabinet members were caught up in formal discussions, Kido, the former foreign minister Shigemitsu Mamoru, Prince Konoe Fumimaro, and others not directly involved in the discussions launched an informal meeting of their own, with the intention of drawing up a "sacred decision" scenario behind the scenes.

The center of gravity in this action was Kido. First, Suzuki approached him after the Big Six meeting on August 9, at about 1:00 P.M., saying "we have decided to accept the Potsdam Proclamation with four conditions." It is not entirely clear whether this reflected what Suzuki understood to be the case at that time or whether it was simply a misunderstanding on Kido's part. Regardless, Kido understood it to reflect what had occurred at the meeting.[21] And he was not the only person who understood it this way: so did Shigemitsu, who had been staying in the Imperial Hotel and encouraging the staff of Foreign Ministry since August 7, and so did Konoe.[22] At this point, it should be noted, the notion of the "sacred decision" did not come up in the minds of the three. When Shigemitsu visited Kido at the request of the Foreign Ministry staff on the previous day (August 8), Kido had informed him of the developments since his resignation in April. As early as 1944, he and Kido had together pledged to "realize the end of the war with the word from the top when the time is right." His notes, published in *Shigemitsu Mamoru shuki*, also reveal that Shigemitsu bore in his mind the "sacred decision" plotted in cooperation with Kido. As for their meeting on August 8, however, no record gives evidence of their discussing the actual procedure of the "sacred decision."[23]

Suzuki's visit to Kido coincided with Konoe's visit, at the suggestion of Prince Takamatsu Nobuhito, an officer of the Navy General Staff, who was thinking of approaching Kido about arrangements for immediate peace. When Konoe was informed of the Soviet entry into the war by his secretary, Hosokawa Morisada, upon the request of Prince Takamatsu, he thought: "[I]t could be a gift from Heaven." Rushing to Kido, he asserted that the conditions should be reduced to the single issue of preserving the emperor system, and it would then be inevitable that the dispute should be settled by "His Majesty's intervention." Kido, however, presented his view that "we have no choice" but to put forward the four conditions.[24] Hosokawa, accompanied by Konoe, rushed to the headquarters of the Navy General Staff, reporting what Kido had told the prince. Urged by Hosokawa, Prince Takamatsu made a call to Kido after 3:00 P.M. and expressed his concern that "the Allied Powers may see the conditions as an expression of intent to not negotiate for peace."[25] Kido relayed this anxiety to the emperor.

The idea soon struck Konoe of asking Shigemitsu to convince Kido. Konoe immediately met Shigemitsu, soliciting his help by saying that there was no alternative to the emperor's intervention, even though the Big Six meeting that morning had agreed on the four conditions, which, he thought, might wreck any hope of peace. Meanwhile, the Foreign Ministry staff learned about the "four-conditions" dispute from Tōgō right after the meeting ended. Deputy Minister Matsumoto frantically urged Tōgō to "stop it by all means, because those conditions would certainly break off the talks."[26]

Recognizing the anxieties prevalent among the Foreign Ministry staff, Shigemitsu drove to the Imperial Household Ministry, in a car arranged by Konoe, and pressed Kido on the need for "His Majesty's intervention." In Konoe's own words, Kido was "in a bad mood." From Kido's point of view, it seemed that "thanks to His Majesty's intervention, at last the way to peace had already been paved," and that the government should now take charge of the measures to follow. In other words, Kido considered "His Majesty's decision" to dispatch the Konoe mission with the emperor's personal message sufficient. He also believed that the problem of determining conditions for peace were within the jurisdiction of the government. Shigemitsu "sympathized deep in his heart" with Kido's remarks, but he then dwelled on the urgent need of seeking "His Majesty's intervention" in order to "reverse what the military is thinking." Kido finally agreed.[27]

Kido had an audience with the emperor at about 4:30 P.M. and secured Hirohito's understanding on the need for intervention at the coming imperial conference. Then he turned to Shigemitsu and asked, "Could we not urge the cabinet to arrange for the imperial conference to convene tonight, during which we could express our opinions in the presence of the emperor and make a decision according to His Majesty's decision?"[28] Shigemitsu consulted with Konoe right away, while communicating this plan to the Foreign Ministry and the cabinet. Meanwhile, Kido forwarded the emperor's intentions to Suzuki, who had suspended the cabinet meeting, and urged him to "carry out things as soon as possible with no conditions."[29]

Initially, Kido did not consider the "sacred decision" necessary, since he believed that the Big Six meeting had already agreed on the four conditions. However, Shigemitsu, Konoe, and Prince Takamatsu, all of whom thought it inevitable that negotiations for surrender would collapse once the four conditions were communicated to the United States, succeeded in persuading Kido to support a "sacred decision" scenario, indicating only one condition (preservation of the emperor system). The emperor also supported this plan. As Kido told Shigemitsu, "His Majesty comprehends everything very well and is firmly determined." The emperor was, in fact, one of the "authors" of the "sacred decision" scenario.[30] Suzuki, fearing that the cabinet might resign owing to lack of unity, suspended the cabinet meeting shortly after 10:00 P.M. and sought an audience with the emperor, accompanied by Foreign Minister Tōgō. Tōgō explained the course of discussion, and Suzuki sought a session of the Supreme War Council in the presence of the emperor. The emperor "granted permission."[31]

In the scenario concocted by Suzuki and Kido, the cabinet would first discuss the original plan of accepting the Potsdam Proclamation with the single condition of preserving the emperor system, and then, with or without consensus, they would seek the "sacred decision," to which the emperor had already assented in advance.[32] Sakomizu took charge of convening the imperial conference upon the emperor's request, but he first had to clear two hurdles. The first was that convening the Supreme War Council in the presence of the emperor required the written approval of both the army and navy chiefs of general staff. The other hurdle was that since the Big Six meeting had been suspended with the understanding that unanimity was the condition for holding an imperial conference, there was much fear about possible disagreements at the conference arising from still unsettled disputes.

As for the first problem, Sakomizu had already obtained both chiefs' signatures on the necessary documents on the condition that "I shall inform you and seek your approval before the imperial conference is convened." Sakomizu later recalled, "I took it upon myself to submit all those documents to the palace without informing both chiefs."[33] At that time, as his memoirs tell us, Chief of the Navy General Staff Toyoda was waiting for the Big Six meeting to reconvene. Having yielded no consensus, it had been in recess since the morning. Toyoda noted his surprise when he "was informed all of sudden at around 11:30 P.M. that the Supreme War Council will be held in the presence of the emperor."[34] Certainly, such an abrupt calling of the conference must have perplexed most members, including the chiefs of the army and navy Bureau of Military Affairs staff. Sakomizu had kept the "sacred decision" scenario secret from everyone gathering at the palace: "Nobody but the prime minister, foreign minister, and I [Sakomizu] knew that the aim of this conference was to solicit the sacred decision."[35]

With the emperor in attendance, the Supreme War Council began its meeting at 11:50 P.M. The members of the council were the six and four senior staffs (three secretaries of Sakomizu, Hoshina Zenshirō, Yoshizumi Masao, and a Planning Agency director, Ikeda Sumihisa), plus the chairman of the Privy Council, Hiranuma Kiichirō, who was included at the emperor's suggestion. Presiding over the conference, Suzuki first summarized the developments up to that point. When the Big Six had met in the morning, the proposal for four conditions had been the major theme of discussion, Suzuki said. In the afternoon cabinet meeting, however, six members supported the foreign minister's proposal of pushing only for the preservation of the emperor system; three other members stood behind the four-conditions proposal, and the remaining five were undecided. Suzuki let Foreign Minister Tōgō explain the reasoning behind his proposal. As for the Potsdam Proclamation, Tōgō said, "all [of the cabinet] reached agreement in accepting this," suggesting that acceptance of the Potsdam Proclamation was a prerequisite for further discussion. "Many conditions would lead to refusal of all," Tōgō continued. He suggested they should make the "preservation and safety of the emperor's family the only condition," adding, "we should consider the problem of disarmament during discussions of the armistice agreement. I think it would be unavoidable to accept military occupation and punishment of war criminals." Navy Minister Yonai agreed with Tōgō, but Anami argued that "these four conditions are absolutely essential to achieve peace, because they are absolute conditions for the preservation of the emperor system." Umezu then repeated his opinion, saying: "I am in total agreement with the army minister. The preparation for the homeland battle has already been completed. Even though the Soviet entry into the war has further complicated the situation, I do not think it is bad enough to give up our chance to deliver the coup de grâce against the United States and Britain."[36]

The most vocal participant in the debate was Hiranuma. Having been quite suddenly notified about the conference, Hiranuma "had no idea or plan in my mind," he later recalled. Overall, he generally seems to have supported Suzuki. While generally in favor of Tōgō's proposal, Hiranuma directed many questions at Tōgō and the army and navy ministers, ranging from background to the Soviet invasion, possible scenarios for a homeland battle, and strategies of defense against the atomic bombs, to the deterioration of domestic security conditions owing to air raids and food shortages. He succeeded in extracting favorable answers from Suzuki and Tōgō concerning the termination of the war.

Hiranuma was particularly unhappy with the phrase "the status of His Majesty established by the constitution," which he suggested should be replaced with "the prerogatives of His Majesty as a sovereign ruler." The emperor's prerogatives, he insisted, dated from the time of the nation's founding and were not just established in law. Tōgō's proposal was therefore modified according to Hiranuma's suggestion without opposition.[37] Hearing Hiranuma's opinion, Tōgō thought, "the prerogative as a sovereign ruler is nothing but just one of those established in the law of the land. Mr. Hiranuma saw it as preceding the constitution, but the other side of the negotiations could hardly grasp such a thing."[38] But Tōgō did not dare to argue any further.

Anami's four-conditions argument ultimately received support from Toyoda as well as Umezu, but the imperial conference concluded with the "sacred decision." The emperor endorsed the proposal of the Foreign Ministry, as designed by Kido and others.[39] The third session of the extraordinary cabinet meeting, which started at 3:00 A.M. on August 10, decided that, "according to His Majesty's will, we shall accept the Potsdam Proclamation only with a prior agreement on the single matter of the national polity [*kokutai*]." If this decision was intact, the Foreign Ministry believed, they could rest on a "unilateral assumption," without any reply from the Allied Powers. At the conference, however, Anami argued: "How can we trust the enemy? As long as we cannot have a firm guarantee on the emperor's prerogatives before our announcement, the army will continue to wage war. It will not be stopped solely by today's decision." He drove home the point to Prime Minister Suzuki and Navy Minister Yonai that "we will continue the war if there is no confirmation of their [the Allies'] agreement on the imperial prerogatives" and he ultimately obtained their assent.[40] How the United States and the Allies would respond to this conditional reply had become all the more important.

At about 4:00 A.M. on August 10, Foreign Minister Tōgō returned from the conference to the Foreign Ministry, where Deputy Minister Matsumoto, Chief of the Treaty Bureau Shibusawa, and others had drafted a telegram to be sent to the Allies to convey acceptance of the Potsdam Proclamation along the lines of Tōgō's proposal. This draft made the "unilateral assumption," not asking the United States to clarify its intentions, that the Potsdam Proclamation would not change the status of the emperor established in the constitution.[41] However, after having gone through the imperial conference and the extraordinary cabinet meetings, the draft required adjustment in two areas. The first point was that the original phrase "the status of the emperor established by the constitution" would be changed to "the prerogatives of His Majesty as a sovereign ruler." The second point was to request a clear answer to the proposal and not merely "unilaterally assume" the safety of the imperial system. Finally, the draft was changed to read, "on the condition that the above declaration [the Potsdam Proclamation] does not include any demand to change the prerogatives of His Majesty as a sovereign ruler, we shall accept it. The empire trusts in the above agreement and hopes for the prompt and clear presentation of your reaction on this point." Deputy Minister Matsumoto was one among several who worried about these changes, but he was nonetheless relieved to see that the other three conditions were not included.[42]

In this way, at dawn on August 10, the first telegram expressing Japan's acceptance of the Potsdam Proclamation was cabled to the United States via the Swiss and Swedish governments. The next day, without prior approval from the army and navy, a telegram was cabled from Foreign Minister Tōgō to Japanese ambassadors in the "independent" nations of Greater East Asia, urging them to inform each government of Japan's acceptance of the Potsdam Proclamation and "forward the empire's deep appreciation for their sincere cooperation in endeavoring to wage the common war, hand in hand with the empire, for the liberation of Greater East Asia."[43]

The Army's Response

When the cabinet meeting session began at 2:00 P.M. on August 10, the focus of discussion shifted to whether the members should announce their decision to accept the Potsdam Proclamation. Advocates of announcement pointed to a variety of positive reasons for doing so. For instance, it would help dampen the arguments for continuation of the war, prevent groundless rumors from spreading, and inform the public of the conciliatory stance on the Japanese side, so that, in the event of an American refusal to accept the proposal, it "will tighten the determination of our people to fight to the death for honor." Those opposed to an announcement, however, ultimately prevailed. First, they pointed out the troublesome possibility that if they announced the termination of the war, the mood of despair and war weariness among the public would certainly gain momentum and weaken Japan's position in the peace negotiations with the United States. As the director-general of the Information Bureau, Shimomura Hiroshi, observed, "once it is announced, some people would be incensed, but most would yearn for the ceasefire to come, because they are tired of incessant air raids and hard lives. It is disadvantageous in any way to let such a situation be known to the other side of the negotiation."[44] The second point of opposition was based on the perceived difficulty of maintaining order among the public, once their morale had been slackened by the announcement, in the event that negotiations stalled. There was a powerful argument that this difficulty was particularly pertinent in the case of the military.

In the end, it was concluded that it would not be wise to inform the public until the "imperial edict" was finally announced, because, in addition to the above misgivings, there was always the possibility that some diehards for continuation of the war might stir up unexpected problems should they know of the surrender before an "imperial edict to terminate of the war" was issued. At the same time, it was also agreed in consultation among the director-general of the Information Bureau and the army, navy, and foreign affairs ministers to "take steps toward gradually directing the mood of the people toward the end of the war."[45] The first step was a statement by the director-general of the Information Bureau released at 4:30 P.M. on August 10 that referred to the brutality of the "new type of bombs" and the Soviet entry into the war, and plainly said: "We now have to admit that we are caught in the truly worst situation. The government has been exerting a final effort to defend the last line of preserving the honor of the nation and the national polity. We expect the hundred million Japanese people as well will overcome all obstacles to preserve the national polity." In short, it tried to imply that peace negotiations were under way and show an alternative to a deadly homeland battle.

This attempt was followed by a statement that Army Minister Anami delivered to all Army Ministry officers on the morning of August 10. Without mentioning his opinion on the other three conditions, he summarized the developments at the imperial conference and gave his men instructions to refrain from "dereliction of duty" and to "follow orders for either war or peace, taking into account further developments in the diplomatic negotiations." In these ways, the domestic mood of war weariness and the arguments for ending the war in the government worked hand in hand to weaken the military's arguments for continuation of the war.

This approach, however, met with strong resistance. "Instructions from the Army Minister" delivered on August 11 began with the phrase "To all officers and soldiers" and appealed strongly for resolute resistance, insisting: "Firmly convinced, we shall wage the holy war to defend our sacred land without fail." According to Lieutenant Colonel Inaba Masao, an officer in the Bureau of Military Affairs who played the main role in drafting the instructions, he wrote the document specifically for overseas troops such as Kwantung Army and had it delivered as instructions from the army minister with approval from the chief of the Bureau of Military Affairs, Arao Okikatsu. Inaba did so out of his conviction that "we should encourage the troops by delivering strong words, lest we disturb them, and we should not relax our offensive posture right through to the very end or until surrender."[46] These instructions contrast with the statement from the Information Bureau's director-general released simultaneously by radio broadcast and in the newspapers.[47] Colonel Hayashi Saburō, secretary to the army minister, approved the announcement of the instructions through the media with Anami's assent, understanding them to be "the epitome of traditional army thinking that the supreme command should be independent of politics while decisions of peace and war should be within the jurisdiction of the government."[48] The idea that the question of a cease-fire should be within the jurisdiction of the supreme command seemed to prevail in the army. It was because of this understanding that Tōgō was forced to concede that "the matter of the cease-fire should be dealt with by the supreme command after a reply has arrived from the other side."[49] Prime Minister Suzuki, however, overrode the opposition by interpreting the sacred decision as if it were intended to "bring about the unification of the military and the government."[50]

On the other hand, the response of the Army General Staff differed from that of the Bureau of Military Affairs. At dawn on August 10, Chief of Staff Umezu gave Deputy Chief Kawabe, who was waiting on the spot, a brief account of developments during the imperial conference and the content of the "sacred decision." On August 9, when Kawabe learned of the Soviet entry, and expressed his determination to "simply fight on, staking all hope on national pride," he was trying to persuade Chief Umezu and Minister Anami to support measures placing the nation under martial law, replace the cabinet, and "take it over with the military."[51] But to his great astonishment, the emperor pointed out delays in the construction of defense trenches in the Kantō area and the growing disparity in preparations for the homeland battle between what they had planned and what they had actually carried out. "Almost all plans the supreme command makes are always disorganized and off schedule," the emperor remarked.[52] Kawabe noted in his diary that day: "Should I be allowed to speculate, His Majesty's state of mind was not brought about as a consequence of the dispute in the imperial conference. After all, His Majesty holds no hope for further operations. To put it in another way, His Majesty's trust in the military has completely evaporated."[53] In a nutshell, the emperor's approval of Tōgō's proposal was owing more to his own distrust of the military leadership, especially those officials responsible for operations, than it was a consequence of the dispute in the imperial conference. Nothing was more crucial to the Army General Staff than this.[54] It may constitute one of the reasons why the arguments among the Army General Staff for continuing the war were finally contained.

Resistance from the Troops Abroad

Seeking to inform frontline troops of Japan's acceptance of the Potsdam Proclamation before they heard of it from their own side, the Foreign Ministry decided to make the decision public, as Deputy Minister Matsumoto had proposed. At about 8:00 P.M. on August 10, in active cooperation with the Dōmei News Agency, the director of the Information Bureau of the Foreign Ministry, Okazaki Katsuo, and Ōta Saburō, chief of the bureau's third division, broadcast the announcement in Morse code to avoid the military's censorship.[55]

The U.S. government received this broadcast before it was informed by the official telegram from Japan via Switzerland and Sweden, and the message was also intercepted by Japanese troops abroad. Numerous telegrams then immediately flowed into Imperial General Headquarters, including one from the Southern Army at dawn on August 11, inquiring whether "the announcement we intercepted in the English-language broadcast from Tokyo at midnight on August 11 is true or not, and the Japanese government is willing to accept the ultimatum of the Potsdam Proclamation." The cable from the Chinese

Theater Expeditionary Army urged "firm vigilance not to be deceived by this propaganda" and called for measures to arrest the growing commotion, reporting that the information on Japan's acceptance of the Potsdam Proclamation had "already been reaching the public in a wide area of China." Cables from the Eighteenth Theater Army in Bangkok and the Seventh Theater Army in Singapore arrived in Tokyo one after another, both loudly appealing for the continuation of the war. The Eighteenth Theater Army insisted: "[W]e shall keep our officers and soldiers firmly united, beat the ugly enemies with grace, and seize control of strategic positions in Thailand until every last one of us falls, in order to buttress the defense of the holy state."[56]

Reviewing these threatening cables, the Army General Staff sought to clarify its position. It cabled a reply from Imperial General Headquarters to each of the armies directly over the signature of chief of staff, saying: "The Imperial Army and Navy will fight to an honorable death rather than lay down their arms. But it is a fact that we have launched negotiations with aims of fulfilling the two primary purposes of the war shown in the above section" (telegram from the Army General Staff, no. 487). In addition, on the same day, the following message signed by the army minister and chief of staff was cabled to the commanders of the Kwantung Army, the China Expeditionary Army, the Southern Theater Army, and the Second General Army in the homeland:

In response to the Soviet entry into the war, the empire, while still conducting powerful operations against the Soviet forces, is now in negotiations with the Soviet Union and the United States, Britain, and China, along the following lines:

1. With the condition that there be no demand for changing the prerogatives of His Majesty as a sovereign ruler, the empire is willing to accept the Potsdam Proclamation.

2. It almost goes without saying that as long as there remains even a shred of doubt about the above condition, the empire will resolutely proceed to accomplish the purposes of the war.[57]

These two telegrams had one key element in common. Both made it obvious that the government was in negotiations to achieve the "purposes of the war." At a minimum, this meant the preservation of the national polity, or *kokutai*—the prerogatives of His Majesty as a sovereign ruler. Mention of the three other conditions was avoided. Of particular significance is the second clause, which read "the empire will resolutely proceed to accomplish the purposes of the war," rather than calling for continuation of the war or homeland resistance. In other words, it can be read as a clear implication that negotiations or continued fighting were both possible measures to accomplish "the purposes of the war," that is, the preservation of the emperor system. It is possible, however, that this message was sent with the understanding that "the purposes of the war" included the other three conditions, because making those three conditions conspicuous would certainly be more upsetting to the army both in and outside Japan. Even if this was the case, this message clearly marks a substantial shift in the attitudes of the army leadership, in that it offered an alternative to homeland resistance in order to attain "the purposes of the war." A similar consideration can be observed in the responses of the Bureau of Military Affairs to the Soviet entry into the war.

Even so, some ten junior officers in the Bureau of Military Affairs saw no option but to wage all-out resistance on the home islands if no positive answer were forthcoming on the preservation of the national polity. Lieutenant Colonel Itō Hiroyuki, an officer of the Bureau of Military Affairs, had no doubt in his mind that the army leadership could "bring the war to an honorable settlement" by inflicting a hard blow on the enemy when the expected landings on the mainland took place that autumn. Kōmura and Colonel Takayama Shinobu, senior officer in the Bureau of Military Affairs, also shared this view.[58] In anticipation of an unclear reply from the United States regarding the preservation of the national polity, the Bureau of Military Affairs was determined to draw up detailed plans including an "Outline for National Martial Law," "Outline for Measures in the Coup," "Outline for Preparation for Launching the War Cabinet," and other documents, all of which anticipated outright military rule of Japan.[59]

Conclusion: Behind the *Ten'yū* (Gift of Heaven) Argument

During the imperial conference of August 9–10, Privy Council Chairman Hiranuma referred to public unrest and deterioration of domestic security owing to air raids and food shortages, driving home the point that "the current situation is very dangerous and a cause for deep anxiety, even though I have no doubt that people are deeply loyal in the depth of their souls." In other words, he called attention to the danger that continuation of the war might alienate the people from the imperial house, leading to a harsher mood of war weariness and the emergence of anti-war movements, which might culminate in popular revolt, terminating both the war and the emperor system. Moreover, Hiranuma was not the only one on the alert against this danger.

For the same reasons, Navy Minister Yonai viewed the atomic bombs and the Soviet entry into the war as a "gift from Heaven." He explained: "I have been insisting on the early settlement of the situation for a long time, but not because of my fear of the enemy's attack, the atomic bombs, or the Soviet entry into the war. It is first and foremost because of my great anxiety about the domestic situation. Therefore, it is now rather fortuitous for us to settle the situation without that matter coming to surface."[60] Given the danger that if the end of the war resulted from the domestic situation, it might bring about a change in the emperor system, the atomic bombs and the Soviet entry seemed like heaven-sent excuses for terminating it without such a fearful change taking place.[61]

On the other hand, Hiranuma expressed his anxiety about "the potential for deteriorating conditions of domestic security as a result of termination of the war." In fact, those who advocated continuing the war, especially in the army, were in a state of turmoil. When told of the Soviet entry by Hosokawa Morisada, Prince Konoe Fumimaro said: "[I]t may be gift from heaven for containing the army."[62] In short, the leadership had been facing the dilemma that a hasty termination of the war might invite an army rebellion, while the protracted continuation of the war would provoke public hostility to the emperor system. The double-shocks of *gaiatsu* (external pressures) of the atomic bombs and the Soviet entry presented themselves as nothing less than a "gift from heaven" to the leadership in escaping from this dilemma. The problem, however, lay in the fact that the Potsdam Proclamation included no reassurance from the Allied Powers on the preservation of the emperor system. It was against this background that U.S. Secretary of State James Byrnes's response on behalf of the United States constituted the new focus of the political process unfolding after August 11.

This chapter does not offer a direct answer to the question of which was the more important factor in ending the war, the atomic bombs or the Soviet entry. The atomic bombings shocked the imperial court and the Big Six as much as the Soviet entry did, but for the Japanese Army, and, in particular, its Bureau of Military Affairs, the Soviet entry played a much more important role and was crucial in prompting a change in its position to one of preserving the emperor system, with the homeland intact, including Korea.[63] In short, the impact of the two factors depended largely upon what sort of scenario for terminating the war one embraced at that point. In any case, in the absence of the two *gaiatsu,* no political process could have broken the deadlock over the Potsdam Proclamation in the Japanese leadership.

4 ∎

The Atomic Bombs and the
Soviet Invasion

Which Was More Important in Japan's Decision to Surrender?

TSUYOSHI HASEGAWA

Almost immediately following the end of World War II, Americans began to question the use of the atomic bomb and the circumstances surrounding the end of the Pacific War. More than half a century later, books and articles on the atomic bomb still provoke storms of debate among readers, and the use of atomic weapons remains a sharply contested subject.[1] As the 1995 controversy over the *Enola Gay* exhibit at the Smithsonian's National Air and Space Museum revealed, the issues connected with the dropping of the bombs on Hiroshima and Nagasaki continue to touch a sensitive nerve in Americans. Among scholars, disagreement remains no less heated. But, on the whole, this debate has been strangely parochial, centering almost exclusively on how the U.S. leadership made the decision to drop the bombs.

There are two distinct gaps in this historiography. First, with regard to the atomic bombs, as Asada Sadao in Japan correctly observes, American historians have concentrated on the "motives" behind the use of atomic bombs, but "they have slighted the *effects* of the bomb."[2] Second, although historians have been aware of the decisive influence of both the atomic bombs and the Soviet entry into the war, they have largely sidestepped the Soviet factor, relegating it to sideshow status.[3]

Two historians, Asada Sadao and Richard Frank, have recently confronted this issue head-on, arguing that the atomic bombing of Hiroshima had a more decisive effect on Japan's decision to surrender than did Soviet entry into the war.[4] This essay challenges that view. It argues that (1) the atomic bombing of Nagasaki did not have much effect on Japan's decision; (2) of the two factors—the atomic bombing of Hiroshima and Soviet entry into the war—the

Soviet invasion had a more important effect on Japan's decision to surrender; (3) nevertheless, neither the atomic bombs nor Soviet entry into the war served as "a knock-out punch" that had a direct, decisive, and immediate effect on Japan's decision to surrender; (4) the most important, immediate cause behind Japan's decision to surrender was the emperor's "sacred decision" to do so, engineered by a small group of the Japanese ruling elite; and (5) that in the calculations of this group, Soviet entry into the war provided a more powerful motivation than the atomic bombs to seek the termination of the war by accepting the terms specified in the Potsdam Proclamation. Further, by posing counterfactual hypotheses, I argue that Soviet entry into the war against Japan alone, without the atomic bombs, might have led to Japan's surrender before November 1, but that the atomic bombs alone, without Soviet entry into the war, would not have accomplished this. Finally, I argue that had U.S. President Harry S. Truman sought Stalin's signature on the Potsdam Proclamation, and had Truman included the promise of a constitutional monarchy in the Potsdam Proclamation, as Secretary of War Henry Stimson had originally suggested, the war might have ended sooner, possibly without the atomic bombs being dropped on Japan.

The Influence of the Hiroshima Bomb on Japan's Decision to Surrender

In order to discuss the influence of the atomic bombs on Japan's decision to surrender, we must examine three separate issues: (1) the effect of the Hiroshima bomb; (2) the effect of the Nagasaki bomb; and (3) the effect of the two bombs combined.

Let us first examine the effect of the Hiroshima bomb. In order to prove that the Hiroshima bomb had a decisive effect on Japan's decision, Asada and Frank use the following evidence: (1) the August 7 cabinet meeting; (2) the testimony of Lord Keeper of the Privy Seal Kido Kōichi concerning the emperor's statement on August 7; and (3) the emperor's statement to Foreign Minister Tōgō Shigenori on August 8.

The Cabinet Meeting on August 7

According to Asada and Frank, the cabinet meeting on August 7 was a crucial turning point. Asada argues that, judging that "the introduction of a new weapon, which had drastically altered the whole military situation, offered the military ample grounds for ending the war," Foreign Minister Tōgō Shigenori proposed that "surrender be considered at once on the basis of terms presented in the Potsdam Declaration [Proclamation]."[5] Frank writes: "Togo extracted from the American statements about the 'new and revolutionary increase in destruct[ive]' power of the atomic bomb a reason to accept the Potsdam Proclamation."[6]

If these arguments are correct, there was indeed a fundamental change of policy, at least on the part of Tōgō, if not the entire cabinet, and the Hiroshima bomb had a decisive effect on Tōgō's thinking, since until then he had been advocating suing for peace through Moscow's mediation before considering the acceptance of the Potsdam Proclamation. In his memoirs, however, Tōgō does not portray this cabinet meeting as a decisive turning point. The following is all he says about the cabinet meeting: "On the afternoon of the 7th, there was a cabinet meeting. The army minister and the home minister read their reports. The army appeared to minimize the effect of the bomb, without admitting that it was the atomic bomb, insisting that further investigation was necessary."[7]

The only source that makes a reference to Tōgō's insistence on the acceptance of the Potsdam Proclamation was the testimony given by Cabinet Minister Sakomizu Hisatsune under postwar interrogation. Citing Sakomizu's testimony, Ōi Atsushi, who interviewed Tōgō in preparation for the Tokyo trial, asked him about his alleged proposal to accept the Potsdam terms. Tōgō replied: "I reported that the United States was broadcasting that the atomic bomb would impart a revolutionary change in warfare, and that unless Japan accepted peace it would drop the bombs on other places. The Army . . . attempted to minimize its effect, saying that they were not sure if it was the atomic bomb, and that since it [had] dispatched a delegation, it had to wait for its report."[8] The picture that emerges from this testimony is that Tōgō merely reported the U.S. message. Perhaps he merely conveyed his preference to consider the Potsdam Proclamation by reporting Truman's message. But when met with stiff opposition from Army Minister Anami Korechika, who dismissed the American atomic bomb message as mere propaganda, Tōgō, without a fight, accepted Anami's proposal to wait until the delegation submitted its official findings. According to Sakomizu's memoirs, Tōgō first proposed, and the cabinet agreed, that Japan should register a strong protest through the International Red Cross and the Swiss legation about the American use of the atomic bomb as a serious violation of international law prohibiting poison gas. Sakomizu further wrote: "There was an argument advocating the quick termination of war by accepting the Potsdam Proclamation," but in view of the army's opposition, the cabinet merely decided to send the investigation team to Hiroshima.[9]

In other words, neither the cabinet nor Tōgō himself believed that any change of policy was necessary on the afternoon of August 7, one day after the atomic bomb was dropped on Hiroshima, although the majority of the cabinet members had already known that the bomb was most likely an atomic bomb, and furthermore that unless Japan surrendered, many atomic bombs might be dropped on other cities in Japan. In fact, far from entertaining the possibility of accepting the Potsdam terms, the cabinet was blatantly more combative against the United States, deciding to lodge a formal protest against the use of the atomic bomb.

What Did the Emperor Say on August 7?

The news of the dropping of an atomic bomb on Hiroshima had already been brought to the emperor early in the morning on August 7, but Kido learned of it only at noon. Kido had an unusually long audience with the emperor that lasted from 1:30 to 2:05 in the Imperial Library. Kido's diary notes: "The emperor expressed his august view on how to deal with the current situation and asked various questions."[10] But Kido's diary says nothing about what the emperor's view was and what questions he asked. Later, Kido recalled that Hirohito had told him: "Now that things have come to this impasse, we must bow to the inevitable. No matter what happens to my safety, we should lose no time in ending the war so as not to have another tragedy like this."[11] Citing Kido's account as the decisive evidence, Asada concludes: "The Emperor . . . was from this time forward Japan's foremost peace advocate, increasingly articulate and urgent in expressing his wish for peace."[12] Frank, however, does not share Asada's description of the emperor as the "foremost peace advocate," viewing him as wavering at times over whether or not Japan should attach more than one condition to its acceptance of the Potsdam Proclamation.[13]

Kido's description of the emperor's reaction to the Hiroshima bomb must be taken with a grain of salt. As Hirohito's closest adviser, Kido worked assiduously to create the myth that the emperor had played a decisive role in ending the war. Kido's testimony under interrogation on May 17, 1949, was designed to create the image of the benevolent emperor saving the Japanese from further devastation. Hirohito's offer of "self-sacrifice" does not correspond to his behavior and thinking during those crucial days. It should be noted that on July 30, three days after he received a copy of the Potsdam Proclamation, Hirohito was concerned above all about the safety of the "three divine treasures" (*sanshu no jingi*) that symbolized the imperial household in the Ise Shrine in the event of an enemy attack. Meanwhile, more than 10,000 Japanese were killed by American incendiary bombings during the eleven days from the Potsdam Proclamation to the Hiroshima bomb. Hirohito's wish to prevent further sacrifice of his "children" (*sekishi*) at his own risk does not ring true.[14] Contrary to Asada's assertion, Hirohito's first and foremost preoccupation was the preservation of the imperial house. Neither does his subsequent behavior indicate that Hirohito was the most persistent, articulate advocate of immediate peace. Here, Frank's skepticism is closer to the truth than Asada's conclusion.

The Emperor's Statement to Tōgō on August 8

On the following morning, August 8, Foreign Minister Tōgō Shigenori went to the imperial palace for an audience with the emperor. According to Asada, using the American and British broadcasts "to buttress his case," Tōgō urged the emperor to agree to end the war as quickly as possible "on condition, of course, that the emperor system be retained." Hirohito concurred and replied:

Now that such a new weapon has appeared, it has become less and less possible to continue the war. We must not miss a chance to terminate the war by bargaining [with the Allied powers, Asada adds] for more favorable conditions now. Besides, however much we consult about [surrender, Asada adds] terms we desire, we shall not be able to come to an agreement. So my wish is to make such arrangements as will end the war as soon as possible.[15]

From this statement, Asada concludes that "the emperor expressed his conviction that a speedy surrender was the only feasible way to save Japan." Hirohito urged Tōgō to "do [his] utmost to bring about a prompt termination of war," and told the foreign minister to convey his desire to Prime Minister Suzuki Kantarō. "In compliance with the imperial wish, Tōgō met Suzuki and proposed that, given the atomic bombing of Hiroshima, the Supreme War Council be convened with all dispatch."[16] Frank's interpretation follows Asada's basic assumption. According to Frank, "Togo called for immediate termination of the war on the basis of the Potsdam Declaration [Proclamation]," but unlike Asada, he asserts that Hirohito "still balked personally at simple acceptance of the Potsdam Declaration [Proclamation]."[17]

The crucial question here, however, concerns the effect of the Hiroshima bomb on the emperor. Both Asada and Frank make the argument that Tōgō's meeting with the emperor was a crucial turning point in both men's decision to seek an immediate end to the war on the terms stipulated by the Potsdam Proclamation. This argument, however, is not convincing.

"We must not miss a chance to terminate the war by bargaining for more favorable conditions now," Tōgō quotes the emperor as saying. Asada adds the words, "with the Allied powers" in brackets after "bargaining," to read: "We must not miss a chance to terminate the war by bargaining [with the Allied powers] for more favorable conditions now." Asada takes this to mean that the emperor wished to end the war by accepting the Potsdam Proclamation.[18] Is it correct, however, to interpret the implied meaning here as "bargaining with the Allied powers"? As I argue below, Tōgō had dispatched an urgent telegram to Japan's ambassador to the USSR, Satō Naotake, only the previous day, instructing the latter to obtain Moscow's answer to Prince Konoe Fumimaro's mission. It is also important to recall that the Japanese government decided to suspend judgment on the Potsdam Proclamation precisely because it had pinned its last hope on Moscow's mediation. Whom was the Japanese government bargaining with at that moment? Certainly, it was not the Allied powers, as Asada has inserted in brackets. The only party with whom Japan was "bargaining" at that moment was the Soviet Union, not the Allied powers, and the Japanese government preferred to suspend judgment over the Potsdam terms as long as the possibility of Moscow's mediation still seemed available to it.[19] Hirohito's statement did not change this position.

Before the Hiroshima bombing, Tōgō had already become convinced that sooner or later, Japan would have to accept the Potsdam terms. It is possible that the Hiroshima bomb further reinforced his conviction. But it bears repeating that he did not take the initiative to reverse the previous course, and that he did not propose direct negotiations with the United States and Britain. As for the emperor, it is possible that the Hiroshima bomb contributed to his urgent desire to terminate the war, but it is erroneous to say that immediately after the Hiroshima bomb, Hirohito decided to accept the Potsdam terms, as Asada asserts.

When Did Suzuki Decide to Terminate the War?

Another piece of evidence on which Asada's and Frank's argument is constructed is Prime Minister Suzuki's statement. According to Asada, on the night of August 8, Suzuki told Sakomizu: "Now that we know it was an atomic bomb that was dropped on Hiroshima, I will give my views on the termination of the war at tomorrow's Supreme War Council."[20] After the war, Suzuki made another statement: "The atomic bomb provided an additional reason for surrender as well as an extremely favorable opportunity to commence peace talks." From these statements, Asada concludes: "The hitherto vacillating and sphinx-like Suzuki had finally made up his mind. It is important to note that Suzuki did so before he was informed of the Soviet entry into the war early on the following day."[21]

Asada's conclusion is based on the 1973 version of Sakomizu's memoirs, according to which, Suzuki called Sakomizu *late at night* and made the statement quoted by Asada. Sakomizu explains that Suzuki relied on a prepared text written by his secretaries in order to make an official statement. Three pages later, Sakomizu writes: "On Prime Minister Suzuki's order, I had been working hard to write a text for the prime minister's statement for the cabinet meeting on the following day *since the evening* of August 8" (emphasis added). At around one o'clock in the morning on August 9, Hasegawa Saiji of the Dōmei News Agency telephoned to inform him of the Soviet Union's entry into the war.[22]

Sakomizu's 1973 memoirs contain crucial inconsistencies with respect to timing. In his earlier memoirs published in 1964, Sakomizu says that after he informed the prime minister of Dr. Nishina's report on the Hiroshima atomic bomb, which he had received on the evening of August 8, Suzuki ordered him to call meetings of the Supreme War Council and the cabinet "tomorrow on August 9 so that we can discuss the termination of the war." It took Sakomizu until 2 A.M. on August 9 to complete the preparations for the meetings on the following day. He finally went to bed thinking about the crucial meeting between Molotov and Satō in Moscow. It was not until three in the morning that Hasegawa called and told him about the Soviet declaration of war on Japan.[23] The timeline described in his 1964 memoirs makes more sense than that in the 1973 memoirs. According to Hasegawa's testimony, it was not until 4:00 A.M. on August 9 that he telephoned Sakomizu about the Soviet declaration of war, a fact that corresponds to Sakomizu's account in the 1964 memoirs, but not to that in the 1973 memoirs.[24] Sphinx-like Suzuki, as Asada calls him, had previously confided his views favoring peace privately on numerous occasions, but for domestic morale reasons, he had trumpeted bellicose statements, to the constant chagrin of the foreign minister. The dropping of the atomic bomb reinforced Suzuki's determination to seek an end to the war, as it did the emperor's. Nevertheless, it is likely that Suzuki, like everybody else, hoped for Moscow's mediation to achieve this, as Sakomizu's 1964 memoirs indicate.[25]

What is important, moreover, is the evidence that Asada chooses to ignore. According to Suzuki's biography, the prime minister came to the clear conclusion after the Hiroshima bomb that there was no other alternative but to end the war. Nevertheless, it was not until he learned of the Soviet invasion of Manchuria that he "was finally convinced that the moment had at last arrived to end the war, since what we had been afraid of and tried to avoid at any cost had finally come about [kitarubekimono ga kita]." He thought that "now is the time to realize the emperor's wish," and "in view of the urgency of the situation, I finally made up my mind to be in charge of the termination of the war, taking all the responsibility upon myself."[26] This biography makes it clear that Suzuki did not make up his mind about terminating the war until the Soviet entry into the war.[27]

Tōgō's Telegram on August 7

That Tōgō did not change the policy even after the atomic bombing of Hiroshima can be ascertained from important evidence that both Asada and Frank ignore. Right after the cabinet meeting on August 7, Tōgō dispatched an urgent telegram, no. 993, to Ambassador Satō in Moscow, saying: "The situation is becoming more and more pressing. We must know the Soviets' attitude immediately. Therefore, do your best once more to obtain their reply immediately."[28] In the context of the effect of the Hiroshima bomb, this telegram shows that the Japanese government as a whole, and Tōgō personally, still clung to the hope that the termination of the war was possible and desirable through Moscow's mediation. This was the line that Tōgō had followed since the Potsdam Proclamation had been issued by the Allies. The Hiroshima bomb did not change this policy.[29]

The emperor's statement to Tōgō, cited by Asada and Frank, can therefore be interpreted as the continuation of, not a departure from, the previous policy. If anything, the Japanese ruling elite pinned their hopes more desperately on Moscow's mediation after the Hiroshima bomb. There is no evidence to show that the emperor's words "We must end the war" should be interpreted as "ending the war by accepting the Potsdam Proclamation," as Asada and Frank argue. When Ambassador Satō cabled to Tokyo that Molotov had finally agreed to see him at 5 P.M. on August 8, no one, including the usually shrewd and hard-nosed Satō himself, doubted that Molotov would give Satō an answer to Japan's long-standing request that Moscow receive Prince Konoe as the emperor's special envoy.

There is no evidence to indicate that the Hiroshima bomb immediately and directly induced either the Japanese government as a whole or individual members, including Tōgō, Suzuki, Kido, and Hirohito, to terminate the war by accepting the terms of the Potsdam Proclamation. Japan could wait until Moscow's reaction before it would decide on the Potsdam terms.

Measuring the Shock Value

Asada argues that the atomic bombs provided a greater shock to Japanese policymakers than the Soviet entry into the war because (1) the bombing was a direct attack on the Japanese homeland, compared with the Soviet Union's "indirect" invasion in Manchuria; and (2) it was not anticipated. As for the first argument, the comparison between atomic bombings of the homeland and the Soviet invasion in Manchuria is irrelevant. American conventional air attacks had had little effect on Japan's resolve to fight the war. What separated the conventional attacks and the atomic bombs was only the magnitude of the one bomb, and it is known that the cumulative effects of the conventional attacks by American air raids caused more devastation in terms of the number of deaths and destruction of industries, ports, and railroads. But the number of sacrifices was not the major issue for Japanese policymakers.

The hierarchy of values under which the Japanese ruling elite operated is crucial in understanding the psychological factor involved in evaluating the effect of the atomic bombs on Japan's decision to surrender. The number of victims and profound damage that the atomic bombs inflicted on the citizens of

Hiroshima and Nagasaki, which the American policymakers had hoped would have a decisive influence on the Japanese government, were not among the top considerations of the Japanese ruling elite. The Japanese policymakers, from the emperor down to the military and civilian leaders, including Tōgō himself, were prepared to sacrifice the lives of millions more Japanese to maintain the *kokutai* (national polity), however they interpreted this nebulous concept. If the effects of the bombs caused concern for the ruling elite—especially to Hirohito, Kido, Konoe, and others closest to the emperor—it was because the devastation caused by the bombs might lead to a popular revolt that could sweep away the emperor system.

If the degree of shock can be measured by the action taken in response to the event, one might argue that the Hiroshima bomb did not have a greater effect than Soviet entry into the war, since no one, including Hirohito, Kido, Suzuki, and Tōgō, took any concrete actions to respond to the Hiroshima bomb. The Supreme War Council was not even convened for three full days after the Hiroshima bomb; not until after the USSR entered the war against Japan did it meet. It is true that the emperor instructed Suzuki to convene the Supreme War Council, and Sakomizu attempted to hold the meeting on Suzuki's orders. But "because some military leaders had prior commitments," he could not arrange the meeting until the morning of August 9. Asada considers this delay "criminal," but this laxity is indicative of the way the ruling elite felt regarding the "shock" of the Hiroshima bomb.

The Supreme War Council that was convened on the morning of August 9 immediately after the Soviet invasion of Manchuria was not the same meeting that Sakomizu had arranged the previous night. The formality of the Supreme War Council meeting required a new summons in order to convene.[30] Sakomizu's previous arrangements made it easier to summon the new meeting, but the speed with which the Supreme War Council was convened indicates the urgency that the Japanese government felt about the situation immediately after the Soviet invasion of Manchuria. Such urgency was absent in its reaction to the Hiroshima bombing. On August 10 and on August 14, Hirohito summoned the imperial conference on his own initiative. It was within his power to do so, but no one believed this was called for immediately after the Hiroshima bombing.

Finally, in his telegram to Satō on August 7, Tōgō described the situation as "becoming more and more pressing," but not completely desperate. The Hiroshima bomb did not make the Japanese ruling elite feel as though their backs were to the wall. It inflicted a serious body blow, but it was hardly a knock-out punch.

The Influence of the Nagasaki Bomb and of the
Two Atomic Bombs Combined

Chronologically, the Soviet entry into the war was sandwiched between the Hiroshima bomb and the Nagasaki bomb. But here, reversing the chronological order, I shall discuss the effect of the Nagasaki bomb first.

The news of the Nagasaki bomb was reported to Japanese leadership during the middle of a heated discussion at the Supreme War Council after the Soviet invasion, but this news had no effect on the discussion. Asada concedes that "[the] strategic value of a second bomb was minimal," but says that "from the standpoint of its shock effect, the political impact of [the] Nagasaki bomb cannot be denied." He explains that Suzuki now began to fear that "the United States, instead of staging the invasion of Japan, will keep on dropping atomic bombs." Asada therefore concludes that the Nagasaki bomb was "unnecessary to induce Japan to surrender, but it probably had confirmatory effects."[31] It is true that Suzuki said at the cabinet meeting on the afternoon of August 13 that the atomic bombs nullified the traditional form of homeland defense. But it appears that the military treated the Nagasaki bomb as a part of the ordinary incendiary air raids. Even after the Nagasaki bomb, and even though Anami made startling assertions that the United States might possess more than 100 atomic bombs, and that the next target might be Tokyo, the military insisted upon the continuation of the Ketsu Gō strategy. Anami's revelation did not seem to have any effect on the positions that each camp had held. The Nagasaki bomb simply did not substantially change the arguments of either side. The official history of the Imperial General Headquarters notes: "There is no record in other materials that treated the effect [of the Nagasaki bomb] seriously."[32]

Thus, it is fair to conclude that the Nagasaki bomb and, for that matter, the two bombs combined, did not have a decisive influence on Japan's decision to surrender. Remove the Nagasaki bomb, and Japan's decision would have been the same.

The Influence of the Soviet Entry into the War

According to Asada, of the atomic bombs and the Soviet entry into the war, the atomic bombings of Hiroshima and Nagasaki gave Japanese leaders the greater shock. He argues:

From the viewpoint of the shock effect, then, it may be argued that the bomb had a greater impact on Japanese leaders than did the Soviet entry into the war. After all, the Soviet invasion of Manchuria gave them an indirect shock, whereas the use of the atomic bomb on their homeland gave them the direct threat of the atomic extinction of the Japanese people.

The shock of the bomb was all the greater because it came as a "surprise attack."[33]

Frank also asserts: "the Soviet intervention was a significant but not decisive reason for Japan's surrender. It was, at best, a reinforcing but not fundamental reason for the intervention by the Emperor."[34]

The Japanese General Staff's Assessment of the Soviet Threat

Asada's assumption that since the Japanese military had anticipated the Soviet attack, it was not a shock to them when it really happened is questionable. The Japanese military began reassessing the Soviet threat even before Germany surrendered in May. On June 8, the imperial conference adopted the document "The Assessment of the World Situation," prepared by the General Staff. This assessment judged that after the German capitulation, the Soviet Union would plan to expand its influence in East Asia, especially in Manchuria and China, when an opportunity arose. The USSR had taken a series of measures against Japan, it continued, to prepare to enter into hostile diplomatic relations, while reinforcing its troops in the east. Therefore, when Moscow judged that the military situation had become extremely disadvantageous to Japan and that its own sacrifice would be small, the document concluded, there was a great probability that the Soviet Union might decide to enter the war against Japan. It predicted that in view of the American military plan, the climatic conditions in Manchuria, and the rate of the military buildup in the Soviet Far East, an attack might come in the summer or the fall of 1945.[35] The General Staff further paid close attention to the rate of Soviet reinforcement of troops and equipment in the Far East. By the end of June, the USSR had already sent troops, weapons, airplanes, tanks, and other equipment far surpassing the level that had existed there in 1941. The General Staff concluded that if this pace were kept up, the Soviet military would reach a preparedness level sufficient to go to war against Japan by August.[36]

In the beginning of July, the General Staff refined this assessment and came to the conclusion that the USSR might likely launch large-scale operations against Japan after February 1946, while the initial action to prepare for this operation in Manchuria might take place in September 1945. This assessment concluded: "It is unlikely that the Soviet Union will initiate military action against Japan this year, but extreme vigilance is required over their activities in August and September."[37] Thus, the General Staff thought that a Soviet attack might be possible, but what dominated its thinking was the hope that it could be avoided. On the basis of this wishful thinking, the General Staff did not prepare the Kwantung Army for a possible Soviet invasion. In fact, despite the General Staff's assessment that the Soviet attack might occur in August–September, the military preparedness of the Kwantung Army was such that had an attack occurred in August–September, it would not have had any possibility of defending itself.[38]

The General Staff was not unanimous in its assessment of Soviet intentions. The Fifth Section of the Strategy Guidance Section of the General Staff was in charge of intelligence regarding the Soviet Army, and it was the conclusions of this section that resulted in the portion of the General Staff's assessment that predicted the possibility of a Soviet attack in August–September. The assessment of the Fifth Section met opposition from the Twelfth Section (War Guidance Section), headed by Colonel Tanemura Suetaka. Tanemura was one of the staunch advocates who insisted upon the need to keep the Soviet Union neutral. At one meeting at the end of July, Tanemura strenuously objected to Colonel Shiraki Suenari's assessment that the Soviet attack might come as early as August. Tanemura assailed this assessment. He argued: "This assessment overexaggerates the danger. Stalin is not so stupid as to attack Japan hastily. He will wait until Japan's power and military become weakened, and after the American landing on the homeland begins." Since the Twelfth Section was closely connected with the Bureau of Military Affairs, the nerve center of the General Staff, Tanemura's view became the prevailing policy of the General Staff, and hence of the Army as a whole.[39]

On August 8, one day before the Soviet invasion, the General Staff's Bureau of Military Affairs produced a study outlining what Japan should do if the Soviet Union issued an ultimatum demanding Japan's total withdrawal from the Asian continent. According to this plan, the following alternatives were suggested: (1) reject the Soviet demand and carry out the war against the Soviet Union in addition to the United States and Britain; (2) conclude peace with the United States and Britain immediately and concentrate on the war against the Soviet Union; (3) accept the Soviet demand and seek Moscow's neutrality, while carrying on the war against the United States and Britain; and (4) accept the Soviet demand and involve the Soviet Union in the Greater East Asian War. Of these alternatives, the army preferred to accept the Soviet demand and either keep the Soviet Union neutral or, if possible, involve the Soviet Union in the war against the United States and Britain.[40]

The Bureau of Military Affairs also drafted a policy statement for the Supreme War Council after it received the news of the Soviet invasion on August 9. To deal with this crisis it envisioned the following policy: (1) fight only in self-defense, without declaring war on the Soviet Union; (2) continue negotiations with the Soviet Union to terminate the war, with the minimal conditions of the preservation of the *kokutai* and the maintenance of national independence; (3) issue an imperial rescript appealing to the people to maintain the Yamato race; and (4) establish a martial law regime.[41] In a document presented to the Supreme War Council, the army recommended that if the Soviet Union continued the war, Japan should "strive to terminate the war with the Soviet Union as quickly as possible, and to continue the war against the United States, Britain, and China, while maintaining Soviet neutrality."[42] In his postwar testimony, Major General Hata Hikosaburō, the Kwantung Army's chief of staff, recalled that the Kwantung Army had believed that it could count on Soviet neutrality until the spring of the following year, although it allowed for the slight chance of a Soviet attack in the fall.[43]

It bears emphasizing that right up to the moment of invasion, the army not only did not expect an immediate Soviet invasion but also it still believed that it could either maintain Soviet neutrality or involve the Soviet Union in the war against the United States and Britain. The thinking that dominated the center of the army and the Kwantung Army was indeed "wishful thinking," that a Soviet attack, although possible, would not happen.[44]

Thus, it is misleading to conclude, as Asada does, that since the army had assessed that the Soviet attack might take place, the Soviet invasion into Manchuria was not a shock to the Japanese military. The Bureau of Military Affairs suppressed the prediction that a Soviet attack was imminent and relied instead on its wishful thinking that it could be avoided. Its strategy was based on this assessment. Therefore, when Soviet tanks crossed the Manchurian border, the news certainly was a great shock to it, contrary to Asada's assertion.

Deputy Chief of Staff Kawabe's Attitude

To support his assertion that the Soviet invasion had little effect on the Japanese military's will to fight, Asada cites the following passage from Deputy Chief of Staff Kawabe Torashishirō's diary entry from the crucial day, August 9, 1945: "To save the honor of the Yamato race, there is no way but to keep on fighting. At this critical moment, I don't even want to consider peace or surrender."[45] But if we examine Kawabe's diary more closely, a slightly different picture emerges.

Kawabe was awakened in bed at the General Staff headquarters at around 6:00 A.M. and received the news from his aide that the Intelligence Division had intercepted broadcasts from Moscow and San Francisco reporting that the Soviet Union had declared war on Japan. Kawabe wrote down his first impressions of the news as follows:

The Soviets have finally risen! [*So wa tsuini tachitari!*] My judgment has proven wrong. But now that the situation has come to this, we should not consider seeking peace. We had half anticipated this military situation and the military fortune. There is nothing to think about. To save the honor of the Yamato race, there is no other way but to keep fighting. When we decided to begin the war, I always belonged to the soft and prudent faction, but once the situation has come to this, I don't like to think about peace and surrender. Whatever the outcome, we have no choice but to try.[46]

Asada is correct in pointing out that despite the news of the Soviet invasion in Manchuria, Kawabe was determined to continue the war. And yet Kawabe's diary also betrays the shock and confusion he felt at the news. Contrary to his "judgment," Kawabe conceded, "the Soviets have risen!" This exclamation mark speaks volumes about Kawabe's shock. In fact, until then all Ketsu Gō strategy had been built upon the assumption that the USSR should be kept neutral, and for that reason, Kawabe himself had campaigned hard for the Foreign Ministry to secure Soviet neutrality through negotiations. He admitted that his judgment had proved wrong. But this admission was immediately followed by a Monday morning quarterback–like reflection that the eventuality of a Soviet attack had been in the back of his mind. This is not necessarily a contradiction. In fact, Kawabe and the Army General Staff had been bothered by the nagging suspicion that the Soviets might strike at Japan. This suspicion, however, prompted the army to double its efforts to secure Soviet neutrality. Moreover, the army did not anticipate, first, that the attack was to come so soon, at the beginning of August, and, second, that the Soviet invasion would take place on such a large scale against the Japanese forces in Manchuria and Korea from all directions.

Kawabe's diary also reveals his confusion. If his judgment proved wrong, logically it should follow that the strategy that he had advocated based on the erroneous assumption should have been reexamined. Instead of adopting this logical deduction, Kawabe "did not feel like peace and surrender in this situation." This was not rational strategic thinking, but a visceral reluctance to accept surrender. The only rationale he could justify for the continuation of war was "the honor of the Yamato race." His insistence on fighting was also a preemptive move, anticipating, quite correctly, that the peace party would launch a coordinated move to end the war. Nevertheless, his argument for the continuation of war indicated the degree of the army's desperation and confusion.

If the Soviet invasion indeed shocked the military, which event, the atomic bombing of Hiroshima or the Soviet attack, provided a bigger shock? In order to answer this question, one must compare the August 9 entry with the August 7 entry in Kawabe's diary. In the entry for August 7, Kawabe wrote: "As soon as I went to the office, having read various reports on the air raid by the new weapon on Hiroshima yesterday morning of the 6th, I was seriously disturbed [*shinkokunaru shigeki o uketari,* literally, 'received a serious stimulus']. . . . With this development [*kakutewa*] the military situation has progressed to such a point that it has become more and more difficult. We must be tenacious and fight on."[47] Kawabe admitted that he was disturbed by, or more literally, received "a serious stimulus [*shigeki*]" from the reports of the atomic bomb at Hiroshima. Nevertheless, he avoided using the term "*shōgeki* [shock]." Compared with this passage describing the news of the atomic bomb as a matter of fact, the first thing that catches the eye in his entry for August 9 is the first sentence, "So wa tsuini tachitari!" ("The Soviets have finally risen!"). As far as Kawabe was concerned, there is no question but that the news of the Soviet attack gave him a much bigger shock than the news of the atomic bomb.

Both diary entries advocated continuing the war. But there was a subtle change. While the effects of the atomic bomb were described as having worsened the military situation, there was no change in the overall assumptions. But Kawabe's insistence on fighting after the Soviet attack is marked by his defensive tone, deriving partly from the anticipated move for peace and partly from the disappearance of the fundamental assumptions on which the continuation of the war had rested. In this respect, too, the shock of the Soviet attack was much greater to the military than the atomic bombing of Hiroshima.

Kawabe's August 9 diary entry goes on to describe the subsequent events at General Staff headquarters. He recorded his decisions in an elliptical memorandum that singles out the continuation of war against the United States as the major task, and suggests the following measures: (1) proclaim martial law, dismiss the current cabinet, and form a military dictatorship; (2) abandon Manchuria, defend Korea, and dispatch troops from northern China to the Manchurian-Korean border; (3) evacuate the Manchurian emperor to Japan; and (4) issue a proclamation in the name of the army minister to avoid disturbances (*dōyō*) within the military. Thus, in Kawabe's mind, the continuation of war was associated with the establishment of a military dictatorship in order to forestall the movement to end the war that would inevitably gather momentum as Soviet tanks penetrated deep into Manchuria.

Kawabe's diary entry for the evening of August 9 also indicates his psychological condition. Unable to sleep because of mosquitoes and Tokyo's tropical heat, he mused on the fate of the country: "To continue fighting will mean death, but to make peace with the enemy will mean ruin. But we have no choice but to seek life in death with the determination to have the entire Japanese people perish with the homeland as their deathbed pillow by continuing to fight, thereby keeping the pride of the Yamato race forever."[48] Insisting on the continuation of the war clearly lacked all strategic rationale.

Kawabe's determination to fight, however, easily collapsed as soon as the emperor's "sacred decision" was made at the imperial conference on August 10. After he was informed of the result of the imperial conference, he noted in his diary: "Alas, everything is over." He was critical of the argument advanced by Anami, Umezu, and Toyoda, because he did not believe the conditions they had insisted upon would be accepted by the enemy. For Kawabe, there were only two options: either accept unconditional surrender or perish to maintain honor. The emperor's decision revealed that he had completely lost his trust in the military. In Kawabe's view, this was not merely the emperor's opinion but the expression of the general view broadly shared by the Japanese people as a whole. Kawabe continues:

How is it that not one military officer from the army and the navy before the emperor could assure [him] that we would be able to win the war? . . . How ambiguous the answer of the two chiefs was: "Although we cannot say that we shall be able to win the war definitely, we have no reason to believe that we shall definitely lose the war." No, I am not criticizing their answer. Their answer reflects reality. Although I have persistently insisted on the continuation of war and have encouraged myself to continue fighting, I would have no choice but to give the same answer as given by the chiefs if I were to be asked about the probability of our victory. I am only driven by the sentiment that "I don't want to surrender; I don't want to say surrender even if I am killed," and wish to limit the conditions for the termination of the war.

Kawabe further noted that the General Staff officers knew more than anyone else about the difficulty of continuing the war.[49]

In November 1949, Kawabe gave this testimony in response to point-blank questions: "[B]etween the atomic bombing and the entry of Soviet Russia into the war, which of the two factors played a greater part in bringing about the cessation of hostilities?" the U.S. GHQ interrogator, Ōi Atsushi, asked. Kawabe replied:

When the atomic bomb was dropped, I felt: "This is terrible." Immediately thereafter, it was reported Soviet Russia entered the war. This made me feel: "This has really become a very difficult situation."

Russia's participation in the war had long since been expected, but this does not mean that we had been well prepared for it. It was with a nervous heart filled with fear that we expected Russia to enter the war. Although it was a reaction of a man who was faced with the actual occurrence of the inevitable, mine was, to speak more exact, a feeling that "what has been most [feared] has finally come into reality." I felt as though I had been given a thorough beating in rapid succession, and my thoughts were, "So not only has there been an atomic bombing, but this has come, too."

I believe that I was more strongly impressed with the atomic bomb than other people. However, even then, . . . because I had a considerable amount of knowledge on the subject of atomic bombs, I had an idea that even the Americans could not produce so many of them. Moreover, since Tokyo was not directly affected by the bombing, the full force of the shock was not felt. On top of it, we had become accustomed to bombings due to frequent raids by B-29s.

Actually, [the] majority in the army did not realize at first that what had been dropped was an atomic bomb, and they were not generally familiar with the terrible nature of the atomic bomb. It was only in a gradual manner that the horrible wreckage which had been made of Hiroshima became known, instead of in a manner of a shocking effect.

In comparison, the Soviet entry into the war was a great shock when it actually came. Reports reaching Tokyo described Russian forces as "invading in swarms." It gave us all the more severe shock and alarm because we had been in constant fear of it with a vivid imagination that "the vast Red Army forces in Europe were now being turned against us." In other words, since the atomic bomb and the Russian declaration of war were shocks in a quick succession, I cannot give a definite answer as to which of the two factors was more decisive in ending hostilities.[50]

Kawabe's testimony repudiates Asada's contention that since it was anticipated, the Soviet attack did not represent a shock to the military. Moreover, up to the last sentence, Kawabe's argument reinforces the view that the Soviet entry into the war had a greater effect on the military than the atomic bomb.

Frank dismisses this statement by arguing that the emperor's decision to surrender was made even before the accurate assessment of the Manchurian situation reached Tokyo.[51] This is hardly a convincing argument. The effect of the Soviet entry had little relation to the military situation in Manchuria. The very fact that the USSR had entered the war shattered Japan's last hope for ending it through Soviet mediation. In other words, the political consequence of the Soviet action, not the military situation in Manchuria, was the crucial factor.

Other Testimonies by Military Leaders

A document in *Arisue Kikan News*, no. 333, which gave the Army Ministry's answer to the prepared questions of the GHQ, provides interesting information. To the question of whether or not the army knew that sooner or later the Soviet Union would join the war with the Allies against Japan, the Army Ministry answered that it had had no knowledge of this. The army had tried to prevent the Soviet Union from participating in the war, because it had believed that Soviet participation would have a great political and strategic effect on major operations against Japan's main enemy, the United States. Japan was prepared to give up Manchuria in order to keep the USSR out of the war. To the question of whether or not Japan would have accepted surrender before the Soviet entry into the war, this document answers: "The Soviet participation in the war had the most direct impact on Japan's decision to surrender."[52]

Major General Amano Masakazu, the operations department chief at Imperial General Headquarters, replied this way to GHQ interrogation regarding the effect of Soviet entry into the war: "It was estimated that the Soviet Union would most likely enter the war in early autumn. However, had the Soviet Union entered the war, the Imperial General Headquarters had no definite plan to resist the Soviet Union for a long period while effectively carrying out a decisive battle with the American forces on the other. There was nothing to be done but hope that . . . the 17th Area Army [of the Kwantung Army], reinforced by crack units from the China area, would do their best and would be able to hold out as long as possible."[53] Amano confessed that the army had possessed no way to counter a Soviet attack, although it thought that this might come in early autumn. It is difficult then to argue from Amano's statement, as Asada does, that simply because it had been anticipated, the Soviet attack was not a great surprise to the army.

Lieutenant General Ikeda Sumihisa, director of the General Planning Agency, testified that "upon hearing of the Soviet entry into the war, I felt that our chances were gone." Having served in the Kwantung Army, he knew its condition well. The Kwantung Army was no more than a hollow shell, largely because it had been transferring its troops, equipment, and munitions to the home islands since the latter part of 1944 in anticipation of homeland defense. Ikeda often told the commander of the Kwantung Army "that if the USSR entered the war, Japan would never be able to continue the war." He firmly believed that "in the event that the Soviet [Union] entered the war, Japan's defeat would be a foregone conclusion."[54]

Colonel Hayashi Saburō, Anami's secretary, was asked by a GHQ interrogator about the influence of the atomic bombs and the Soviet entry into the war on Anami's views regarding the termination of the war. Hayashi did not say anything about the effect of the atomic bomb, but he was confident that the Soviet entry into the war reinforced Anami's feelings about the need to hasten the end of the war.[55]

Chief of the Navy General Staff Admiral Toyoda Soemu also gave revealing testimony to the GHQ interrogators. He admitted that the atomic bomb had been a shock, but he believed that the United States would not be able to continue to drop atomic bombs "at frequent intervals," partly because of the difficulty of securing radioactive materials, and partly because of world public opinion against such an atrocity. "I believe the atomic bombing was a cause for the surrender," Toyoda testified, "but it was not the only cause." In contrast to the atomic bombs, the Soviet entry into the war was a greater shock to the military. "In the face of this new development," Toyoda continued, "it became impossible for us to map any reasonable operation plan. Moreover, the peace program which we had so far relied upon [i.e., through Moscow's mediation] came to naught. Therefore, an entirely different program had to be sought out. At the same time we could not expect to obtain a good chance for peace by merely waiting for such a chance. It was time for us to accept the terms of the Potsdam Declaration [Proclamation]." Toyoda concluded: "I believe the Russian participation in the war against Japan rather than the atomic bombs did more to hasten the surrender."[56]

Asada ignores all this overwhelming evidence that stresses the importance of the Soviet entry into the war. In the face of this evidence, his contention that because the military had expected the Soviet invasion, it did not shock them when it actually happened cannot be sustained.

Frank casts doubt on the reliability of Kawabe's and Toyoda's testimonies because they were given some years after the events. Although he does not quote from Ikeda and Hayashi, he would likely discount them on the same grounds. Frank's methodology of separating contemporaneous sources from evidence that came after the events is commendable. One cannot apply this method too rigidly, however. In the first place, what benefits did Kawabe, Toyoda, Ikeda, and Hayashi gain by emphasizing the Soviet factor rather than the atomic bomb years after the events? One may even argue that their statements carry more weight because they were made to American interrogators, who had a vested interest in proving that the atomic bombs were more decisive than the Soviet entry.

After dismissing Kawabe's and Toyoda's recollections years after the events, Frank extensively quotes from Suzuki's testimony in December 1945:

The Supreme War Council, up to the time [that] the atomic bomb was dropped, did not believe that Japan could be beaten by air attack alone. They also believed that the United States would land and not attempt to bomb Japan out of the war. On the other hand there were many prominent people who did believe that the United States could win the war by just bombing alone. However, the Supreme War Council, not believing that, had proceeded with the one plan of fighting a decisive battle at the landing point and was making every possible preparation to meet such a landing. They proceeded with that plan until the atomic bomb was dropped, after which they believed the United States would no longer attempt to land when it had such a superior weapon . . . so at that point they decided that it would be best to sue for peace.[57]

Relying on Suzuki's statement, Frank concludes: "Suzuki's assessment goes to the heart of the matter: Soviet intervention did not invalidate the Ketsu-Go military and political strategy; the Imperial Army had already written off Manchuria."[58] But this statement cannot persuasively prove that Suzuki had already decided to seek the termination of the war according to the Potsdam terms before the Soviet invasion. It must be kept in mind that these testimonies are English translations of the original Japanese statements. When Suzuki referred to the "atomic bomb," he must have used the term, *genbaku* or *genshi bakudan*. A peculiarity of the Japanese language is that it makes no distinction between a singular and a plural noun. Therefore, when Suzuki said *genbaku*, he was likely referring to the atomic bombs, meaning the bomb at Hiroshima *and* the bomb at Nagasaki. In fact, it is better to interpret these terms as referring to the plural form. Taken as such, what Suzuki meant must have been the effect of the two bombs in a general sense. Therefore, it is erroneous to conclude, as Asada and Frank do, that Suzuki's decision to end the war predated the Soviet attack on Japan, since Suzuki was comparing the atomic bombs with conventional air attacks, not with Soviet entry into the war.[59]

Furthermore, although Suzuki may have believed that the atomic bombs had nullified the basic assumption on which the Ketsu Gō strategy was based, his view was not necessarily shared by the Army officers. Anami consistently argued throughout the critical days even after the Hiroshima and Nagasaki bombs that the army was confident it could inflict tremendous damage on the invading American troops, indicating that Anami and the army officers continued to believe that despite the atomic bombs, the Americans still planned to launch a homeland invasion. And this assessment was fundamentally correct, since American military planners never substituted atomic bombing alone for the plan to invade Japan.

In fact, as the Bureau of Military Affairs report to the Diet in September 1945 indicated, army planners rejected the "counterforce" effects of atomic weapons in a battleground situation. It states: "It is true that the appearance of the atomic bomb brought a great psychological threat, but since its use would be extremely difficult on the battleground, in view of the close proximity of the two forces and scattered units, we were convinced that it would not directly affect our preparations for homeland defense."[60] Toyoda's testimony, quoted above, also questioned the American intention to rely on the atomic bombs. When it came down to the military plan, it was not Suzuki's view, but the views of the Army and Navy General Staff that mattered most.

As for Soviet entry into the war, the report of the Bureau of Military Affairs states: "Although the Soviet participation in the war was expected from the analysis of the general world situation, we did not anticipate the situation where we would have to fight on the two fronts from the point of view of the nation's total power. Throughout we had decided to focus our major strategy on the homeland defense, while preparing to sacrifice the operations in the continental defense. Therefore, Soviet entry into the war did not directly affect our conviction that we would score victory in the decisive homeland battle."[61] This is an ambiguous and contradictory statement. On the one hand, it states that Soviet participation in the war was unexpected, forcing Japan to fight on two fronts. On the other, it takes the view that the Ketsu Gō strategy had already written off Manchuria, which did not substantially affect homeland defense. The latter conclusion seems to support Frank's argument that since the Japanese Army had already written off Manchuria, Soviet entry into the war did not substantially change the army's strategy of putting all its eggs in the one basket of the Ketsu Gō strategy. The problem with this argument is that it ignores the assertion that Japan did not anticipate having to fight on two fronts.

To be fair to the arguments advanced by Asada and Frank, Imperial General Headquarters anticipated the possibility of Soviet participation in the war and adopted a strategy to cope with this worse-case scenario. Already in September 1944, Imperial General Headquarters summoned the Kwantung Army's operational chief, Colonel Kusachi Sadakichi, and issued Continental Order 1130, by which it ordered the Kwantung Army to concentrate on the defense of a small strip of Manchukuo and Korea against Soviet attack with the strict orders not to provoke any military confrontations with the Red Army.[62] The Kwantung Army mapped out the final operational plan against the Soviet attack on July 5, which basically followed Continental Order 1130.[63] As for Hokkaidō, Imperial General Headquarters issued Continental Order 1326 on May 9, 1945, which defined the task of the Fifth Area Army in Hokkaidō as the defense of Hokkaidō itself. For this purpose, the Fifth Area Army was ordered to direct the defense of southern Sakhalin primarily against the possible Soviet attack, while blocking a U.S. and Soviet landing on the Kurils and crossing the Sōya Straits. As for the possible Soviet invasion of Hokkaidō, the Fifth Area Army was "to attempt to repulse the enemy depending on circumstances and points of attack and to secure important areas of Hokkaidō."[64]

Alongside with these military plans, however, Imperial General Headquarters harbored wishful thinking that there was unlikely to be a Soviet attack. The Kwantung Army had little confidence in its ability to hold the last defense line. As for the Fifth Area Army, it expected that in the event of the anticipated American invasion of the homeland, Hokkaidō would be left to defend itself against a possible combined attack by the United States and the Soviet Union. The problem with Hokkaidō's defense was its size, which was as big as the whole of Tōhoku and Niigata prefectures combined. The Fifth Area Army had to disperse 114,000 troops to three possible points of attack: one division in the Shiribetsu-Nemuro area in the east, one division at Cape Sōya in the north, and one brigade in the Tomakomai area in the west. The fortification of the Shibetsu area had not been completed, and the defense of the Nemuro area was considered hopeless because of the flat terrain. The defense of the north was concentrated at Cape Sōya, but nothing was prepared for Rumoi, where the Soviet forces intended to land.[65] The inadequacies of these operational plans, both in the Kwantung Army and the Fifth Area Army, were exposed when the actual Soviet attack came. The military planners had no confidence in the army's ability to repulse a Soviet invasion of Korea and Hokkaidō. As Frank writes, "the Soviet Navy's amphibious shipping resources were limited but sufficient to transport the three assault divisions in several echelon[s]. The Red Army intended to seize the northern half of Hokkaido. If resistance proved strong, reinforcements would be deployed to aid the capture the rest of Hokkaido. Given the size of Hokkaido, the Japanese would have been hard pressed to move units for a concerted confrontation of the Soviet invasion. The chances of Soviet success appeared to be very good."[66] Soviet occupation of Hokkaidō was thus within the realm of possibility.

The Soviet Factor in the Emperor's "Sacred Decision"

Although Soviet entry into the war played a more decisive role in Japan's decision to surrender, it did not provide a "knock-out punch" either. The Supreme War Council and the cabinet found themselves confronted by a stalemate between those who favored acceptance of the Potsdam terms with one condition, the preservation of the imperial house, and those who insisted in addition that there be no Allied occupation and that demilitarization and any war crimes trials be conducted by Japan itself. Given the political weight of the army and an overwhelming sentiment among army officers in favor of continuing the war, the war party might have prevailed had there not been a concerted effort to impose peace on the reluctant army by imperial fiat. Tōgō, Prince Konoe, and Shigemitsu Mamoru were instrumental in persuading the wavering Kido and Hirohito, but more important were second-echelon players such as Sakomizu (Suzuki's cabinet secretary), Deputy Foreign Minister Matsumoto Shun'ichi, Colonel Matsutani Makoto (Suzuki's secretary and crucial liaison with the army), Matsudaira Yasumasa (Kido's secretary), and Rear Admiral Takagi Sōkichi (Navy Minister Yonai's closest confidant).[67] Throughout this complicated political process, in which the emperor intervened twice to impose his "sacred decision" to accept the Potsdam terms, first with one condition and the second time unconditionally, the Soviet factor, more than the atomic bombs, played the decisive role.

Political Calculations

Soviet entry into the war was indeed a shock to the Japanese ruling elite, both civilian and military alike. Politically and diplomatically, it dashed any hope of ending the war through Soviet mediation. But Soviet entry meant more than merely precluding the option of Soviet mediation for peace. Here, we must consider the political calculations and psychological factors apparent in dealing with Japan's two enemies. Before the invasion of Manchuria, the Soviet Union had been Japan's best hope for peace, while the Japanese ruling elite felt bitter resentment toward the United States, which had demanded unconditional surrender. After August 9, this relationship was reversed. The small opening that the United States had intentionally left ajar in the Potsdam terms, which Japanese foreign ministry officials had astutely noticed as soon as the Potsdam Proclamation was issued, suddenly looked inviting, providing the only room in which the Japanese could maneuver. They concluded that suing for peace with the United States would confer a better chance of preserving the imperial house, if not the *kokutai* as it was envisaged by ultranationalists. No sooner had the marriage of convenience uniting right-wing Japan and the communist Soviet Union broken down than the Japanese ruling elite's fear of communism sweeping away the emperor system was reawakened. To preserve the imperial house, it would be better to surrender before the USSR was able to dictate terms. On August 13, rejecting Anami's request that the decision to accept U.S. Secretary of State James Byrnes's counteroffer (the "Byrnes note"), which rejected Japan's conditional acceptance of the Potsdam terms, be postponed, Suzuki explained: "If we miss today, the Soviet Union would take not only Manchuria, Korea, [and] Karafuto [Sakhalin Island], but also Hokkaidō. This would destroy the foundation of Japan. We must end the war when we can deal with the United States."[68] Furthermore, when Shigemitsu had a crucial meeting with Kido on the afternoon of August 9 at Prince Konoe's request, which eventually led to Kido's meeting with Hirohito that persuaded the emperor to accept the "sacred decision" scenario, Shigemitsu stressed the negative effect of further Soviet expansion on the fate of the imperial household.[69]

What motivated Hirohito was neither a pious wish to bring peace to humanity nor a sincere desire to save the people and the nation from destruction, as his imperial rescript stated and as the myth of the emperor's "sacred decision" would have us believe. More than anything else, it was a sense of personal survival and deep responsibility to maintain the imperial house, which had lasted in unbroken lineage since the legendary Jinmu emperor. For that purpose, Hirohiro was quick to jettison the pseudo-religious concept of the *kokutai*, and even the emperor's prerogatives as embodied in the Meiji Constitution. What mattered to him was the preservation of the imperial house, and to that end, he was willing to entrust his fate to the will of the Japanese people. Hirohito's transformation from a living god (*arahitogami*) to a human emperor (*ningen tenno*), which is seen as having occurred during the American occupation, actually took place during the final "sacred decision" at the imperial conference.

With astonishing swiftness, the members of the imperial house closed ranks and defended Hirohito's decision. To attain this objective, Hirohito was prepared to part with the military and the ultranationalists, who were major obstacles.

It is difficult to document just how the Soviet factor influenced the emperor's decision and the thinking of his close advisers. It is possible to conjecture, however, that the emperor and his advisers wished to avoid any Soviet influence in determining the fate of the imperial household and the emperor's status. It is not far-fetched to assume that Suzuki's statement and Shigemitsu's thinking quoted above, which explain the need to accept the Byrnes note before the Soviet Union expanded its conquered territories, was widely shared by the ruling circles in Japan.

There was another factor in the political calculations of the Japanese ruling elite: fear of popular unrest. On August 12, Navy Minister Yonai Mitsumasa told Takagi Sōkichi: "They may not be the appropriate words, but the atomic bombs and the Soviet entry into the war are in a way a godsend, since we don't have to decide to stop the war because of the domestic situation. The reason why I have advocated the end of war is not that I was afraid of the enemy's attack, nor was it because of the atomic bombs or the Soviet entry into the war. It was more than anything else because I was afraid of domestic conditions. Therefore, we were fortunate to [be able to] end the war without pushing the domestic situation to the fore."[70] Yonai's fear was widely shared by the ruling elite. Konoe's advocacy of peace, which he had submitted to Hirohito in February 1945, was motivated by his fear of a communist revolution. Whether or not such a revolution was actually likely or even possible, the fear among the ruling elite of such popular unrest sweeping away the entire emperor system was quite real. On August 13, 14, and 15, Kido met Machimura Kingo, chief of the Metropolitan Police, to hear reports of possible political and social turmoil at home.[71]

The Psychological Factor

The complicated political calculations of the Japanese leadership were closely intermingled with crucial psychological factors. In particular, there were two different psychological elements at work. The first was the reversal of the degree of hatred attached to two enemies, as described above. The second was a profound sense of betrayal.

Soviet entry into the war had double-crossed the Japanese in two distinct senses. In the first place, the Kremlin had opted for war just when Japan was pinning its last hopes of peace on Soviet mediation. Furthermore, the invasion was a surprise attack. True, Molotov had handed a declaration of war to

Satō in Moscow. Satō then asked for Molotov's permission to transmit the declaration of war to Tokyo by ciphered telegram, but the ambassador's dispatch never reached Tokyo. In fact, it never left Moscow, most likely having been suppressed by the telegraph office on the orders of the Soviet government. Molotov announced that the declaration of war was also to be handed by Soviet Ambassador Iakov Malik to Tōgō in Tokyo simultaneously. But the Japanese government learned of the Soviet invasion of Manchuria only from a news agency report at around 4:00 A.M. on August 9.[72]

Matsumoto Shun'ichi explained Tōgō's rage when he received the news of the Soviet invasion of Manchuria. Tōgō had gullibly believed assurances about the Soviet commitment to the neutrality pact, and he had pinned his hopes on Soviet mediation to terminate the war. Not only did this turn out to be a mistake, but the Soviet action also revealed that the Japanese government had been consistently and thoroughly deceived. Tōgō's determination to end the war by accepting the Potsdam terms was thus motivated by his desire to compensate for his earlier mistake in seeking Moscow's mediation.[73] Hirohito's monologue also had a tinge of resentment toward the Soviet Union, which he too had mistakenly relied upon to mediate a termination to the war.[74] Tōgō and his colleagues were also anxious to deny the Soviet Union any advantage, since it had perpetrated such a betrayal. After the Soviet entry into the war, the USSR and matters related to the military situation in Manchuria suddenly disappeared from the discussions of Japanese policymakers. This does not mean that the Soviet factor had lost importance. In fact, their silence on the Soviet factor in these discussions was proof of both a conscious and unconscious attempt at denial. The greater their sense of betrayal, the more determined Japanese leaders became to deny the importance of Soviet entry into the war. They avoided denouncing Moscow's perfidy because they did not want to reveal the colossal error they themselves had committed in seeking Soviet mediation. And now that the fate of the emperor and the imperial house hung in the balance, they wished those issues to be determined by the United States rather than the Soviet Union. These conscious and unconscious manipulations of memory and historical records began simultaneously with events as they unfolded and continued subsequently in order to reconstruct these crucial events.

Interpreting the Evidence

To prove the decisiveness of the atomic bomb, Asada cites the testimonies given by Kido and Sakomizu. Kido, he says, stated: "I believe that with the atomic bomb alone we could have brought the war to an end. But the Soviet entry into the war made it that much easier."[75] Sakomizu's testimony to Allied interrogators stated: "I am sure we could have ended the war in a similar way if the Russian declaration of war had not taken place at all."[76] To borrow Frank's expression, these testimonies "should be approached with circumspection," not because they were given years after the events, but because their veracity is questionable. Kido was prominent among those who attempted to create the myth that the emperor's "sacred decision" had saved the Japanese people and the Japanese nation from further destruction. On different occasions, both Kido and Sakomizu told a different story.

In an interview with the Diet Library in 1967, Kido stated: "Things went smoothly. The atomic bombs served their purpose, and the Soviet entry served its purpose. They were both crucial elements [*umaku iku yōso to natta*]. I believe that Japan's recovery as we see it today was possible because of the Soviet [entry into the war] and the atomic bombs."[77] Sakomizu's memoirs also convey a different picture from that put forward by Asada. When Sakomizu heard the news of the Soviet invasion of Manchuria from Hasegawa Saiji of the Dōmei News Service, he writes, he was "really surprised" and asked: "Is it really true?" He says that he felt "as if the ground on which I stood was collapsing." While Hasegawa was double-checking the accuracy of the report, Sakomizu "felt the anger as if all the blood in the body was flowing backward."[78] This testimony was corroborated by Hasegawa, who remembered: "When I conveyed the news [about the Soviet declaration of war] to Tōgō and Sakomizu, both were dumbfounded. Tōgō repeatedly asked me: 'Are you sure?' since he was expecting Moscow's answer regarding mediation."[79]

Many in the ruling elite considered the atomic bombs and Soviet entry into the war as god-given gifts (*tenyū*). Like Kido, in the statement quoted above, Yonai thought both the atomic bomb and the Soviet entry into the war were gifts from heaven,[80] and when Konoe heard the news of the Soviet invasion, he said "in order to control the Army, it may be a god-sent gift."[81] Surveying the discussions at Supreme War Council meetings and cabinet meetings, there are some references only to the atomic bombs (such as Suzuki's statement quoted above), others to Soviet entry into the war alone (such as Konoe's statement), and still others to both (such as Yonai's remarks) in advocating peace. Choosing passages that merely emphasize the effect of the atomic bombs and ignoring other passages is not sound analytical practice. It should be noted, too, that all these references were made only after the Soviet Union entered the war.

To prove that the atomic bombing on Hiroshima had a decisive effect on Hirohito's "sacred decision," Asada cites the emperor's statement at the imperial conference on August 9–10. According to Asada, Hirohito allegedly said that it would be impossible to continue the war, "since the appearance of the atomic bomb."[82] Frank also singles out the emperor's speech on August

10 as one of the most crucial pieces of evidence proving the decisiveness of the atomic bomb. According to Frank, "the Emperor also explicitly cited two military considerations: inadequate preparations to resist the invasion and the vast destructiveness of the atomic bomb and the air attacks. He did not refer to Soviet intervention."[83] For this assertion, both Asada and Frank rely on a single source: Takeshita Masahiko's *Kimitsu sakusen nisshi*.[84] The emperor's reference to the atomic bombs appears only in *Kimitsu sakusen nisshi*. Since Takeshita did not participate in the imperial conference, his account must have come from Anami, who was his brother-in-law. None of the participants recall that Hirohito referred to the atomic bombs in his speech. In fact, Tōgō's memoirs and Sakomizu's memoirs, quoted in *Shūsen shiroku*, which Asada cites as the evidence that the emperor specifically cited the atomic bomb as the major reason for his decision, actually does not contain this reference.[85] Frank concedes that at the meeting with Japan's most senior military officers on August 14, the emperor cited both Soviet intervention and "the enemy's scientific power." This was "the only contemporary instance where the Emperor saw Soviet intervention as significant," Frank writes, adding, "and even then he coupled it with the atomic bomb." In the imperial rescript, Frank says, "the emperor spoke explicitly on one point: the enemy's employment of a 'new and most cruel bomb.' "[86]

Silence, however, does not necessarily mean that the Soviet entry had little effect on Hirohito's decision to surrender. It is true that the emperor did not refer to the Soviet entry in his imperial rescript to the general Japanese population on August 15. But Frank ignores another important document: the imperial rescript addressed to the soldiers and sailors, issued on August 17, which states:

Now that the Soviet Union has entered the war against us, to continue . . . under the present conditions at home and abroad would only recklessly incur even more damage to ourselves and result in endangering the very foundation of the empire's existence. Therefore, even though enormous fighting spirit still exists in the imperial navy and army, I am going to make peace with the United States, Britain, and the Soviet Union, as well as with Chungking, in order to maintain our glorious *kokutai*.[87]

To the soldiers and sailors, especially die-hard officers who might still wish to continue fighting, the emperor did not mention the atomic bomb. Rather, it was Soviet participation in the war that provided a more powerful justification to persuade the troops to lay down their arms.[88]

Frank is absolutely right in pointing out that "[t]he end of hostilities required both a decision by a legitimate authority that Japan must yield to Allied terms and compliance by Japanese armed forces with that decision," and that such legitimate authority was the emperor. He is also right about the inability of the

Suzuki government to accept unconditional surrender without the emperor's intervention.[89] It is true that the emperor's strong desire to terminate the war played a decisive role in his "sacred decision." Nevertheless, it seems errone-ous to attribute the emperor's motivation for this decision to what he said in the imperial rescripts. Now united behind the "sacred decision," the cabinet set out to persuade the Japanese people, both civilians and men in uniform, to accept surrender. The cabinet therefore made a few revisions to Sakomizu's draft of the imperial rescript.

Two documents issued by the cabinet need to be examined. The first is a cabinet statement released after the imperial rescript was broadcast, which re-fers to both the use of the atomic bomb, which changed the nature of war, and the Soviet entry as two important reasons for ending the war.[90] The second is the prime minister's radio announcement of August 15, in which he stated that Soviet entry into the war had prompted the cabinet to make the final decision to end the war, and that the atomic bomb, which "it was evident the enemy will continue to use," would destroy both the military power of the empire "and the foundation of the existence of the nation, endangering the basis of our kokutai."[91] Both documents cite the atomic bomb and the Soviet entry into the war as the two important reasons that had prompted the government to seek the termination of the war, thus invalidating Frank's claim that the atomic bomb had a more decisive effect on the emperor's decision to end the war.

Counterfactual Hypotheses

A series of counterfactual hypotheses can help clarify the question of which factor, the atomic bombs or Soviet entry into the war, had the more decisive effect on Japan's decision to surrender. We might ask, in particular, whether Japan would have surrendered before November 1, the scheduled date for the start of Operation Olympic, the U.S. invasion of Kyūshū, given (a) neither the atomic bombings of Hiroshima and Nagasaki nor Soviet entry into the war; (b) Soviet entry alone, without the atomic bombings; or (c) the atomic bombings alone, without Soviet entry.[92]

Let us examine the first proposition. The *Summary Report (Pacific War)* of the United States Strategic Bombing Survey, published in 1946, concluded that Japan would have surrendered before November 1 without the atomic bombs and without the Soviet entry into the war. This conclusion has become the foundation on which the revisionist historians constructed their argument that the atomic bombs were not necessary for Japan's surrender.[93] Since Barton Bernstein has persuasively demonstrated in his devastating critique of the U.S. Strategic Bombing Survey that its conclusion is not supported by its own evidence, I need not dwell on this supposition.[94] It suffices to state that, contrary to its conclusion, the evidence the Strategic Bombing Survey relied on overwhelmingly demonstrates the decisive effect of the atomic bombs and Soviet entry on Japan's decision. As Bernstein asserts: "[A]nalysts can no longer trust the *Survey*'s statement of counterfactual probabilities about when the Pacific War would have ended without the A-bomb or Soviet entry. On such matters, the *Survey* is an unreliable guide." I concur with his conclusion: "[I]t is time for all to stop relying upon the United States Strategic Bombing Survey's pre-November 1945, surrender-counterfactual for authority."[95]

For the second counterfactual hypothesis, that is, surrender with the Soviet entry alone, Asada contends: "[T]here was a possibility that Japan would not have surrendered before November 1."[96] By making this assertion, Asada ignores an important conclusion made by Bernstein. Bernstein states: "In view of the great impact of Soviet entry, however, in a situation of heavy conventional bombing and a strangling blockade, it does seem quite probable—indeed, far more likely than not—that Japan would have surrendered before November without the use of the A-bomb but after Soviet intervention in the war. In that sense . . . there may have been a serious 'missed opportunity' in 1945 to avoid the costly invasion of Kyushu without dropping the atomic bomb by awaiting Soviet entry."[97] However, since it was inessential at that point in his essay, Bernstein does not fully develop his argument.

As I have argued above, Japan relied on Soviet neutrality both militarily and diplomatically. Diplomatically, Japan pinned its last hope on Moscow's mediation for the termination of the war. Only by Soviet entry into the war was Japan forced to make a decision on the Potsdam terms. Militarily as well, Japan's Ketsu Gō strategy was predicated on Soviet neutrality. That was why the General Staff's Bureau of Military Affairs constantly overruled the Fifth Section's alarming warnings that a Soviet invasion might be imminent. Manchuria was not written off, as Frank asserts; rather, the military was confident that it could keep the USSR neutral, at least for a while. When the Soviet invasion of Manchuria occurred, the military was taken completely by surprise. Even Asada admits, "[T]he Soviet entry spelled the strategic bankruptcy of Japan."[98] Despite the repeated bravado calling for the continuation of the war, it pulled the rug right out from underneath the Japanese military, puncturing a gaping hole in their strategic plan. Their insistence on the continuation of the war lost its rationale.

Without Japan's surrender, it is reasonable to assume that the USSR would have completed the occupation of Manchuria, southern Sakhalin, the entire Kurils, and possibly even the Korean peninsula, by the beginning of September. Inevitably, Soviet invasion of Hokkaidō would have emerged as a pressing issue to be settled between the United States and the Soviet Union. The United States might have resisted a Soviet operation against Hokkaidō, but given Soviet military strength, and given the enormous casualty figures the American high command had estimated for Olympic, the United States might have agreed to a division of Hokkaidō as Stalin envisaged. Even if it succeeded in resisting Stalin's pressure, Soviet military conquests in the rest of the Far East might have led the United States to concede some degree of Soviet participation in Japan's postwar occupation. Whatever the United States might or might not have done regarding Soviet operations in Hokkaidō or the postwar occupation of Japan, Japanese leaders were well aware of the danger of allowing continued Soviet expansion beyond Manchuria, Korea, and Sakhalin. That was one of the very powerful reasons why the Japanese ruling elite coalesced at the last moment to surrender under the Potsdam terms, why the military's insistence on continuing the war collapsed, and why the military relatively easily accepted surrender. Japan's decision to surrender was above all a political decision, not a military one. It was more likely, therefore, that even without the atomic bombs, the war would have ended shortly after the Soviet entry into the war, most likely before November 1.

Asada does not ask whether Japan would have surrendered with the atomic bombing of Hiroshima and Nagasaki alone, without the Soviet entry into the war. It is most likely that the two bombs alone would not have prompted Japan to surrender, as long as it still had the hope of attaining a mediated peace through Moscow. As I have shown, the Hiroshima bomb did not significantly change Japan's policy except for injecting a sense of urgency in seeking an end to the fighting. Without the Soviet entry into the war, I do not see how the Nagasaki bomb would have changed the situation. Japan would most likely still have waited for Moscow's answer to the Konoe mission even after the Nagasaki bomb. The most likely scenario would have been that while waiting for an answer from Moscow, Japan would have been surprised by the Soviet invasion of Manchuria sometime in the middle of August and would have sued for peace on the Potsdam terms. We would then have debated endlessly about whether the two atomic bombs preceding the Soviet invasion or the Soviet entry had the greater influence on Japan's decision to surrender. In this case, too, however, Soviet entry would clearly have had a more decisive effect, for the reasons stated above.

Without Soviet participation in the war in the middle of August, the United States would have faced the question of whether it should use a third bomb sometime after August 19, and then a fourth bomb early in September, most likely on Kokura and Niigata. It is hard to say how many atomic bombs it would have taken to compel the Japanese ruling elite to abandon their approach to Moscow. It is possible to argue, although it is impossible to prove, that the Japanese military would still have argued for the continuation of the war even after the dropping of a third bomb, and even after a fourth bomb. Could Japan have withstood the attacks of all seven atomic bombs scheduled to be produced before November 1?[99] Would the United States have had the resolve to use seven atomic bombs in succession? What would have been the effect of these bombs on Japanese public opinion? Would the continuing use of the bombs have solidified the resolve of the Japanese to fight or eroded it? Would it have hopelessly alienated the Japanese from the United States, to the point where it would have been difficult to impose the American occupation on Japan? Would it have encouraged the Japanese to welcome a Soviet occupation instead? These are the questions I cannot answer with certainty.

But what I can state is that the two atomic bombs on Hiroshima and Nagasaki were not likely to be decisive in inducing Japan to surrender. Without the Soviet entry into the war between the two bombs, Japan would most likely have continued the war.

There still remains one important hypothesis to consider. What if Truman had asked Stalin to join the Potsdam Proclamation *and* retained the promise to the Japanese to allow the preservation of a constitutional monarchy, as Stimson's original draft of the proclamation had suggested? This scenario would not have assured Japan's immediate acceptance of the Potsdam terms, since it would surely have encountered the army's insistence on three other conditions. It is not even certain that the army would have accepted a constitutional monarchy, which was certainly not consistent with its understanding of the *kokutai*. Nevertheless, it would have strengthened the resolve of the peace party to seek the termination of the war, and would have made it easier for it to accept the terms, knowing that a monarchical system would be preserved and that Moscow might be harsher and demand the elimination of the emperor system.

But inviting Stalin to join the joint ultimatum and compromising on the unconditional surrender terms were not an option that Truman and Secretary of State James Byrnes would have considered. Although Secretary of War Henry Stimson, Admiral William Leahy, General George Marshall, Assistant Secretary of War John McCloy, Secretary of the Navy James Forrestal, and Acting Secretary of State Joseph Grew would all have preferred this, to Truman and Byrnes, it was anathema. Ironically, it was the atomic bomb that made it possible for Truman to be able to issue the Potsdam Proclamation, demanding unconditional surrender, without Stalin's signature. The atomic bomb also changed the very nature of the Potsdam Proclamation. Instead of being a final warning before Olympic, as originally intended, it became the justification for the use of the atomic bomb. In this sense, the revisionist historians' claim that the atomic bomb delayed rather than hastened Japan's surrender merits serious consideration.

Conclusions

The argument presented by Asada and Frank that the atomic bombs rather than Soviet entry into the war had a more decisive effect on Japan's decision to surrender cannot be supported. The Hiroshima bomb, although it heightened the sense of urgency to seek the termination of the war, did not prompt the Japanese government to take any immediate action that repudiated the previous policy of seeking Moscow's mediation. Contrary to the contention advanced by Asada and Frank, there is no evidence to show that the Hiroshima bomb led either Tōgō or the emperor to accept the Potsdam terms. On the contrary, Tōgō's urgent telegram to Satō on August 7 indicates that, despite the Hiroshima bomb, they continued to stay the previous course. The effect of the Nagasaki bomb was negligible. It did not change the political alignment one way or the other. Even Anami's fantastic suggestion that the United States had more than 100 atomic bombs and planned to bomb Tokyo next did not change the opinions of either the peace party or the war party at all.

Rather, what decisively changed the views of the Japanese ruling elite was the Soviet entry into the war. It catapulted the Japanese government into taking immediate action. For the first time, it forced the government squarely to confront the issue of whether it should accept the Potsdam terms. In the tortuous discussions from August 9 through August 14, the peace party, motivated by a profound sense of betrayal, fear of Soviet influence on occupation policy, and above all by a desperate desire to preserve the imperial house, finally staged a conspiracy to impose the "emperor's sacred decision" and accept the Potsdam terms, believing that under the circumstances surrendering to the United States would best assure the preservation of the imperial house and save the emperor.

This is not, of course, to deny completely the effect of the atomic bomb on Japan's policymakers. It certainly injected a sense of urgency in finding an acceptable end to the war. Kido stated that while the peace party and the war party had previously been equally balanced in the scale, the atomic bomb helped to tip the balance in favor of the peace party.[100] It would be more accurate to say that the Soviet entry into the war, adding to that tipped scale, then completely toppled the scale itself.

Jockeying for Position in the Postwar World

Soviet Entry into the War with Japan in August 1945

DAVID HOLLOWAY

On August 8, 1945, two days after the bombing of Hiroshima, the Soviet Union declared war on Japan, thereby allying itself with China, the United States, and Britain, which had been fighting Japan for years. Less than a week later, on August 14, the Japanese emperor publicly declared Japan's willingness to surrender. Japan signed the formal act of surrender on September 2 on the battleship USS *Missouri* in Tokyo Bay less than four weeks after Soviet entry into the war.

Japanese defeat was already certain when the Soviet Union declared war. Perhaps for that reason, Western historians have until recently written little about the Soviet war with Japan. For those interested in World War II in the Pacific, the atomic bombing of Hiroshima and Nagasaki diverted attention from the Soviet role in the defeat of Japan.[1] For those writing about the Soviet Union in World War II, the war against Japan has been little more than a postscript to the titanic struggle in Europe.[2] Western military historians have written studies of the Soviet-Japanese war, but they have focused on military strategy and operational matters rather than on broader military-political questions.[3] Tsuyoshi Hasegawa's *Racing the Enemy* marks an important new stage in the historiography of the Soviet-Japanese war and, more generally, of the end of the war in the Pacific.[4] Based on extensive Russian, Japanese, and American archives, Hasegawa provides a detailed international history of the end of the war in the Pacific and argues that the Soviet attack was crucial in forcing Japan to surrender.

For Russian historians, the Soviet-Japanese war has been a more important subject of research, but here too the literature has been unsatisfactory. In the

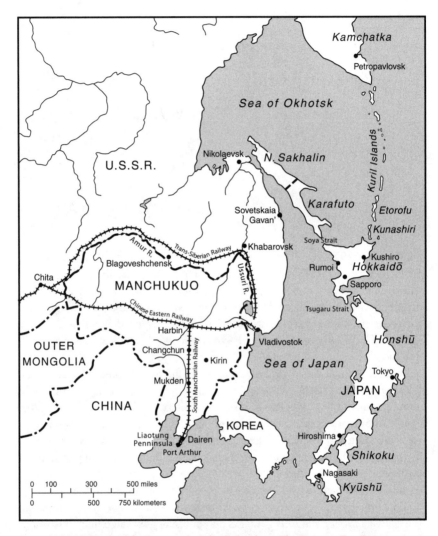

Japan in 1945. Revised from a map in John J. Stephan, *The Russian Far East:
A History* (Stanford University Press, 1994).

Soviet period, historians focused on the military operations of the Soviet Army and paid less attention to the strategic and political issues surrounding the war.[5] They routinely claimed that it was the Soviet attack, and not the atomic bomb, that caused Japan to surrender. It followed, in this analysis, that the bombing of Hiroshima and Nagasaki was unnecessary from a military point of view and must therefore have been intended primarily to intimidate the Soviet Union.[6] It is only in the post-Soviet years that Russian historians have begun to explore in depth the political dimensions of Soviet entry into the war on the basis of new archival evidence.[7] Thanks to the work of Russian historians and to the partial opening of Russian archives, it has become possible, as Hasegawa's work shows, to take a fresh look at the Soviet war with Japan.

Japan's defeat was certain when the Soviet Union entered the war, but the timing and the conditions of its surrender remained undetermined. The Soviet-Japanese war was thus a vital element in the closing chapter of World War II. It also had important consequences for the postwar world, because it played a role in the breakdown of the wartime alliance. Stalin had ambitious strategic goals in the Far East. Some of these he achieved by entering the war against Japan, but he was thwarted in the pursuit of others by American policy. The way in which the war in the Pacific ended had a profound effect on later relations among Japan, the Soviet Union, and the United States.

The Soviet-Japanese war was a point of transition in another sense as well. Japan surrendered in response to two military blows—the atomic bombings and the Soviet attack. The Soviet Manchurian campaign is widely regarded as a masterpiece of Soviet military art, a culmination of the bitter and bloody learning process the Red Army underwent during World War II. The use of the atomic bomb, with its unprecedented capacity for destruction, opened a new phase in the history of warfare. August 1945 was a pivotal month in the history of international relations, the hinge between the pre-atomic and atomic ages. This gives the Soviet-Japanese war an additional importance; it is crucial for understanding not only the end of the war in the Pacific but also the origins of the Soviet-American competition in nuclear arms.

The central question in the historiography of Soviet foreign policy at the end of World War II has been whether it was realist in character or driven by Marxist-Leninist ideology.[8] In other words, did the Soviet Union behave as any great power would do, consolidating and seeking to enhance its power, or did it aim above all to create conditions in which the international communist movement would flourish? Recent research based on Russian archives suggests that this dichotomy is not always useful. Stalin, whose central role in policymaking is confirmed by the new archival materials, was certainly a realist in his assessment of power and power relationships, but he was also deeply interested in, and concerned about, ideological issues and questions of Marxist-Leninist theory. It is difficult to call him either a realist or an ideologue *tout court*. Moreover, realism and Marxism-Leninism are rather broad categories and may therefore be too crude to use in an undifferentiated way in historical analysis. Lenin's theory of imperialism, for example, overlaps with some realist approaches to international relations in its pessimism about the inevitability of war in the international system—although Leninism has a specific analysis of the causes of war and predicts peace once socialism prevails around the world.

If the role of ideology were the central question, the entry into the war against Japan would not be a particularly good case study of Soviet policy at the end of World War II. It does not present the same problems of interpretation as Soviet policy in Europe: did the Soviet Union plan all along to establish communist regimes, or were those regimes a response to deteriorating relations with the West? Nor does it involve the complexities of policy toward China, where the Soviet Union was dealing with both the Nationalist government and the Chinese Communist Party.[9] Entry into the war with Japan did not confront the Soviet leadership with choices of the kind that would shed light on the role of Marxist-Leninist ideology in Soviet policy.

There are nevertheless important issues that the Soviet war with Japan does illuminate. This chapter uses recent studies and collections of documents to explore two questions about Soviet policy before, during, and after the war. The first is: why did the Soviet Union enter the war? The terrible struggle with Germany had inflicted enormous suffering and destruction on the country. Japanese defeat was already certain. Why then did Stalin decide to declare war on Japan? What goals was he pursuing? What do those goals tell us about his overall policy at the end of World War II? How should we understand the relationship between Europe and Asia in Soviet policy at the end of the war?

Access to new Russian archival materials has made it possible to explore the tactical intricacies of Soviet policy on a day-to-day basis.[10] This is an important corrective to earlier approaches that focused on Stalin's broad intentions, because intentions have to be adjusted to the realities of specific contexts. It would be a mistake, however, if this were to lead to neglect of the role of ideas and strategic concepts in policy. To understand the development of policy, it is necessary to examine the interaction between strategic goals and tactical choices. This chapter tries to do just that by looking at Stalin's conception of postwar international politics and the way in which—and the degree to which—that shaped his policy.

The second question is: what impact did the atomic bomb have on Soviet policy, both before and after Hiroshima? Stalin had authorized a small atomic project in September 1942, and during the war, the Soviet Union received extensive and detailed intelligence about the Manhattan Project. Did atomic intelligence shape Stalin's policy on entry into the war with Japan? If so, how? Was he surprised by Hiroshima, or had intelligence forewarned him? What was his immediate response to the use of the atomic bomb on Hiroshima and Nagasaki? The answers to these questions have obvious relevance to our understanding not only of the end of the war in the Pacific but also of the origins of the U.S.-Soviet nuclear arms race.

I touched upon these two sets of questions in my book *Stalin and the Bomb*, which was published in 1994.[11] What prompted me to write this chapter was the appearance of new sources that would, I hoped, shed new light on questions that merited more detailed exploration. Three sets of documents are of particular importance for this chapter. The first is a two-volume collection of documents on the Soviet-Japanese war published under the auspices of the Institute of Military History of the Russian Ministry of Defense, the Historical-Archival and Military-Memorial Center of the Russian General Staff, and the Central Archive of the Russian Ministry of Defense.[12] The second is a two-volume set of documents on Soviet-Chinese relations in 1937–45 published by the Institute of Far Eastern Studies of the Russian Academy of Sciences, the Russian Ministry of Foreign Affairs, and the Russian Federal Archival Service.[13] The third is a series of documents on the Soviet atomic project in 1938–54 published by the Russian Ministry for Atomic Energy.[14] Some of the documents in these collections have been published before, but most are new and many come from archives that are still not generally open to researchers, especially foreign scholars.

These collections are, as I hope will become clear, very helpful in addressing the questions set out above. The documents are well annotated, and helpful context is provided. It is important, however, to recognize the limitations of these collections. First, it is in most cases not possible for the individual researcher to look at the documents in their files, and this makes it more difficult to understand the context in which the documents were produced. Second, not all archives have provided documents for these collections. For example, the compilers of the invaluable series on the atomic project did not have access to Stalin's papers.[15] Third, there are some important gaps. There are, for example, no records of deliberations in the Soviet leadership before or during the Potsdam Conference about the significance of the bomb. Nor have any records been made public of messages between Moscow and the Soviet Embassy in Japan in the immediate aftermath of Hiroshima, though it would be very interesting to know what the embassy reported to Moscow and what questions Moscow put to the embassy.

These limitations mean that there are still important gaps in our knowledge.

In this chapter, I have stayed close to the documents in order to weigh their significance as carefully as possible, precisely because there is no agreement about the answers to some of the questions I examine. I try to set out as clearly as I can the evidence for the judgments I make.

Russo-Japanese Rivalry

Russia became a major power in East Asia in the second half of the nineteenth century, when it exploited Chinese weakness to gain formal control over large territories in the Far East. This expansion brought Russia into conflict with Japan, which had expansionist ambitions of its own in East Asia. In 1896, after the first Sino-Japanese war, Russia formed a secret alliance with China against Japan. The Chinese Eastern Railway Company, which was owned by the Russian government, built and managed a railway line that cut across Manchuria and eased communications with Vladivostok, the most important Russian port on the Pacific Ocean. Two years later, Russia obtained from China a twenty-five-year lease on the Liaotung (Liaodong) peninsula in Manchuria, including the ports of Port Arthur (Lüshun) and Dalian (Dairen). It also obtained the right to build another railway line, the Southern Manchurian Railway, linking Harbin and Port Arthur, an ice-free naval base. (See map.)[16]

Russia's expansion was halted by Japan, which launched a surprise attack on the Russian fleet in Port Arthur in February 1904. The war went badly for Russia on land and at sea. The defeat of the Russian fleet in the Straits of Tsushima in May 1905 destroyed Russia's illusions about the strength of its navy and opened the way to peace negotiations. The Treaty of Portsmouth, signed by Japan and Russia in September 1905, was a blow for Russia, which had to give up many of its recent gains in the Far East. It handed over to Japan the southern portion of Sakhalin and the lease to the Liaotung Peninsula, including Port Arthur and Dalian, and also a large section of the Southern Manchurian Railway.[17] One of Stalin's major goals in 1945 was to restore the losses incurred in the Russo-Japanese War. Defeat at the hands of Japan, he said in his victory address on September 2, 1945, had "left a dark stain on our country. Our people believed and expected that the day would come when Japan would be beaten and the stain removed. For forty years we people of the older generation waited for this day. And now that day has come."[18]

Relations with Japan did not improve after the Bolshevik Revolution. Japan intervened in Russia in 1918 and maintained military forces in the Maritime Province until 1922. Japan's military intervention in Manchuria in 1931 posed a threat to the Soviet Union. Japan began to expand into Inner Mongolia and North China in the middle of the decade. In November 1936, Japan and

Germany (soon joined by Italy) signed the Anti-Comintern Pact, confronting the Soviet Union with the prospect of war on two fronts. The Soviet government viewed Japan's expansion with alarm and took the danger of war very seriously. It built up the Red Army in the Far East and provided the Nationalist government in China with military aid for its war against Japan.[19]

By the end of the decade, the Soviet Union and Japan confronted each other in the Far East with forces that included about 25 percent of each country's military manpower.[20] They clashed in battle in July 1938 at Lake Khasan, near the Korean border, where the Red Army regained the territory taken by the Japanese in the initial attack. In 1939, following a series of battles beginning in May, the Red Army inflicted a decisive defeat on the Kwantung Army in August–September at Khalkhin-Gol (Nomonhan) on the Chinese-Mongolian frontier. By showing the Red Army to be a capable force, these two battles influenced Japan's later decision to pursue a policy of expanding to the south rather than to the north.[21]

The Soviet-German Non-Aggression Pact of August 23, 1939, severely upset Japan's strategic calculations. The Japanese government had had no warning of the pact or of the German attack on Poland, which followed on September 1, and was shocked that Germany had taken such steps without consulting its ally. It could not now count on being able to force the Soviet Union into a two-front war. The Soviet Union and Japan signed a neutrality pact in April 1941, agreeing to remain neutral in the event of an attack by any other power on either signatory. The pact reflected the Japanese desire for peace in the north while it pursued expansion to the south. The Soviet Union, for its part, wanted peace on its eastern border because the situation in Europe was so dangerous. The possibility of attacking the Soviet Union was raised once again in Tokyo after June 22, 1941, when the Germans invaded the Soviet Union. The imperial conference on July 2 decided to press ahead with Japan's southward expansion, but it also authorized preparations for a war against the Soviet Union.[22] Less than six months later, Japan struck at the U.S. Pacific Fleet in Pearl Harbor.

Japan and the Postwar World

Three memoranda written in the People's Commissariat of Foreign Affairs in 1944 and early 1945 provide some insight into Soviet wartime thinking about Japan. They cannot be taken as a direct expression of Stalin's thinking, but they do set out lines of argument, and give voice to attitudes, that recur in Stalin's discussions in late 1944 and in 1945. These memoranda provide a useful benchmark against which to assess Soviet policy. Above all, they show that Japan occupied a crucial place in the Soviet conception of the postwar order.

The first memorandum was written in January 1944 by I. M. Maiskii, deputy people's commissar of foreign affairs and until recently ambassador in London. Maiskii sent his thoughts "On the Desirable Bases of a Future Peace" to V. M. Molotov, people's commissar of foreign affairs.[23] This was one of a number of papers in which leading figures in the People's Commissariat of Foreign Affairs outlined their ideas about the postwar world.[24] After reading it, Molotov passed it on to Stalin and other members of the Politburo.[25] Maiskii argued that the Soviet Union, in constructing the postwar order, ought to aim to create a situation in which peace—at least in Europe and Asia—would be maintained for a period of thirty to fifty years. That would give enough time for the Soviet Union to become so powerful that no state or combination of states in Europe or Asia would even think of attacking it. And in that period, Europe—or at least continental Europe—would become socialist, thereby excluding wars in that part of the world.[26] In order to achieve this postwar order, Germany would have to be "rendered harmless" for thirty to fifty years, while France should not be allowed to challenge the Soviet Union's position as "the single mighty land power in Europe."[27]

Maiskii applied similar reasoning to Japan:

The USSR has no interest in unleashing war with Japan, but it is very interested in the complete military defeat of Japan, because without the latter condition we cannot count on a long peace in Asia. Before the final victory over Germany, the allies, in all probability, will not officially pose us the question of entering into the war with Japan. However, it is almost certain that after the defeat of Germany, they will do so (especially the USA). Our tactics evidently ought to amount to avoiding, by means of clever maneuvering, our open involvement in the war with Japan. It would be far more advantageous from the point of view of the USSR to let the British and the Americans have the "honor" of smashing Japan. That would save us human and material losses and besides would force the USA and Great Britain to expend some of their human and material resources. That would somewhat cool the imperialist ardor of the USA in the postwar epoch. It would also be our revenge for the position of the Anglo-Americans on the question of the second front.[28]

Maiskii argued that it was important for the Soviet Union to have "strategically advantageous" borders:

Above I referred to the fact that the Soviet Union ought to obtain from this war in the Far East southern Sakhalin and the chain of Kuril Islands. I do not think that, in order to achieve that, we must necessarily without fail take part in the war with Japan. It is perfectly possible that at a peace conference, with a general redrawing of the map of the world and complex maneuvering by large and small powers, the USSR could obtain the goals I have just named without firing a shot in the Far East. That is of course on the indispensable condition that the USA and Britain really do defeat Japan utterly. After that, more or less the same kind of regime as that established for Germany should be set up for Japan.[29]

Maiskii explained the importance of the Kuril Islands by noting that they "fenced off" the Soviet Union from the Pacific Ocean.[30] Control of southern Sakhalin and the Kurils would give the Soviet Union unimpeded access to the Pacific Ocean.

The dispatches of the Soviet ambassador in Tokyo, Iakov Malik, provide further evidence on Soviet thinking about the Far East in 1944. News of the Allied landings in Normandy in June 1944 had caused alarm and despondency among the Japanese population, Malik reported. In political and military circles, he wrote, it had elicited the fear that, once Germany had been defeated, Britain and the United States would press the Soviet Union to enter the war against Japan. These fears meant, in Malik's view, that Japan would seek better relations with the Soviet Union and would try to prevent it from cooperating actively with the Western Allies in the Far East. It would seek to interest the Soviet Union in carving up China and try to frighten it with the threat of American imperialism. The Americans and the British, in Malik's view, now had a great interest in having the Soviet Union join the war against Japan, because Soviet forces could play a major role in defeating Japan and because Soviet participation would make it easier to create a stable peace in the Pacific after the war. From this analysis Malik drew the prescient conclusion that the two warring sides in the Pacific would be forced to regard the Soviet Union as a crucial factor in the Far East.[31]

In June 1944, Malik returned to Moscow for consultations. The following month, he wrote a paper on the issues that would have to be dealt with once Japan was defeated.[32] Among the twenty-seven items he listed were the status of Manchuria, the Treaty of Portsmouth, the Kurils, and the future of China. Malik noted that the Soviet Union would have to define its attitude to the occupation of Japan—should it take part or leave the task to the Allies? He doubted that it could be left to the Allies without harming Soviet state interests. Russia, he wrote, could not stand by while Britain and the United States destroyed the Japanese empire.[33] The task for the Soviet Union was to work out a careful plan of action for the Pacific Basin, "possibly in connection with problems in Europe and other parts of the world." The Soviet Union would be involved in dealing with these issues after the defeat of Japan, he wrote, possibly without having taken part in the Pacific War and still bound to Japan by the neutrality pact. It might therefore be appropriate for the Soviet government to point out that the problem of postwar order affected both east and west and to apply the "principle of interrelationship" between the two. By this Malik implied that the Soviet Union's victories in the west would enable it to play its part in determining the postwar order in the east, even if the Soviet Union did not enter the war against Japan.[34]

S. A. Lozovskii, deputy people's commissar of foreign affairs, provided another analysis of American and British policy in a memorandum he sent to Molotov on January 14, 1945. Lozovskii, who oversaw Soviet Far Eastern policy, warned that the Americans and the British were "doing everything to draw us into the war with Japan." The neutrality pact had remained in force because "the Soviet Union did not wish to create a second front in the Far East, while Japan had likewise no interest in opening for itself a 5,000-kilometer land front on the borders of Korea, Manchuria, and the MPR [Mongolian People's Republic]." After Stalingrad, he wrote, there had been a shift in the balance of interest in keeping the pact: the Soviet Union was more interested beforehand, Japan more interested afterward. The Soviet Union would still be involved in the final settlement of all Far Eastern questions, he argued, even if it did not enter the war. "We must not forget," he wrote, "that the time is coming when we shall be able to annul the Treaty of Portsmouth with all its territorial, political, and economic consequences."[35] If Roosevelt and Churchill brought up the issue of entry into the war at Yalta, he wrote, the Soviet leaders could say that they had a neutrality pact with Japan and intended to adhere to it until it ran out in April 1946. They could add that Soviet public opinion would look very unfavorably on complications in Soviet-Japanese relations before Germany was defeated and European questions settled. They could, besides, remind the Western Allies that the Soviet Union had large interests in the Pacific and was ready to discuss all Pacific questions with the United States and Britain on the basis of the interests of the three great powers.

These memoranda give an insight into Soviet goals in the Far East. Malik provided an astute tactical assessment, and according to Slavinskii, his analysis played a significant role in the preparation of the Soviet position at Yalta.[36] Maiskii painted a much broader strategic picture. Although it is difficult to say how far his ideas influenced Stalin and Molotov, Stalin's ideas about the postwar world did correspond in part with Maiskii's analysis. Maiskii and Lozovskii argued that the Soviet Union could achieve its strategic goals without entering the war, and Malik appeared to take the same view, though in a less definite fashion. Stalin, however, had already made it clear to the Western allies in November 1943 that the Soviet Union was willing to enter the war against Japan after Germany had been defeated. It appears that Maiskii and Malik, and perhaps Lozovskii too, were unaware of this. This indicates how tightly information about policy was held at the center.

Maiskii, Malik, and Lozovskii were very largely in agreement on the goals the Soviet Union should pursue, but on another important issue, Malik and Lozovskii did not see eye to eye. As Jonathan Haslam reports, Lozovskii responded within a month to Malik's July 1944 memorandum, attacking it as un-Marxist. Malik had not produced a class analysis of Japanese politics, Lozovskii wrote. He had paid no attention to the political parties that had been driven underground, to the fierce struggles in the ruling class, to the oppression of the working class and the peasantry, or to the role of fascist elements in the state. This shortcoming was a common failing among Soviet diplomats, in Lozovskii's view, for they "think that if in notes and memoranda we do not speak about classes, then one can get by without a Marxist analysis in one's internal reports for the commissariat as well." There is no record of a response by Malik to this criticism, which in any event does not seem to have done him harm, for he soon returned to his post in Tokyo.[37]

The Yalta Agreement

On the day after Pearl Harbor, Roosevelt sounded out Maksim Litvinov, the new Soviet ambassador, on the Soviet attitude to the Japanese-American war. Three days later, Molotov, Litvinov's successor as people's commissar of foreign affairs, instructed Litvinov: "We do not consider it possible at the present moment to declare a state of war with Japan." Litvinov reported to Moscow that when he informed Roosevelt of this, the latter replied that he was sorry to hear it, but that in the Soviet position, he would have taken the same view.[38]

Soviet unwillingness to enter the war with Japan in December 1941 is not hard to understand. The Soviet Union was still reeling from the onslaught of Operation Barbarossa. It had suffered stunning military defeats at the hands of the Wehrmacht and had lost control of huge parts of the country. Stalin had no incentive to open a second front in the Far East while the fate of the Soviet Union hung in the balance in Europe. The Americans realized that the Soviet Union would not now join the war against Japan, but they did seek indirect assistance from the Soviet Union, asking that American bombers be allowed to make preparations to use Soviet airfields in the event of a Japanese attack on the Soviet Union. Stalin adamantly refused these requests.[39]

It was only after the Soviet victories at Stalingrad in February 1943 and at Kursk in July 1943, when the initiative had passed from Germany to the Soviet Union, that Stalin gave a clear indication of Soviet willingness to enter the war against Japan. In October 1943, during a meeting of foreign ministers in Moscow, he told U.S. Secretary of State Cordell Hull that the Soviet Union would join the war against Japan once Germany was defeated.[40] He repeated that assurance to Roosevelt and Churchill at the Teheran conference in November.[41] By making Soviet entry into the war with Japan conditional on the defeat of Germany, he apparently hoped to encourage the Western allies to move with greater urgency to open a second front in Europe; that was his way of using the "principle of interrelationship" that Malik had invoked.

In mid-October 1944, in response to inquiries from the American Chiefs of

Staff, Stalin told W. Averell Harriman, the U.S. ambassador in Moscow, that it would take three months after the defeat of Germany for the Soviet Union to be ready for war against Japan. Two or three months' supplies would have to be stockpiled in Siberia before operations could begin, Stalin explained, because the Trans-Siberian Railroad could not fully support the forces needed to launch and sustain a big offensive. Stalin had consulted the General Staff before giving this response.[42] He also told Harriman that "certain political aspects" would have to be clarified for the Soviet Union to take part in the war.[43] On December 14, Harriman, on Roosevelt's instructions, drew Stalin out on those "political aspects." Harriman reported to Roosevelt:

> After bringing out a map from the next room, the Marshal said that Lower Sakhalin and the Kurile Islands should be returned to Russia. The approaches to Vladivostok are now controlled by the Japanese, he explained. He considered that the U.S.S.R. is entitled to protection for its communications to this important port and remarked that "all outlets to the Pacific Ocean are now held or blocked by the enemy." He stated, drawing a line around the southern part of the Liaotung Peninsula including Dairen and Port Arthur, that Russia again wished to lease these ports and the area surrounding them.[44]

Stalin explained to Harriman that the Soviet Union would also wish to lease the Russian-built railway lines in Manchuria, that is, the Chinese Eastern Railway and the Southern Manchurian Railway.

At Yalta, Roosevelt and Churchill agreed to these political demands, to Stalin's evident satisfaction.[45] The secret Yalta Agreement, which was signed by the three leaders on February 11, 1945, stated that the Soviet Union would enter the war against Japan on the side of the Western Allies two or three months after the capitulation of Germany and the end of the war in Europe. It spelled out the conditions for Soviet entry:

> 1. The *status quo* in Outer Mongolia (the Mongolian People's Republic) shall be preserved;
> 2. The former rights of Russia violated by the treacherous attack of Japan in 1904 shall be restored, viz.: (a) the southern part of Sakhalin as well as all the islands adjacent to it shall be returned to the Soviet Union, (b) the commercial port of Dairen shall be internationalized, the preeminent interests of the Soviet Union in this port being safeguarded and the lease of Port Arthur as a naval base of the USSR restored, (c) the Chinese-Eastern Railroad and the South-Manchurian Railroad which provides an outlet to Dairen shall be jointly operated by the establishment of a joint Soviet-Chinese company it being understood that the preeminent interests of the Soviet Union shall be safeguarded and that China shall retain full sovereignty in Manchuria;
> 3. The Kuril Islands shall be handed over to the Soviet Union.[46]

The agreement also stated: "[I]t is understood that the agreement concerning Outer Mongolia and the ports and railroads referred to above will require concurrence of Generalissimo Chiang Kai-shek." Roosevelt promised to obtain Chinese agreement when Stalin indicated that it was time to do so. Stalin, for his part, promised to conclude a treaty of friendship and alliance with China. Roosevelt and Churchill pledged: "[T]hese claims of the Soviet Union shall be unquestionably fulfilled after Japan has been defeated." Stalin asked for the document to be signed by all three leaders; Roosevelt and Churchill agreed.[47]

The willingness of Roosevelt and Churchill to accede to Stalin's claims shows how eager they were to have Soviet participation in the war. The U.S. Chiefs of Staff had concluded on the eve of the Yalta conference that, while Soviet participation was not essential for victory over Japan, it would be desirable to have "Russian entry at the earliest possible date consistent with her ability to engage in offensive operations."[48] They did not expect Soviet entry into the war to relieve the United States of the need to invade the Japanese home islands. They did, however, hope that the Red Army would tie down the Kwantung Army in Manchuria and prevent the movement of Japanese forces from the Asian mainland to the home islands to counter an invasion. That would weaken Japanese resistance to an invasion and thereby save the lives of American troops.

The claims codified in the Yalta Agreement were essentially those defined by Maiskii, Malik, and Lozovskii in their memoranda, though Maiskii had not mentioned the railways. By restoring the rights Russia had lost in 1905, the Soviet Union would redress the humiliation of defeat in the Russo-Japanese War. It would also succeed in reinstating the strategic advantage that imperial Russia had had and that the Soviet Navy sought—unimpeded access to the Pacific Ocean and a strong naval position vis-à-vis Japan.[49] To that extent, the agreement reflected the advice of officials in the People's Commissariat of Foreign Affairs. But on one crucial issue Stalin did not follow the advice of his officials. Maiskii and Lozovskii had argued that entry into the war was unnecessary, while Malik, who adopted a less clear-cut position, had hinted at the same conclusion.

Stalin decided otherwise. Why did he do so? There is no record of any debate or discussion on the issue, and indeed Stalin seems to have had it in mind since 1941 to enter the war against Japan, if and when the time was right.[50] He evidently did not believe that the Western Allies would pay regard to Soviet interests in the Far East if the Soviet Union did not enter the war. His insistence on obtaining Roosevelt's and Churchill's signatures on the Yalta Agreement suggests that he was afraid they might renege on their commitments when it suited them. Soviet occupation of territory, he may have thought, was a more reliable guarantee of Soviet interests than the goodwill of the Allies. Another factor, perhaps, was that Stalin had additional gains in mind beyond those codified in the agreement. In the months after Yalta, he set his sights on occupying at least part of Hokkaidō, the northernmost of the Japanese home islands. Whether he already had that goal in mind at Yalta is not clear; in any event, he did not voice it there.

Soviet Preparations for War

The danger of a Japanese attack did not disappear entirely after the signing of the neutrality pact. During World War II, the Soviet Union still faced the Kwantung Army, which had close to a million men in Manchuria and was supported by the forces of Manchukuo (the Japanese puppet regime), and by Japanese forces in Korea. The Kwantung Army continued to pose a threat, even though its best units were redeployed to other theaters and replaced with inexperienced troops.[51] In the desperate early months of the war, the Stavka (headquarters of the Soviet Supreme High Command) moved eighteen divisions from the Far East to take part in the defense of Moscow and in the subsequent counteroffensive.[52] But it could not reduce the number of forces below the level needed for defense against a Japanese attack, and it maintained at least 700,000 troops (thirty-two division equivalents) in the Far East during the war.[53]

Soviet preparations for war against Japan began in earnest after the Yalta conference. Stalin's instructions to the General Staff were straightforward: plan for war against Japan and make the war as short as possible.[54] The General Staff considered various options, including invasion of the home islands. It concluded, however, that such an operation would be very difficult because it would require cooperation with Allied navies, which were still far from Japan, and would entail great losses by Soviet forces. Ultimately, the General Staff decided that defeat of the Kwantung Army in Manchuria would do most to destroy Japanese military resistance and bring the war to an end.[55] Between April and June, the General Staff drew up plans for the Manchurian campaign.

The aim of the campaign was to liberate Manchuria as well as the northern part of Korea from the Japanese.[56] The basic concept was to attack Manchuria simultaneously from a number of different directions and destroy the Kwantung Army with maximum speed. The Japanese would then be unable to bring in reinforcements from Korea or northern China. The two most powerful blows would come from Soviet forces deployed in the Mongolian People's Republic and those in the Maritime Province, forcing the Kwantung Army to conduct a defense on two fronts. Several auxiliary strikes toward the center of Manchuria from Transbaikal and Priamur'e were also planned. To isolate the Kwantung Army from the Japanese Expeditionary Forces in China and from the home islands, it was planned to carry out strikes in the Kalga-Beijing direction exiting on the Yellow Sea and along the eastern coast of northern Korea. If the Japanese forces in Manchuria were defeated quickly, it was planned to liberate southern Sakhalin and the Kuril Islands as well. Plans were also drawn up to land troops on Hokkaidō.[57]

Stalin approved the General Staff's plan at a meeting on June 26–27.[58] On the 28th, the Stavka sent directives to the Soviet forces in the Far East. These were organized into three fronts or army groups.[59] The Stavka ordered the Transbaikal Front, which was deployed mainly in the Mongolian People's Republic, and the Maritime Group (renamed the First Far Eastern Front on August 5), which was deployed in the Maritime Province, to be ready for offensive operations by July 25. The Second Far Eastern Front, which was deployed to the north, was to be ready by August 1. The Pacific Fleet was assigned the mission of covering the ports and the sea-lanes. Together with the ground forces, it was to secure the ports and naval bases in northern Korea and Sakhalin and to seize the Kuril Islands. These directives made no mention of landing troops on Hokkaidō; there was apparently no agreement at the June 26–27 meeting on the occupation of Hokkaidō. The Soviet plan was nevertheless an ambitious one, aiming to defeat the Kwantung Army in Manchuria in a strategic offensive lasting no more than one or two months.[60] By doing so, it would achieve what the U.S. Chiefs of Staff hoped that Soviet entry into the war would do: tie down the Kwantung Army and prevent the movement of Japanese troops from the Asian mainland to the home islands. It would also secure the territorial gains promised to the Soviet Union by the Yalta Agreement.

In April 1945, Stalin brought in Marshal A. M. Vasilevskii, former chief of the General Staff and one the ablest commanders to emerge during the war, to help plan the war in the Far East and to take command of Soviet forces there.[61] In May, a special Far Eastern High Command was established in Chita (it later moved to Khabarovsk) to coordinate the operations of the three Fronts. Vasilevskii, who had moved to Chita on July 5, was named commander-in-chief of Soviet Forces in the Far East on August 1, as Soviet forces were making their final preparations.[62] To support him he had commanders and staff officers who had already demonstrated their considerable abilities in the war against Germany.[63]

The Soviet plan involved the movement of huge numbers of troops and equipment from the European theater, almost 10,000 kilometers away. Between April and August, the Soviet Army transported more than half a million troops, along with thousands of tanks, artillery pieces, and trucks, as well as 36,000 horses, along the Trans-Siberian Railway to the Far East.[64] By August, the

Soviet Union had over 1.6 million troops in place for the war. Movements on this scale could not be kept secret, and the General Staff feared that the increased military activity might prompt the Japanese to launch a preemptive strike. The Stavka instructed Soviet forces to make themselves ready for a possible attack by Japan while taking deceptive measures to mislead the Japanese.[65]

Japanese Peace Feelers

On April 5, 1945, the Soviet Union informed the Japanese government that it was denouncing the neutrality pact on the grounds that Japan was helping Germany in its war with the Soviet Union and was, besides, at war with the United States and Britain, allies of the Soviet Union.[66] Under the terms of the five-year pact, this meant that it would not be renewed when it expired in April 1946; it was, however, supposed to remain in effect until then in spite of the denunciation. On May 29, Molotov misled the Japanese ambassador when he told him that "we did not tear up the pact, but refused to prolong it, because we considered that the situation had changed since it was concluded."[67]

The Soviet government was of course aware that Japan's military position was growing weaker. Against fierce Japanese resistance, American forces took the island of Iwō Jima in March and on April 1 landed on Okinawa. On March 9, American bombers inflicted enormous damage on Tokyo, leaving more than 75,000 people dead and one million homeless.[68] In the following months, the United States carried out a series of intensive bombing raids on Japanese cities. It was clear that the United States was winning the war, but it was equally clear that victory could be very costly if Japan continued to resist as it had been doing.

The Soviet government was also aware that the Japanese government—or at least some elements of it—was looking for a way out of the war. On February 18, Ambassador Malik reported from Tokyo that the Japanese consul general in Harbin, Miyagawa Funao, had paid him a visit in order to sound him out on the Yalta conference. Malik noted that Miyagawa twice made the point that the war was now at a stage where a person with great authority might be able to demand an end to hostilities. Only Stalin could play that role, according to Miyagawa.[69]

On March 22 the GRU *rezidentura* (i.e., Soviet military intelligence) in Tokyo reported:

Among Japanese, the opinion has recently been spreading that a Japanese victory is impossible. They think that the moment has come when it is necessary to conclude peace with America through the mediation of the Soviet Union; however, before concluding peace they consider it necessary to choose a suitable moment to give decisive battle to the Americans using all the Japanese armed forces.[70]

The Koiso government fell on April 5, and six days later Soviet intelligence reported that the new cabinet under Baron Suzuki Kantarō, "proceeding from the very unfavorable military situation and the ever growing difficulties in the country, has set the goal of creating conditions for Japan's exit from the war."[71] On April 14, it reported that the new foreign minister, Tōgō Shigenori, had been given the task of establishing better relations with the Soviet Union in order to obtain Soviet help in securing peace between Japan and the United States.[72] On April 21, Tōgō informed Malik of his strong "personal wish" to meet Molotov and inquired whether Molotov would be traveling to, or returning from, the San Francisco conference through Siberia. If so, Tōgō very much wanted to meet him.[73]

The Soviet response to these approaches was completely noncommittal, and it remained so even when Japanese overtures intensified after the surrender of Germany on May 8. The Japanese government was divided between those who wanted to end the war short of unconditional surrender and those who wanted to continue the war so that better terms could be secured in a peace settlement. The Soviet Union was crucial for both groups: for the peace party, it could serve as a mediator; for the war party, it was important to secure the most favorable military conditions for Japan by preventing Soviet entry into the war.[74] Moscow was aware of these differences. On May 18, the Tokyo *rezidentura* reported: "Army circles are trying to take power into their own hands and to carry on the war to the last possibility."[75] Five days later, it informed Moscow that there were persistent rumors from the Foreign Ministry that Japan was attempting to conclude a peace agreement with the United States through mediation by the Soviet Union. Japan would be willing to give southern Sakhalin and the Kuril Islands to the Soviet Union for acting as mediator. Some people thought, the *rezidentura* reported, that Japan might even cede Hokkaidō to the Soviet Union.[76]

In the middle of May, Tōgō asked the former Prime Minister Hirota Kōki to explore with Malik how far Japan could count on Soviet good offices. Malik had four conversations with Hirota in June. Hirota insisted that Japan wanted peaceful, friendly relations with the Soviet Union and set out the details of a plan, which included a non-aggression treaty and the neutralization of Manchukuo, as well as a number of concessions to Soviet interests.[77] Malik reported these exchanges to Moscow. On July 8, Molotov instructed Malik to avoid giving the Japanese any pretext for presenting these talks as negotiations. "Hirota's proposals," Molotov wrote, "testify to the fact that, as its military situation deteriorates, the Japanese government is willing to make ever greater concessions to prevent our intervention in the war in the Far East."[78]

Four days later, on July 12, Soviet intelligence reported to Moscow that

the Japanese government is already now strenuously seeking ways to get out of the war without having to make an unconditional surrender. This desire of Japan reaches us by all channels. Leading figures in Japan have more than once approached the ambassador semi-officially about peaceful mediation between Japan and America, as the ambassador has reported to the government.[79]

The same message went on to say that, according to a Japanese informant, only Stalin's mediation could help Japan, because the United States was insisting on unconditional surrender. Japanese naval circles, he said, were willing to reach a compromise with political and government circles in order to get out of the war. On the following day, July 13, Satō Nataoke, the Japanese ambassador in Moscow, asked the Soviet government to receive Prince Konoe Fumimaro, a former prime minister, whom the Japanese government had decided to send to Moscow to seek Soviet assistance in negotiating a cease-fire as a first step toward a peace agreement.[80] That was four days before the start of the Potsdam Conference. Sato did not believe that the Japanese approach would yield results until it became much more specific. "As you are well aware," he wrote to Tōgō, "the Soviet authorities are extremely realistic and it is extremely difficult to persuade them with abstract arguments."[81] The vagueness of the Japanese approach reflected the inability of the Japanese government to agree on proposals for a peace settlement. The peace party and the war party concurred on the need for an approach to Moscow, but their reasons for the approach were different and they were consequently unable to agree on the terms on which they would be willing to conclude peace.[82]

Soviet Goals

The Soviet Union gave no sign of being tempted by the Japanese approaches. It showed not the slightest inclination to help Japan negotiate a peace agreement with the United States; nor was it interested in staying out of the war in return for Japanese offers of greater Soviet influence in Asia. There were probably several reasons for this, including the fear that Japan might be trying to trick or embarrass the Soviet Union, but the two most important were surely Stalin's determination to see Japan eliminated as a great power and his desire to strengthen the Soviet Union's strategic position in the Far East by securing the gains promised at Yalta. He had no interest in negotiating a peace treaty that would allow Japan to remain a powerful military-political force in East Asia or deprive the Soviet Union of the gains promised at Yalta.

In his conversations with American and Chinese officials, Stalin made it clear that he wanted to see Japanese power destroyed. On May 28, he told Harry Hopkins that

There is a possibility that Japan will be ready to capitulate, but not unconditionally. In that case the allies as one of the options can resort to occupation of the islands, treating Japan more gently than Germany. The second option is unconditional surrender, which will allow the allies to crush Japan. From the point of view of the fundamental interests of the allies, he, Stalin, personally would prefer unconditional surrender of Japan, since that would mean Japan's complete and utter defeat.[83]

Stalin consistently supported the goal of unconditional surrender, which he interpreted in the harshest terms.

Stalin's insistence on unconditional surrender sprang in part from his concern about what might happen to Japan after the war. He elaborated on this point in his negotiations with the Chinese government in July. It is worth quoting at length what he said to T. V. Soong, the head of the Chinese delegation, on July 11, two days before the Japanese ambassador asked the Soviet government to receive Prince Konoe and six days before the start of the Potsdam Conference:

Comrade Stalin said that governments, if only in the US and Britain, changed and with time they would forget about the sufferings inflicted by the current war and would begin to give Japan various privileges, as happened with Germany after the first World War. . . . Comrade Stalin pointed out that . . . Germany could restore its strength in 20–30 years. Comrade Stalin remarked that now, of course, Germany had fewer possibilities for doing that than after the First World War. But now too it could restore its strength in 40 years. Comrade Stalin said that in America and Britain there would be people who would help Japan. Soong did not know, said Comrade Stalin, how the representatives of the Soviet Union had had to fight at Yalta and Teheran for acceptance of the demand of unconditional surrender by Germany under tough conditions. The Americans and the English had not agreed that all German troops should be taken prisoner after the occupation and taken away to the rear. That question was resolved in a natural way on the day of Germany's surrender. We simply rounded up all the German troops and the Americans did the same. We kept making the point that the best part of the German nation is to be found in the army and on that basis demanded that all German troops be taken prisoner. I cannot say, said comrade Stalin, that the English and the Americans would not understand that, they merely wanted to keep Germany for a political game, for balance [*ravnovesie*]. Doubtless there will be people in the US and England who will help Japan. To stop that from happening we will have to dispose of great strength.

Soong said that China and the Soviet Union should reach agreement to be merciless in relation to the Japanese.

Comrade Stalin agreed with that and said that China and the Soviet Union had already had the pleasure of Japanese occupation, while neither the Americans nor the British had ever been occupied by the Japanese. That is why, said Comrade Stalin, we wish to have a powerful naval base on the Liaotung Peninsula and such a base would correspond to the interests of China.[84]

Stalin's strategic goal was to remove Japan as a great power from the international scene and to make territorial gains that would strengthen the Soviet position in the Far East. Maiskii had put forward the same idea in his January 1944 memorandum: Soviet security would be best served by the complete annihilation of Japanese power, just as it would be by the elimination of German power. The Soviet Union would then be the dominant power in Asia and in Europe for a long period. Stalin drew a parallel with the years after World War I. He hoped that the restoration of Japanese—and German—power would take longer than the revival of German power had taken after the previous war. The timescales he mentioned were not very different from the 30–50 years discussed by Maiskii in his memorandum to Molotov. In the meantime, Stalin wanted to strengthen the Soviet Union's strategic position in the Far East so that it could resist the reemergence of Japanese power.

From his conversations with Soong, it is evident that Stalin feared that after the war, Britain and the United States would try to build up Japan as a counterweight to the Soviet Union. He apparently also worried that Britain and the United States might not be as single-minded as the Soviet Union about destroying Japanese power. On April 13, the day after Roosevelt's death, he asked Harriman if American policy toward Japan would be softened. That was out of the question, Harriman replied, especially in view of American public opinion about Japan.[85] On May 28, in his conversation with Hopkins, Stalin mentioned that there were rumors that the British and the Japanese were engaged in peace negotiations.[86] The secret *Bulletin of the Central Committee Information Bureau* reported in its July 1 issue that "reactionary circles" in Britain wanted a compromise peace with Japan in order to prevent the Soviet Union from strengthening its position in the Far East. The same question, it noted, was being raised in American newspapers and journals too.[87]

This suspicion of British and American motives may help to explain why Stalin did not stand aside to allow the Japanese and the Western Allies to fight it out, as both Maiskii and Lozovskii had recommended. He might have feared that, rather than fight to the finish, Britain and the United States would conclude a compromise peace that would leave Japan as a powerful force in Asia and deprive the Soviet Union of the gains it hoped to make in the Far East. That might also have been a factor in Stalin's response to the Japanese peace feelers. If he had rejected the feelers out of hand, Japan might have been more willing to make concessions to the United States in order to bring the war to an end. If he had shown real interest in mediating, that might have incurred American resentment and jeopardized the Yalta Agreement. He did not inform the United States or Britain about the Japanese peace feelers until the Potsdam Conference in July, nor did he share with them the intelligence he had about Japanese political opinion.[88]

It is clear that the Soviet Union had more to gain from participation in the war under the terms of the Yalta Agreement than from responding positively to the proposals put forward by Hirota.[89] Besides, Stalin hoped for even more. At the end of May, he told Harry Hopkins that he expected the Soviet Union to share in the occupation of Japan and wanted an agreement with the United States and Britain on zones of occupation.[90] That would give the Soviet Union a continuing voice in determining the future of Japan. The Yalta Agreement and occupation rights in Japan would both contribute to the overriding goal of destroying Japanese power and preventing, or hindering, its reemergence.

Negotiations with China

The Yalta Agreement required that China as well as Japan make concessions to the Soviet Union. Roosevelt and Churchill had insisted that Chiang's concurrence be obtained before the agreement could enter into effect, and Stalin had promised to conclude a treaty of friendship and alliance with China. Negotiations between the Soviet Union and China began in Moscow on June 30, three days after Stalin had approved the General Staff's plan for war against Japan. The first round lasted until July 12; the second round began on August 7, after the Potsdam Conference and after Hiroshima.

Stalin took a very active part in the talks, meeting six times between June 30 and July 12 with T. V. Soong, the head of the Chinese delegation. Stalin wanted a treaty signed quickly so that the Soviet Union could enter the war on the basis of the Yalta Agreement as an ally of China. But the negotiations proved to be difficult. The Chinese government was very unhappy with the Yalta Agreement. It regarded Outer Mongolia as part of China and objected to the clause preserving the status quo in Mongolia, which Stalin interpreted as recognition of Mongolian independence. It objected also to the clause relating to railways and ports in Manchuria. It resented the idea that the Soviet Union could have "preeminent" interests on Chinese territory and disagreed with the practical arrangements proposed by the Soviet Union for Port Arthur and Dalian and for the railways.[91]

Stalin claimed that, beyond the immediate goal of defeating Japan, the Soviet Union and China shared a long-term interest in countering Japanese power and restraining Japanese aggression. He explained that the Soviet Union wanted to strengthen its strategic position in the Far East and argued that that would be in China's interest too. He told Soong on July 2 that

Japan will not perish, even if it is forced to make an unconditional surrender. History shows that the Japanese are a powerful nation. After the Versailles Treaty everyone thought that Germany would not rise again. But some 15–17 years passed and it restored its strength. If Japan is forced to its knees, then it too will in time be able to repeat what Germany did. The Soviet Union has to ensure that it has the right to defend Outer Mongolia with its own forces, and that is also in the interests of China. If we are strong, then China will be strong.[92]

Later in the same meeting, Stalin said: "[I]f the Kuril Islands are Soviet, and Formosa and other territories are returned to China, then we will always have the possibility of keeping Japan squeezed from the east, the south and the west."[93]

Stalin pressed the Chinese hard. It is true that he was eager to gain China's acceptance of the Yalta Agreement so that the Soviet Union could attack Japan as China's ally. But, as the Chinese understood, there was in the end nothing to prevent Soviet forces from occupying Manchuria without a treaty. Stalin took a tough line on Mongolia, an issue of considerable strategic importance to the Soviet Union. He accepted the Chinese proposal to hold a plebiscite on independence once the war was over. Since the outcome of the plebiscite was a foregone conclusion, this was a concession on the Chinese rather than the Soviet part. Stalin pushed for strong Soviet control over the ports and the railways, but Soong was strenuous in resisting his demands.

Stalin tried to reassure the Chinese delegation about Soviet intentions in China, and particularly about the degree of Soviet support for the Chinese communists. When Soong asked him on July 9 what he thought of the Chinese communists, Stalin replied by asking "what the Chinese government wanted from the Soviet Union."[94] Evidently, he went on, "the issue was that the Soviet Union should not arm the Chinese communists and that all aid should go directly to the government of Chiang Kai-shek to dispose of." When Soong replied in the affirmative, Stalin said that he agreed with that. Soong went on to say that the Chinese government was trying to resolve the communist question by political means. That would be desirable, Stalin responded, because the Chinese communists were good patriots and would fight well against the Japanese. Soong told Stalin that the central government was trying to merge the armies and create a unified system of power. Stalin replied that that was a completely legitimate wish, for "in a state there should be one army and one government."[95]

It proved impossible to reach agreement quickly. Soong told Stalin on July 11 that he wanted to return to China for consultations with Chiang Kai-shek while Stalin and Molotov were in Berlin for the Potsdam Conference.[96] Stalin said he could not agree to that, because the question of Soviet entry into the war would be discussed at Potsdam. Without an agreement with China, he would not be able to say definitely when the Soviet Union would attack Japan. He needed an agreement before the Potsdam meeting, so that he could speak clearly about his plans in the Far East. Stalin proposed that he and Molotov delay their journey to Berlin by one day. Soong agreed to this, but a further meeting, on July 12, failed to resolve the outstanding issues.[97] Soong returned to Chungking for consultations, and Stalin left for Berlin.

The Atomic Bomb and the Date of Soviet Entry into the War

One of the key questions about Soviet entry into the war against Japan is when and how the atomic bomb entered into Stalin's calculations. The historian Antony Beevor has argued that the desire to seize German uranium as well as nuclear scientists and research laboratories was a major reason for Stalin's determination to take Berlin before the Western allies did. Beevor's claim is founded on faulty evidence, but it is appropriate to ask when and how the atomic bomb first had an impact on Soviet policy.[98] The Soviet Union had been receiving detailed intelligence about foreign nuclear research since 1941, and in September 1942, Stalin had authorized a small Soviet project to investigate whether an atomic bomb could be built.[99] That had grown during the war, but it was still a laboratory project, rather than an industrial one, and certainly not comparable to the American effort.

Soviet intelligence had good, though not always accurate, information on the progress of the Manhattan Project in 1945. On February 28, People's Commissar of State Security V. Merkulov reported to L. P. Beria that the "first [American] experimental 'combat' explosion is expected in 2–3 months."[100] On July 2, the Commissariat of State Security informed I. V. Kurchatov, the scientific director of the Soviet project, that the first explosive test of an atomic bomb would take place in July, probably about the 10th; this would be a plutonium bomb, and the yield was expected to be equivalent to 5,000 tonnes of TNT.[101] On July 10, a week before the opening of the Potsdam Conference, Merkulov wrote to Beria that several reliable sources had reported that the United States would conduct its first experimental test of an atomic bomb in July, probably on July 10 (the test took place on the 16th).[102] Merkulov's memorandum, like the report to Kurchatov, said that this would be a plutonium bomb, with an expected yield of five kilotons. It is very likely that Beria gave this memorandum to Stalin before he left for Potsdam.[103] In his memorandum, Merkulov said nothing about the war or about the possible use of the bomb against Japan.

Did this information affect the timing of Soviet entry into the war? Stalin had told Harry Hopkins on May 28 that Soviet forces would be ready to enter the war by August 8, but that the actual date of entry would depend on conclusion of the negotiations with China.[104] The Stavka orders of June 28 instructed the Soviet forces to be ready for attack by July 25 and August 1, but according to General S. M. Shtemenko, who as chief of the Operations Directorate of the General Staff was deeply involved in planning the war, it was planned in the middle of June to start operations between August 20 and 25.[105] That plan seems to have held firm for some weeks, for in a meeting with T. V. Soong on July 10, Molotov indicated that the Soviet Union would declare war on Japan in late August.[106] Between July 10 and July 16, however, the planned date of entry into the war seems to have been advanced to August 11.[107] Stalin evidently wanted to move the date even further forward, for on July 16, the day he arrived in Potsdam, he telephoned Marshal Vasilevskii in the Far East to ask him to advance the date of entry into the war by ten days and begin the offensive on August 1. Vasilevskii told Stalin that Soviet forces would not be ready by August 1. He asked that the previous date, August 11, remain in effect and Stalin agreed.[108] This was a provisional date, because the Stavka had not yet issued an order to begin operations against Japan. On the following day, July 17, Stalin told U.S. President Harry S. Truman that the Soviet Union would be ready to enter the war by the middle of August; this seems quite compatible with the planned date of August 11.[109] A week later General A. I. Antonov, chief of the General Staff, gave a more cautious assessment when he told his American and British counterparts that the Soviet Union would join the war in the second half of August.[110]

In 1967, Vasilevskii wrote that Stalin's request on July 16 to advance the date of the Soviet attack had been connected with the atomic bomb test, which took place on the same day. But in his memoirs, published in 1974, Vasilevskii stated that Stalin could not have known of the test when he telephoned and that the phone call must therefore have been prompted by general military-political considerations.[111] It is of course conceivable that in making the call, Stalin was motivated not by news of the test, but by the intelligence that the test was due to take place.[112] It is more likely, however, that the call reflected more general military-political considerations, as suggested by Vasilevskii. There was growing evidence of Japanese desperation to bring the war to an end: the GRU had reported from Tokyo on July 12 on the strenuous Japanese efforts to get out of the war, short of unconditional surrender; and on the following day, Satō had asked the Soviet government to receive Prince Konoe. Moreover, the negotiations with the Chinese had not been going well. The first round of talks had ended on July 12, with no indication that final agreement would be reached quickly. These two factors could have forced a reconsideration of the date of entry into the war, because they showed that Japan might be willing to end the war quickly if offered terms other than unconditional surrender, and that the talks with China might drag on for a long time.

As long as Stalin believed that the United States wanted the Soviet Union to enter the war, it made sense for him to tell the Americans that the date of entry depended on conclusion of the Sino-Soviet Treaty, because he could then expect them to press China to accept Soviet terms for the treaty. But once it became clear that Japan was eager to end the war and that the talks with the Chinese might drag on, he was willing to attack Japan without the treaty with China, as his request to Vasilevskii to make Soviet forces ready for entry into the war by August 1 indicates. There was nothing to stop Soviet forces invading Manchuria with or without a treaty, as Stalin and the Western Allies knew, and once Soviet forces had occupied Manchuria, Stalin would have another instrument of pressure on the Chinese government.

At Potsdam, Truman approached Stalin after a plenary session on July 24, as the latter was about to leave the conference room. He casually mentioned that the United States "had a new weapon of unusual destructive force."[113] He did not say, however, that this was the atomic bomb. According to Truman's memoirs, Stalin replied that "he was glad to hear it and hoped we would make 'good use of it against the Japanese.'"[114] It is open to question, however, whether Stalin actually said that. Anthony Eden, who was watching from a few feet away, wrote in his memoirs that Stalin had merely nodded his head and said, "Thank you," without further comment.[115] Stalin's interpreter, who translated Truman's remark, confirmed Eden's account, but recalled that Stalin merely nodded his head, without saying thank you.[116]

Molotov and Marshal G. K. Zhukov, who were both at Potsdam, later claimed that Stalin knew that Truman had the atomic bomb in mind; and A. A. Gromyko recalled a conversation with Stalin at Potsdam about the atomic bomb.[117] Although there is no contemporary documentation to confirm it, it seems clear that Stalin understood what Truman was referring to. Molotov, Zhukov, and Gromyko all report that what concerned Stalin at Potsdam was that the United States and Britain would use the bomb to put pressure on the Soviet Union, but none of them recalled him saying anything about the influence of the bomb on the war against Japan.[118] General Antonov told General Shtemenko that Stalin had said to him at Potsdam that the Americans had a new bomb of great destructive power. According to Shtemenko, neither Stalin nor Antonov understood the significance of the bomb; at any rate, they did not give the General Staff new instructions for the war against Japan.[119] After his conversation with Vasilevskii on July 16, Stalin appears to have taken no action at Potsdam to advance the date of the attack on Japan, in spite of the fact that Vasilevskii reported to him by phone every day during the conference.[120]

It is clear that Stalin was eager to enter the war before Japan surrendered. There were two things to cause him anxiety: the increasingly active Japanese approaches to Moscow, which suggested growing desperation on the part of the Japanese government to find a way out of the war, and Stalin's chronic suspicion that the Western Allies would conclude a compromise peace with Japan, thereby thwarting Soviet aims in the Far East and allowing Japan to remain a powerful military-political force. These factors are sufficient to explain Stalin's anxiety. There is no clear evidence that before August 6, Stalin's policy was driven by the fear that the United States would use the atomic bomb to end the war at a stroke; indeed, Shtemenko's testimony suggests otherwise. If Stalin had understood just how destructive the atomic bomb was, and that it would soon be used against Japan, he would surely have applied further pressure on Vasilevskii to speed up preparations for war. That he did not do so indicates that he did not understand the impact the atomic bomb was about to have on the war.

This interpretation differs from that of Tsuyoshi Hasegawa, who claims that the atomic bomb was a factor in Stalin's calculations about the war against Japan as early as 1943. This claim seems implausible, and Hasegawa offers no evidence to support it.[121] If Stalin had believed in 1943 that the atomic bomb was so important, he would have given greater priority to the Soviet nuclear project. But the main burden of Hasegawa's argument is that during the Potsdam Conference, Stalin realized that the United States now had the bomb, that it would use it against Japan, and that the use of the bomb would lead Japan to surrender.[122] As a consequence, he claims, it was only late in the conference that Stalin advanced the date of attack from August 20–25. This contradicts the testimony of Vasilevskii and Shtemenko discussed above. Besides, it seems unlikely that Stalin would have told Truman on July 17 that he would be ready to enter the war by August 15 if he was in fact planning to do so on August 20–25. That would leave him open to recriminations from his allies if he failed to enter the war as early as he said he would. More significantly, it might spur them to hasten their efforts to finish the war before the Soviet Union was ready to join in.

It is very likely that Stalin knew about the forthcoming nuclear test. It is not clear when he learned that the test had been successful, though he might well have deduced that from Truman's remark. There is no evidence that Stalin expected the bomb to be used against Japan. Neither Molotov, nor Zhukov, nor Gromyko recalled any apprehension on that score; in fact, Gromyko refers in his memoirs to the danger of pressure in Europe, not to the war against Japan. Stalin might well have assumed that the period between the first test and actual use in war would be much longer than three weeks. And finally, even if Stalin did anticipate early use of the bomb against Japan—for which there is no evidence—there is no indication that he believed before Hiroshima that the bomb would greatly hasten Japan's surrender.

The Potsdam Conference

The Potsdam Conference initially appeared to go well from the Soviet point of view. At their first meeting, on July 17, Truman told Stalin that he expected Soviet help in defeating Japan. Stalin replied that Soviet forces would be ready to enter the war by the middle of August. He would keep the commitment he had made at Yalta, he said, but agreement would have to be reached with China first.[123] Truman was happy with this answer. He wrote in his diary for that day of Stalin's promise to "be in the Jap War on August 15th. Fini Japs when that comes about."[124] To his wife he wrote, "I've gotten what I came for; Stalin goes to war August 15 with no strings on it. . . . [W]e'll end the war a year sooner now."[125] A week later, on July 24, General Antonov assured the Allied Chiefs of Staff that the Soviet Union would be ready to start operations in the latter half of August, though the exact date would depend on completion of the negotiations with the Chinese.[126] Two days later, the American and Soviet Chiefs of Staff negotiated an agreement to coordinate military operations against Japan.[127]

On the second day of the conference, July 18, Stalin told Truman about the Japanese request to send Prince Konoe to Moscow. He handled the issue very delicately, asking whether it might be best to make no response, since the Soviet Union was about to declare war on Japan. Truman said that it was for Stalin to decide. Stalin replied that it might be advisable to lull the Japanese to sleep. He proposed therefore to say that the Soviet government could not give a definite reply to the Japanese message because it was not clear what the purpose of Konoe's mission was.[128] Ten days later, Stalin told Truman and Clement Attlee (who had replaced Churchill as prime minister) that Tokyo had made a new approach. Konoe, the Japanese had explained, was to ask the Soviet government to serve as a mediator to bring the war to an end. Stalin said that this approach contained nothing new and recommended an answer similar to that given the last time. Truman and Attlee agreed.[129] Stalin had thus informed Truman about the Japanese approaches without provoking any American interest in using them to explore the possibility of a compromise peace.

Stalin could take satisfaction from the military coordination with the Allies, and from the lack of American interest in pursuing a compromise peace. Below the surface, however, a serious shift was taking place. American enthusiasm for Soviet entry into the war had waned considerably since Yalta, largely because of differences over the postwar settlement in Europe. By the time of Germany's capitulation in early May, there was a "current of uneasiness" in Washington about Soviet policy in the Far East, and some discussion of the possibility of withdrawing from the Yalta Agreement.[130] Stalin had reassured Harry Hopkins at the end of May that China would be unified under the Nationalists, and that the Soviet Union had no territorial claims on China, but apprehensions remained in Washington about Soviet ambitions in the Far East.[131]

Truman was nevertheless still counting on Soviet help against Japan. General George C. Marshall, the U.S. Army chief of staff, told Truman on June 18: "[O]ur objective should be to get the Russians to deal with the Japs in Manchuria (and Korea if necessary)." Truman reassured him that "one of his objectives in connection with the coming conference [i.e., Potsdam] would be to get from Russia all the assistance in the war that was possible."[132] At his first meeting with Stalin at Potsdam, Truman raised the issue of Soviet help and received Stalin's assurance that the Soviet Union would enter the war.

American interest in Soviet help declined, however, when news arrived of the successful testing of the atomic bomb at Alamogordo in the early morning of July 16. At 7:30 that evening in Potsdam, Secretary of War Henry L. Stimson received a telegram from Washington to say that the test had been successful.[133] Two days later Truman wrote in his diary: "Believe Japs will fold before Russia comes in. I am sure they will when Manhattan appears over their homeland."[134] On July 21, Stimson received a detailed report about the test. Truman said it gave him "an entirely new feeling of confidence," when Stimson read it to him. "The bomb as a merely probable weapon had seemed a weak reed on which to rely," Stimson realized, "but the bomb as a colossal reality was very different."[135] The successful test made Soviet entry into the war much less important to the Americans. "Marshall felt as I felt he would," Stimson wrote in his diary on July 23, "that with our new weapon we would not need the assistance of the Russians to conquer Japan."[136] On the same day, U.S. Secretary of State James Byrnes told Churchill that he had cabled Soong, advising him not to give way on any point in the negotiations. Churchill concluded: "[I]t is quite clear that the United States do not at the present time desire Russian participation in the war against Japan."[137]

On July 26, Truman, Churchill, and Chiang Kai-shek issued the Potsdam Proclamation, calling on Japan to surrender and threatening prompt and utter destruction if it did not do so. An ultimatum had been under discussion in Washington for some weeks. The key point at issue was whether the demand for unconditional surrender should be modified to make Japanese surrender more likely, and specifically whether the proclamation should say that Japan could keep an imperial system. There were those—including Stimson and Undersecretary of State Joseph Grew, a former ambassador to Japan—who argued that the Japanese would fight to the bitter end unless they were reassured that the imperial dynasty could be retained.[138] This reassurance did not find its way into the proclamation, whose final paragraph read: "We call upon the government of Japan to proclaim now the unconditional surrender of all

Japanese armed forces, and to provide proper and adequate assurances of their good faith in such action. The alternative for Japan is prompt and utter destruction."[139] The proclamation did not mention the atomic bomb.

Stalin was neither asked to sign the proclamation nor consulted about its terms. Hopkins had suggested to Stalin in May that Truman and Stalin could discuss the terms of Japanese surrender when they met, but that did not happen.[140] Molotov received a copy of the proclamation as soon as it was issued, at about 9 o'clock on the evening of July 26.[141] At 11.55 P.M., V. N. Pavlov, Stalin's interpreter, phoned a member of the American delegation to ask that the proclamation not be made public for about three days. It had already been given to the press, he was told, and publication could not be postponed.[142] Stalin was unhappy with this lack of consultation, as he made clear at the conference two days later.[143]

The Soviet delegation had prepared a document of its own, which reads in full:

The time has come when the governments of the allied democratic countries—the United States of America, China, Great Britain, and the Soviet Union—have recognized the necessity of declaring their attitude to Japan.

Eight years ago, Japan attacked China and since then has conducted a bloody war against the Chinese people. After that Japan treacherously attacked the United States and Great Britain, beginning a war of brigandage in the Pacific. And this time, Japan used the same method of perfidious surprise attack as forty years ago when it attacked Russia.

Throwing itself into war, Japan tried to exploit the situation created as a result of Hitler's aggression in Europe. The tenacious resistance of the Chinese people and the courageous struggle of the American and British armed forces upset the predatory plans of Japanese militarists.

Like Hitler's Germany in the West, bellicose Japan has caused, and continues to cause, countless disasters to peace-loving peoples. In spite of the defeat of Germany and the end of the war in Europe, Japan continues to drag out the bloody war in the Far East. The calamities of peoples and the victims of war continue to grow, in spite of the futility of prolonging the war. It is impossible to tolerate this situation any longer.

Throughout the world, the peoples are full of a desire to put an end to a war that has dragged on. The United States, China, Great Britain, and the Soviet Union consider it their duty to come forward with joint decisive measures that ought to lead to an end to the war.

Japan should understand that further resistance is futile and presents the greatest danger for the Japanese people itself. Japan must end the war, lay down its arms, and surrender unconditionally.[144]

This document was clearly intended as an alternative to the Potsdam Proclamation, but Stalin did not give it to his allies; there was no point in doing so once the proclamation had been made public.

The Soviet document is nonetheless important for the light it throws on

Soviet thinking. Like the Potsdam Proclamation, it calls for unconditional surrender, which was the position that Stalin had taken consistently toward Japan.
It lacks the subtle formulation of the proclamation—"unconditional surrender
of all Japanese armed forces"—and bluntly calls for Japan to surrender unconditionally. Unlike the proclamation, it says nothing about the treatment of
Japan after the war. The proclamation had said that Japanese military forces,
after being completely disarmed, "shall be permitted to return to their homes
with the opportunity to lead peaceful and productive lives"; the Soviet statement makes no such commitment. Nor does the Soviet document say anything explicit about Soviet entry into the war, though its reference to "decisive measures" hints at it. The most important difference from the Potsdam
Proclamation is that Stalin would have been one of the signatories.

An ultimatum signed by Stalin, along with Truman, Churchill, and Chiang,
would have made it clear to the Japanese that they could not hope to avoid
unconditional surrender through Soviet mediation. Such an ultimatum would
have been more likely than the Potsdam Proclamation to persuade the Japanese
to surrender, because it would have put an end to Japanese illusions about
Soviet policy. This suggests that Stalin's objection to the Potsdam Proclamation
was not that it would end the war too quickly—that is, before Soviet forces
could begin military operations—but that it neither provided the justification
for Soviet entry into the war nor conferred the legitimacy on Soviet claims in
the Far East that a joint declaration would have done. It is possible, of course,
that Stalin intended the ultimatum to be issued just before Soviet entry into the
war. Perhaps he also calculated that if Japan surrendered in response to an ultimatum signed by him as well as the other leaders, the Soviet Union would still
obtain what had been promised to it under the Yalta Agreement and perhaps
also a role in the occupation of Japan. In that case, it would achieve its strategic
aims without having to fight for them.

Japan did not surrender in response to the Potsdam Proclamation. The absence of Stalin's signature may have encouraged the Japanese government to
believe that the Soviet Union would remain neutral and act as a mediator.[145]
Prime Minister Suzuki informed the press on July 28 that his government intended to ignore the ultimatum.[146] On the following day, July 29, Molotov
told Truman that Stalin would find it helpful if the United States and Britain
would formally request the Soviet Union to enter the war against Japan. This
request might be based, he suggested, on the Japanese rejection of the proclamation.[147] Truman was reluctant to do as Stalin wished, and Byrnes even more
so. Byrnes wanted the war over before the Soviet Union joined in. On the day
before, he had told Secretary of the Navy James Forrestal that "he was most
anxious to get the Japanese affair over with before the Russians got in, with

particular reference to Dairen and Port Arthur. Once in there, he felt it would not be easy to get them out."[148] On Byrnes's advice, Truman sent Stalin a note saying that under international law, "it would be proper for the Soviet Union to indicate its willingness to consult and cooperate with other great powers now at war with Japan with a view to joint action on behalf of the community of nations to maintain peace and security."[149] This response, which was hardly what Stalin was seeking, reflected the waning American interest in—and, on the part of some officials, growing hostility to—Soviet participation in the war with Japan.

There was little coordination between the United States and the Soviet Union on the question of ending the war with Japan. It is true that the two governments agreed on the coordination of military operations. They also concurred on the issue of unconditional surrender, although that was a term subject to different interpretations. But the two sides were not open with each other. Stalin was guarded in informing Truman about Japan's efforts to end the war, short of un-conditional surrender; and the U.S. government did not consult Stalin about the Potsdam Proclamation or ask him to sign it.[150] The most significant failure in co-ordination was that the two main factors bearing on the Japanese surrender—the atomic bomb and Soviet entry into the war—were never considered together, jointly by the two countries, in the formulation of a strategy to end the war.

The Soviet War with Japan

On August 3, Vasilevskii sent Stalin a report on the state of Soviet forces in the Far East. All three fronts would be ready on August 5 for the order to begin military operations; it would take another three to five days to cross the frontier into Manchuria. Taking account of logistical factors and of the weather fore-cast, the best time for the offensive would be August 9–10; Shtemenko notes that this was a slight change from the provisional date of August 11. Vasilevskii wrote that any delay beyond August 9–10 would be inadvisable and asked that final instructions be given to him no later than August 5.[151]

Stalin accepted Vasilevskii's advice, and on August 4 or 5—it is not clear which—he sent the order to launch the attack on August 10 at 18.00 hours Moscow time, or 24.00 hours Transbaikal time. On August 7, however, Stalin sent Vasilevskii a new order, at 16.30 hours (Moscow time), advancing the attack on Manchuria by forty-eight hours.[152] Soviet forces were now to begin their offensive on August 8, not August 10, at 18.00 hours Moscow time, or 24.00 hours Transbaikal time. At 5 P.M. on August 8, Molotov informed the Japanese ambassador that the Soviet Union would consider itself to be at war with Japan "from tomorrow," August 9.[153] By using the expression "from tomorrow," he may have hoped to create the illusion that a few hours remained before the Soviet Union attacked, but the attack started in the first minutes of August 9, Transbaikal time, that is, at 6 P.M. on August 8 Moscow time, one hour after the ambassador had been notified.[154]

Stalin's order to Vasilevskii on August 7 contained no explanation of the change of date, but it seems obvious that it was the atomic bombing of Hiroshima the day before that impelled him to speed up Soviet entry into the war. There was still no Sino-Soviet Treaty to legitimize Soviet entry into the war; nor was there a public request from the United States or Britain to help in the defeat of Japan. (Molotov nevertheless told the Japanese ambassador that the Western Allies had asked the Soviet Union to enter the war in view of the Japanese refusal to surrender.)[155] Yet it was vital for the Soviet Union to enter the war before it was over, in order to ensure that it obtained the gains promised at Yalta. On the evening of August 8, three hours after the Soviet attack had begun, Stalin told Harriman and George Kennan, charge d'affaires at the U.S. Embassy, that "he thought the Japanese were at present looking for a pretext to replace the present government with one which would be qualified to undertake a surrender. The bomb might give them this pretext."[156] This suggests that Stalin believed that the bomb would precipitate a quick surrender by Japan.

Hasegawa claims that Stalin was so stunned by the news of Hiroshima that he refused to see anyone on August 6, and that he was convinced that the bomb would bring the war to an end at once.[157] According to Hasegawa, it was only when Stalin realized that Japan might not surrender immediately that he issued the new order for Soviet forces in the Far East to attack. I do not find this persuasive. Hiroshima was certainly a shock for Stalin, but the fact that there are no entries for August 6 in his Visitors Book does not mean that he saw no one that day. Visitors to Stalin's dacha, where he often held meetings, were not recorded in his Visitors Book. Stalin's daughter Svetlana writes in her memoirs that her father was very preoccupied on the day after the bombing of Hiroshima. When she went to her father's dacha that day, she found that "he had his usual visitors. They told him that the Americans had dropped the first atomic bomb over Japan. Everyone was busy with that, and my father paid hardly any attention to me."[158] It is not clear whether this means August 6 or 7. The bomb was dropped on Hiroshima on the 6th at about 0:15 A.M. Moscow time, so Svetlana is probably referring to August 6. It would have taken time for an assessment to be made of the bombing of Hiroshima and of its likely political effects—after all, it took the Japanese some time to assimilate what had happened. Consultations would have been needed with Vasilevskii and with the Soviet Embassy in Japan before the new order went out. Moreover, one cannot assume that Stalin concluded at once that Japan would surrender immediately. Well-informed senior members of the Truman administration continued to think, even after Hiroshima, that an invasion would be necessary.[159] Stalin surely thought that the bombing of Hiroshima would speed up the Japanese surrender, since he said as much to Harriman. His decision on August 7 to advance Soviet entry by forty-eight hours also indicates that he thought Japan would surrender quickly. But there is no evidence to suggest that on August 6 he thought the war would be over so quickly that it was now pointless for the Soviet Union to attack.

The Soviet Union achieved strategic surprise in its attack on Manchuria. The chief of staff of the Kwantung Army, General Hata Hikosaburō, told his Soviet captors in September: "We did not think that the Soviet Union would suddenly declare war on Japan this year."[160] Soviet forces advanced rapidly from the west, the east, and the north, demoralizing the Japanese with the speed of their advance. The Kwantung Army proved to be weaker than the Soviet planners had expected, but the occupation of Manchuria was even so achieved in remarkably quick time: the campaign has been widely regarded as an outstanding example of military strategy in both conception and execution.[161] The Soviet Army suffered 36,000 casualties (12,000 dead and 24,000 wounded).[162] Japanese losses were higher, with over 80,000 men killed, and about 640,000 taken prisoner.[163]

The impact on Japan of Soviet entry into the war was all the greater because it followed the destruction of Hiroshima. The new Russian documents cannot settle the argument about the relative weight to be given to Soviet entry and the atomic bomb in explaining the Japanese decision to surrender. That explanation has to be sought in Japanese sources. But it is worth pointing out that the new Russian documents—especially the military intelligence reports and the messages from the embassy in Tokyo about Japanese peace feelers—do convey the impression that Japan was very much looking to the Soviet Union for help in ending the war on terms other than unconditional surrender. It does not seem altogether surprising, when one looks at the evidence, that Stalin was worried that the offer of a compromise peace by the United States would bring the war to an end quickly. It is precisely because Japanese government circles looked to the Soviet Union that Soviet entry came as such a shock. For those in the Japanese government who wanted to continue the war, the Soviet attack was a great setback, because Japan now faced the combined military might of all the world's most powerful states. For the peace party, too, the Soviet attack was a blow, because it destroyed any hope of using Soviet good offices to bring the war to an end. There was now no government to which Japan could turn for help in mediating a peace agreement. And Soviet entry came at just the moment when the Americans showed that they could now inflict a new and terrible form of destruction on Japanese cities.

On the morning of August 9, at 11 A.M. (Japanese time)—eleven hours after the start of the Soviet offensive—the United States dropped another atomic bomb on Nagasaki. Early on the morning of August 10, the emperor sided with the peace party and expressed his will that the Potsdam Proclamation be accepted, on the single condition that the emperor's role be preserved. That decision was communicated to the Allies on the same day. The Allied reply, which was agreed to by Moscow, insisted that the emperor be subject to the supreme commander of the Allied Powers but also stated that "the ultimate form of government of Japan shall, in accordance with the Potsdam Declaration, be established by the freely expressed will of the Japanese people."[164] Following a new round of debate in Tokyo, the emperor publicly accepted the Allied terms on August 14. Four days later, on August 18, Imperial General Headquarters ordered Japanese troops to "suspend all operational tasks and stop all hostilities."[165]

On August 19, a cease-fire was agreed between the Soviet forces and the Kwantung Army. Soviet forces pressed on to occupy the territories ceded to the Soviet Union by the Yalta Agreement.[166] They had made very rapid progress in Manchuria, but it was only after August 20 that they occupied the major cities of Changchun, Mukden, and Harbin. They landed troops on airfields at Port Arthur and Dalian on August 22–23 in order to forestall an American attempt to seize those ports; ground forces soon followed. They conducted operations to take over southern Sakhalin (August 11–26) and the northern Kuril islands (August 18–27), meeting stiff resistance before they were able to establish control.[167]

On August 15, Truman sent Stalin a copy of General Order No. 1, which set out in detail the procedures for the surrender of Japanese forces. According to the order, Japanese forces in Manchuria, in Korea north of the 38th parallel, and on Sakhalin were to surrender to the Soviet Far Eastern Command; no mention was made of the Kuril Islands. Stalin replied the following day, August 16, agreeing with the order, as long as Manchuria was understood to include the Liaotung peninsula. He also made two proposals. The first was that Soviet forces accept the Japanese surrender on all the Kuril Islands, which, he said, were to become Soviet possessions under the Yalta Agreement. The second proposal was that Soviet forces accept the Japanese surrender also on Hokkaidō, north of a line between the towns of Rumoi and Kushiro. "This last proposal," he wrote, "has particular significance for Russian public opinion. As is known, the Japanese in 1919–1921 held the whole of the Soviet Far East under the occupation of its forces. Russian public opinion would be seriously offended if Russian forces had no zone of occupation on some part of Japan's own territory." Two days later, on August 18, Stalin received a terse reply from Truman agreeing to his proposal about the Kurils but stating that General Douglas MacArthur, the supreme commander of the Allied Powers, would accept the surrender of all Japanese forces on the home islands.[168]

Stalin was unhappy with Truman's response on Hokkaidō, as he made very clear in his reply to Truman four days later, on August 22: "I must say that I and my colleagues did not expect such an answer from you."[169] He was, moreover, unwilling to give up all thought of landing forces on Hokkaidō. The General Staff had drawn up plans for the Hokkaidō operation, but the meeting of Party and military leaders on June 26–27 had deferred a decision on it.[170] The idea of landing on Hokkaidō presented itself again, now that Japan had been defeated and Soviet forces were occupying southern Sakhalin. Vasilevskii sent a cable to the Stavka about the operation on August 18, and on the same day he assigned to the First Far Eastern Front the mission of occupying the northern half of Hokkaidō and the southern Kurils in the period from August 19 to September 1.[171] The Commander of the Pacific Fleet reported to Vasilevskii on August 19 on his plans for landing two divisions (about 20,000 troops) of the 87th Rifle Corps on Hokkaidō at Rumoi.[172]

On August 20, Vasilevskii reported to the Stavka: "[A]t present I and the command of the First Far Eastern Front are seriously occupied with preparation of the landing operation on the island of Hokkaidō. . . . With your permission we will begin the sea operation shortly after the occupation of the southern part of Sakhalin, on about August 22, 1945."[173] On the same day, Stalin confirmed the order to make the 87th Rifle Corps ready for landing on Hokkaidō.[174] Early on August 21, Vasilevskii instructed his forces to complete their preparations and report back to him on their readiness. He wanted them to be prepared to begin the operation to land on Hokkaidō by the end of the day on the 23rd, though the actual date for the attack would be set by a further order from the Stavka.[175] Everything was being made ready, when Stalin, on the morning of August 22, ordered Vasilevskii to stop preparations. This was the same day on which he replied to Truman, expressing his unhappiness at, but also implicitly accepting, Truman's decision not to permit Soviet occupation of northern Hokkaidō. Vasilevskii sent out an order later the same day, stating that the operation would begin only "on the special orders of the Stavka."[176] On August 23 Vasilevskii reported to the Stavka: "[T]he operation on Hokkaidō will be started only on your further order, before that not one ship will be sent there."[177]

The available documents explain neither Stalin's desire to occupy the northern part of Hokkaidō nor his decision to abort the operation. He had made it clear to Harry Hopkins at the end of May that he wanted a zone of occupation on the home islands. In his August 16 letter to Truman, he stressed the historical reasons for wanting such a zone, but the main reasons were surely strategic. Occupation of northern Hokkaidō, along with southern Sakhalin and the Kurils, would turn the Sea of Okhotsk into a Soviet lake and give the Soviet Union control over the vital La Pérouse Strait, which separates the Sea of Okhotsk from the Sea of Japan. Occupation of northern Hokkaidō would also give the Soviet Union a voice in determining the postwar future of Japan. That Stalin still thought of occupying Hokkaidō after Truman's rebuff shows how important a goal this was for him. In the end, however, he decided that it was not worth risking conflict with the United States. It is true that Japanese resistance on southern Sakhalin and the northern Kuril Islands was delaying the progress of Soviet operations, and the operation to occupy northern Hokkaidō might have dragged on in an embarrassing way; as it was, the occupation of the southern Kurils (the northern territories), which began on August 28, was not completed until September 5.[178] But the political motive of avoiding conflict with the United States appears to have been even more important than the operational delays in Stalin's decision to abort the Hokkaidō operation.[179]

On August 17, before he had received Truman's rejection of his proposal about Hokkaidō, Stalin instructed General K. N. Derevianko, the Soviet representative to General MacArthur, to insist that Japanese forces in northern Hokkaidō surrender to the Soviet Union.[180] Eight days later, on August 25, he changed this instruction, writing to Derevianko: "[Y]ou should not raise the question of Japanese armed forces surrendering to Soviet forces on the northern part of Hokkaidō, as you were instructed to, since President Truman has denied us that."[181] Two days later the chief of staff of the Soviet forces in the Far East sent an order to the commander of the Pacific Fleet categorically forbidding him to send any ships or aircraft whatever in the direction of Hokkaidō, "in order to avoid the creation of conflicts and misunderstandings in relation to the allies."[182]

Stalin secured the territorial gains that had been assigned to the Soviet Union in the Yalta Agreement, but he failed to achieve the additional goal of occupying the northern half of Hokkaidō. It is interesting to compare Stalin's desire to land troops on Hokkaidō with his acceptance of the 38th parallel as the demarcation line in Korea. Truman proposed this line in General Order No. 1, which he sent to Stalin on August 15. Stalin asked for changes in the order with respect to the Kurils and Hokkaidō, but accepted the 38th parallel without demur, even though there were no American troops in the south and Soviet forces had already landed on the northern Korean coast, with more forces to follow before long. It is unclear why Stalin did not press for a change in the line of demarcation or even present the United States with a fait accompli by moving forces south of the parallel. Five years later, that must have seemed like a missed opportunity; but in August 1945 his attention was very much focused on Japan, and evidently the most important goal with respect to Korea was to ensure its independence from Japan, not its subordination to the Soviet Union.[183]

The Sino-Soviet Treaty

When Stalin said that the date of Soviet entry into the war depended on China's acceptance of the terms of the Yalta Agreement, he doubtless hoped that the Americans, in their eagerness for Soviet participation, would put pressure on the Chinese to accept those terms. In the event, the Soviet Union entered the war without having completed negotiations with China. There is no evidence to suggest that Soviet military preparations were at any time held back by the need to reach agreement with the Chinese. On the contrary, the Red Army, under pressure from Stalin, made every effort to be ready for war as soon as possible. When Stalin telephoned Vasilevskii on July 16 to ask him to advance the date of the attack to August 1, he was clearly prepared to attack Japanese forces in Manchuria without a treaty with China; he may have been hoping that an ultimatum signed by all the Allied leaders, including himself, would provide the pretext for entering the war.

T. V. Soong returned to Moscow on August 7 and had his first meeting with Stalin at 10 o'clock that evening, five and a half hours after Stalin had given the order to invade Manchuria. Stalin did not mention this to Soong. He opened the meeting by asking what news Soong had brought.[184] When it became clear that Chinese positions had not changed, Stalin explained at some length the Soviet need for Port Arthur and Dalian, in view of the possibility that Japanese power might be restored. "We need thirty years to build and equip our own ports," he said. "And since now these ports—Petropavlovsk, Olga, Sovetskaia Gavan, and others—are badly equipped, they need to be reequipped and turned into modern naval bases. Japan needs to be held in check, and for that the Soviet Union needs to build strong naval bases on its own territory, which will require a minimum of thirty years. When that time has run out, we will need neither Chinese ports nor Chinese railways."[185] In spite of the break of more than three weeks in the negotiations, very little progress was made at this meeting.

On the following evening, August 8, Harriman discussed the terms of the Sino-Soviet Treaty with Stalin.[186] Harriman had remained in close contact with Soong during the negotiations. He had resisted Soong's efforts to draw the United States into mediating between the Soviet Union and China. At first he had encouraged Soong to reach an agreement, but later he urged him not to make further concessions. Harriman wanted to defend U.S. interests by ensuring that Dalian be maintained as an open port, so that unrestricted trade could take place in Manchuria and in China as a whole.[187] At their meeting on August 8, Harriman told Stalin that Truman was especially concerned that the arrangements for managing the ports and the railways in Manchuria not interfere with the open door policy.[188] He repeated Truman's request for a written statement from Stalin saying that he supported the open door policy. Stalin agreed amiably to this request—though he never fulfilled it. But when Harriman pressed him on the specific arrangements for the ports and railways, Stalin parried his arguments. He insisted that the master of the port of Dalian be a Russian, and that Dalian be included in the Soviet military zone on the Liaotung peninsula.

Stalin and Soong met again on August 10, after the Soviet Union had entered the war. Once Soviet forces had crossed into Manchuria, Stalin had a new means of pressure on China. The Chinese government wanted to be sure that Soviet forces would leave Manchuria when Japan was defeated and therefore had an interest in signing a treaty. Stalin too had an interest in concluding negotiations quickly because the treaty would acknowledge formal Chinese acceptance of the Yalta Agreement and—if only retroactively—provide a rationale for Soviet entry into the war as an ally of China. Stalin opened the meeting by reporting that Japan had announced it would surrender. Japan wished to make a conditional surrender, he said, but it was an unconditional surrender that was needed. It was now high time to sign the agreements, he added.[189] He made a series of specific proposals on the outstanding issues, brushing aside Chinese objections. At the end of the meeting, Soong later reported to Harriman, Stalin told Soong that he had better come to an agreement quickly or the "communists will get into Manchuria."[190] Following intensive negotiations at the level of foreign ministers, Stalin and Soong met again on August 13, and the next day, the two countries signed a Treaty of Friendship and Alliance, along with a series of other agreements covering the railways and ports, as well as Outer Mongolia.[191]

Stalin did not get everything he had pressed for in the negotiations. He compromised on several issues. While the master of the port of Dalian, for example, was to be a Soviet citizen, as Stalin wanted, the port itself would become part of the military zone only in the event of war with Japan. Nevertheless, Stalin had achieved most of what he sought: the independence of Mongolia from China and recognition of Soviet interests in Manchuria. Molotov told Harriman that the Soviet government was satisfied with the results of the negotiations, even though it had made concessions to the Chinese.[192] The subsequent history of political relations between the two countries indicates that the Soviet Union was much happier than China with the agreements reached in these negotiations.[193]

Conclusions

We can now return to the questions raised at the start of this chapter. In his victory address on September 2, Stalin explained his reasons for entering the war against Japan. He emphasized that the Soviet Union, although it had fought against Japan as part of the general war against world fascism, had had its own account to settle with Japan.[194] Japanese aggression against Russia had started in 1904, he said, with the Japanese attack on a Russian naval squadron near Port Arthur. Victory in 1945 had removed the dark stain of defeat in 1905. But the war against Japan was not a mere atavism for Stalin. He was pursuing broader strategic goals as well. He asserted in his victory address that southern Sakhalin and the Kuril Islands would no longer serve as a means of separating Russia from the ocean and as a base for Japanese attacks on the Soviet Far East; they would now serve as a means of direct communication between the Soviet Union and the Pacific Ocean and as a base for defending the Soviet Union against Japanese aggression.

Stalin's vision of the postwar world was very much colored by the revival of German power after World War I and by the dual threat posed to the Soviet Union in the 1930s by Germany in the west and Japan in the east.[195] He foresaw the eventual reemergence of Japanese and German power after World War II but wished to postpone it for as long as possible. He feared that Britain and the United States would seek to restore the power of those two countries in order to counterbalance the Soviet Union. That was why it was important to secure positions that would make it possible to prevent, delay, or counter the restoration of German and Japanese power and to ensure a dominant Soviet position in Europe and in Asia. That also helps to explain why in both Europe and the Far East, Stalin insisted on unconditional surrender, and why he was anxious about the possibility that the Western Allies might conclude separate, compromise peace agreements with Germany and Japan.[196] This is not the place to pursue further the interesting parallels and interconnections between Stalin's policies in Europe and in the Far East. But it is worth noting that the new documentary evidence underlines the importance of Japan in Stalin's conception of the postwar world, and hence the importance of the strategic goals he was pursuing in the war against Japan. This should not be surprising in view of the turbulent history of Russo-Japanese relations, but it has not been reflected in studies of Soviet policy in World War II and the early Cold War, where Germany has received far more attention than Japan.

Stalin emerges from the new documents on the Soviet-Japanese war as very much a realist, assessing international politics in terms of power relations among states. Given the wartime context, this is to be expected. But even where class analysis would be appropriate—as, for example, in judgments about postwar Japanese politics or the character of states in the postwar international system—it is conspicuously lacking. As Jonathan Haslam points out, Stalin appears to have been closer to Malik than to Lozovskii in his interpretation of international politics.[197] Nevertheless, when Stalin gave his most considered analysis of postwar international politics, in his speech on February 9, 1946, he based that analysis on Lenin's theory of imperialism, and in particular on Lenin's prediction that war was inevitable as long as imperialism existed.[198] This view was quite compatible with the realist assumption that war is an intrinsic feature of the international states system. It is difficult therefore to draw a clear distinction, on this specific issue, between Leninist and realist theory; each reinforces the other. That is one reason why it is not always helpful to think of Stalin's foreign policy in terms of a dichotomy between realism and Marxism-Leninism.

One striking aspect of Stalin's policy before and during the war with Japan is his persistence in seeking the agreement of the Allies for what he wanted to do. He was very pleased, for example, when Roosevelt agreed at Yalta to his political conditions for entering the war. He very much wanted the Yalta Agreement to be signed by Roosevelt and Churchill. He tried to conclude the treaty with China in time to enter the war as China's ally. He prepared an alternative to the Potsdam Proclamation to be signed by himself as well as the Western Allies. He asked Truman for a public invitation to join the war; when that was denied, he nevertheless portrayed Soviet entry into the war as a response to the Allies' request for help. He sought Truman's agreement to occupy the southern Kurils and northern Hokkaidō. In all these cases, he was looking for acceptance of the legitimacy of Soviet claims and interests by the Western Allies. He was testing how far he could go without provoking hostility or resistance on their part, establishing the limits of what they would accept. Stalin was of course quite ruthless in pursuing his strategic goals, as his violation of the neutrality pact and his treatment of Japanese peace feelers show. But his abandonment of the Hokkaidō operation indicates that he was willing—even if ungraciously—to acknowledge that there were limits to what the Western Allies would accept. So too does his decision to stop his forces at the 38th parallel in Korea. This suggests that before and during the war with Japan he neither wanted nor anticipated a complete rupture in the alliance.

The second set of questions raised in the introduction to this paper concern the atomic bomb. Contrary to Hasegawa's claim, there is no evidence that calculations about the bomb shaped Soviet policy on entry into the war before August 6. It is true that the planned date of entry into the war was apparently advanced in mid-July from August 20–25 to August 11, but the signs of growing Japanese desperation and Stalin's fears of a compromise peace provide a plausible explanation for this. Stalin may well have believed, when he arrived in Potsdam, that the atomic bomb test had already taken place. He surely understood Truman's cryptic remark about "a weapon of unusual destructive force," and perhaps took it as an indication that the test had been successful. But there is no good evidence that he advanced the date of entry into the war during the Potsdam Conference.

Stalin's decision on August 7 to advance entry into the war by forty-eight hours suggests that Hiroshima took him by surprise and that he was worried by the possibility of an immediate Japanese surrender. Although he almost certainly knew at Potsdam that the atomic test had taken place and had been successful, he may not have grasped that it would take so little time to move from testing to first use; nor does he seem to have understood just how destructive the bomb would be. This is not surprising. Stimson drew a sharp distinction between "the bomb as a merely probable weapon" and "the bomb as a colossal reality."[199] A similar psychology may have been at work in Stalin's case, with Hiroshima as the demonstration of this new "colossal reality."

On August 20, two weeks to the day after Hiroshima, Stalin signed a decree setting up a "Special Committee of the State Defense Committee" to take charge of all work connected with the use of atomic energy, including first of all the building of the atomic bomb.[200] He made Beria the chair of this committee, which was given extraordinary powers to achieve what had now become an overriding priority for the Soviet Union. The leaders of the atomic project had several times during the war advocated the creation of just such a body, but it was the American success in building the bomb and the American use of the bomb in Japan that convinced Stalin of the need for an all-out effort.[201] The decision to set up the special committee marked the beginning of the nuclear arms race that was to dominate world politics for most of the next fifty years.

According to Gromyko, Stalin told him at Potsdam that Washington and London doubtless hoped that it would take the Soviet Union a long time to build the bomb. During that time, he continued, they would use their atomic monopoly to impose their plans for Europe and the rest of the world on the Soviet Union. But "no," said Stalin, "that will not be."[202] Even though we have no contemporary documents to support it, this account rings true. Zhukov records that at Potsdam Molotov expressed a similar sentiment about Truman applying pressure.[203] If this was Stalin's view before Hiroshima, he must have regarded the bombing of Hiroshima and Nagasaki as being directed against the Soviet Union. "They are killing the Japanese and intimidating us," he is reported to have said to Molotov.[204] None of the newly declassified materials give us a good contemporary account of Stalin's reaction to the bombing of Hiroshima. But it seems reasonable to conclude from the analysis in this chapter that Stalin took the view that the United States had used the atomic bomb to thwart Soviet ambitions in the Far East, and that it would try to exploit its atomic monopoly for political gain in the coming years.

It is therefore appropriate, finally, to comment on Soviet foreign policy after the Japanese surrender. Stalin managed to enter the war and secure the terms of the Yalta Agreement, and he presented this as a great achievement in his victory address on September 2. But he did not attain all his goals. He did not gain a Soviet zone of occupation in Japan, nor did he get an effective Soviet voice in governing Japan. It did not take long for Soviet dissatisfaction with this situation to manifest itself. On September 22, during the Foreign Ministers' Conference in London, Molotov, on Stalin's instruction, proposed to Byrnes that the Soviet Union and the United States conclude a treaty against the possible revival of Japanese aggression.[205] When Byrnes asked why, Molotov replied that demobilized Japanese soldiers were not being taken prisoner on the home islands. The Americans were leaving Japanese soldiers at liberty without consulting their allies, he complained. Japan would have at its disposal experienced officers and soldiers and would thus be able to renew aggression in the near future. Byrnes explained to Molotov that the Western Allies were bound by the Potsdam Proclamation (which said that soldiers could return to their homes once they had been disarmed) and by their reply to the Japanese message of August 10 about the status of the emperor. Molotov asked, rather pointedly, which policy the Allies were pursuing with respect to Japan: unconditional surrender or conditional surrender?[206]

A month later, Stalin made clear his deep unhappiness with American policy when he received Harriman at his retreat in Gagra on the Black Sea at the end of October.[207] When Stalin remarked that his offer to land troops on Hokkaidō had been rejected, "it was quite obvious from the tone of his voice and from the expression on his face that he was still very irked at our refusal to permit Soviet troops to land at Hokkaidō."[208] Stalin complained: "[T]he Soviet Union had become an American satellite in the Pacific. This was a role it could not accept. It was not being treated as an Ally."[209] He later went on to ask: "Would it not be better for the Soviet Union to step aside and let the Americans act as they wished in Japan? The Soviet Union would not interfere. For a long time the isolationists had been in power in the United States. He had never favored a policy of isolation, but perhaps now the Soviet Union should adopt such a policy. Perhaps in fact there was nothing wrong with it."[210] This curious remark makes more sense if one recalls a conversation that Stalin had had with Cordell Hull at a banquet in the Kremlin two years earlier, on October 30, 1943. "Later in the evening," Hull writes in his memoirs:

Stalin said that the Soviet Union was not for isolation. I emphasized the soundness of that view by pointing out that isolation had almost ruined my country and his.

The Marshal stressed the necessity for collaboration and cooperation between the United States and Russia in the most sympathetic manner.[211]

Stalin's comment to Harriman was a warning, or a threat, that the Soviet Union might abandon the search for collaboration and cooperation with the United States.

Stalin had by this time decided to adopt a tough line in his dealings with the United States and Britain. This first became apparent in September at the London meeting of the Council of Foreign Ministers, where Molotov took unyielding positions on a number of issues to do with the postwar settlement. On December 9, Stalin wrote from Gagra to Molotov, Beria, G. M. Malenkov, and A. I. Mikoian (the "Quartet") to explain that the policy pursued since the London meeting was essential in dealing with the Western Allies: "It is obvious that in dealing with such partners [*s takimi partnerami*] as the United States and Britain, we cannot achieve anything serious if we begin to give in to intimidation or show hesitation. To get anything from such partners, we must arm ourselves with a policy of tenacity and steadfastness."[212] He claimed in this letter that the policy of tenacity had already yielded results in Europe, but he did not mention Japan or the Far East. He had been very critical of Molotov for being too willing to make concessions on the arrangements for control of occupied Japan.[213] He had been particularly incensed that Molotov had given preliminary agreement to an American proposal for voting procedures in the Commission on the Far East that would have allowed majority voting on the four-member Commission, as long as the United States was one of the majority. In a letter to the "Quartet" from Gagra on November 4, Stalin called this a "swindle" designed to isolate the Soviet Union. He insisted on the principle of unanimity.[214]

"Tenacity and steadfastness" were, in Stalin's mind, the appropriate response to what he saw as intimidation—or the potential for intimidation—on the part of the Western Allies. Although there is no explicit documentary evidence to support the connection, it is clear that the intimidation he feared was diplomatic pressure backed by the atomic bomb.[215] Molotov expressed this fear plainly when he warned in a speech on November 6: "[T]he discovery of atomic energy must not encourage . . . enthusiasm for using this discovery in a foreign-policy power game."[216]

Stalin had striven hard to obtain strategic gains in the Far East, and to ensure that the Soviet Union was not threatened by a revival of Japanese power. He had achieved a great deal by securing the gains promised in the Yalta

Agreement. But he was ultimately frustrated in his efforts to gain a voice in the arrangements for the control and administration of occupied Japan, and, as he feared, the United States did help in the longer term to build up Japan, though as an economic great power, not a military one. Stalin had jockeyed for a strong position in the Far East in the postwar world, but he had achieved only partial success, and now postwar international politics had been transformed by the atomic bomb, which the United States had but the Soviet Union did not yet possess.

The Soviet Factor in Ending the Pacific War

From the Neutrality Pact to Soviet Entry into the War in August 1945

TSUYOSHI HASEGAWA

The Soviet factor in ending the Pacific War has been a neglected subject. Although it has been touched on in the voluminous books and articles on the atomic bomb in American historiography, the discussion has almost exclusively centered on how the Truman administration factored the Soviet Union into its decision to drop the bomb. Left unexplored are the questions of how the USSR was involved in Japan's surrender, what significance the Japanese government attached to the Soviet Union in its foreign and military policy, and how Stalin took the American atomic bomb into consideration in his decision to enter the war against Japan.

This chapter aims to bring the Soviet factor to center stage in the drama of the Pacific War's ending by examining the crucial period from the neutrality pact in April 1941 to the Soviet entry into the war against Japan on August 9, 1945. The process of ending the Pacific War must be examined through the complicated interplays of various actors—Soviet, American, Japanese, and Chinese—and this chapter, although focusing on the Soviet side of the story, attempts to view Stalin's policy in the context of his dealings with Japan, China, and the United States. It argues that although he concluded the neutrality pact with Japan in 1941 to avoid a two-front war in Europe and Asia, he intended to wage war against Japan all along when an opportune moment provided itself. Following the Moscow Foreign Ministers' Conference and the Teheran Conference in 1943, Stalin carefully and methodically took measures to build his case with the Western Allies, and he finally succeeded in obtaining major concessions from President Franklin D. Roosevelt about the territorial and other rewards that would accrue to the USSR for entering the war against

Japan. His objectives were avowedly geopolitical, not ideological, focusing on territorial gains, and control of railways and strategic ports in Manchuria to protect Soviet security against future aggression from Japan. After successfully concluding the Yalta Agreement, Stalin's objective was to join the war against Japan in order to obtain the geopolitical gains promised at Yalta. In other words, for Stalin, the war had to last long enough for the Soviet Union to join it. Nevertheless, he faced four dilemmas in achieving his goal. Although the Soviet government renounced the Soviet-Japanese Neutrality Pact in April, it assured the Japanese that the pact was still in force. This assurance was given so that under the cloak of neutrality, the USSR could secretly transport troops and equipment to the Far East in preparation for war. The first dilemma was how long this deception would work before the Japanese discovered Stalin's true intentions and perhaps launched a preemptive attack on the still unprepared Soviet Army. Second, the tactical need to maintain the façade of neutrality created the strategic problem of how to justify the Soviet attack on Japan in violation of the neutrality pact. Third, Stalin feared that in view of the increasing conflict with the United States over Poland and in view of the increasingly anti-Soviet attitude displayed by the new president, Harry S. Truman, who succeeded Roosevelt in April, the United States might renege on the Yalta Agreement and seek to achieve Japan's capitulation unilaterally before the USSR joined the war. Finally, Stalin had to gain China's acceptance of the Yalta terms that violated China's sovereign rights, a precondition set in the Yalta Agreement for Soviet entry into the war.

This chapter argues that in order to solve the first dilemma, Stalin skillfully and successfully manipulated the policy of the Japanese government, for which Soviet neutrality and later the possibility of Soviet mediation to end the war became the top priority. In fact, by April 1945, the Soviet Union occupied the most prominent place in Japan's foreign and military policy. The chapter also argues that to Stalin, the Potsdam Conference provided a crucial arena in which to resolve three other dilemmas. First, he attempted to obtain Truman's commitment to the Yalta Agreement by assuring him that the Soviet Union was prepared to join the war against Japan. Second, after he failed to achieve China's approval of the Yalta terms in the negotiations preceding the Potsdam Conference, he attempted to mobilize the support of the United States to put pressure on the recalcitrant Chinese. Third, and most important, he expected Truman and Churchill to consult him fully on the joint ultimatum to be issued to Japan, which would override the neutrality pact and provide a convenient justification for waging war on Japan. On all three scores, Stalin failed.

The reason for his failure was the atomic bomb. Before Potsdam, Truman faced his own dilemmas. The first dilemma was how to deal with the Soviet Union. On the one hand, he needed Soviet entry into the war in order to shorten the fighting and reduce the cost in American lives. But, on the other hand, he feared the consequences of Soviet expansion in the Far East, and if possible, he wished to avoid it. The second dilemma was his commitment to the unconditional surrender demand to Japan. In order to shorten the war, especially before the USSR joined it, his advisers recommended, it might be wise to modify the unconditional surrender demand by promising the Japanese that they could retain the monarchical system. But because of the pressure of domestic American public opinion, which was strongly against the Japanese emperor, and, more important, because of his own strong conviction that America's national mission in the Pacific War lay in avenging the humiliation of Pearl Harbor, Truman was not willing to accept this recommendation. The atomic bomb solved these dilemmas. Truman chose not to tell Stalin the whole truth about the atomic bomb and decided to exclude Stalin completely from the deliberations leading to the Potsdam Proclamation, which sought to impose unconditional surrender on Japan. Stalin was totally outmaneuvered by Truman. He belatedly attempted to request an invitation to participate in the Potsdam Proclamation from Truman, but Truman flatly rejected this request.

The result of the Potsdam Conference was a race between the atomic bomb and Soviet entry into the war. The issue was whether the atomic bomb would compel Japan to surrender before the USSR entered the war or whether Stalin would manage to enter the war before the Japanese surrendered. This chapter argues that after the Potsdam Conference, Stalin attempted to change the date of the Soviet attack on Japan twice, first, right after the Potsdam Conference, and second, after the United States dropped the atomic bomb on Hiroshima. The news of the Hiroshima bomb was a great shock to Stalin, who was almost convinced that he had lost the race. But the Japanese attempt to seek Moscow's mediation for peace revived Stalin's hopes. He advanced the date of attack by forty-eight hours, achieving his goal of joining the war just in the nick of time.

Two important issues are outside the scope of this chapter. First, it does not deal with the question of whether Soviet entry into the war or the atomic bombs dropped on Hiroshima and Nagasaki played a more crucial role in Japan's decision to surrender, since this is covered by Chapter 4 in this volume. Second, space does not permit discussion of Soviet military operations in the Kurils, although these operations are important in validating the major argument that this chapter advances: that Stalin's major objective in the war against Japan was to secure the geopolitical gains promised at Yalta.[1]

From the Neutrality Pact to the Yalta Agreement

It was strategic calculations by both the Soviet Union and Japan that led to the conclusion of a neutrality pact in April 1941. Moscow needed peace in the Far East in order to avoid a two-front war if Nazi Germany invaded the Soviet Union. Japan also needed peace in the north if it wished to move south to exploit the vacuum in Southeast Asia created by World War II. When Germany invaded the Soviet Union in June 1941, the Japanese government debated whether it should join Germany and attack the Soviet Union or move south at the risk of war with the United States. In July, the government decided to advance south and not to intervene in the Soviet Union "for the time being," but to make secret preparations for war in case the German-Soviet war provided a favorable opportunity.[2] Japan decided to wait for the ripe persimmon to fall to the ground, as one General Staff officer put it.[3] But to prepare for war against the Soviet Union just in case, the Japanese army implemented a large-scale mobilization of troops along the Manchurian border under the guise of "special maneuvers" of the Kwantung Army, doubling its size from 400,000 to 700,000.[4]

In view of the Japanese reinforcements along the Manchurian border, Stalin was forced to maintain a sufficient number of troops in the Far East, while giving the Far Eastern Military District the strict order to refrain from actions that might provoke military action by Japan.[5] Only when he received reliable information in October that Japan was unlikely to attack the Soviet Union did he send troops from the Far East to the defense of Moscow.[6] On December 7, Japan attacked Pearl Harbor, and the Pacific War began. Stalin must have breathed a sigh of relief, since Japan's war against the United States made it unlikely that Japan would attack the Soviet Union.

Immediately after Japan's attack on Pearl Harbor, the United States requested Soviet participation in the war against Japan, but Foreign Commissar Viacheslav Molotov rejected this request for two reasons. First, with the Soviet Union devoting all its energies to the war against Germany, it could not afford to divert any effort and resources to a war against Japan. Second, the Soviet Union was bound by the neutrality pact with Japan.[7] This did not mean that Stalin did not harbor any intention to wage war against Japan at this time. In fact, when British Foreign Secretary Anthony Eden came to Moscow only ten days after Molotov's rejection, Stalin told Eden that sooner or later the Soviet Union would join the war against Japan. But the best way to enter the war against Japan would be to induce Japan to violate the neutrality pact.[8] Although Stalin made no concrete plans at this time, it is important to note that from the very beginning of the Pacific War, Stalin's intention was to join the war against Japan. Furthermore, it bears remembering that Stalin was already concerned with the potential problem of reconciling the neutrality pact with the war against Japan.

Throughout 1942, Tokyo carefully monitored developments in the German-Soviet war to see if an opportune moment might arise for Japan to attack the Soviet Union. But the persimmon never fully ripened. Japan's policy remained to "maintain tranquility" in the north, and Tokyo rejected the German request to join the war against the Soviet Union.[9] Already in the second half of 1942, the tide of military fortunes had begun to turn against Japan, which lost the battle of Midway in June 1942, and the battle of Guadalcanal in February 1943. From this time on, Japan could no longer afford to wait for a propitious moment to attack the Soviet Union. The positions of the Soviet Union and Japan had reversed. Japan now needed Soviet neutrality more than the USSR needed Japan's. Now it was Stalin's turn to look for the ripe persimmon to fall to the ground.[10]

While Tokyo was interested in enhancing its relations with the Soviet Union in 1943, the Moscow's approach to Japan became noticeably cooler, and Soviet relations with the United States and Britain improved by a few notches.[11] At the Foreign Ministers' Conference at Moscow in October 1943 and at the Big Three Conference at Teheran in November, Stalin promised to enter the war in the Pacific after the Germans had been defeated in Europe, in return for the Western Allies' promise to open a second front.[12] He made it clear that he wanted various "desiderata" in return for Soviet entry into the war, but at this time he did not specify what they were. It is possible to speculate, however, that in private conversation with Roosevelt, he revealed roughly what he wished to obtain, though there is no record of this. In January 1944, Roosevelt explained at the Pacific War Council that he had agreed to grant to Stalin what he was to give later at Yalta.[13] It is important to note that the objectives Stalin revealed to Roosevelt were purely geostrategic gains, not ideological ones, something that Roosevelt found it easy to accept.

Stalin's promise to enter the war against Japan was closely connected with his bargaining to extract concessions from the Americans and the British on the opening of the second front. But it was not merely a negotiating ploy. He had already secretly begun preparing for the war against Japan. As soon as the victory of the battle of Stalingrad became certain in August 1943, the State Committee of Defense ordered the People's Commissariat of Internal Affairs (NKVD) to construct a railway line between Komsomolsk-na-Amure to Sovetskaia Gavan as its top priority project.[14] Stalin thus laid the first foundations for massive transportation of troops and equipment to the Far East. But if he secretly initiated preparations for the war against Japan, he kept his intentions close to his chest, confiding the secret merely to a few key Politburo members such as Molotov and the NKVD chief, Lavrentii Beria.[15]

During 1944, two important reports on Soviet policy toward Japan were written by Ivan Maiskii, former ambassador to Britain, and Iakov Malik, Soviet ambassador to Japan. Maiskii advocated that the USSR's concern in the postwar world should be above all its security, and that for that purpose, the Soviet government should obtain southern Sakhalin and the Kurils. More important was Malik's 73-page report. Malik argued that Japan's defeat was only a matter of time, and that the Soviet Union should act before the United States and Britain dismembered the Japanese empire. According to Malik, the Soviet objectives should be to secure passage to the Pacific by occupying strategic points such as Manchuria, Korea, Tsushima, and the Kurils. He then made twenty-seven specific proposals, which served as the basis for the Yalta Agreement.[16]

The reports by Maiskii and Malik indicate two important points that characterized the fundamental nature of Soviet foreign policy toward Japan during the war. First, the tenor of the reports was overwhelmingly geostrategic rather than ideological. In fact, it appears that both Molotov and Stalin rejected a stridently ideological criticism of Malik's report by Deputy Foreign Commissar Solomon Lozovskii, who charged that it was devoid of any analysis of class struggle in Japan. Second, both Maiskii and Malik believed that the USSR's territorial demands should be based on Soviet security requirements that went far beyond historical legitimacy, enunciated as the Allied war objectives in the Atlantic Charter and the Cairo Declaration. It is important to note that Stalin's objectives were not merely the Soviet dictator's wild plan, but were widely shared by the Soviet foreign policy elite. There was nonetheless an important difference between Maiskii and Malik, on the one hand, and Stalin, on the other. Both Maiskii and Malik thought that the Soviet Union would be able to obtain these gains without participating in the war. But Stalin knew that without waging war on Japan, the Soviet Union would never be able to secure these gains. Stalin never thought it possible to obtain these gains through a peace conference, as these foreign policy advisers had advocated.

While his diplomats believed that Moscow could stand to gain by maintaining neutrality, Stalin was thus secretly planning a war against Japan. In the summer of 1944, he recalled Marshal Aleksandr Vasilevskii to the Kremlin from the Belorussian front and told him that he intended to appoint him commander of the Far Eastern Front for the war against Japan. In September, Stalin instructed the General Staff to conduct a detailed study as to the number of troops, weapons and equipment, logistical support, points of concentration, and possible operational plans in the war against the Japanese forces in Manchuria.[17]

Approximately at the same time, American military planners had mapped out the plan for invasion of Japan. Overcoming disagreements as to the best methods to achieve Japan's capitulation among the services, the Joint Chiefs of Staff approved a two-stage invasion of Japan, first Kyūshū and then a decisive invasion of the Kantō Plain. In that plan, the JCS envisaged collaboration with the Soviet Union as an essential prerequisite. Before the U.S. forces invaded Kyūshū, it was deemed absolutely essential to pin down the Japanese forces in Manchuria and North China. For this purpose, the USSR would have to enter the war against Japan before the United States launched the Kyūshū invasion. Nevertheless, the Soviet military specialists remained exceedingly reluctant to provide the American military planners with necessary information. As far as Stalin was concerned, collaboration with the United States was essential to secure military supplies through Lend-Lease, but he did not want to give the Japanese any opportunity to learn about the Soviet intention, fearing that this would give them a pretext to launch a preemptive attack on the Soviet Union. Thus, when the Combined Chiefs approved the overall strategy for the defeat of Japan at the Quebec Conference in September 1944, they had no choice but to proceed without counting on Soviet participation in the war.[18] Divergences between the United States and the Soviet Union on their respective strategic needs for collaboration became more and more pronounced as the more concrete operations plans were mapped out on both sides.

After the fall of Saipan in July 1944, the Tōjō Hideki government was finally forced to resign, and the Koiso Kuniaki government was formed. As the military situation worsened day by day, the importance Japan attached to the Soviet Union increased proportionally. In September, the government resolved to seek to maintain Soviet neutrality and, if possible, to elevate Soviet-Japanese relations to a higher level. It also attempted to mediate a peace between the Soviet Union and Germany. Foreign Minister Shigemitsu Mamoru decided to send a special envoy to Moscow and Berlin to achieve these goals.[19]

It is interesting to point out the degree of concessions that the Japanese government was willing to make to achieve its policy toward the Soviet Union. It was willing to allow Soviet ships to pass through the Tsugaru Strait and to abolish the Soviet-Japanese Basic Agreement of 1925 as well as the Anti-Comintern Pact and the Tripartite Pact. Japan was thus prepared to abandon its alliance with Germany. Furthermore, it was prepared to accept Soviet activities in Manchuria and Inner Mongolia, give up the coveted Chinese Eastern Railway, and return southern Sakhalin and the northern Kurils to the Soviet Union. The list of concessions indicates that Japan was willing to make drastic concessions, giving up vital interests in Manchuria and sacrificing territories gained by the St. Petersburg Treaty of 1875 and the Portsmouth Treaty of 1905 after the Russo-Japanese War. Nevertheless, it is doubtful whether this list would have satisfied Stalin's voracious appetite. The list said nothing about the South Manchurian Railway, Dairen (Dalian), and Port Arthur. Neither Korea nor the southern Kurils were included. Perhaps the Japanese government still clung to possession of Korea as vital to its interests. As for the southern Kurils, it never occurred to it that Moscow would be bold enough to claim what the Japanese considered to be intrinsically Japanese territory. The Japanese government proceeded on the assumption that the Soviet demand for territories would be limited to those that they could claim on grounds of historical legitimacy, without realizing that the Soviet foreign policy elite were claiming them on the basis of Soviet security requirements.[20]

Not surprisingly, Molotov flatly rejected Japan's idea of sending a special envoy. He explained that Soviet-Japanese relations remained firmly based on the neutrality pact. Besides, receiving an envoy might wrongly signal to the USSR's allies that it was committed to a separate peace with Japan at a time when Stalin was conducting a delicate maneuver by which to extract maximum concessions from the United States in return for his promise to enter the war against Japan.[21] As far as Stalin was concerned, the time to engage in real bargaining with Japan had passed. Negotiations with Japan were useful only to prolong the war. Despite the existence of the neutrality pact, the Soviet Union was definitely "leaning to one side," to use Mao Zedong's famous phrase from a later period.

But the Allied differences had to be adjusted. In September, Stalin raised a question about the Allied decision at Quebec. Obviously disturbed by the Allied military plan, which did not mention Soviet participation in the war, Stalin asked if the United States was still interested in Soviet entry into the war, bluffing that if that was the American intention, it would be fine with the Soviet Union. The U.S. ambassador in Moscow, W. Averell Harriman, hastened to disabuse him of any such misconception. He was eager to please Stalin by confirming the continuing commitment to Soviet entry into the war.[22] Stalin was clearly gambling on the American need to secure Soviet entry into the war to extract maximum concessions from the Americans.

In October, Stalin told Harriman that he could not give a definite date for the Soviet attack on Japan but said that "planning should begin at once." He also requested "food, and fuel for aircraft and motor transport, sufficient to constitute a two to three months' reserve," indicating that he envisaged a short operation. But he was still reticent about his price for entering the war, although he made it clear that "consideration would have to be given to certain political aspects."[23]

On October 15, Stalin held another meeting devoted to the Far Eastern theater with military representatives from the Soviet Union, the United States, and Britain. For the first time, General Aleksei Antonov, chief of the Soviet General Staff, gave a detailed explanation of the Soviet operational plan in the Far East, describing where Manchuria would be invaded, how many Japanese divisions there were in Manchuria and North China, and how many divisions Moscow expected to dispatch to the Far East. He revealed that at present the USSR had thirty divisions in the Far East, but that to obtain a margin of superiority against the Japanese forces, thirty additional divisions would have to be added. Stalin said that for the operation against Japan, the USSR would need stockpiles of food, fuel, rails, and railway stock—essential items that only the United States could supply by sea. Harriman was quick to oblige such requests. Finally, Stalin talked about "political consideration" for Soviet entry into the war against Japan, but did not reveal what this political consideration was at this time.[24]

While he was maneuvering to gain the maximum concessions from the United States, Stalin began a propaganda campaign to prepare the USSR for the impending war against Japan. In his speech on the anniversary of the October Revolution on November 7, he raised the eyebrows of the audience, including the Japanese, by identifying Japan as an aggressor and comparing its attack on Pearl Harbor with the Nazis' invasion of the Soviet Union. A book on the siege of Port Arthur in the Russo-Japanese War was published and favorably reviewed in the Soviet press.[25]

Stalin correctly believed that he could extract concessions from the United States by promising to enter the war against Japan. In a study of the Soviet participation in the war against Japan completed in November 1944, the U.S. Joint Chiefs of Staff concluded that "Russian entry at the earliest possible date" was desirable, considering Soviet military action essential, not only to pin down Japanese forces in Manchuria and North China, but also "to interdict lines of communication between Japan and Mainland Asia."[26]

Finally, on December 14, Stalin named the price for Soviet entry. Harriman asked a question about the "political considerations" that Stalin had referred to previously for Soviet participation in the war. Stalin brought out a map from the next room and said that southern Sakhalin and the Kuril Islands should be returned to the Soviet Union. It should be noted here that Stalin was lumping together the Kurils, which Japan had peacefully acquired from Russia in 1875 in exchange for southern Sakhalin, which Japan had obtained after the Russo-Japanese War in 1905. He justified the claim to southern Sakhalin and the Kurils in terms of the Soviet right to have access to the Pacific Ocean. Stalin then said that the Soviet Union desired leases on the port facilities of Dairen and Port Arthur, the Chinese Eastern Railway, and the South Manchurian Railway. Finally, he demanded recognition of the status quo in Outer Mongolia. Stalin's gigantic ambitions were now fully revealed. His demand for the Kurils clearly contradicted the principle of territorial integrity enunciated by the Atlantic Charter and the Cairo Declaration. His avaricious claims to the railways and ports in Manchuria violated the sovereign rights of China, a major ally of the United States and Britain. But the important fact is that Harriman was not surprised by Stalin's demands, at least at this time. The only concern that the American ambassador expressed was that Dairen should become an international port rather than the port facilities being leased to the Soviet Union. Harriman was more interested in securing the port for U.S. commercial interests than he was concerned with China's sovereign rights. The high-sounding principles in the Atlantic Charter and the Cairo Declaration could be thrown out of the window, as long as the pressing strategic need to secure Soviet entry into the war was assured.[27]

The Yalta Agreement

In February 1945, the Big Three met at Yalta. Roosevelt and Stalin had an unofficial discussion on the Far Eastern question on February 8, during which Stalin presented the demands outlined in his conversation with Harriman. It took Roosevelt merely fifteen minutes to accept them. The Secret Protocol, or Yalta Agreement, that came out of this brief fifteen-minute talk became the foundation of U.S.-Soviet relations in their war against Japan. It stipulated that in return for Soviet entry into the war against Japan on the side of the Western Allies "in two or three months," the status of Outer Mongolia would be preserved; southern Sakhalin would be returned to the Soviet Union; Dairen would be internationalized, "with the preeminent interests of the Soviet Union in this port being safeguarded"; the lease of Port Arthur would be restored to the Soviet Union; the Chinese Eastern Railway and the South Manchurian Railway would be operated by a joint Soviet-Chinese company, taking into consideration the "preeminent interests of the Soviet Union"; China would retain full sovereignty in Manchuria; and the Kuril Islands would be "handed over" to the Soviet Union. The agreement was made conditional on the approval of Chiang Kai-shek.[28]

Stalin was pleased. The Soviet ambassador to the United States, Andrei Gromyko, noted that when Stalin succeeded in obtaining Roosevelt's consent, Stalin was elated, walking back and forth in his room repeating: "Good. Very good!"[29] He had reason to be elated: he had got what he wanted. He had received the approval of Roosevelt and Churchill for his insistence on the principle based on the security demands of the USSR for settling territorial issues in the postwar world, overruling the principle based on historical legitimacy, enunciated by the Atlantic Charter and the Cairo Declaration. To obtain the gains promised at Yalta, however, Stalin had to do two things: to join the war against Japan and to obtain Chiang Kai-shek's acceptance of these terms. The latter condition, which Stalin himself had insisted on including, was advantageous to the Soviet Union, he believed, inasmuch as without Chinese consent, the provisions of the Secret Protocol would inevitably be a bone of contention with China. In addition, the fact that the USSR would regain privileges that the Russian empire had once enjoyed under the tsar, and that had subsequently been abandoned under the Soviet Union, would boost the support of the Soviet people for war against Japan. It would be wrong to assume that the Soviet dictator could impose his will on his people all the time and on all issues. Even Stalin had to be concerned with the reaction of the Soviet people to a war in which they might feel they had little stake.

Moscow's Renunciation of the Neutrality Pact

With the Yalta Agreement concluded and the objectives of the war against Japan established, Stalin now had to prepare for the war. The first question he had to deal with was the neutrality pact. Article 3 of the pact stipulated that unless one party notified the other of the intention not to renew it, it was to be extended for the next five years. Therefore, unless the Soviet Union informed the Japanese government of its intention to abrogate the pact before April 26, it would automatically be renewed, and the deadline was fast approaching.

Lozovskii had already recommended in January that the Soviet government should notify the Japanese that it did not intend to renew the pact. He suggested that lest Japan infer that Allied pressure had forced the Soviet government to take this step, the Japanese should be notified of this before China's foreign minister, T. V. Soong, visited Moscow at the beginning of April.[30]

Stalin faced a dilemma. On the one hand, he had no choice but to renounce the pact before the deadline. Although this renunciation did not free the Soviet Union from its obligation to neutrality until the pact expired in April 1946, at least psychologically and morally, it would diminish the impact of the war against Japan as a violation of the pact and avoid comparison with Hitler's violation of the non-aggression pact between Germany and the USSR. And it would serve as a clear signal to the United States, with whom conflict had emerged over Poland and eastern Europe, of the Soviet commitment to honor the promise made at Yalta to enter the war against Japan.[31]

The renunciation of the neutrality pact, on the other hand, would give the Japanese a clear signal that the Soviet Union intended to join the war against them, and it might therefore trigger a Japanese attack on Soviet forces in the Far East before all the preparations were completed. The Soviet government could explain that even though the pact had been renounced, it would still be in force until it expired in April 1946. This explanation would lead Japan to believe that it was still possible to keep the Soviet Union neutral, while under the cloak of neutrality, the USSR could secretly transport men and matériel to the Far East to prepare for the war. This solution would conveniently satisfy the immediate tactical need to "lull the Japanese to sleep," as Stalin put it, but it still left the strategic question of how to justify the violation of the neutrality pact if the USSR launched a surprise attack on Japan sometime in the summer, as the General Staff was planning to do.

On April 5, Molotov summoned Ambassador Satō Naotake to his office and read the Soviet official statement renouncing the neutrality pact. The exchange between Satō and Molotov indicates that the Soviet government was ambiguous about its intention. Molotov initially indicated that with this renunciation, the Soviet government was freed from any obligation under the pact. Reminded by Satō that Article 3 stipulated otherwise, Molotov immediately retracted his statement and affirmed that the pact would be in force until it expired in April 1946. For the time being, Stalin and Molotov decided to opt for the tactical advantage, leaving the solution of the strategic problem of how to justify the war against Japan for a later date and by other means.[32]

With regard to the risk that this renunciation might trigger a preemptive attack by Japan on the Soviet forces along the Manchurian border, Stalin had received reasonable and unanimous assurances from Malik and other intelligence sources that Japan was so reliant on Soviet neutrality that it was unlikely to attack the Soviet Union. But just in case, before he renounced the pact, he placed the Far Eastern military district on high military alert, instructing that the defenses of railways and major cities, including Vladivostok and Khabarovsk, be reinforced.[33]

Truman's Policy Toward the Soviet Union and the Issue on Unconditional Surrender

By the time Truman assumed the presidency in April 1945, the military and the political situation in Europe and Asia had drastically changed. With victory over Germany now only a matter of time, conflict between the Anglo-American Allies and the Soviet Union over Poland intensified. The military situation in the Pacific changed so favorably for the United States that the Joint Chiefs of Staff became confident that the United States alone could force Japan to surrender without Soviet participation in the war. Stalin became tormented by two possibilities. First, he suspected that the new president, known for his anti-Soviet views, might renege on the Yalta Agreement. Second, he feared that the war in the Pacific might be over before the USSR entered the war.

As the American military planners mapped out concrete plans for the invasion of Japan's homeland, two mutually connected issues were raised and debated among the military and civilian policymakers: how to deal with Soviet entry into the war against Japan and how to define the unconditional surrender demand to Japan.[34] Ambassador W. Averell Harriman and Acting Secretary of State Joseph Grew, among others, took the position that the United States should take a tougher stand toward the Soviet Union. Following Harriman's advice, Truman delivered a stern lecture to Molotov on April 23 to "carry out the agreements" reached at Yalta. His "cock-like" belligerency and the tone with which he spoke shocked the Soviet leaders.[35] Stalin immediately reacted. On April 24, he sent a telegram to Truman rejecting the American-British proposal on the Polish question as a violation of the Yalta Agreement. Stalin's tone was almost as strident as Truman's with Molotov.[36] Furthermore, on May 10, Truman signed a presidential directive to cut off shipments of Lend-Lease goods to the Soviet Union, provoking the Soviet diplomat's reaction that this was a deliberate hostile act designed to break with the Soviet Union.[37]

Truman's belligerent attitude toward the Soviet Union exceeded even Harriman's expectations. Harriman was anxious to use the Lend-Lease issue to extract Soviet concessions on Poland, but not to break decisively with the USSR. Truman, too, had second thoughts about the abrupt deterioration of U.S.-Soviet relations. He sought advice from Joseph Davies and Harry Hopkins, two pro-Soviet advisers to Roosevelt. In order to mend fences with Stalin, Truman decided to send Hopkins to Moscow.[38]

Truman's zigzag course with regard to the Soviet Union reflected the ambivalence of the U.S. policymakers about the role the Soviet Union should play, not merely in Europe but also in Asia. On the one hand, Soviet entry into the war against Japan would hasten the end of the Pacific War. Despite the change in the military fortunes in favor of the United States, the military planners in the War Department favored Soviet entry. But, on the other hand, in view of the troubles over Poland, other policymakers feared the consequences of Soviet military actions in Asia. The U.S. Navy, represented by Admiral Ernest King, commander in chief of the U.S. Fleet, Navy Secretary James Forrestal, and Chief of Staff William Leahy became more skeptical about the utility of Soviet participation in the war. Harriman, Grew, and former President Herbert Hoover were alarmed by the possibility of expansion of Soviet influence in Asia. Truman was torn between these two views, though his sympathy clearly lay with the anti-Soviet camp. He wished to avoid Soviet entry into the war, but he needed it to minimize the sacrifices of American soldiers. This was a conundrum for which Truman could find no easy solution.

The Soviet question was closely connected with the issue of defining the unconditional surrender demand that the United States was imposing on Japan. Groups emerged in policy circles that favored redefining this demand by allowing the Japanese to retain the monarchical system under the current dynasty. In May and June, this view was championed by Grew, who suggested to Truman that the president issue a statement to "clarify" the unconditional surrender demand by allowing the possibility of retention of a monarchical system. But Truman was deeply committed to unconditional surrender and was not prepared to compromise on this point, not only because American public opinion was decidedly against Hirohito, but also because he was determined to avenge the humiliation of Pearl Harbor. Grew's attempt failed, and with this failure, his influence waned. The leadership for redefining unconditional surrender shifted from Grew to Secretary of War Henry L. Stimson.[39]

Japan Seeks to Maintain Soviet Neutrality

Stalin was relieved to know from Ambassador Malik's dispatches that despite the Soviet renunciation of the neutrality pact, the Japanese government was even more eager to seek Soviet neutrality.[40] This did not mean that the Japanese were so gullible as not to notice the transfer of Soviet troops from the European theater to the Far East. The Fifth Section of Japan's Army General Staff was in charge of intelligence on the Soviet military, and on the basis of unassailable evidence, it came to the conclusion that Soviet entry into the war was inevitable.[41] But this view was overruled by the Twelfth Section, in charge of operations, which was to merge with the Army Ministry's powerful Bureau of Military Affairs. The head of the Twelfth Section was Colonel Tanemura Suketaka, a staunch supporter of the continuation of the war, for which he considered Soviet neutrality the most essential prerequisite.

Tanumura expressed his view on the Soviet Union in an influential report he distributed to the army authorities. In this report, he underscored the importance of preserving Soviet neutrality for the continuation of the war with the United States and Britain. Now that the USSR had renounced the neutrality pact, he calculated, there was a 90 percent probability of Soviet entry into the war. Nevertheless, Japan would have no choice but to gamble on the remaining 10 percent. Japan would have to pay a high price in order to entice the USSR into remaining neutral, including the complete abandonment of Manchuria, southern Sakhalin, Taiwan, the Ryūkyūs, the northern Kurils, and Korea. This would be tantamount to returning to the status before the Sino-Japanese War of 1894–95.[42] In including the Liaotung Peninsula (Dairen and Port Arthur) and Korea, Tanemura's concessions were far more extensive than Shigemitsu's concessions in 1944. But Tanemura still operated on the assumption that the

USSR would be satisfied with possession of the territories and rights on the principle of historical legitimacy, not realizing that Soviet thinking far exceeded that.

Tanemura's argument swayed the High Command, which having put all its eggs in the one basket of the last-ditch Ketsu Gō strategy of fighting off the expected U.S. invasion of Kyūshū, considered it essential to keep the Soviet Union out of the war. On April 22, Deputy Chief of Staff Kawabe Torashirō paid a visit to Foreign Minister Tōgō Shigenori and requested that Tōgō do his utmost not only to preserve Soviet neutrality but also to improve Japan's relations with the Soviet Union.[43]

The army's proposal was more than welcome to Tōgō, since he, Navy Minister Yonai, and the Lord Keeper of the Privy Seal, Marquis Kido Kōichi— key members of the peace party—harbored a secret plan to end the war through the mediation of the Soviet government. Although their policy was not clearly defined and they were uncoordinated, they were unanimous in their view that as long as the Allies insisted on unconditional surrender, which they interpreted to be the destruction of the *kokutai* (national polity) centering on the emperor system, the only chance of ending the war while assuring the preservation of the *kokutai* would be Moscow's mediation.

The army and the peace party thus shared the need to rely on the Soviet Union, but their objectives for approaching Moscow greatly differed. The army wanted to assure Soviet neutrality so as to continue the war, while the peace party wished to use Moscow's mediation to end it. It should be emphasized, however, that mollifying the Soviet Union had now become the topmost priority in Japan's foreign and military policy.

The army high command was aware of the desperate situation in which Japan found itself and reluctantly concluded that defeat was inevitable. But they were confident that their Ketsu Gō strategy would be able to inflict such tremendous damage on the invading American forces that the United States would be forced to terminate the war by accepting terms favorable to Japan. However, the high command had to resolve the conflict between the Fifth Section of the General Staff, which by June was predicting that a Soviet attack might occur in late August or in September 1945, and the Army Ministry's Bureau of Military Affairs, which dismissed that possibility. A compromise was reached in early June, and Imperial General Headquarters presented the war plan to the Supreme War Council (Supreme Council for the Direction of the War), which identified the continuation of the war against the United States and Britain as Japan's top priority. While warning of the possibility of Soviet attack in August and September, it insisted on the need to preserve Soviet neutrality. This decision was eventually approved at the imperial conference.

The intransigence with which the army steered Japan's policy toward the continuation of war alarmed Japan's peace party. As the defeat of the battle of Okinawa became apparent, Emperor Hirohito finally abandoned the hope of waging a last decisive battle before ending the war. The peace party made a decisive move to approach Moscow.[44]

The Hopkins Mission to Moscow

To repair the damage done by Truman's anti-Soviet stance, Harry Hopkins was sent to Moscow, where he remained from May 26 to June 6. The Hopkins-Stalin talks dealt with three important issues directly bearing on the Pacific War. First, Hopkins asked Stalin when the Soviet Union would enter the war. Stalin answered that "the Soviet armies would be in a sufficient state of preparedness and in position by August 8, 1945." This statement has been taken by many historians as Stalin's pledge to attack Japan on August 8; and thus that the actual Soviet attack on August 9 was exactly what Stalin had promised Hopkins in May. This is hardly the case. What Stalin spoke of was the completion of "a state of preparedness" by August 8, not the definite date of attack, which would be determined by a number of intangible factors, such as weather and the completion of negotiations with the Chinese.[45]

The second question was the issue of unconditional surrender and the position of the emperor. When Hopkins asked about unconditional surrender, Stalin responded that the USSR would prefer this, since it would mean the complete military destruction of Japan. As for the emperor system, Stalin categorically stated that he favored the abolition of the emperor system.[46] Hopkins reported to Truman: "Stalin made it quite clear that the Soviet Union wants to go through with unconditional surrender and all that is implied in it. However, he feels that if we stick to unconditional surrender the Japs will not give up and we will have to destroy them as we did Germany."[47]

Stalin's position on unconditional surrender and the emperor system suggests the fundamental objective that Stalin pursued in waging war against Japan. He was determined to destroy Japan's military potential and weaken Japan's political structure so that Japan would never again pose a security threat to the Soviet Union. Ironically, Stalin and Truman shared the same value in demanding the unconditional surrender of Japan. But in Stalin's case, there was another motivation behind demanding unconditional surrender. He knew that doing so would prolong the war.

The third important question raised by Stalin was the question of "zones of operations for the armies and zones of occupation in Japan." He took it for granted that the Soviet Union would share in the occupation, as it had in

Germany. Hopkins did not reject this suggestion, and proposed that the question of surrender and occupation of Japan be discussed at the forthcoming Big Three meeting between Truman, Churchill, and Stalin.[48] Then Hopkins made an important proposal to Stalin: he promised the question of a U.S.-Soviet joint ultimatum to Japan would be placed on the agenda of the Big Three meeting.[49] According to the American version, "Mr. Hopkins said he thought at the next meeting of the three heads of Government all these matters should be discussed." But the Russian version is more specific, stating: "Hopkins said that at the next meeting Marshal Stalin and Truman can discuss possible proposals for Japanese capitulation and also plans for occupation of Japan, and other urgent matters." [50] This is an enormously important point that historians have previously ignored. Hopkins promised the possibility of a joint ultimatum to Japan at the Potsdam Conference and gave Stalin the impression that the United States had already agreed to let the USSR participate in Japan's occupation. In Stalin's mind, this invitation gave him a perfect solution to the problem that the Soviet government had been struggling with. It had explained to the Japanese government that the neutrality pact was still in force, while Stalin and his close advisers intended to launch a surprise attack on Japan violating it. The invitation to the joint ultimatum by the Allies would give Stalin a perfect justification for the violation of the neutrality pact.

Secretary of War Henry L. Stimson's Draft
Proposal for the Ultimatum to Japan

When Truman met T. V. Soong in early June, he informed him for the first time of the contents of the Yalta Agreement and suggested that China should come to an agreement with the Soviet Union, since Stalin had told Hopkins that he would support Nationalist China as the sole legitimate power in a unified China. When Soong asked Truman if he was contemplating issuing an Allied joint declaration specifying the terms of surrender, Truman answered that such a general statement "would be both necessary and desirable, but he thought it should be done when the Soviet Union entered the war." At this stage, Truman was clearly committed to the Yalta Agreement and desired Soviet entry into the war.[51]

On June 18, Truman held a military conference at the White House to hear from the military leaders about plans for the invasion of Japan. General of the Army George C. Marshall said that for Japan to capitulate, short of complete military defeat, it would, in addition to bombing and naval blockade, have to be faced with a U.S. landing in the home islands and "entry or threat of entry of Russia into the war." Although Marshall intentionally gave Truman the lower numbers of estimated American casualties, even these numbers must have had a sobering effect on the president. In the end, Truman approved only Operation Olympic, suspending his judgment on the second, final stage, Operation Coronet.[52]

But some policymakers were already exploring the possibility of amending the unconditional surrender terms as an alternative to invasion. Forrestal submitted this proposal to the president on June 13, and Grew met Truman on June 18, telling him that "the preservation of the Throne and non-molestation of Hirohito" would be "the irreducible Japanese terms." On both occasions, Truman refused to accept their recommendations and deferred the issue either to a consensus on the part of the state, war, and navy secretaries or to James Byrnes, soon to be secretary of state.[53]

After the White House meeting that approved Operation Olympic on June 18, Stimson took an active role in amending the unconditional surrender demand. Unlike Grew, who was by then marginalized as an influential policy adviser, Stimson brought with him the formidable influence of military planners. On June 26, the Committee of Three—Henry Stimson, James Forrestal, and Joseph Grew—approved the basic outline of Stimson's rough draft, but it created a subcommittee headed by Assistant Secretary of War John McCloy to work out a more detailed draft. During the two-day subcommittee meetings, it was the War Department's Operations Division that played a key role in writing the final version of the draft, which was submitted by Stimson to the president on July 2.[54]

Three important points should be noted in Stimson's draft proposal. First, it called for unconditional surrender, but the formulation of this demand was changed to "unconditional surrender of the armed forces." Second, it contained a provision that allowed the Japanese to retain "a constitutional monarchy under the current dynasty." Third, it envisioned the Soviet Union as one of the signatories of a joint ultimatum, and phrases about Soviet contributions to the war effort were inserted in brackets in anticipation that the Soviet Union would participate.[55]

It should be noted that the Operations Division, which did not know of the ongoing atomic bomb project, except for McCloy, contemplated five possible timings for issuing the ultimatum, and concluded that "the best time would be immediately after Russia's entry into the war." The Operations Division therefore suggested: "It would be very desirable if by prior agreement, perhaps arising from the next conference, the proclamation could be tied in with Russian entry into the war. If this date could be about 15 August to 1 September and if surrender were accepted, the Allies would be in the best military position to exploit the situation."[56] The Operations Division's timing coincided uncannily with what Stalin must have been thinking about the timing of a joint ultimatum.

Although the Operations Division had no knowledge of the atomic bomb, McCloy knew about it. What McCloy wrote to Stimson is revealing about their thinking about the role of the atomic bomb in relation to Japan's surrender. McCloy wrote: "You will appreciate that this has no relation to S–1 [Manhattan Project] element but as it discussed other factors which relate to the timing, I think that the S–1 element can be readily introduced in it."[57] The meaning of McCloy's memo is somewhat ambiguous. It could be taken as an indication that McCloy and Stimson thought of the threat of the atomic bomb as an additional element for inducing Japan to surrender. In that case, the atomic bomb and Soviet entry into the war would be complementary factors. But it could also mean that the atomic bomb could serve as an independent factor, detached from Soviet entry into the war, and that the warning should be timed with the use of the atomic bomb, not with Soviet entry into the war. This important question needs further study.

The Hirota-Malik Negotiations

Japan's Foreign Ministry gingerly explored the possibility of terminating the war by unofficially contacting Ambassador Malik. As far as Tōgō was concerned, before he officially approached Moscow, he had to know the Kremlin's assessment of its relations with Japan. Thus began a clumsy, bizarre attempt on Japan's part to conduct unofficial negotiations by sending the former prime minister and foreign minister Hirota Kōki to Ambassador Malik in June.

Hirota's mission was never clearly specified. He was to sound out Soviet intentions with regard to Japan's wish not only to keep the Soviet Union out of the war but also to develop closer friendly relations by settling outstanding bilateral issues and making major concessions with regard to rights and territories in East Asia. But because of the fear of alienating the army, he was enjoined from requesting Moscow's mediation to terminate the war.[58] Hirota pursued the elusive Soviet ambassador in Hakone and the Soviet Embassy in Tokyo with persistence, and yet when they met four times in June, Hirota did not reveal anything concrete. While Malik kept insisting that he would not be able to do anything without Japan's specific proposals, Hirota dwelled on generalities, repeating that Japan would consider any specific requests from the Soviet side.[59]

Details of these fruitless negotiations do not concern us here. What is important is to place the negotiations in the context of Stalin's overall policy toward Japan. Having closely monitoring Malik's detailed reports about the first two meetings, Molotov sent his instructions to the ambassador on June 15. Molotov enjoined Malik from taking the initiative in seeking meetings with Hirota. "If he again requests a meeting," Molotov ordered, "then you may receive him and listen to him. If he again talks about general matters, you must limit yourself to stating that you will inform Moscow of the talks at the first possibility (but through diplomatic pouch). You should not go beyond that."[60] Molotov's intention is unmistakable: he wanted to use the Hirota-Malik negotiations to prolong the war. Stalin was directly involved in this. A photocopy of Molotov's message bears his handwritten note "To Stalin, Request approval, V. Molotov" and Stalin's signature indicating his approval.

By sending Hirota to Malik, Japan fell right into the trap of Stalin's machinations to prolong the war. The Hirota-Malik negotiations represented a gross failure of Japan's diplomacy at this critical juncture.

Stalin Decides to Attack Japan and Japan Requests Moscow's Mediation

On June 22, the emperor summoned the so-called Big Six—Prime Minister Suzuki Kantarō, Foreign Minister Tōgō Shigenori, Army Minister Anami Korechika, Chief of the Army General Staff Umezu Yoshijirō, Navy Minister Yonai Mitsumasa, and Chief of the Navy General Staff Toyoda Soemu—to the Imperial Palace.[61] At the outset of this meeting, Hirohito asked their views about the possibility of terminating the war. Although Hirohito's opinion was couched in the form of a question, such direct intervention by the emperor was unprecedented. At the end of the meeting, Hirohito urged them to proceed with the negotiations with the Soviet Union. However, Hirota's two subsequent meetings with Malik failed to produce any results.[62]

On June 26 and 27, Stalin convened a combined conference of the Politburo, the government, and the military, at which the closely guarded secret decision to wage war against Japan was revealed and adopted as government policy. The General Staff's recommendation of a simultaneous all-out thrust from three fronts toward the center of Manchuria also received final approval.[63] On June 28, three directives were issued by Stalin, the first to the commander of the Far Eastern Front to complete all the preparations for an attack by August 1 and the second and the third to the commander of troops of the Maritime groups and the commander of the Transbaikal Front respectively to complete the preparations for attack by July 25.[64]

Only after the USSR had made the final decision did the Japanese government belatedly decide to send Prince Konoe as the emperor's special envoy formally to request the Soviet government's mediation to terminate the war. The war party in the Big Six (Anami, Umezu, and Toyoda) gave their tacit approval for this secret mission without informing their subordinates, but in view of radical staff officers' expected opposition, the cabinet could not come up with specific conditions for the termination of the war. Konoe welcomed this arrangement, since the absence of specific instructions gave him wide leeway. He assembled a handful of trusted advisers and drafted a negotiating position that made the preservation of the *kokutai* the sole condition. It recommended territorial concessions except for Japan's homeland, acceptance of a democratic form of government headed by the emperor, acceptance of an occupation government and occupation force for a limited period, acceptance of punishment of war criminals by the occupation powers, and complete disarmament for a definite period of time. Preserving the *kokutai* was defined as perpetuating the emperor system, but it was conceded that if it came to the worst, Hirohito's abdication should be considered. It is important to note that this was broadly compatible with Stimson's draft proposal for the Potsdam Proclamation, described above.[65] Stalin had no knowledge of Konoe's draft, of course, but from Malik's dispatches, he must have known that a powerful group around the emperor advocated surrender on condition that some form of the emperor system be preserved. This would doom Stalin's plan and made it all the more imperative for him to insist on unconditional surrender.

On July 12, Tōgō sent an "extremely urgent" and "strictly secret" telegram to Satō in Moscow, instructing the ambassador to see Molotov immediately. Tōgō told Satō to present the message to Molotov, informing him that it was the emperor's desire to terminate the war. The emperor asked the Soviet government to accept Prince Konoe Fumimaro as his special envoy, who would go to Moscow to seek Soviet mediation to terminate the war. Tōgō made it clear, however, that so long as the Allies demanded unconditional surrender, Japan would have "no alternative but to fight on with all its strength for the honor and existence of the Motherland."[66]

Tōgō's telegrams and Satō's replies were intercepted by the American code-breaking operation known as Magic. The Magic decrypts of the Satō-Tōgō exchanges were immediately delivered to the highest American policymakers, including Truman (through Leahy), Byrnes (who had been sworn in as secretary of state on July 3), Stimson, McCloy, and Forrestal. Finding it significant that the Japanese government indicated its willingness to terminate the war in the emperor's name, Stimson, Forrestal, and McCloy attempted to persuade the president to allow the Japanese to retain a constitutional monarchy to speed up Japan's surrender. Truman and Byrnes, who were wedded to unconditional surrender, rejected their recommendation.[67] Clearly, it was Truman and Byrnes who called the shots on this issue. Stimson, who was not even invited to attend the Potsdam Conference, was excluded from the decision-making process.

Stalin closely watched these events, which were moving with breathtaking speed, and carefully planned his next move. He initially thought that he would not be able to conceal his intention to wage war against Japan from the Japanese beyond the first weeks of July.[68] He must have been delighted to learn that the Japanese were still requesting Moscow's mediation to terminate the war in the middle of July. Stalin exploited this request to further prolong the war, but he was keenly aware that Japan's surrender was imminent. He was also keeping abreast of intelligence reports from Beria concerning the progress of the American atomic bomb project. The Americans were close to possessing a nuclear weapon. Stalin must have been consumed by the fear that the war might end before the Soviet Union could join the fray. Before the Potsdam Conference began, Stalin called Vasilevskii in Chita from Potsdam, presumably using a military telephone line, and asked the commander of the Far Eastern Front if it would be possible to move up the date of attack by ten days from the August 11 set by the Military High Command, or Stavka. Vasilevskii answered that "the concentration of the troops and the transportation of essential war supplies would not allow" the change. Stalin for the time being accepted Vasilevskii's cautious judgment.[69]

Two obstacles still stood in the way of the Soviet attack plan. The first was the neutrality pact. Stalin had to come up with an excuse that would override this commitment. At the end of May, it should be recalled, Hopkins had suggested the possibility of placing the specific surrender terms on the agenda of the Potsdam Conference. Just as the United States had carefully prepared a draft ultimatum under Stimson's leadership, Stalin also ordered the Foreign Commissariat to work on a draft of its own. In Stalin's mind, this joint ultimatum would have cardinal importance. Not only would it justify the violation of the neutrality pact, but, if the timing of the issuance was well coordinated with the Soviet military plan, it would also serve as a declaration of war against Japan.

The second obstacle was the provision in the Yalta Agreement that made Chiang Kai-shek's consent a precondition for Soviet entry into the war. The provisions of the Yalta Agreement grossly violated the sovereign rights of the Chinese government. Although Chiang Kai-shek was informed about the Yalta Agreement weeks after the conference, he was not formally told of its specific provisions until June 15.[70] The Chinese Foreign Minister, T. V. Soong, arrived in Moscow on June 30, and the Stalin-Soong negotiations began two days later. Stalin needed an agreement with the Chinese to fulfill the obligations of the Yalta Agreement, and he was eager to close the deal before he left Moscow for Potsdam. But Soong was adamant about China's rights with respect to Outer Mongolia and railways and ports in Manchuria. Finally, the negotiations were broken off, and Stalin and Molotov left for Moscow to meet Truman and Churchill at Potsdam. The Yalta provision on Chinese consent, which he himself had inserted to advance Soviet interests in China, now came to haunt Stalin.

Thus, the Potsdam Conference loomed large as the crucial moment for Stalin's plan to wage war against Japan. He expected to close the deal by using the bait of Soviet participation in the war to extract concessions from Truman, as he had done successfully with Roosevelt at Yalta.

The Potsdam Conference

The Truman-Stalin Meeting on July 17

Stalin arrived in Berlin on July 16. He immediately asked, through Truman's special assistant Joseph Davies, to meet Truman that evening. Davies was horrified to learn, however, that Truman did not want to see Stalin that evening. According to Davies, Stalin was "tired, worried and irritated over something." We do not know what led Truman to shun such an important meeting, but it is possible to speculate that he was eagerly waiting for the news of the atomic test at Alamogordo.[71] At noon on the following day, Stalin had the first meeting with the American president in Truman's "Little White House" in Babelsberg. According to Charles Bohlen's note, at this meeting, Stalin, "reverted to the Yalta Agreement concerning Soviet entry into the Pacific war and told the President that the Soviets would be ready for such entry *by the middle of August*, but said that prior to acting they would need to complete their negotiations and reach agreement with the Chinese [emphasis added]."[72] It is important to note that it was Stalin who without Truman's prodding volunteered to enter the war as he had pledged at Yalta, and that it was Stalin who brought up the issue of the Sino-Soviet negotiations. But according to the Soviet record, it was Truman who requested that the USSR join in the war against Japan. The Soviet record states: "Truman said [that] . . . the United States expects assistance from the Soviet Union. Stalin answered that the Soviet Union is prepared to enter into action *by the middle of August* and that it will keep its word. Truman expressed his satisfaction on this matter and asked Stalin to tell him about his negotiations with Soong."[73]

In contrast to the Bohlen note, according to the Soviet version, Truman requested Soviet entry into the war and Stalin complied with this request. Also, the Soviet record takes the view that it was Truman who asked about the progress of the Sino-Soviet negotiations. The Bohlen note then records that Stalin talked about the state of negotiations with the Chinese. He assured Truman that the Soviet Union would stand firm on its pledge to support Chinese sovereignty in Manchuria under the Nationalist government. Stalin then explained in detail the current conditions of the Sino-Soviet negotiations. All these portions are omitted from the Soviet record.[74] According to the Soviet version, Stalin said: "[T]he Chinese do not understand what constitutes Soviet preeminent interests in the railways and ports in Manchuria"; according to Bohlen's notes: "Chungking did not understand horse trading; they were very slow and tried to wrangle every little thing. They did not seem to be aware of the big picture." The Soviet version has Truman express the desire that the USSR and the Chinese would soon come to an agreement, but according to the Bohlen notes: "The President and Secretary Byrnes both indicated that the main interest of the United States was in a free port." Stalin expected Truman to support the Soviet demands, which, as far as he was concerned, were etched in stone in the Yalta Agreement, and to put pressure on the Chinese in return for the firm commitment he had made to enter the war. He was immediately disappointed, because although Byrnes committed himself to the Yalta Agreement, he warned that the United States would not support any provisions that went beyond that.[75]

Differences between the two versions speak volumes about the different expectations each leader had of the other. Stalin felt that Truman should feel grateful for his commitment to enter the war "by the middle of August," just as FDR had felt grateful for his commitment and rewarded the USSR with rights and concessions at China's expense. For this commitment, he expected Truman to reward him by putting pressure on the Chinese to come to an agreement with the USSR. But as far as Truman was concerned, Soviet entry into the war against Japan was an obligation under the Yalta Agreement. He did not feel grateful for Stalin's assurance that the USSR would do so. Moreover, he had doubts about the consequences of Soviet entry into the war in the Far East. He was thus in no mood to help Stalin reach an agreement with the Chinese. Not only did he not help the USSR on this matter, but also he made a point of disagreeing with Stalin's attempt to establish Soviet preeminence in Dairen.[76] He wrote in his diary: "[H]e had some more questions to present. I told him to fire away. He did and it is dynamite—but I have some dynamite too which I'm not exploding now."[77] Truman's memoirs explained: "[W]e might know more about two matters of significance for our future effort: the participation of the Soviet Union and the atomic bomb. We knew that the bomb would receive its first test in mid-July. If the test of the bomb was successful, I wanted to afford Japan a clear chance to end the fighting before we made use of this newly gained power."[78] Truman did not come to Potsdam to actively seek Soviet entry into the Pacific war, which to him remained an insurance policy. In fact, he had profound misgivings about Soviet involvement. He wanted to avoid it if at all possible, which hinged on the atomic bomb test.

The first Stalin-Truman conversation also contained another important piece of information: the date of the forthcoming Soviet attack on Japan. Stalin at first explained that the Soviet Union was ready to join the war by the second half of August. Toward the end of his conversation, however, according to the Bohlen note, Stalin suddenly reverted to the question of Soviet entry into the war, "Stalin repeated that the Soviets would be ready in mid-August, as was agreed at Yalta, and said they would keep their word."[79] There was a discrepancy between Stalin's two statements on the date of Soviet entry into the war: "by the middle of August" or "in mid-August." The former might mean that Stalin had in mind August 11 as the day of attack as set by the Stavka, but Truman took it to be August 15. If he was interested in forcing Japan's surrender before the USSR entered the war, he thus had to do it before August 15. This gave him a benchmark against which to construct a timetable.

The Truman-Stalin Meeting on July 18

After the meeting with Truman on July 17, Stalin had a separate meeting with Churchill. As it turned out, Stalin revealed to the prime minister a piece of confidential information about Japan's peace overtures to Moscow. When Churchill asked why he had not conveyed this news directly to Truman, Stalin answered that he had feared that Truman might think "that the Russians were trying to influence him towards peace" or "that Russia was reluctant to go to war."[80] On July 18, when Truman paid a return visit to Stalin's villa, Stalin revealed the information he had shared on the previous day with Churchill: the Japanese had asked Moscow to mediate in ending the war. He showed Truman Satō's note that explained the emperor's desire to terminate the war but warned that the demand for unconditional surrender would force Japan to fight to the bitter end. Stalin asked Truman if it was worthwhile answering this communication. Truman answered that he had no respect for the good faith of the Japanese. "Stalin pointed out that the Soviet Union was not at war with Japan and that it might be desirable to lull the Japanese to sleep, and possibly a general and unspecific answer might be returned, pointing out that the exact character of the proposed Konoye [sic] mission was not clear. Alternatives would be that they might ignore it completely and not answer, or send back a definite refusal." Truman said that the first course of action—asking for clarification—would be satisfactory.[81]

Truman had already known from the Magic intercepts about Japan's overtures to Moscow. It is not clear whether Stalin knew that the Americans were eavesdropping on Japan's diplomatic dispatches, but he may have had an inkling of it. Whether he knew of or suspected the existence of the Magic, however, he was in any case trying to impress Truman with his goodwill. In the end, it was Truman who suggested the course Stalin had all along intended to take: not to reject, not to ignore, but to reply to the Japanese that the purpose of the Konoe mission was unclear, in order "to lull the Japanese to sleep."

The Atomic Bomb Test in New Mexico

The first news of the successful detonation of the atomic bomb at Alamogordo on July 16, New Mexico time, reached Stimson on the evening of July 17, shortly after the first session of the Potsdam Conference was over. He brought the news to President Truman on the morning of July 18. But the first reports were so sketchy that it was not until General Groves's full report arrived on July 21 that the atomic bomb factor began to influence the American decisions.

The news of the successful atomic bomb test solved the fundamental dilemmas that had vexed Truman. With the atomic bomb, the president became confident that the United States could unilaterally force Japan to surrender without the Soviet Union. In fact, it became important to exclude the Soviet Union from the joint ultimatum and to drop the bomb before the USSR joined the war. Truman therefore did not even tell Stalin that the United States now possessed the atomic bomb. He only told him during the recess of the Potsdam Conference on July 24 that he now had in his possession "a new weapon of unusual destructive force."[82] More important than this half-truth about the atomic bomb in terms of arousing Stalin's suspicion was Truman's handling of the Potsdam Proclamation. Truman was now determined to impose unconditional surrender on Japan without any consultation with the Soviet Union. The crucial question regarding the exact process in which the final form of the Potsdam Proclamation was adopted is not clear. We know that the initial proposal to strike out the promise regarding "a constitutional monarchy under the present dynasty," as Stimson's original draft had it, came from the Joint Strategic Survey Committee (JSSC) in Washington. This proposal met with an angry reaction from the Operations Division, which presented a counterproposal by amending JSSC's amendment to read: "The Japanese people will be free to choose whether they shall retain their Emperor as a constitutional monarchy."[83] When the Joint Chiefs of Staff met on July 16 and 17 at Potsdam, they unanimously adopted the JSSC's proposal. The promise of a constitutional monarchy disappeared from the Potsdam Proclamation.

It is not clear who was behind this amendment. Although no evidence exists, it is possible to speculate that the real actors working behind the scenes for this were Truman and Byrnes. Tōgō's July 12 dispatch to Satō informing him of the emperor's wish to terminate the war jolted Stimson and McCloy with excitement. Stimson sent a memo to Truman on July 16, and urged Truman to retain the original phrase promising a constitutional monarchy in the ulti-matum. Truman told Stimson to see Byrnes. When Stimson went to see the secretary of state on the following day, Byrnes rejected Stimson's proposal. According to Stimson, "He [Byrnes] outlined a timetable on the subject [of a] warning which apparently had been agreed to by the President, so I pressed it no further."[84] Furthermore, Byrnes and Truman struck out the passage from the text that the Joint Chiefs of Staff recommended that indicated that the ultimate form of government would be left to the Japanese, thus making the text even harsher to those in Japan who advocated the preservation of the monarchical system.[85] Why did Truman and Byrnes write an ultimatum that demanded un-conditional surrender without any reference to the emperor's status that they knew full well that the Japanese government would surely reject? It is impor-tant to remember that the order to drop the atomic *bombs* (note the plural) was issued by the acting chief of staff, General Handy, with the prior approval of Stimson and Marshall, to General Carl Spaatz, commander of the U.S. Army Strategic Air Forces, on July 25, one day before the Potsdam Proclamation was issued. If one takes into consideration the following five crucial facts—(1) that Truman knew that Japan would reject unconditional surrender; (2) that the order to drop the atomic bombs was issued on July 25; (3) that the Potsdam Proclamation was issued on July 26; (4) that the atomic bombs were ready to be dropped in the first week of August; and (5) that Truman knew that the USSR would enter the war on August 15—two conclusions are inescapable: (1) that the purpose of the Potsdam Proclamation was to justify the dropping of the atomic bombs, and (2) Truman wanted to drop the bombs before the USSR entered the war.[86]

Truman Issues the Potsdam Proclamation

Stalin's suspicion was piqued by Truman's half-truth about the atomic bomb, since he knew full well from his intelligence source what Truman was talking about. But an even greater shock awaited Stalin. Stalin had wished and expected to be asked to affix his signature to the joint ultimatum, which would serve as the Soviet declaration of war against Japan and justify the violation of the neutrality pact. He fully expected to be consulted on the joint ultimatum. In anticipation of the discussion on the joint ultimatum, Stalin had come to Potsdam with a Soviet draft for the ultimatum, which began: "The time has come when the governments of the allied democratic countries—the United States of America, China, Great Britain, and the Soviet Union—have recog-nized the necessity of declaring their attitude to Japan." It went on: "Eight years ago, Japan attacked China. . . . After that Japan treacherously attacked the United States and Great Britain. . . . Japan used the same method of perfidious surprise attack as forty years ago when it attacked Russia." The aggressive plans of the Japanese militarists had been thwarted, however, by the "tenacious resistance of the Chinese people and the courageous struggle of the American and British armed forces." The draft then stated: "The United States, China, Great Britain, and the Soviet Union consider it their duty to come forward with joint decisive measures that ought to lead to an end to the war." Finally, it called upon Japan to "lay down its arms, and surrender unconditionally."[87]

The document was filled with effusive praise of the Western Allies, closely linking Soviet interests with theirs. This draft indicates how badly Stalin wished to be invited to participate in the joint ultimatum. There remains one question, however. If Japan's last hope was to end the war through Moscow's mediation, didn't Stalin fear that the issuance of the joint ultimatum might bring Japan to surrender prematurely before the USSR joined the war, by shattering Japan's last hope? In order to prevent this, Stalin had two escape hatches. First, Stalin must have hoped that the issuance of the ultimatum might be postponed to coincide with the Soviet attack. This expectation was by no means far-fetched, since, as stated above, even the Americans, or, more precisely, the Operations Division of the War Department, which had composed Stimson's draft of the Potsdam Proclamation, had originally envisaged that the optimal time to issue the ultimatum was at the moment of Soviet entry into the war. Second, the draft itself contained a provision that would likely prevent Japan's premature surrender. It called for Japan's unconditional surrender, and Stalin knew from Tōgō's telegrams what Truman and Byrnes knew, that is, that if the Allies insisted on unconditional surrender, Japan would fight the war to the bitter end. To make it more difficult for Japan to accept surrender, he would therefore definitely insist on elimination of the emperor and the emperor system, as he had said at his meeting with Hopkins in May.

All this careful planning came to naught, because Truman completely excluded Stalin from the deliberation of the joint ultimatum, although he fully consulted Churchill and the British delegation behind Stalin's back. Finally, the Potsdam Proclamation, without Stalin's signature and with the unconditional surrender demand but without promising a constitutional monarchy, was issued on July 26. The text of the proclamation was released to the press even before Byrnes sent it to Molotov. Molotov immediately telephoned Byrnes and requested that the release of the proclamation be postponed. Byrnes told Molotov that it was too late, since the text had been released to the press. Stalin was completely outmaneuvered by Truman.

On July 28, Stalin made the last attempt to invite himself to participate in the joint ultimatum. He showed Truman Japan's formal request for Moscow's mediation to terminate the war, which the Soviet government had received on

July 25, remarking that although the Soviet delegation had not been consulted by the Allies about the Potsdam Proclamation, he wished to keep the Allies informed of Japan's further approach to Moscow. After he had his interpreter read the English translation of Japan's request, he dismissed it as nothing new, and declared that he would give the Japanese a more definite negative answer.[88]

On the following day, Stalin did not attend the conference, since he had allegedly caught a cold. At the end of the conference, Molotov told Truman that Stalin had instructed him to tell the president that "the best method would be for the United States, England, and the other allies in the Far Eastern war to address a formal request to the Soviet Government for its entry into the war."[89] This request could be made on the basis of Japan's rejection of the Potsdam Proclamation, and for the purpose of "shortening the war and saving lives."[90] It is interesting to note that Molotov's request was entirely deleted from the Soviet record.

This request put Truman and Byrnes in an awkward situation. Under no circumstances were they willing to comply with it, because the exclusion of the Soviet Union from the Potsdam ultimatum was their major purpose since the successful atomic bomb test. And yet, since it had been a consistently declared U.S. policy, and Truman had publicly stated, that the United States desired Soviet participation in the war, and since Soviet entry into the war might still serve as an insurance policy to assure Japan's surrender if the atomic bombs failed to do so, they could not flatly reject this request. In order to get out of this dilemma, Truman and Byrnes concocted tortuous legal arguments that the Soviet Union could justify entering the war against Japan on the basis of the Moscow Declaration of October 30, 1943, and Articles 103 and 106 of the still unratified United Nations Charter.[91]

According to Truman's memoirs: "I did not like this [Stalin's] proposal for one important reason. I saw in it a cynical diplomatic move to make Russia's entry at this time appear to be the decisive factor to bring about victory." As far as Truman was concerned, Soviet participation in the war was a treaty obligation, but there was "none obliging the United States and the Allies to provide Russia with a reason for breaking with Japan."[92] Byrnes also writes: "I must frankly admit that in view of what we knew of Soviet actions in eastern Germany and the violations of the Yalta agreements in Poland, Rumania and Bulgaria, I would have been satisfied had the Russians determined not to enter the war. Notwithstanding Japan's persistent refusal to surrender unconditionally, I believed the atomic bomb would be successful and would force Japan to accept surrender on our terms."[93] Truman and Byrnes knew that these legal explanations were not sufficient to justify the Soviet violation of the neutrality pact, but they were not about to help Stalin on this issue by inviting him to join the Potsdam Proclamation.

Japan's Reaction to the Potsdam Proclamation

Stalin was a master strategist, but he did not always get what he wanted. On the Potsdam joint ultimatum, he was completely outmaneuvered by Truman. He was also lucky, because his failure was unexpectedly turned into a serendipitous windfall for him. When the Potsdam Proclamation was relayed to the Japanese by short-wave radio, their immediate attention was drawn to two facts: first, the Potsdam Proclamation demanded unconditional surrender, but kept silent about the fate of the emperor and the monarchical system; and second, Stalin had not signed it.

The Japanese Foreign Ministry took note of the ambiguous formulation of the Potsdam terms, which might leave the possibility of retention of the monarchical system, and argued for the eventual acceptance of the terms. But as long as the promise to retain a monarchical system was not clearly spelled out and until the Soviet government responded to Japan's request to receive the Konoe Mission, it was quite reasonable, given the delicate balance between the peace party and the war party in the government, for the Japanese government to continue the policy of seeking Moscow's mediation to end the war. It is doubtful that Prime Minister Suzuki actually used the term *mokusatsu* (ignore, or, literally, silently kill) at his news conference. The Japanese government was suspending judgment on the Potsdam terms, rather than rejecting them, pending Moscow's reply to the Konoe Mission.[94]

For Truman, it was sufficient to learn that the Japanese government did not accept the ultimatum. It is a myth he himself helped to create that he ordered the use of the atomic bomb only after the Japanese government promptly rejected the ultimatum.[95] The Japanese government never rejected the Potsdam Proclamation, and Truman never issued an order to use the atomic bombs. He did not have to, since the order had been given before the Potsdam Proclamation was promulgated. It is more accurate to say that the Japanese government's inaction did not give Truman sufficient grounds to intercede to rescind the order to use the atomic bomb.

The Atomic Bomb and Soviet Entry into the War

Stalin Attempts to Change the Date of Attack

The fiasco of the Potsdam Proclamation convinced Stalin that Truman had finally decided to force Japan to surrender unilaterally without any Soviet help. He was alarmed, and he acted quickly while he was still in Berlin. On July

30, he appointed Marshal Vasilevskii as supreme commander of the Soviet troops in the Far East as of August 1, thus removing all secrecy with which he had prepared for the attack on Japan.[96] On August 2, the Stavka made official the reorganization of the Far Eastern Front into three separate fronts: the First Far Eastern Front, made up of the Maritime group of troops, commanded by Marshal K. A. Meretskov; the Second Far Eastern Front, formerly the Far Eastern Front, commanded by General M. A. Purkaev; and the Transbaikal Front, commanded by Marshal Rodion Malinovskii.[97]

The Potsdam Conference was over on August 2, and the Soviet delegation left Berlin that day and arrived in Moscow on August 5. On August 3, Chief of Staff Colonel-General S. P. Ivanov and "Colonel General Vasiliev" (Vasilevskii's nom de guerre) sent an important report on the situation at the front to Stalin and Antonov, presumably responding to their order:

In the Transbaikal Front, the 39 A Liudnikov Army [Voiska] and the 53A Managarov Army are completing the advancement to the designated district of concentration, so that by the morning of August 5, 1945, with the rest of the troops of the front, they will be ready, in accordance with your instructions, in the areas about fifty to sixty kilometers from the border, to take the command for the initiation of the action.

From the moment of receiving the order to cross the border, and then to the actual beginning of action, for the supply of troops and their final preparations a minimum of three and a maximum of five full days [sutok] will be required.

Taking into consideration all the problems of securing and stockpiling the equipment and provisions for the troops, the optimal time for the initiation of action of front[line] troops (I have in mind crossing the border) will be August 9–10, 1945.

In addition, the armies of the First and the Second Far Eastern Front should be able to initiate action on the same day and at the same time after the troops of the Transbaikal Front go into action. Military preparedness of all these fronts should be completed by August 5.[98]

This report suggests that the change of the date of attack from the previously agreed August 11 to August 9–10 was more likely written in response to Stalin's earlier request to change the date. Since this report was sent on August 3, Stalin's request must have been sent earlier than that date. It is most likely, although it cannot be determined from the documentary evidence, that the order was issued from Potsdam on July 30, at the same time when Vasilevskii was officially and openly appointed the commander of the Soviet Army in the Far East, after Stalin's last attempt to obtain the Western Allies' invitation to join the Potsdam Proclamation was rejected by Truman. It is likely, absent other documentary evidence, that Stalin proposed to advance the date of attack in response to what he perceived as the American maneuver to achieve Japan's surrender before the Soviet entry into the war. Vasilevskii requested instructions regarding questions of a "political and diplomatic nature," strongly suggesting that the change of date was dictated by political motivation arising from the Potsdam Proclamation.

After receiving Vasilevskii's recommendation to advance the date of attack by one to two days, however, the Stavka seems to have turned down this request, presumably judging that to do so would be too risky. As previously agreed, the precise time of attack was set at midnight Transbaikal time on August 11 (6 P.M. Moscow time on August 10).[99]

The race between Truman and Stalin, and between the atomic bomb and Soviet entry into the war against Japan, was on in earnest.

The Hiroshima Bomb

Stalin returned to Moscow on the evening of August 5. His appointment log for August 5 shows that immediately after his arrival at the Kremlin, he frantically resumed activities. He met Molotov, Mikoian, Beria, and Malenkov from 19:45 to 23:00. Kaganovich joined the meeting at 20:40, Voznesenskii came at 20:55 and left at 21:40; Vyshinskii came at 21:40 and left at 22:00, and finally Kuznetsov joined the meeting between 21:55 and 22:10.[100] Considering the participation of Molotov (foreign commissar), Vyshinskii (deputy foreign commissar), Beria (NKVD chief), Kuznetsov (navy commissar), and Mikoian (in charge of Lend-Lease), it is almost certain that at least part of this meeting was devoted to the war in the Far East and the possibility of the Americans using the atomic bomb. It is also safe to assume that Stalin was constantly in touch with General Antonov of the General Staff, most likely through direct military telephone lines.

The Kwantung Army noticed an increase in Soviet reconnaissance activities from the end of July all along the borders from Manchouli to Korea. The most daring actions took place on the night of August 5 on the eastern border along the Ussuiri. An observation post manned by thirty Japanese soldiers near Hulin was attacked by a group of a hundred Soviet soldiers, who had crossed the river. The fight continued until August 6, but eventually the Soviet forces withdrew.[101] Whether it was an intentional diversionary action or an unintended breach of discipline, it reinforced the Kwantung Army's conviction that Soviet military actions would likely be border incursions, not a mass invasion.

Then the shocking news reached Moscow. The Americans dropped the first atomic bomb on Hiroshima at 8:15 A.M. (Hiroshima time: 0.15 Moscow time) on August 6. Truman received the news on the USS *Augusta* on the way back to the United States. He could not hide his excitement, and exclaimed, jumping to his feet: "This is the greatest thing in history." He then released a statement that had been previously arranged by Stimson: "It was to spare the Japanese people from utter destruction that the ultimatum of July 26 was issued at Potsdam.

Their leaders promptly rejected that ultimatum. If they do not now accept our terms they may expect a rain of ruin from the air, the like of which has never been seen on earth."[102]

In contrast to Truman, the news of the atomic bomb crushed Stalin. *Pravda* did not report anything about the atomic bomb on Hiroshima on August 7, and only on August 8 did it report Truman's statement on the atomic bomb in a lower column on page 4 without comment.[103] Stalin's appointment log shows that he refused to see anyone on August 6, reminiscent of his behavior immediately after the Nazi invasion of the Soviet Union on June 22, 1941.[104] It is reasonable to assume that Stalin was completely devastated by the news, believing that the game was over and that the Americans had won.

On the afternoon of August 7, T. V. Soong and the Chinese delegation arrived in Moscow. While waiting for the arrival of the Chinese delegation at the airport, Molotov and Harriman exchanged a brief conversation. Harriman asked Molotov how he thought the Japanese would react to the atomic bomb on Hiroshima. Molotov said that he had heard nothing yet and rather belligerently commented: "You Americans can keep a secret when you want to." It is difficult to say what Molotov meant by this comment, but it is possible to interpret it as a tacit and sour-grape acknowledgment of defeat. At the arrival of the Chinese delegation, Molotov told Soong that Japan was on the verge of collapse. Considering Molotov's dejected mood, it is likely that the foreign commissar did not know at this time that the Kremlin had received new information about Japan's reaction to the atomic bomb.[105] At least, Molotov did not look at this moment like a foreign commissar prepared to declare war on Japan.

The dropping of the atomic bomb on Hiroshima did not have an immediate, decisive impact on Japan's decision to surrender. It did not change Japan's policy of seeking Moscow's mediation, and it did not immediately lead to the government's acceptance of the Potsdam Proclamation. On August 7, one day after the atomic bomb was dropped on Hiroshima, Foreign Minister Tōgō sent an urgent telegram to Ambassador Satō in Moscow, instructing him to seek an appointment with Molotov immediately to obtain Moscow's answer on the subject of the Konoe mission.[106] On August 6, having learned that Molotov had returned to Moscow, Satō had contacted Deputy Foreign Commissar Solomon Lozovskii, requesting a meeting with Molotov. Satō received no reply, but on August 7, he again contacted Lozovskii requesting an appointment with Molotov, although he had not yet received Tōgō's August 6 telegram. Satō's request on August 7 had special meaning: it was an unmistakable sign that Tokyo had not surrendered despite the atomic bomb, and it was the first reaction of the Japanese government to the Hiroshima bomb.

Having received this news, Stalin leapt to action. At 4:30 P.M., he ordered Vasilevskii to begin the Manchurian operation at midnight on August 9 (6 P.M., August 8, Moscow time), thus moving up the date of attack by forty-eight hours. Accordingly, Vasilevskii issued four directives between 10:35 and 11:10 Transbaikal time (4:35 to 5:10 Moscow time), each ordering all forces on the Transbaikal Front, the First and Second Far Eastern Fronts, and the Pacific Fleet to begin operations at 6 P.M. Moscow time on August 8 (12 midnight Transbaikal time and 1 A.M. Khabarovsk time on August 9).[107] The die was cast. The Soviet forces were about to cross the Manchurian border at midnight on August 9.

In the meantime, Satō received the news that he had been looking for. He was told to come to see Molotov at 6 P.M. on August 8 at the Foreign Commissariat. Later, the appointment time was changed to 5 P.M., giving the USSR one hour to hand a declaration of war to the Japanese government before the Soviet attack began. At 7:50 P.M. on August 7, Satō dispatched a telegram to Tōgō, informing the foreign minister that Molotov would meet with him at 5 P.M. the following day.[108] In addition, Stalin decided to begin negotiations with the Chinese at 10 P.M., giving the Chinese only a few hours of rest.

Sino-Soviet Negotiations, August 7

The Sino-Soviet negotiations began at 10 P.M. in the Kremlin. Stalin was impatient. He wanted to conclude an agreement that night so that he could observe the provision of the Yalta Agreement for the Soviet entry into the war, but he was not ready to sacrifice any rights and territories promised at Yalta.

As soon as Soong entered the room, he was greeted by Stalin's impetuous question: "What news have you brought?" Soong only referred to Chiang Kai-shek's meeting with Soviet Ambassador Apollon Petrov on July 16. That was not what Stalin wanted to hear, and at the first encounter, Stalin must have realized that he would have to enter the war with the Yalta provision unfulfilled.

Soong was prepared to sacrifice Outer Mongolia, railways in Manchuria, and Port Arthur, but he stood firm on Dairen. During the negotiations Stalin revealed why he was so persistent on Soviet rights and concessions in Manchuria. He explained that the Soviet ports in the Far East were not connected with railways. Therefore the railways, Port Arthur, and Dairen were important to keep under Soviet control as a defense against a future Japanese threat. Japan would surrender, but it would revive in thirty years.[109] Both sides stood firm. The negotiations did not produce an agreement.

Stalin's interest in the Far East was not ideological, but geostrategic in the classical sense. He was not prepared to sacrifice what he regarded as Soviet entitlements for the sake of formally fulfilling the Yalta Agreement. He gambled on the assumption that once Soviet tanks rolled into Manchuria, the Americans and the Chinese would not condemn the USSR for violating the Yalta provision, for fear that Stalin might change his mind about supporting the Nationalist government as the sole legitimate government in China. Even worse, he might claim Manchuria as a Soviet sphere of influence.

Moscow Declares War on Japan

As soon as Satō came to the Foreign Commissariat at 5 P.M. on August 8, Molotov began to read the Soviet declaration of war on Japan. The declaration asserted that since Japan had rejected the Potsdam Proclamation, "the proposal of the Japanese Government to the Soviet Union concerning mediation in the war in the Far East thereby loses all basis." This was a tortured logic, since Japan had suspended judgment on the Potsdam Proclamation precisely because its request for mediation by the Soviet government was still pending. The declaration further explained: "The Allies approached the Soviet government with a proposal to join in the war against Japanese aggression and thereby shorten the length of the war, reduce the number of victims, and assist in the prompt reestablishment of general peace." The Soviet government did not use either the Moscow Declaration or Articles of the United Nations Charter to justify its violation of the neutrality pact, as suggested by Truman and Byrnes, and opted instead to concoct a brazen lie that the Allies had requested it to join the Potsdam Proclamation. It was Stalin's open and bold challenge to Truman to see if the president dared to protest. The declaration finally served notice: "The Soviet government declares that as of tomorrow, that is, as of August 9, the Soviet Union will consider itself in a state of war with Japan."[110]

Satō had harbored no illusion about the Soviet reply to Japan's request to receive the Konoe mission, but the declaration of war was the last thing he had expected. Having read the declaration several times, Satō asked Molotov if he could send a coded telegram to his government before midnight. Molotov raised no objection. Satō was a brilliant diplomat, but he made a fatal mistake here. He took it for granted that the phrase "as of tomorrow that is, as of August 9" in the Soviet declaration of war meant August 9, Moscow time, without realizing that in Far Eastern time, August 9 would arrive in less than one hour. He accordingly asked Molotov for permission to send a telegram to Tokyo to alert the Japanese government that the Soviet government had declared war on Japan. Satō's telegram never reached Tokyo, or rather it never left Moscow, since within less than one hour after his meeting with Molotov, the USSR was at war with Japan, and therefore, for security reasons, severed all the communications with Japan.[111]

Less than one hour after Satō left Molotov's office, Soviet tanks, troops, and airplanes crossed the Manchurian border from all directions. Stalin had managed to join the war against Japan in the nick of time.

Truman's Reactions to Soviet Entry into the War

A few minutes after 3 P.M. in Washington, Truman held a news conference at the White House. The president appeared and read a statement to the reporters: "I have only a simple announcement to make. I can't hold a regular press conference today, but this announcement is so important I thought I would call you in. Russia has declared war on Japan. That's all."[112] This terse statement betrays Truman's profound disappointment. Things had not gone according to his timetable. The Japanese did not immediately surrender, and he had let the USSR manage to join the war.

After Truman's short announcement, a statement by the secretary of state was released to the press. Byrnes welcomed the Soviet declaration of war against Japan, which he believed would "shorten the war and save . . . many lives." He further stated that at the Potsdam Conference, the president had conveyed to Stalin that Soviet participation in the war would be justified on the basis of Paragraph 5 of the Moscow Declaration of 1943 and Articles 103 and 106 of the United Nations Charter.[113]

Clearly Byrnes's statement was directed at the Soviet claim that the Soviet government had been asked by the Allies to join the Potsdam Proclamation. Byrnes implied that this was not true, hinting at the illegitimacy of the Soviet government associating itself with the Potsdam Proclamation. Nevertheless, Byrnes's statement fell far short of condemning the Soviet declaration of war as a deception. Stalin's gamble had worked.[114]

Space does not permit description here of the tortuous process by which the Japanese government came to accept the Potsdam terms, thanks to the emperor's unprecedented "sacred decision," first, on August 10, with one condition, preservation of "the prerogatives of His Majesty as the sovereign ruler," and, finally, on August 14, unconditionally, at the second imperial conference.[115] The Truman government was divided over the issue of whether it should accept Japan's first reply. Over the objections of Stimson, Leahy, and Forrestal, Truman accepted Byrnes's recommendation that the United States should reject this reply. After this decision, Truman had a meeting with Congressman Mike Mansfield (D-Mont.) and told him the reason why he had rejected Japan's reply: to accept Japan's offer "would constitute something less than unconditional surrender," and would permit the emperor to become "the nuclear rallying point for future nationalism."[116] It is ironic that Stalin could have uttered the same words. After the Byrnes note was presented to the cabinet in the afternoon on August 10, Truman said that he expected Britain and China to acquiesce promptly to the document, and that if he did not hear from Moscow, the United States would proceed with the occupation of Japan without the USSR.[117] It is not clear why Truman thought that Moscow would reject the Byrnes note. Perhaps, he expected Soviet objections to the provision in the Byrnes note that stipulated that the future form of government should be determined by the will of the Japanese people themselves. To Truman's surprise, however, Moscow promptly accepted the Byrnes note. Stalin was pleased with the U.S. rejection of Japan's reply, since it gave the Soviet troops more time to expand the territory under Soviet occupation. U.S. policymakers were not unaware of this danger, but in counterposing the danger of Soviet expansion in Asia and the need to avenge the humiliation of Pearl Harbor, Truman and Byrnes gave more weight to the unconditional surrender of Japan than to the need to prevent Soviet expansion.

Stalin also gambled on the Chinese response. He expected the Soviet advance deep into Manchuria would induce the Chinese to make concessions for fear that the Soviet influence in Manchuria would lead to the establishment of a communist regime in Manchuria. He gambled and won. The Chinese finally came around to an agreement on August 15, three hours after Japan announced unconditional acceptance of the Potsdam terms.

Conclusions

The Soviet Union played a central role in the drama of the ending the Pacific War. Stalin was determined to enter the war against Japan in order to obtain the geopolitical gains promised at Yalta. He had to balance Japan and the United States for this purpose. While he was transporting troops and equipment to the Far East with frantic speed in preparation for the war against Japan, he deceived the Japanese government into believing that the neutrality pact would remain in force until it expired in April 1946. He fully exploited Japan's clumsy diplomatic faux pas of sending Hirota to Malik to keep the Soviet Union out of the war. He let Hirota pursue Malik, but instructed Malik not to refuse to meet him, in order to "lull the Japanese to sleep," while he was frantically putting the last touches on the preparations for the war against Japan. In fact, the Politburo and the State Defense Committee made the final decision to wage war against Japan on June 26 and 27. It was only after this decision that the Japanese government decided to request Moscow's mediation by sending Prince Konoe as the emperor's special envoy. This move merely served Stalin's purpose. It was exploited to prolong the war and gave Stalin a bargaining chip in his dealings with Truman.

Stalin came to Potsdam to achieve three objectives. First, he wanted to reaffirm Truman's commitment to the Yalta Agreement by promising Soviet entry into the war. Second, he wanted to mobilize Truman's support to put pressure on the recalcitrant Chinese to conclude a treaty endorsing the Yalta Agreement. Third, he wanted to join the Allies' joint ultimatum to Japan. Such an ultimatum would justify Soviet entry into the war against Japan in violation of the neutrality pact. It would also serve as a declaration of war on Japan.

The successful detonation of the atomic bomb in New Mexico spoiled Stalin's plans. Truman did not share the secret of the atomic bomb with Stalin and excluded him completely from the deliberations leading to the Potsdam Proclamation, which was issued without Stalin's knowledge and without Stalin's signature. Truman did little to influence the Chinese, who were adamantly resisting Stalin's bullying to accept the Yalta terms. Stalin made a desperate attempt to request an invitation from Truman to join in the Potsdam Proclamation, but Truman coldly refused. This fiasco finally convinced Stalin that the United States was determined to force Japan's surrender unilaterally without Soviet help. If this were allowed to happen, Stalin would be deprived of the fruits promised at Yalta.

The race between the atomic bomb and Soviet entry into the war was on. Stalin accordingly ordered Vasilevskii to hasten all the preparations to attack by August 5 (Moscow time) and attempted to change the date of the attack to August 10. But the Stavka did not agree with this change at this late stage. Stalin returned to Moscow on August 5 and resumed frantic activities to prepare for the war against Japan.

But the Americans moved first. They dropped the first atomic bomb on Hiroshima. Stalin was crushed. He was convinced that the game was over.

But the game was not played out yet. The Hiroshima bomb failed to deal a coup de grâce to the Japanese. The Japanese government continued to cling to the hope that it could end the war through Moscow's mediation. Satō's approach to the Foreign Commissariat on August 7 launched Stalin into action. He ordered the date of attack to be advanced by forty-eight hours to midnight on August 9 (6 P.M., August 8, Moscow time). He had Molotov tell Satō to see him in his office at 5 P.M. on August 8 and hastily arranged the meeting with T. V. Soong and the Chinese delegation at 10 P.M. in the Kremlin.

Soong was as adamant as before, and the negotiations with the Chinese did not yield a treaty with China. But Stalin was in a hurry. He decided to plunge into the war without a treaty with China, thereby violating a provision of the Yalta Agreement. He gambled. Once the USSR had entered the war, neither the Americans nor the Chinese would condemn the Soviet government for violating the Yalta Agreement.

At 5 P.M. on August 8, Molotov handed the Soviet declaration of the war to the unsuspecting Satō on the grounds that the Allies had invited the Soviet government to join in the Potsdam Proclamation. It was a blatant lie, but as Stalin suspected, no one protested. Within one hour after Satō left Molotov's office, Soviet tanks rolled into Manchuria. Stalin had managed to enter the war, fulfilling a goal he had aimed at since 1941. Now he had to conquer physically what he had been promised at Yalta. During the war that lasted from August 9 through September 5, the USSR occupied all the territories that were promised by the Yalta Agreement.

In the end, Stalin succeeded. He achieved what he wanted through Machiavellian diplomacy and ruthless execution of military plans. But we should not portray Stalin as an infallible strategist who anticipated everything with clairvoyance and executed everything flawlessly. He failed miserably in his attempt to join in the Potsdam Proclamation, and he let Truman drop the atomic bomb before the USSR entered the war. He was lucky, because he was greatly assisted by catastrophic mistakes committed by the Japanese government. But in the end, did he really win? He managed to obtain the war trophies he was after, but at the cost of the long-term enmity of the Japanese, which lingers on to this day.

Conclusion

The Interpretive Dialogue, 1989–2005, and Various
Proposals for Understanding the Ending of the War
and Why and How Japan Surrendered

BARTON J. BERNSTEIN

> [Dismayed that Japan had not surrendered on America's
> August 11 terms,] the President remarked sadly that he
> now had no alternative but to order an atomic bomb to be
> dropped on Tokyo.
>
> —British Chargé d'Affaires John Balfour to the
> Foreign Office, sent 1:08 P.M., August 14, 1945

> What worried JFB [Secretary of State James F. Byrnes]
> was the knowledge that we would not have more atomic
> bombs [ready for use against Japan] before August 22.
> WJB [Walter J. Brown] wrote message for JFB [to in-
> form Japan]: "Unless we receive a reply to our message
> of August 11 by [date left blank], we shall conclude that
> your message of August 10 was not in good faith . . . and
> we shall proceed to act accordingly, unleashing the full
> fury of attacks in the air, on the sea and on the land."
>
> —Special Assistant Walter Brown, diary notes,
> for about 1–2 P.M., August 14, 1945

To some scholars in history and political science, and in the often political-sci-
ence-related communities of strategic studies and policy studies, the division
in America (far more than elsewhere) between political science and history in
dealing with Japan's surrender may suggest the need to close the gap between
political science theory and historical research. That may be an admirable
hope, and even a worthy aim.

But that gap is, in practice, hard to bridge for most practitioners in these
disciplines, particularly in the United States. It is often a difference about what

the important questions are, what kinds of evidence (and thus research) count, how to assess evidence, how to focus the dialogue, and what literature is relevant. Related to that is the political science quest, often shared by many in strategic studies and policy studies, for larger generalizations ("theories"), and frequently the distrust by historians for such a quest on the grounds that it erodes crucial differences in studying events. That gap between these fields is often related to differences over the acceptable and appropriate levels of abstraction undergirding such an enterprise. These differences generally seem sharpest, especially in the United States, between international-relations theorists in political science, on the one side, and foreign policy analysts and area studies scholars in the history field, on the other.

For various reasons, there has been much less focused dialogue across these disciplinary boundaries in America on end-of-the-Pacific/Asian War studies than on the Cuban missile crisis. Part of the reason may be that the landmark book in political science on the missile crisis, Graham Allison's *Essence of Decision*, which made contributions to security studies and policy studies, came along at a time (the early 1970s) and out of an institutional domain (Harvard) distinguished by an intellectually powerful seminar in history *and* political science on decision making. Rooted initially in an interdisciplinary academic seminar, with notables in the political science field (frequently with interests in strategic studies and policy studies) and sometimes with governmental experience participating and including at least one prominent diplomatic historian (Ernest May), and meeting at one of America's preeminent universities, there was, predictably, going to be more spillover and better communication across traditional academic boundaries.

Nonetheless, *Essence of Decision* seemed uninformed about what foreign policy historians actually did, and remarkably, and uncritically, trusting about oral history sources. The scholarly dialogue resulting from that book was often rather flawed and truncated, with little awareness by political scientists and security studies scholars, frequently smitten by Allison's emphasis on bureaucratic/governmental politics, that historians had long been using a form of bureaucratic/governmental politics, but without explicit theory, to look at the formation of policy within government.[1]

Now, at a time when the study of foreign-relations history has generally lost prestige in the American academy, and when the scholarly practitioners of foreign policy history feel often undervalued in academic history departments in America, there has been a frequent call to do "international history." That call, while often suggesting more newness than is warranted for such history, may be most important for further emphasizing the need, usually based on language skills, to examine in depth the interaction between nations and to use their archives. That may be a useful exhortation, if not a daunting admonition, to much American foreign-relations writing to broaden, deepen, and expand its purview for some subjects.

Yet the obvious problem in the efforts of American scholars and others in the West focusing on Japan's surrender, and conceivably broadening that study to examine not simply Japanese actions but also related American and Soviet actions in 1945, is the substantial language difficulty. Scholars in the West who have examined the Soviet efforts—Soviet-Japanese negotiations and Soviet decision making—usually know the Russian language and can read the Russian sources. But much, if not most, of the work in the Western world dealing with Japan's surrender has not been written by Japan specialists who know the Japanese language. Indeed, despite shifts in the past seventeen years, many writing on Japan's ending of the war do not know the Japanese language, but have worked from English-language sources and sometimes from specially arranged translations.

Perhaps it is time, in some form of international consortium, to seek to arrange the translation into English of a number of key documents on Japan's ending of the war and related policy matters—the emperor's monologue, the volumes of important imperial army documents and other valuable Japanese military materials on the last months of the war, large sections of *Shūsen shiroku*, more of Privy Seal Kido's writings, parts of Navy Minister Yonai's writings and those of Rear Admiral Takagi Sōkichi, and some still-untranslated memoirs, including Cabinet Secretary Sakomizu's, or at least relevant parts, and Army Minister Anami's diary. This would be in keeping with the admirable effort years ago in the West in the study of Japanese-American road to Pearl Harbor and war, and more recently by the Cold War International History project to reach across national and language boundaries to expand and nurture international, and transnational, scholarship.

Scholars in the West, as well as in Japan and Russia and elsewhere, undoubtedly regret the severe limitations on Russia's and Japan's making important archival sources available. In the case of Russia, the key presidential archives for World War II are not open to non-Russian scholars and usually not to Russian scholars, other than a few briefly privileged individuals. In the case of Japan, the presumably very important imperial household archival materials are entirely closed to scholars. It is an irony worth pondering that had the United States chosen to depose Hirohito, try him as a war criminal (as Truman apparently briefly thought of doing), and seize the imperial household archives for a war-crimes trial, analysts would be better able to study and explain Hirohito. The United States, in contrast, after sometimes lengthy, hard-to-fathom delays, opened most of its relevant archives, though new decisions since 9/11 have led to severe restrictions on access to some A-bomb-related archival materials that were once open.

Beyond the serious problem of sources, and the warranted encouragement of more informed scholarship and a more focused dialogue, there are the related questions of determining what interpretive matters seem settled and where future analysis should focus in discussing Japan's surrender. There was probably less agreement among publishing scholars in 1989–2005 than in 1946–55 on what strategy of research and of focus, as well as what questions, should guide the inquiry. Certainly, Koshiro's recent bold work has thrown down an interesting challenge.

Even aside from Koshiro's work, which seeks partly to reorient the field, there was in 1989–2005 probably less *scholarly* agreement than in the first post-Hiroshima decade, 1946–55, on why and how Japan surrendered, and whether the atomic bombing was necessary. In that early postwar period, some of the prominent scholarly writers and many other seemingly thoughtful publications in the West on these interpretive problems were influenced by, or at least loosely reflected, the U.S. Strategic Bombing Survey's assertion that the A-bomb had "in all probability" been unnecessary to avoid a November 1 invasion, and certainly to end the war in 1945. Perhaps more important, all of those 1946–55 studies, explicitly or implicitly, shared a similar conception of the Japanese emperor system and of Hirohito in particular. In those studies, Hirohito was regarded mostly as having been, until about June–August 1945, a figurehead, a symbolic emperor, who managed only in the last week or possibly the last few months of the war to expand his influence and to exercise power in a unique way to push toward surrender.

Since about 1989–91 in the West, however, and somewhat earlier in Japan, there has been a serious reconsideration and a dispute about Hirohito's role during the war and about the nature of the wartime emperor system, ranging from Asada Sadao and Stephen Large on what may be usefully designated the right to Herbert Bix and Irokawa Daikichi on the left, with Edward Drea closer to Bix at times on Hirohito and Richard Frank often near Drea. There is no consensus on these crucial interpretive issues. The interpretive differences in the conception of Hirohito and the emperor system easily spilled over, in recent years, into disputed interpretations of why Hirohito acted to move toward surrender in August 1945, why he did not act energetically earlier, and whether he was hemmed in by the militarists or whether he often shared their hopes and goals in the quest for a decisive battle.[2]

Differences in interpreting Hirohito are often related to disputes—not always made fully explicit—about the nature of the *kokutai* in World War II and how various Japanese leaders, including Hirohito himself, conceived of it. Because the conception is often rather elusive, and because the meaning of the *kokutai* was normally not a subject for explicit analysis among Japan's top leaders, with perhaps the exception of Baron Hiranuma in the troubled days of August, historians in dealing with Japan's end-of-the-war policies usually tend not to look closely at the often implicitly competing conceptions of *kokutai*.

There is also need to examine more closely the relationship of Hirohito and the so-called military diehards on the Supreme War Council. How much can their behavior, including their yielding to Hirohito's pleas on the 10th and 14th for Japan's surrender, be explained by their respect for and loyalty to him and to the emperorship? Might it be possible further to parse the issues by seeking to distinguish between loyalty to Hirohito himself and to the emperorship, or is that a case where the questions reach beyond the likelihood of useful analysis, in view of the nature of existing documentation? In turn, even though the archives of the imperial household remain closed after more than sixty years, there are troubling questions—perhaps answerable more fully if those documents ever become available—about what Hirohito thought of those so-called diehards.

Even the issues of the relationship of Hirohito to Privy Seal Kido and to Prince Konoe warrant careful reconsideration in depth. Most of the Western literature describes the Kido-Hirohito relationship as close, but important questions linger in determining how much Kido pushed Hirohito on crucial matters and how much Kido's prodding may have been mostly confirming Hirohito in his inclinations. In turn, there are still crucial questions about why Hirohito turned to Konoe as the special intermediary for Japanese-Soviet matters, and how much authority Hirohito was bestowing on Konoe.

Analyses of Hirohito and the so-called diehards also raise questions about how deeply, in summer 1945, he and other Japanese leaders feared a leftist upheaval if the war was not ended and whether their fear was reasonable and accurate. Such a set of questions has both a liberating and a complicating effect, by moving the scholarly study of Japan's surrender to a deeper analytical level than one that just examines governmental decision making. At that deeper level, the decision making can be related to basic questions of social structure and of the social history in 1945 Japan. Thus, in analyzing the surrender, there is an opportunity, reaching beyond Bix's 1995–2000 work and Irokawa's mid-1990s translated work, to seek to combine social history and foreign-policy history.

Frequently, in orthodox foreign-policy history, there is an unfortunate wariness of seeking closely to link foreign policy and social history. Such efforts do require some thoughtful attention to social theory, and reaching beyond an empiricism that assumes that connections are self-evident.

Perhaps that analytical enterprise of linking social history and foreign policy in the case of 1945 Japan can be profitably further expanded by looking closely at business interests in Japan starting in mid 1945, or slightly earlier, to consider their position on ending the war and the possible terms for surrender. In the West, mostly Bix—and, then, too briefly—has dealt with this interesting set of issues. Such inquiry can be usefully expanded to the questions about the power and influence of big business, and especially particular industries and aggregations, on the Japanese government in 1945.

Though the U.S. Strategic Bombing Survey's two key 1946 reports undoubtedly ignored considerable contrary evidence in making their case, the question, raised by Joseph Grew and Robert Butow, of whether a June or July 1945 promise to allow an emperor-as-figurehead system might well have produced an earlier Japanese surrender, without the atomic bombing, remains an interesting one. Bix, Asada, and Frank reject this notion in their recent work. Drea, albeit without directly addressing the issue, also seems to lean in a negative direction, as does Tsyuoshi Hasegawa, much as he regrets the atomic bombing.

The even more speculative questions of what the outcome would have been of continuing the blockade and conventional bombing without either the A-bomb or Soviet entry, or without both, may continue to tantalize some interpreters. Richard Frank has briefly addressed small parts of this question—mostly regarding the bombing of the railroad system and increasing food shortages—and so has Bernstein. Robert Pape, with far less evidence than Frank and Bernstein, stressed the importance of the sea blockade and too easily minimized the influence of conventional strategic bombing.

Based partly on the work of Richard Frank and others, there are important questions, requiring research in U.S. and Japanese sources, on battle casualty/fatality estimates by each nation's military of what would happen to both countries' forces, and possibly to the Japanese civilian population, in Ketsu Gō, Olympic, and similar operations. To put that material in appropriate perspective, it should be compared when possible to pre-battle estimates and post-campaign reports for a number of major 1944–45 confrontations including, ideally, Saipan, Luzon, Iwō Jima, and Okinawa. Such a comparison of pre- and post-event studies might also indicate what casualty/fatality numbers reached higher-level officials in the military and among the civilian leadership and analyze, if possible, how well the estimators were trusted at crucial junctures in 1945 at these higher levels. All this could help explain what various officials in each nation expected if an invasion occurred. In turn, that may or may not provide significant leverage on the interesting, controversial counterfactual issue of what might in fact have happened in late 1945 military campaigns and perhaps related operations in the home islands. Projecting to the counterfactual situation of what might have happened itself involves controversial assumptions, sometimes with the use of soft data, and will probably trigger vigorous disputes.[3]

Interpreters of alternative ways of ending the war, and of seeking to force Japan's surrender without the atomic bombing, if partly propelled by the wish that the atomic bomb had not been used, have to keep in mind that some alternative scenarios, involving a war that might have continued for some weeks if not months, might have resulted in more, not fewer, deaths. Such reckoning, with the conclusion that many more would have died, helped lead the anti-revisionist Robert Newman to defend the 1945 atomic bombing yet again in 2004, in *Enola Gay and the Court of History*, and, indeed, to dedicate his book to Paul Tibbets, the pilot of the B-29 (the *Enola Gay*, named for Tibbets's mother) that dropped the first atomic bomb on Japan. Similar pro-Tibbets sensibilities seem to infuse Robert J. Maddox's vigorously anti-revisionist introduction to a 2004 paperback edition of his 1995 volume *Weapons for Victory*. Of the other authors treated in Chapter 1's extended historiographical essay, only Edward Drea would be inclined to join Newman and possibly Maddox in leaning toward such a dedication to Tibbets. To the anti-revisionist Frank, in contrast, such a dedication seems celebratory and unacceptable. To a number of other authors, it even seems ghoulish.[4] The matter of such dedications, reaching beyond strictly analytical categories in explaining Japan's surrender, is a useful way of more deeply understanding many of the authors' moral assessments of the crucial events—the atomic bombings—in August 1945.

It is certainly imaginable that Asada, who greatly respects Hirohito, might be inclined to dedicate a book to the Shōwa emperor's memory. Hatano's inclinations are more difficult to discern. Certainly Bix, Drea, Frank, Irokawa, and Hasegawa would find such a dedication distasteful for multiple and obvious reasons. It is highly unlikely that any of the American-based A-bomb revisionists or the anti-revisionists would seriously entertain the thought of such a dedication, and most are privately, if not publicly, critical of Hirohito and Japan's pro-war leadership, yet some of the A-bomb revisionists do acknowledge the importance of Hirohito's interventions on the 10th and 14th for Japan's surrender.

Returning to analytical categories and departing from the realm of dedications and moral assessments, an important question involves the comparative weight of the first A-bomb and Soviet entry, and the role of the second bomb, in producing Japan's mid-August surrender. Hasegawa, though disputing other matters with Asada and Frank, and implicitly sometimes with Hatano, does not deny that the first A-bomb was also important and indeed essential in producing Japan's mid-August surrender. And Asada and Frank also sees Soviet entry, though less important, as essential. Hatano asserts that the two factors were of equal importance, though his actual essay often seems less certain on this matter.

As suggested by some writers, there is a need to distinguish carefully between why and how the central government in Tokyo surrendered, and how and why the Japanese armed forces, especially those outside the home islands, complied with that decision. So far, aside from some suggestive pieces of work, there has been no substantial attention to this problem. Put bluntly, how and why was compliance achieved, and how narrowly did the surrender avoid coming unstuck, and to many Japanese forces rejecting it? Did Soviet entry or the A-bomb play a more important role in securing compliance, especially outside the home islands? Were both necessary? Or only one, or neither?[5]

Related questions—often minimized or neglected—involve why ordinary Japanese citizens accepted their government's surrender decision and abided by it. Why were there not pockets of insurrection and resistance, or even more than pockets?

Such questions may usefully spill over into a deeper study, at various social levels and regions, of the nature of the wartime experience by 1945 in Japan, and how it was remembered in the early period of the occupation. Contrary to some formulations, there were competing memories, not a single collective memory. That raises, implicitly, the question of how in the then-recent memories the atomic bombing was regarded by Japanese at various levels and when and how sharp analytical and emotional differences began to emerge between perceptions of the atomic bombing and conventional bombing. Such questions reach beyond the issues of how and why Japan surrendered in mid 1945, but they may bear, even indirectly, on why and how Japanese accepted the surrender.[6]

In the aftermath of the atomic bombings, it became customary in both the West and in Japan for many to draw a sharp dividing line—morally, emotionally, strategically, and on other grounds—between atomic bombing and conventional bombing, with the normal conclusion that atomic bombing was in every way worse. Such distinctions were not easily rooted in the numbers actually killed by each means in the war against Japan, because by nearly all estimates, conventional bombing killed more overall than did the two atomic bombings. If, however, the distinction was rooted in the number killed in particular attacks, then the rank ordering, in terms of the number of dead, would most likely be Hiroshima (A-bomb), Tokyo (fire-bombing), and Nagasaki (A-bomb), with other conventional bombing of Japanese cities totaling far fewer deaths for any particular set of attacks. In some subtle but powerful way, the fact of radiation death (and injury) probably significantly contributed to the sense of a moral, emotional, and even strategic dividing line. Yet how and why that line emerged is not self-evident. There are deep issues here meriting cultural analysis.[7]

To note such troubling questions is not to legitimize the atomic bombings but, rather, to ask basic questions about how the bombings were understood, and why. Had the Japanese surrender not so closely followed the two atomic bombings, would the moral, emotional, and strategic dividing lines—in post-war Japan and in the postwar West—have developed as they did? What if there had instead been many atomic bombings—say, six or seven, or eight—of Japanese cities? Or if, as General George C. Marshall contemplated, a batch of A-bombs had been used in connection with Operation Olympic?[8]

The many issues in interpreting Japan's surrender and often in considering alternatives to the A-bomb are, ultimately, not questions only involving scholars and scholarship. The issues cut more deeply and more widely. In Japan and in America, and sometimes elsewhere in the West and possibly at times in Russia, too, the questions reach out to popular conceptions about how major nations worked or did not work to end World War II in Asia, which national leaders chose the right or wrong policies, whether Hirohito was in fact long peace-loving or seeking a final battle victory, whether the atomic bombing was necessary in August 1945 to end the war that month, or at least before the November invasion, and whether more lives were lost or saved by the A-bombs' use in early August 1945. The answers to such questions, often spilling well beyond scholarly discourse, help shape different national peoples' self-conceptions even more than sixty years after Japan's formal surrender on September 2, 1945, on the USS *Missouri*. The answers, in a sense, are part of the shaping of modern memories, and the answers at the popular level—especially if the United States and Japan are compared—widely diverge on some crucial matters.

Certainly, far more remains to be done at the scholarly level. Analyses of Japan's end-of-the-war policy and the surrender decisions themselves must more closely look at the top Japanese military officials—Anami, Umezu, and Toyoda—and seek to determine whether they were acting mostly on behalf of their own values or whether they substantially felt hamstrung by the expectations of their subordinates. Especially for Army Minister Anami, who was key in some analyses of Japan's surrender, did he fear, even on the 9/10th, as on the 13/14th, a dangerous coup attempt, and might that help explain his reluctance on the 9/10th, before Hirohito's intervention, to settle for Japan's surrender with only a provision for the emperor?

Will biography, or some other form of historical study, or, most likely, a combination of analytical modes, allow interpreters to understand the different conclusions at various junctures in 1945 of the navy leaders, Yonai and Toyoda? And how sincere, and at what point, were the various civilians—Foreign Minister Tōgō, Premier Suzuki, and Privy Seal Kido—in wanting a surrender on reasonable terms? Was Kido simply an alter ego to the emperor? Or far more, as seems very likely? And how, in explanations, do analysts link the efforts and influence of these men to the emperor's own views and conclusions at crucial junctures, especially in about mid 1945?

With the invigorated controversy about Hirohito, and in recent Japanese literature about that nation's wartime civilian leaders, many once-accepted operating assumptions have been challenged. What will continue to be argued about is how to conceive of Japan's leaders by summer 1945, whether the atomic bombings and Soviet entry in the war were essential in producing Japan's mid-August surrender, and whether other plausible policies might have ended the war in a better way and before the scheduled November 1 invasion.

All that, as Koshiro has boldly suggested, may be further complicated by looking closely at Japanese-Soviet relations in 1945 well before August 8 and by asking whether understanding the war itself partly in terms of competing imperialisms usefully influences how one should explain why and when Japan surrendered, and on what terms. As the recent work of David Holloway and of Hasegawa has suggested, understanding such issues deeply also allows analysts to move to the broader terrain of Soviet purposes and more fully to embed the problem of Japan's defeat and surrender within a broad interpretive framework of truly multinational, or international, history.[9] Such work by the U.K.-trained Holloway, who is now teaching at Stanford, and by the now virtually bi-national Hasegawa, a Japanese-born and -raised man, who is teaching at the University of California, Santa Barbara, underscores the fruitful internationalization of the scholarship in recent years.

The important interpretive differences between Holloway and Hasegawa on Soviet purposes, on whether there was truly a "race" between the USSR and the United States to end the war, on Stalin's schedule for Soviet entry into the war, and on the relationship of the A-bomb to his wartime policy, open major areas for further historical work. In that scholarship, it is important to recognize, as Holloway indicates, that Japan itself, and not just the "spoils" promised Stalin at Yalta, was a large issue for Stalin. How much, for example, should the origins of the Cold War be explained partly by Truman's successful exclusion of the USSR from a role in postwar Japan, and what is the significance of the fact that Stalin—albeit unhappily—acceded to Truman's urging and that though militarily able to take all of Korea, the USSR stuck by its August agreement with the United States and stopped at the 38th parallel?

Reaching beyond Holloway's essay, it would be valuable to have a somewhat comparative study focusing on Stalin's wartime fears, hopes, and expectations regarding the roles of both Germany and Japan in the postwar world. Prior to Holloway's essay, there was an unfortunate tendency in much of the Western scholarship on Stalin and the Soviet Union to focus heavily on Stalin's concerns about Germany and eastern Europe, and to minimize or forget issues of Japan.

It would be interesting to speculate on whether the national origin, or the country in which the scholar was working and writing, had a clearly discernible effect on the nature, and especially the conclusions, of recent scholarship in the West on the ending of the Pacific/Asian War. If the names and backgrounds of the authors were removed, could an intelligent reader determine this? If so, as may only sometimes occur, on what basis? If not in some or many cases, does that suggest the capacity of some authors, perhaps especially those born in one nation and living elsewhere, to transcend national background in their scholarship? Do they also, as immigrants, transcend the possible influence of the nation in which they are writing and teaching?

There is a somewhat related question of whether gender in the structure of arguments, in the phrasing of points, in the use of language, in the intermixture of narrative and analysis, and in the conception of a particular analysis is clearly discernible in scholarly literature in the West on the end of the Pacific/Asian War. Saki Dockrill's work in the mid 1990s was co-authored with Lawrence Freedman, and Koshiro is the only woman to have published an individual study on the subject in the West in recent years, so the comparative evidence for useful gender distinctiveness may be too limited.

There is far more to the ending of the Pacific/Asian War than the questions about Japan's surrender, as scholars of Soviet and Asian issues, as well as American foreign policy, recognize. Reaching beyond Soviet-Japanese relations, the employment of an interpretive framework with a multinational focus, properly broadened, might even extend to further investigating issues of the surrender and ending the war in the frameworks of Chinese-Soviet relations, American-Chinese relations, and Japanese-Chinese relations in 1945. In looking at the ending of the war on the Asian continent, that would mean examining the wartime concerns about power in postwar Asia, where the Chinese nationalist-communist rivalry would predictably be important. The politics of World War II in each wartime nation clearly had important postwar meanings. The task is to examine and explain those meanings, and to determine how intimately the surrender issues are related to the postwar world that various parties in the late wartime period desired and that ultimately— whether foreseen or not—emerged. How much, for example, can the nature of postwar Japan, in the occupation and later, be explained by the nature of the surrender? What would have happened on the Asian mainland, in particular involving China and Korea, if the war had ended differently in form, and earlier or later in time?[10]

Such questions always involve some sense of the tug, or tension, between contingency and inevitability in the historical process. To help guide such considerations, a few counterfactual questions, suggesting plausibly different events, may be interesting and useful: How would Japan's surrender have turned out if Army Minister Anami had not backed the emperor but instead supported the coup? If Hirohito in August had chosen differently and not chosen surrender? If, in particular, he had counseled rejection of America's somewhat ambiguous terms of the 11th? If Truman had earlier (in July) offered softer terms, including allowing a constitutional monarchy, or not used the atomic bomb in early August but delayed instead, at least for a few weeks? If Stalin had chosen not to enter the war in early August but a few weeks later? If the Pacific/Asian War for various reasons had dragged on for a few more months? Would there have been more atomic bombings, as is very likely, and quite possibly the use of chemical warfare (called biological warfare at the time) on Japanese crops, and gas on Japanese forces? Added to all that, one might ask—in a subject still little investigated—what if Japan's military on the home islands, or beyond, or in both sets of areas, had not generally acceded when Japan's government did formally announce that nation's surrender? Might the war have continued on the continent, at considerable human cost, adding especially to the millions of noncombatants already slain in the Pacific/Asian War?

Perhaps it would also be appropriate to seek to conduct systematically, though based on admittedly soft data, an analysis of whether more people would have died or not if the A-bombs had not been used and if the war had ended at various hypothetical but not clearly implausible junctures—say, variously, late August, early September, late September, early October and late October—before the November 1 invasion. Such a study, looking carefully at different categories of people by nationality and by noncombatant versus combatant status, could provide useful perspective on various counterfactual analyses.

Such multiple questions about how and why the war ended, and the suggestion of lines of future analysis including counterfactual speculation, may take scholars along paths that the poet T. S. Eliot, in a different context, wrote of more than a half-century ago in what can be viewed as thoughts also about historical inquiry:

> We shall not cease from exploration
> And the end of all our exploring
> Will be to arrive where we started
> And know the place for the first time.[11]

Undoubtedly, in practice, as normally on important contested historical issues such as how and why wars end and start, there will not be consensus but richer dialogue in interpreting the end of the Pacific/Asian War. Despite likely differences, perhaps many scholars and lay readers, as well as journalists and popular historians, will feel after more historical inquiry that they better, though not yet fully, "know the place."

Will other scholars, including those social scientists in security studies and policy studies, and those who wish to place Japan's surrender in a framework of social-science theory on how and why nations surrender, be able, in a meaningful way, to "know the place"? And can evolving social-science theory of nation-state surrender, and how wars end, help historians in getting to "know the place"—understanding deeply the rich events, the essential details, the key actors, and the complicated context, in mid 1945, of Japan's surrender?

For nearly all analysts, understanding and assessing Japan's surrender, because of that event's linkage to the atomic bombings, takes on great—really, added—importance. For some writers, again because of the fact of the atomic bombings, this leads to analyses—varyingly sometimes mixed with condemnation or approval—of American policy in mid 1945 in the effort to end the war. For most, however, the question of Soviet motives and behavior in dealing with Japan in mid 1945 is considerably less freighted, perhaps because Cold War passions have ebbed and because the USSR did not gain a footing on Japan's home islands. All of which raises the tantalizing question of what the literature on the surrender and the end of the war would look like if Soviet troops had penetrated and occupied part of Japan.

Reference Matter

Notes

Hasegawa: Introduction

1. David M. Kennedy, "Crossing the Moral Threshold: Why U.S. Leaders Never Questioned the Idea of Dropping the Bomb," *Time*, Aug. 1, 2005, 50. The issue of whether the use of the atomic bombs was immoral is another controversial one, which we do not choose to deal with in this volume.

2. "Japan Started the War in Asia 76 Years Ago: It's Time to End It," an advertisement in the *New York Times*, Sept. 13, 2005, A29, vividly illustrates that the memory of the war is a contemporary issue.

3. For historiography on the U.S. use of the atomic bombs on Hiroshima and Nagasaki, see Barton J. Bernstein, "The Struggle over History: Defining the Hiroshima Narrative," in Philip Nobile, ed., *Judgment at the Smithsonian* (New York: Marlowe, 1995), 127–256; Samuel Walker, "Recent Literature on Truman's Atomic Bomb Decision: A Search for Middle Ground," *Diplomatic History* 29, no. 2 (2005): 311–34, and Barton Bernstein's Chapters 1 and 7 in this volume.

4. Robert J. C. Butow, *Japan's Decision to Surrender* (Stanford: Stanford University Press, 1954). Tsuyoshi Hasegawa, *Racing the Enemy: Stalin, Truman, and the Surrender of Japan* (Cambridge, Mass.: Belknap Press of Harvard University Press, 2005) and its revised version in Japanese, *Antō: Sutārin Torūman to nihon no kōfuku* (Tokyo: Chūōkōron shinsha, 2006), are in part intended to correct this historiographical gap.

5. Leon V. Sigal, *Fighting to a Finish* (Ithaca, N.Y.: Cornell University Press, 1988); Richard Frank, *Downfall: The End of the Imperial Japanese Empire* (New York: Random House, 1999).

6. Herbert P. Bix, *Hirohito and the Making of Modern Japan* (New York: HarperCollins, 2000).

7. None of the authors of the present volume deal directly with the issue of the *kokutai*. For a fuller discussion on this issue, see Hasegawa, *Racing the Enemy.*

8. B. N. Slavinskii, *Sovetskaia okkupatsiia Kuril'skikh ostrov (avgust–sen-*

tiabr' 1945 goda): Dokumental'noe issledovanie (Moscow: TOO "Lotos," 1993); *Pakt o neitralitete mezhdu SSSR i Iaponiei: Diplomaticheskaia istoriia, 1941–1945 gg.* (Moscow: TOO "Novina," 1995); *Ialtinskaia konferentiia i problema "severnykh territorii"* (Moscow: TOO "Novina," 1996); *SSSR i Iaponiia—na puti k voine: Diplomaticheskaia istoriia, 1937–1945 gg.* (Moscow: ZAO "Iaponia segodnia," 1999).

1. Bernstein: Introducing the Interpretive Problems
of Japan's 1945 Surrender

AUTHOR'S NOTE: The author is grateful for assistance over the years from Gar Alperovitz, Sadao Asada, Kai Bird, Robert J. C. Butow, Alvin Coox, Conrad Crane, Edward Drea, Peter Duus, Richard Frank, Gian Gentile, Alexander George, Tsuyoshi Hasegawa, David Holloway, Sean Malloy, Robert Newman, Scott Sagan, Martin J. Sherwin, J. Samuel Walker, and Shintaro Yamaguchi, and more recently from Herbert Bix, John DeBoer, Michael Gordin, Yukiko Koshiro, and Richard Minear, and for support from the Ford Foundation, the MacArthur Foundation, the National Science Foundation, and the Harry S. Truman Library Institute; and to the 2001 University of California, Santa Barbara, conference and seminar members of the Peace Studies group in the early 1990s and at CISAC (now the Center for International Security and Cooperation) at Stanford University in 1994–2004, where parts of earlier versions of this paper were presented. The essay sometimes criticizes the work of people whose aid I have cited. It is important that readers understand that interpretive disagreements in such cases (as with others) are intellectual differences, not personal matters, and that sincere appreciation for assistance does not bar emphasizing interpretive differences, which sometimes emerge forcefully in this essay, because those authors are important, and their work therefore warrants critical comment.

Readers may be perplexed by references in the text and notes to me in the third person, but that seemed preferable to use of the first person. An initial effort, in an early draft, to avoid all references in the text to my work seemed evasive or coy, or both.

EPIGRAPH: Edwin Reischauer, foreword, in Robert J. C. Butow, *Japan's Decision to Surrender* (Stanford: Stanford University Press, 1954), vi.

1. See on the other unusual case in the first half of the twentieth century, H. E. Goemans, *War and Punishment: The Causes of War Termination and the First World War* (Princeton, N.J.: Princeton University Press, 2000).

2. There is a large theoretical literature on the general problem of war termination and surrender, mostly by political scientists. See, e.g., C. R. Mitchell and Michael Nicholson, "Rational Models and the Ending of Wars," *Journal of Conflict Resolution* 27 (September 1983): 494–520; Francis Beer and Thomas Mayer, "Why Wars End: Some Hypotheses," *Review of International Studies* 12 (1986): 95–106; and Christopher Mitchell, "Ending Conflicts and Wars: Judgement, Rationality, and Entrapment," *International Social Science Journal* 43 (February 1991): 35–59. Two thoughtful pre-1989 efforts by political scientists to combine theory and empiricism on Japan's surrender are Paul Kecskemeti, *Strategic Surrender: The Politics of Victory and Defeat* (Stanford: Stanford University Press, 1958), and Leon Sigal, *Fighting to a Finish: The Politics of War Termination in the United States and Japan, 1945* (Ithaca, N.Y.: Cornell University Press, 1988).

3. James Fearon, "Counterfactuals and Hypothesis Testing in Political Science," *World Politics* 43 (January 1991): 165–95.

4. U.S. Strategic Bombing Survey, *Japan's Struggle to End the War* (Washington, D.C.: Government Printing Office, 1946), 13; Hanson Baldwin, "Our Worst Blunders in the War," *Atlantic Monthly* 185 (February 1950): 30–38, and *Great Mistakes of the War* (New York: Harper, 1950), 88–102, esp. 98–102; and Butow, *Japan's Decision to Surrender*, 131–33. Also see U.S. Strategic Bombing Survey, *Summary Report (Pacific War)* (Washington, D.C.: Government Printing Office, 1946), 26.

5. This is based on various letters and some conversations, partly with Robert Newman.

6. Part of the problem is the considerable range of uncertainty on how many died in the atomic bombings then and later, and on how many had died through mid-August in the conventional bombing of Japan, because the latter number (the dispute ranges between about 213,000 and about 800,000) would be a basis for later extrapolations.

7. See Barton J. Bernstein, "Ike and Hiroshima: Did He Oppose It?" *Journal of Strategic Studies* 10 (September 1987): 386–89; and for sources, Committee for a National Discussion of Nuclear History and Current Policy, "Views of American Military Leaders on the Atomic Bombings of Japan" (n.d. [1994–95]).

8. Joseph Grew and Walter Johnson, with assistance of Nancy Hooker, eds., *Turbulent Era: A Diplomatic Record of Forty Years, 1904–1945*, vol. 2 (Boston: Houghton Mifflin, 1952), 1432–40.

9. See also Herbert Bix, "Japan's Delayed Surrender: A Reinterpretation," *Diplomatic History* 19 (Spring 1995): 197–203.

10. Tsuyoshi Hasegawa, *Racing the Enemy: Stalin, Truman, and the Surrender of Japan* (Cambridge, Mass.: Belknap Press of Harvard University Press, 2005). Richard Frank, though not an academic, also produced an important volume, *Downfall: The End of the Imperial Japanese Empire* (New York: Random House, 1999), that paid serious attention to A-bomb issues.

11. Barton J. Bernstein, "The Atomic Bomb and American Foreign Policy, 1941–1945: A Historiographical Controversy," *Peace & Change* 2 (Spring 1974): 1–16; J. Samuel Walker, "The Decision to Use the Bomb: A Historiographical Update," *Diplomatic History* 14 (Winter 1990): 97–114; Barton J. Bernstein, "The Struggle over History: Defining the Hiroshima Narrative," in Philip Nobile, ed., *Judgment at the Smithsonian* (New York: Marlowe, 1995), 127–256; J. Samuel Walker, "The Decision to Use the Bomb: A Historiographical Update," and "History, Collective Memory, and the Decision to Use the Bomb," in Michael Hogan, ed., *Hiroshima in History and Memory* (New York: Cambridge University Press, 1996), 11–37 and 187–99; and J. Samuel Walker, "Recent Literature on Truman's Atomic Bomb Decision: A Search for Middle Ground," *Diplomatic History* 29 (2005): 311–34. On criticisms of some of the literature, also see Barton J. Bernstein, ed., *The Atomic Bomb: The Critical Issues* (Boston: Little, Brown, 1975).

12. Gar Alperovitz, *Atomic Diplomacy: Hiroshima and Potsdam: The Use of the Atomic Bomb and the American Confrontation with Soviet Power* (New York: Simon & Schuster, 1965), 238.

13. On Sherwin, see especially his *A World Destroyed: The Atomic Bomb and the Grand Alliance* (New York: Knopf, 1975).

14. Barton J. Bernstein, "Roosevelt, Truman, and the Atomic Bomb: A Reinterpretation," *Political Science Quarterly* 90 (Spring 1975): 48–59; id., "Doomsday II," *New York Times Magazine*, July 27, 1975, 7, 21ff. Bernstein on some later occasions—rather loosely—varied his phrasing on the Nagasaki's bomb's "necessity."

15. Barton J. Bernstein, "The Perils and Politics and Politics of Surrender: Ending the War with Japan and Avoiding the Third Atomic Bomb," *Pacific Historical Review* 46 (1977): 1–27.

16. Alperovitz, *Atomic Diplomacy* (rev. ed., New York: Penguin Books, 1985), 1–60, esp. 11–15; and see also 386–87n35.

17. Ibid., 11–15, 27–32.

18. Ibid., 30.

19. Gar Alperovitz et al., *The Decision to Use the Atomic Bomb and the Architecture of an American Myth* (New York: Knopf, 1995). See Ian Buruma, "The War over the Bomb," *New York Review of Books,* Sept. 21, 1995, 26–34; and for Buruma-Alperovitz differences, see "The New War over Hiroshima: An Exchange," ibid., Nov. 30, 1995. Also see Brian Villa and John Bonnet, "Understanding Indignation: Gar Alperovitz, Robert Maddox, and the Decision to Use the Atomic Bomb," *Reviews in American History* 24 (September 1996): 529–36; Eric Bergerud, "Dropping the Bomb," *Newsday,* Aug. 6, 1995; and Michael King, "Bombs Away," *National Review*, Nov. 4, 1995, 60–61, 64–65, which are favorable to anti-revisionists—Maddox in the first essay, Maddox and Polmar and Allen in the second, and Maddox, Newman, and Bruce Lee in the third. Cf. Marilyn Young, review, *American Historical Review* 100 (December 1995): 1515–16; and Alonzo Hamby, review, *Journal of American History* 84 (September 1997): 609–14. For a strongly anti-Alperovitz and pro-Maddox review in a military journal, see James Auer and Richard Halloran, "Looking Back at the Bomb," *Parameters* 26 (Spring 1996): 127–35, significantly based on Halloran, "The Useful Bomb," *Far Eastern Economic Review*, Aug. 17, 1995. Alperovitz's views receive oblique criticism and some acceptance in Arnold Offner, *Another Such Victory: President Truman and the Cold War, 1945–1953* (Stanford: Stanford University Press, 2002), esp. 97–99, which devotes a few paragraphs to Japanese policy, including some on 73, 78, 93–95, and 97–99. Dorothy Rabinowitz assailed two Alperovitz-based TV documentaries in the *Wall Street Journal*, Aug. 7, 1995.

20. Robert J. Maddox, *Weapons for Victory: The Hiroshima Decision Fifty Years Later* (Columbia: University of Missouri Press, 1995); and Robert P. Newman, *Truman and the Hiroshima Cult* (East Lansing: Michigan State University Press, 1995). Because this essay mostly focuses on serious scholarship, with only an occasional discussion of some notable popular history, such as Edward Behr's volume on Hirohito, it does not discuss the anti-revisionist work by the popular historians Thomas Allen and Norman Polmar, *Code-Name Downfall: The Secret Plan to Invade Japan—and Why Truman Dropped the Bomb* (New York: Simon & Schuster, 1995), which devotes little space to Japan and often errs severely on facts, arithmetic, and sources; Bruce Lee, *Marching Orders: The Untold Story of World War II* (New York: Crown, 1995), which errs on various matters and claims unwarranted newness; Sidney Weintraub's anti-revisionist *The Last Great Victory: The End of World War II, July/August 1945* (New York: Dutton, 1995), which lacks specific source notes and is skimpy on archival materials, and J.

Robert Moskin's *Mr. Truman's War* (New York: Random House, 1996), which has comparatively little to say on Japanese policy and uncritically trusts secondary sources; its author apparently did not examine archival material. Nor does the essay treat the pro-A-bombing biographies of Truman by David McCullough, Robert Ferrell, and Alonzo Hamby, because they give little attention to Japanese policy in 1945. Among other recent books not treated are J. Samuel Walker, *Prompt and Utter Destruction: Truman and the Use of Atomic Bombs Against Japan* (Chapel Hill: University of North Carolina Press, 2004), a slender, intelligent middle-way synthesis focusing mostly on U.S. policy and providing limited attention to Japanese policy; Thomas Zeiler, *Unconditional Defeat: Japan, America, and the End of World War II* (Wilmington, Del.: Scholarly Resources, 2004), which is really a text supplement and whose author apparently eschewed archival research; Alan Levine, *The Pacific War: Japan Versus the Allies* (Westport, Conn.: Praeger, 1995), which seems designed for similar purposes and is without archival work, while also devoting only about one and one-third chapters to the ending of the war; David Rees, *The Defeat of Japan* (Westport, Conn.: Praeger, 1997), which depends mostly on published books and disregards much of the journal literature and many relevant books; and Tim Maga, *America Attacks Japan: The Invasion That Never Was* (Lexington: University of Kentucky Press, 2002), which is remarkably unreliable. I have not listed books (or essays) of 1989–2005 that bear on end-of-the-war Japan policy that either do not focus sufficiently on such policy or are excluded here because of other relevant criteria (especially involving serious original scholarship).

21. Maddox, *Weapons for Victory* (1995) 189n7 and 194 (bibliography), cites Newman's book manuscript *Truman and the Hiroshima Cult*, which relies heavily on U.S. Strategic Bombing Survey records (on microfilm).

22. Gar Alperovitz, *Cold War Essays* (Garden City, N.Y.: Anchor Books, 1970), 51–74.

23. Various discussions with Newman and a letter of Oct. 18, 2004. The influence of the Lattimore project is mentioned in Newman, *Truman and the Hiroshima Cult*, xiii, and the influence of some related research besides the U.S. Strategic Bombing Survey materials is somewhat speculative, and not adequately confirmed, but no larger interpretation rests on this.

24. Newman, *Truman and the Hiroshima Cult*, passim, and esp. 29 (briefly stated anti-Soviet purposes). For Maddox's brief implication and perhaps acknowledgment of anti-Soviet purposes of some Truman associates, see *Weapons for Victory*, 155.

25. Newman, *Truman and the Hiroshima Cult*, 73 (possibly briefly dampened peace forces), and 108–9 (Hirohito and Nagasaki). See ibid., 214n72, on Butow, *Japan's Decision to Surrender*, chs. 7-9, but also see 131–33. On Stimson, see Stimson and McGeorge Bundy, *On Active Service in Peace and War* (New York: Harper, 1948), 628–29; and Newman, "Hiroshima and the Trashing of Henry Stimson," *New England Quarterly* 71 (March 1998): 5–30, esp. 19–21. Readers should know that I read this pro-Stimson essay in manuscript for Newman and recommended (despite our interpretive disagreements on Stimson) that he send it to the *NEQ*, which I thought would probably publish it.

26. Newman, *Truman and the Hiroshima Cult*, 185–93.

27. Maddox, "The Biggest Decision: Why We Had to Drop the Atomic Bomb,"

American Heritage 466 (June 1995): 71–77; Donald Kagan, "Why America Dropped the Bomb," *Commentary* 100 (September 1995): 17–23. Also see Newman, "What New Consensus?" *Washington Post,* Nov. 30, 1994, responding to Alperovitz, "Beyond the Smithsonian Flap: Historians' New Consensus," ibid., Oct. 16, 1994.

28. As of early 2005, JSTOR (www.jstor.org), an on-line service covering more than eighty-five history and political science scholarly journals and about fifteen others in Asian studies, listed only two reviews of Newman's book and three of Maddox's, with one of the reviews (by Sanho Tree) treating both books together. Newman, when queried, could not locate his file of reviews. Maddox never responded to a similar query about reviews, but his publisher, the University of Missouri Press, provided helpful materials. Both JSTOR-listed reviews of Newman's book were by Alperovitz's collaborators—Sanho Tree in the *Journal of American History* 90 (March 1997): 1475–76, and Robert Messer in the *American Historical Review* 102 (October 1997): 1253. The three JSTOR-listed reviews of Maddox's volume were by Tree, dealing also with Newman's book in *JAH* (March 1997), by Gregg Herken in the *American Historical Review* 102 (February 1997): 212–13, and by Brian Villa and John Bonnet, with Alperovitz's book, in *Reviews in American History.* Of the four separate reviews so far listed here, only Villa and Bonnet's was favorably inclined to anti-revisionism, though Villa would years later somewhat change his position on the atomic bombing in private correspondence. Not listed on JSTOR, the *Pacific Historical Review* 65 (August 1996): 501–3, published Newman's favorable review of Maddox's book and Norman Graebner's rather agnostic but not unfriendly review of Newman's volume. Looking through state history journals might pick up more reviews of Maddox's and Newman's books, but the focus is to locate *major* scholarly reviews, not all reviews. A mixed review of Maddox by Paul Rorvig appeared in *Presidential Studies Quarterly* (Fall 1996), also not listed on JSTOR. An uninformed, enthusiastic review of Maddox by Arch Frederic Blakey appeared in the *Florida Historical Quarterly* 75 (Summer 1996): 106–7, which constituted the basis for the advertisement in 2004 for a new paperback of the book. See the advertisement in the *New York Review of Books,* Nov. 18, 2004, 31, and also Maddox's new introduction in *Weapons for Victory: The Hiroshima Decision* (2004), xi–xvii, for a remarkably selective presentation of recent scholarship, a surprising error in not realizing that the U.S. Strategic Bombing Survey is the agency author (not the title, as Maddox mistakenly contends) of the key 1946 survey, and minor difficulty in spelling the name of one anti-revisionist ally, D. M. Giangreco. Giangreco had reviewed both Newman and Maddox in a strongly favorable but unfortunately error-studded review, "To Bomb or Not to Bomb," *Naval War College Review* 51 (Spring 1998): 141–45.

29. All sales figures by American authors of books are drawn from each author's replies to my queries, with the exception of Maddox's book. The numbers for Maddox's sales are inferred from the report that his publisher produced 3,000 copies in hardback, and that most (if not all) were reportedly sold before the first paperback edition in mid 2004. Newman's number was about 500 in Newman to Bernstein, Oct. 18, 2004; Maddox's sales numbers inferred from a phone conversation with Eve Kidd of the University of Missouri Press, Nov. 15, 2004. For sales numbers, most authors relied upon memory, not checking royalty statements, so their numbers may often be wrong by about 15–25 percent on average, but such error, if it occurred, is undoubtedly hon-

est and would not in any case distort the general pattern. Efforts to update all the sales numbers in 2005–6 were unsuccessful. The first few authors consulted simply did not have the data readily accessible and did not want to be burdened.

30. U.S. Strategic Bombing Survey, *Japan's Struggle to End the War*, 13, and *Summary Report (Pacific War)*, 26.

31. Barton J. Bernstein, "Compelling Japan's Surrender Without the Atomic Bomb, Soviet Entry, or Invasion: Reconsidering the US Bombing Survey's Early-Surrender Conclusions," *Journal of Strategic Studies* 18 (June 1995): 101–48; and Robert P. Newman, "Ending the War with Japan: Paul Nitze's 'Early-Surrender' Counterfactual," *Pacific Historical Review* 64 (May 1995): 167–94, which with minor revisions appears as chap. 2 ("Was Japan Ready to Surrender?") in Newman, *Truman and the Hiroshima Cult*. Bernstein's 1995 criticism of the U.S. Strategic Bombing Survey reports first appeared briefly at a 1985 American Historical Association meeting, but evoked no interest from the panel members, or from others then. The subsequent paragraphs in this section on the two authors are drawn from Bernstein, "Compelling Japan's Surrender," and Newman, *Truman and the Hiroshima Cult*, chap. 2. For the best study of the U.S. Strategic Bombing Survey, see Gian Gentile, *How Effective Is Strategic Bombing? Lessons Learned from World War II to Kosovo* (New York: New York University Press, 2002), 1–166. In his 2004 introduction, Maddox, *Weapons for Victory* (2004), xiv, implies that Newman's critique was unavailable to him in 1994–95, but Maddox's 1995 volume, 189n7, actually mentions Newman's book-chapter critique of the U.S. Strategic Bombing Survey (although citing it as chap. 6), and Maddox's 1995 bibliography, on page 194, also cites Newman's book manuscript. In his new introduction in 2004, Maddox omits any reference to other critiques of the U.S. Strategic Bombing Survey that were published in 1995–2001.

32. Robert A. Pape, "Why Japan Surrendered," *International Security* 18 (Fall 1993): 154–201, and id., *Bombing to Win: Air Power and Coercion in War* (Ithaca, N.Y.: Cornell University Press, 1996), chap. 4 ("Japan, 1944–1945"), 87–136. A somewhat critical, but often approving, review is Stephen Biddle, "Why You Can't Get a Lot for a Little," *Mershon International Studies Review* 41 (1997): 113–16, which pays only slight attention to the issue of the A-bomb in relation to Japan's surrender.

33. Robert A. Pape, "The Air Force Strikes Back: A Reply to Barry Watts and John Warden," *Security Studies* 7 (Winter 1997–98): 191–214; and Barry Watts, "Ignoring Reality: Problems of Theory and Evidence in Security Studies," ibid., 152–55. In *Bombing to Win*, 94–95 and n. 29, Pape briefly, but rather obliquely, addresses part of the A-bomb revisionist position.

34. Pape, "Why Japan Surrendered," 154–55n2, and *Bombing to Win*, 87–88n2, cite K. T. Compton, who fits Pape's civilian vulnerability framework, and two others. But those other two authors—Louis Morton, "The Decision to Use the Atomic Bomb," *Foreign Affairs* 35 (January 1957), and Herbert Feis, *The Atomic Bomb and the End of World War II* (Princeton, N.J.: Princeton University Press, 1966, 1970)—seem highly questionable. Pape provides no page citation to either source. Ascribing an assumption of civilian vulnerability in those two studies seems without clear warrant, though it would be incorrect to state that Pape is clearly wrong. How and why Pape seems so sure on this matter, and without even the hedge of a "probably," is unclear. Pape's n. 5

in his book chapter and essay also cite Kecskemeti's *Strategic Surrender*, which seems to assume civilian vulnerability. Queries by letter to Pape in 1994–95 and in 2004–5 failed to elicit any response from him on these matters.

35. Pape, "Why Japan Surrendered," 155, and *Bombing to Win*, 88.

36. For relevant data, see U.S. Strategic Bombing Survey, *The War Against Japanese Transportation, 1941–1945* (Washington, D.C.: Government Printing Office, 1947), 3–5, 8, 54, 116; id., *Japan's Struggle to End the War*, 11; and id., *Summary Report (Pacific War)*, 11, 14–15.

37. Pape, "Why Japan Surrendered," 184–86, esp. paragraphs one, six and seven in that section on the emperor; and see *Bombing to Win*, 121–23, for similar key sentences amid slightly different paragraphing. Also, for other problems in Pape's work, see Pape, "Why Japan Surrendered," 183–84, and *Bombing to Win*, 121, which contend that the atomic bombing of the 6th and Soviet entry "raised both civilian and military vulnerability to very high levels," and thus "for this final change in civilian views, it is impossible to determine whether military or civilian vulnerability had the greatest impact." Pape in this segment has apparently undermined part of his larger interpretive framework about the preeminence of military vulnerability in producing the surrender.

38. Pape, "Why Japan Surrendered," 197, and *Bombing to Win*, 133. He seemed to be saying far more than that counterfactual conclusions in historical analysis cannot be certain.

39. Pape, "Why Japan Surrendered," 155–56, and *Bombing to Win*, 88 ("already dead"); and "Why Japan Surrendered," 166; and possibly in a small retreat on the cost in cities, *Bombing to Win*, 106 ("nearly dead"). Pape concludes in "Why Japan Surrendered," 165, and *Bombing to Win*, 104, that 22 million were rendered homeless, because he erroneously adds together (1) *all evacuees* and (2) *all those* whose housing was too badly damaged to permit continued domicile, and he assumes, contrary to direct evidence in the U.S. Strategic Bombing Survey reports, that these were *always different* people. Thus, he is often double-counting. See e.g., U.S. Strategic Bombing Survey, *Effects of Air Attack on Urban Complex Tokyo-Kawasaki-Yokohoma* (Washington, D.C.: Government Printing Office, 1947), 8, and *Effects of Air Attack on Osaka-Kobe-Kyoto* (Washington, D.C.: Government Printing Office, 1947), 26–38, 162–64, 243–44.

40. Joint interrogation of Suzuki, no. 531, Dec. 26, 1945, U.S. Strategic Bombing Survey Records, RG 243, National Archives, quoted in Bernstein, "Compelling Japan's Surrender," 116, and in Newman, *Truman and the Hiroshima Cult*, 49.

41. Pape, "Why Japan Surrendered," 156–57, 186–90, and *Bombing to Win*, 89, 124–26. See Newman, *Truman and the Hiroshima Cult*, 208n46, and Bernstein, "Compelling Japan's Surrender," 148n112. Pape relies upon Sigal, *Fighting to a Finish*, 226, who somehow, in an honest error, omits a crucial part of Kawabe's postwar statement. In "Why Japan Surrendered," 187, and in *Bombing to Win*, 125, Pape relies for his second military source (besides Kawabe) upon a postwar quotation from Admiral Toyoda, in which Toyoda said that Soviet entry was more important but did not deny the importance of the atomic bombing. Adding to problems, Pape, in "Why Japan Surrendered," 178–79, and *Bombing to Win*, 116–17, claims—apparently only on the basis of S. Woodburn Kirby et al.'s book *The War Against Japan*, 5: 193–96—that Japanese military leaders considered the Kwantung Army "Japan's premier fighting

force" (Pape's phrase); but careful examination of Kirby et al., 193–96 provides strong *contrary* evidence. Kirby et al. report that Japanese leaders knew that the Kwantung Army had been depleted, that new recruits were often undertrained, and that equipment was often inadequate.

42. Pape, "Why Japan Surrendered" and *Bombing to Win,* both n. 6, cite Sigal, *Fighting to a Finish,* but Pape omits any page number. See also n. 5 in Pape, "Why Japan Surrendered," and in *Bombing to Win,* and "Why Japan Surrendered," 197n147, and *Bombing to Win,* 133n164, which cite Kecskemeti, *Strategic Surrender,* 204–5, which actually explains the subtle U.S. formulation.

43. On the surrender, see, inter alia, Butow, *Japan's Decision to Surrender,* 195–209, and Bernstein, "Perils and Politics," 17–27.

44. No A-bomb historian I know of, other than a few revisionists, finds Pape's work useful on A-bomb/end-of-the-Japanese/Asian War issues. Significantly, in a lengthy essay, the effort by a 1990s political scientist critic to fault Pape on his interpretation of the political effects of conventional bombing and the atomic bombing in Japan does not go much beyond citing two scholarly synthetic books on these issues. See Watts, "Ignoring Reality," 153–55. A Pape student, Alexander Downes, "Targeting Civilians in War" (Ph.D. diss., University of Chicago, 2004), 238–43, notes some problems, while accepting parts of Pape's analysis.

45. Lawrence Freedman and Saki Dockrill, "Hiroshima: A Strategy of Shock," in Dockrill, ed., *From Pearl Harbor to Hiroshima: The Second World War in Asia and the Pacific, 1941–45* (New York: St. Martin's Press, 1994), 191–212.

46. Lawrence Freedman, "The Strategy of Hiroshima," *Journal of Strategic Studies* 1 (1977): 93.

47. Ibid., 93–94.

48. Lawrence Freedman, *The Evolution of Nuclear Strategy* (New York: St. Martin's Press, 1981), 21, quoting B. H. Liddell Hart, *The Revolution in Warfare* (London: Faber & Faber, 1946), 83. Also see Liddell Hart, *Revolution,* 74–75.

49. Freedman and Dockrill, "Hiroshima," 193.

50. Ibid., 205.

51. Ibid., 204.

52. Ibid., 206–7, and "*indirect*" is emphasized in the essay.

53. Ibid., 209. Their phrasing—that the United States "can claim" moral equivalency—may be interpreted by some in a strained (but not totally implausible) effort as not endorsing but simply noting the possibility of such a claim.

54. Ibid., 191 and 193.

55. Saki Dockrill, "Hirohito, the Emperor's Army, and Pearl Harbor," *Review of International Studies* 18 (October 1992), deals briefly with these issues for the earlier period.

56. Sadao Asada, "The Shock of the Atomic Bomb and Japan's Decision to Surrender—A Reconsideration," *Pacific Historical Review* 67 (November 1998): 477–512. I read and recommended the article to the journal for publication, though I did not agree with part of the interpretation, but deemed the essay important and meriting a place in the scholarly dialogue.

57. On an earlier indictment, see Inoue Kiyosho, *Tennō no Sensō Sekinin,* the spirited exchange in *Shokun* (May through July 1977), and the added defense by Charles

Sheldon, "Scapegoat or Instigator of Japanese Aggression: Inoue Kiyoshi's Case Against the Emperor," *Modern Asian Studies* 12 (February 1978): 1–35; and Sheldon, "Japanese Aggression and the Emperor, 1931–1941, from Contemporary Diaries," ibid. 10 (Feb. 1976): 1–40.

58. David Bergamini, *Japan's Imperial Conspiracy* (New York: Morrow, 1971) and reviews, e.g., James Crowley, *New York Times Book Review*, Oct. 29, 1971, 3 and 66; Shumpei Okamoto, *Journal of Asian Studies* 31 (February 1972): 414–16; and (a more ambivalent assessment) Barbara Tuchman, *Book World,* Oct. 24, 1971. Tuchman thought that Hirohito should have been tried (she doesn't say convicted) for war crimes.

59. Edward Behr, *Hirohito: Behind the Myth* (New York: Villard, 1989). The present historiographical essay, in dealing with works on the emperor published in the West in 1989–2005, has intentionally omitted some that are clearly journalistic or unduly brief, or both, and some other marginal studies, including Edward Hoyt, *Hirohito: The Emperor and the Man* (New York: Praeger, 1992), which is mostly journalistic; general histories like Takafusa Nakamura, *A History of Showa Japan, 1926–1989*, trans. Herbert P. Bix et al. (Tokyo: University of Tokyo Press, 1993), which has little on the surrender period; and the otherwise important *Cambridge History of Japan*, vol. 6: *The Twentieth Century* (Cambridge: Cambridge University Press, 1988), ed. Peter Duus, which appeared before 1989 and does very little with diplomacy and ending the war, though it contains much by the military historian Alvin Coox on the military (not the diplomatic) conduct of the war. See Herbert Bix, "Review Essay: Japan Studies Old and New at the End of the Eighties," *Bulletin of Concerned Asian Scholars* 23 (April–June 1991): 84–89.

60. Behr, *Hirohito*, 293–94.

61. Ibid., 297–99.

62. John Dower, review, *New York Times Book Review*, Oct. 8, 1989.

63. Stephen Large, review, *Journal of Japanese Studies* 17 (Summer 1990): 508–12; Toshiaki Kawahara, *Hirohito and His Times: A Japanese Perspective* (New York: Kodansha, 1990).

64. Stephen Large, "Emperor Hirohito and Early Showa Japan," *Monumenta Nipponica* 46 (Autumn 1991): 366.

65. Stephen Large, *Emperor Hirohito and Showa Japan: A Political Biography* (New York: Routledge, 1992), 102–15.

66. Ibid., 116.

67. Ibid., 125.

68. Daikichi Irokawa, *The Age of Hirohito: In Search of Modern Japan*, trans. Mikiso Hane and John Urda (New York: Free Press, 1995). On Irokawa's earlier work in the context of Japanese history writing, see Carol Gluck, "The People in History: Recent Trends in Japanese Historiography," *Journal of Asian Studies* 38 (November 1978): 25–50.

69. Irokawa, *Age of Hirohito*, 75–78, 81, and 86–91.

70. Ibid., 120–22.

71. Ibid., 91 (on 1943) and 31 (on 1945).

72. For reviews, see Ben-Ami Shillony, *Journal of Japanese Studies* 23 (Summer 1997), 450–54; Sharon Minichiello, *Journal of Asian Studies* 55 (May 1996), 458–

59; and Frank Gibney, *New York Times Book Review*, Sept. 24, 1995, 36. Gluck in "Foreword" to Irokawa, *Age of Hirohito*, vii–xii.

73. Irokawa, *Age of Hirohito*, 33.

74. Kurita Wataru, "Making Peace with Hirohito and a Militaristic Past," *Japan Quarterly* 36 (April–June 1989): 186–92; Awaya Kantaro, "Emperor Showa's Accountability for War," ibid., 39 (October–December 1991): 386–98. Also see Herbert P. Bix, "Hirohito's War," *History Today* 12 (December 1991): 12–19; and Nakamura Masanori, *The Japanese Monarchy: Ambassador Joseph Grew and the Making of the "Symbol Emperor System," 1931–1991*, trans. Herbert P. Bix et al. (Armonk, N.Y.: M. E. Sharpe, 1992).

75. Herbert P. Bix, "The Showa Emperor's 'Monologue' and the Problem of War Responsibility," *Journal of Japanese Studies* 18 (Summer 1992): 298–301; Edward Drea, *In the Service of the Emperor: Essays on the Imperial Japanese Army* (Lincoln: University of Nebraska Press, 1998), 171.

76. Bix, "Japan's Delayed Surrender," esp. 197–201.

77. Herbert P. Bix, "Rethinking 'Emperor System Fascism': Ruptures and Continuities in Modern Japanese History," *Bulletin of Concerned Asian Scholars* 14 (April–June 1982): 2–19, and see 19 for warning. See also id., "Kawakami Hajime and the Organic Law of Japanese Fascism," *Japanese Interpreter* 12 (Winter 1977): 118–33. For early Japanese studies on the emperor-fascism issue, see the anti-Marxist essay by Hatano Sumio, "Japanese Foreign Policy, 1931–1945: Historiography," in Sadao Asada, ed., *Japan and the World, 1853–1952* (New York: Columbia University Press, 1989), 217–23, 230–35, plus bibliography (with Asada).

78. Bix, "Showa Emperor's 'Monologue,' " 299 (first quotation), and see 324–26, 340, 350–54, 363. Bix, "Japan's Delayed Surrender," 212, frames what is quoted in this historiographical essay from Bix, *Hirohito and the Making of Modern Japan*, 520. On imperialism, with a critique of the work of Akira Iriye, see Herbert P. Bix, "Imagistic Historiography and the Reinterpretation of Japanese Imperialism," *Bulletin of Concerned Asian Scholars* 8 (July–September 1975): 51–68.

79. Bix, "Japan's Delayed Surrender," 217–23.

80. Bix, *Hirohito and the Making of Modern Japan*.

81. See, for critical reviews, Ben-Ami Shillony, *Journal of Japanese Studies* 28 (Winter 2002): 141–46; and Stephen Large, *Monumenta Nipponica* 56 (Spring 2002): 107–10. More favorable reviews are Carol Gluck, "Puppet on His Own String," *Times Literary Supplement,* Nov. 10, 2000, 3–4; Ian Buruma, "The Emperor's Secrets," *New York Review of Books,* Mar. 29, 2001, 24–28; Ronald Spector, *New York Times Book Review*, Nov. 19, 2000, 14; and Patrick Smith, *Business Week*, Oct. 16, 2000, on-line, with Smith, a former *International Herald Tribune* and *New Yorker* journalist who covered Japan in Hirohito's last years, calling the book "faultlessly researched."

82. Peter Wetzler, *Hirohito and War: Imperial Tradition and Military Decisionmaking in Prewar Japan* (Honolulu: University of Hawai'i Press, 1998), esp. 180.

83. Bix, "Japan's Delayed Surrender," 224.

84. Ibid., 208; Bix, *Hirohito*, 503.

85. Bix, *Hirohito*, 523.

86. Bix, "Japan's Delayed Surrender," 220, and *Hirohito*, 503.

87. Bix, *Hirohito*, 511. Also see Herbert P. Bix, "Japan's Surrender and the Monarchy: Staying the Course in an Unwinnable War," *Japan Focus* (2005), on-line.

88. Bix, "Japan's Delayed Surrender," 217–18, and later in *Hirohito*, 509. For similar wording but not quoting both sentences, see Asada, "Shock," 498.

' 89. Bix, *Hirohito*, 520–23, and "Japan's Delayed Surrender," 223–25.

90. Gar Alperovitz, *Book World*, Sept. 3, 2000, and Richard Frank, ibid., Oct. 8, 2000, 12. Alperovitz's review was sometimes critical of Bix's harshness toward Hirohito.

91. Telephone discussion with Bix, Oct. 14, 2004. Bix's judgment seemed very surprising to some history/international relations students and scholars (myself included) who had read both his book and Alperovitz's interpretation. I have not found any analyst of Japan-surrender issues in the United States or abroad (admittedly, I only checked with five, and no later than 2005) who agrees with Bix on his conclusion about Alperovitz's interpretation.

92. Telephone discussion with Bix, Oct. 14, 2004, on book sales.

93. Edward Drea, "Chasing a Decisive Victory: Emperor Hirohito and Japan's War with the West," in id., *In the Service of the Emperor*, 169–215. See Drea, "Hirohito, Accomplice or Villian: A Man of His Times" (1995 paper for the Society of Military History Annual Meeting; courtesy of Drea).

94. Drea, "Chasing a Decisive Victory," 188.

95. Ibid., 205.

96. Ibid., 201 and 188.

97. Ibid., 209.

98. Ibid., 211.

99. Ibid.

100. Ibid., 215.

101. Drea, *In the Service of the Emperor*, 277–78.

102. See Akira Iriye, *Journal of Asian Studies* 58 (November 1998): 1138; Leonard Humphreys, *Journal of Military History* 63 (January 1999): 204–5; and Alvin Coox, *Historian* 62 (Summer 2000): 677. A harsh review was published in the *Journal of Japanese Studies* 27 (Winter 2001): 219–22, by Takashi Fujitani, who, probably writing in about 1999–2000, favorably quoted J. Samuel Walker's 1995 analysis (published in 1996 in Hogan et al., *Hiroshima*) of the consensus in A-bomb literature, which was written *before* Maddox, Newman, and other anti-revisionist works appeared in 1995. A very favorable review of Drea's book, with mostly favorable judgments of Large's and Wetzler's books, appeared in Michael Barnhart, "Hirohito and His Army," *International History Review* 21 (September 1999): 696–703, who concludes that Hirohito was "not a ceremonial cipher, but neither was he a kaiser" (703).

103. Forrest Morgan, *Compellence and the Strategic Culture of Imperial Japan: Implications for Coercive Diplomacy in the Twenty-First Century* (Westport, Conn.: Praeger, 2003), and chap. 6 (185–250) on Japan's surrender.

104. Forrest Morgan, "Compellence and the Strategic Culture of Imperial Japan" (Ph.D. diss., University of Maryland College Park, 1998; copy made available through UMI dissertation services).

105. Morgan, *Compellence*, 65–68, on hypotheses, and 238–50 for endnotes.

106. Ibid., 187–88 and 215–27.

107. Ibid., 217.

108. Ibid., 238 (quotation) and 236–38.

109. Ibid., 229–37, 238.

110. Ibid., 212–15 and 235–38.

111. Ibid., 216–19, and also see 247n154.

112. Ibid., 246–47n153 and 217.

113. Ibid., 250n190; and Bix, *Hirohito*, 515.

114. Morgan, *Compellence*, 250n190. See also ibid., 270–71n6, for an additional statement of interpretive differences with Bix. In that note, which may have been belatedly inserted, Morgan seems close to Drea's view but indicates no knowledge of Drea's work. As of mid 2005, JSTOR listed no reviews of Morgan's book. Mid-2005 efforts to secure book reviews from the publisher failed, aside from Praeger's providing a copy of *Choice*'s brief statement: "Highly recommended. All levels, libraries."

115. Yukiko Koshiro, "Japan's World and World War II," *Diplomatic History* 25 (Summer 2001): 440; and id., "Eurasian Empire: Japan's End Game in World War II," *American Historical Review* 109 (April 2004): 417–44. Readers might want to consider Koshiro's study in comparison with Bix, "Imagistic Historiography and the Reinterpretation of Japanese Imperialism," *Bulletin of Concerned Asian Scholars* 8 (July–September 1975): 51–68

116. Koshiro, "Eurasian Empire," 417–19.

117. Ibid., 417–418 ("adopted"), 434 ("plan . . . made"), and 439–44. In a letter to me of Oct. 31, 2004, Koshiro stressed that her essay, in her judgment, contended that the policy had been fully adopted and was not simply under consideration.

118. Ibid., 417–18, and nn. 1–2.

119. Ibid., 426 (Tōgō), 426, 430, and 442–43 (Foreign Ministry), 419 (Suzuki), and 428 and 442 (Hirohito). Note that Koshiro, 442, states that the Foreign Ministry on August 7 "was still making a diplomatic attempt, *sincere or not*, to forestall war with the Soviet Union" (emphasis added). The gap between "sincere" and "not" is huge for her central set of arguments.

120. Ibid., 417nn1–2.

121. Initially, I had intended to include in this book an in-depth discussion of the end-of-the-war/Japan-surrender work, including the essays in this volume, by Asada (based mostly on his 1998 essay), Frank, Hatano, and Hasegawa, but space limitations led to my deleting those forty pages, which may appear elsewhere. After my essay was in the editorial process, Asada withdrew from this book project, but by then it was not possible to restore to this essay my nine-page critique of his 1998 article or of his 1998–2004 unpublished revised version.

122. Hasegawa, *Racing the Enemy*, 105; David Holloway, *Stalin and the Bomb: The Soviet Union and Atomic Energy, 1939–1956* (New Haven, Conn.: Yale University Press, 1994). See also the H-Diplo roundtable discussion on Hasegawa's *Racing the Enemy* in January–February 2006, in which Gar Alperovitz, Michael Gordin, Richard Frank, David Holloway, and Barton Bernstein participated, with Thomas Maddux's introduction and Hasegawa's rebuttals. This roundtable is available at www.h-net.org/~diplo/roundtables/#hasegawa (March 2006). There is also a discussion of Hasegawa's book on History News Network and spirited critiques by Asada, Newman, and others, with a rebuttal by Hasegawa in 2006.

2. Frank: Ketsu Gō

1. Michael S. Sherry, "Patriotic Orthodoxy and American Decline," in David T. Linenthal and Tom Engelhardt, eds., *History Wars: The Enola Gay and Other Battles for the American Past* (New York: Holt, 1996), 97.

2. The summary of themes from the postwar critical literature is drawn from J. Samuel Walker, "The Decision to Use the Bomb: A Historiography Update," *Diplomatic History* 14 (Winter 1990): 97–114, and Barton J. Bernstein, "The Struggle over History," in Philip Nobile, ed., *Judgment at the Smithsonian* (New York: Marlowe, 1995), 127–256, esp. 162–67, 173, 178, 195–98.

3. Herbert P. Bix, *Hirohito and the Making of Modern Japan* (New York: HarperCollins, 2000), 496–98; id., "Japan's Delayed Surrender: A Reinterpretation," *Diplomatic History* 19, no. 2 (Spring 1995): 204; Michael D. Pearlman, *Unconditional Surrender, Demobilization and the Atomic Bomb* (Fort Leavenworth, Kans.: Combat Studies Institute, U.S. Army Command and General Staff College, 1996), 1–8. U.S. officials treated Japan's surrender as unconditional and initially kept the status of the emperor and the imperial institution vague to pressure Japanese elites into accepting the first occupation reforms. John Dower, *Embracing Defeat: Japan in the Wake of World War II* (New York: Norton / New Press, 1999), 81–84.

4. Edward S. Miller, *War Plan Orange: The U.S. Strategy to Defeat Japan, 1897–1945* (Annapolis, Md.: Naval Institute Press, 1991), 4, 29, 150, 164–65.

5. JCS 924/15, April 25, 1945; CCS 381 Pacific Ocean Operations (6–10–43), sec. 11, Record Group [hereafter RG] 218, National Archives and Records Administration [hereafter NA]. On May 25, the JCS by "informal action" approved the draft directive for the invasion issued in Joint Chiefs of Staff to MacArthur, Nimitz, and Arnold, WX 87938 25th (May) (the Signal Corps Message form for MacArthur is dated May 26 1945), RG 4, box 17, folder 4, MacArthur Memorial Archive, Norfolk, Va. [hereafter MacArthur Archive].

6. Edward Drea, *In Service of the Emperor: Essays on the Imperial Japanese Army* (Lincoln: University of Nebraska Press, 1998), 11–13, 26–34, 45–46, 63, 89–90; Gerhard L. Weinberg, *World at Arms: A Global History of World War II* (Cambridge: Cambridge University Press, 1994), 245–59.

7. Drea, *In Service of the Emperor*, 187, 191–92.

8. For the assessment at Imperial General Headquarters, see generally Bōeichō Bō-ei Kenshūjo Senshi Shitsu, *Senshi Sōsho*, no. 57, *Hondo Kessen Junbi*, vol. 2: *Kyūshū no bōei* (Tokyo: Asagumo shinbunsha, 1972), 159–61 [hereafter *Hondo kessen junbi (2) Kyūshū no bōei*]; Supreme Commander for the Allied Powers, *Reports of General MacArthur*, vol. 2, *Japanese Operations in the Southwest Pacific Area*, pt. 2 (Washington, D.C.: Government Printing Office, 1966), 577; and Center for Military History [hereafter CMH], statement of Baron Suzuki, Dec. 26, 1945, interrogation no. 531, p. 308.

9. *Hondo kessen junbi (2) Kyūshū no bōei*, 161–64; Edward J. Drea, *MacArthur's ULTRA: Codebreaking and the War Against Japan* (Lawrence: University of Kansas Press, 1992), 202.

10. *Hondo kessen junbi (2) Kyūshū no bōei*, 167–70; Office of the Chief of Military History, U.S. Department of the Army, *Air Defense of the Homeland*, Japanese Monograph No. 25 (1952), 11–15, 19–20, 25; Leon V. Sigal, *Fighting to a Finish: The*

Politics of War Termination in the United States and Japan, 1945 (Ithaca, N.Y.: Cornell University Press, 1988), 35, 38–39; Supreme Commander for the Allied Powers, *Reports of General MacArthur*, 2, pt. 2, 588–89.

11. *Hondo kessen junbi (2) Kyūshū no bōei*, 177–82, 211–16, 278–92; Supreme Commander for the Allied Powers, *Reports of General MacArthur*, 2, pt. 2, 591–92, 605–7.

12. April 8 Imperial General Headquarters Directive no. 2438: "Outline of Preparations for the Ketsu Gō Operation": *Hondo kessen junbi (2) Kyūshū no bōei*, 164–66, 264; Supreme Commander for the Allied Powers, *Reports of General MacArthur*, 2, pt. 2, 601. A complete translated copy of this order is found in *War in Asia and the Pacific*, vol. 12: *Defense of the Homeland and End of the War* (New York: Garland, 1980), 201–31.

13. Supreme Commander for the Allied Powers, *Reports of General MacArthur*, 2, pt. 2, 612.

14. *Hondo kessen junbi (2) Kyūshū no bōei*, 211–25; Supreme Commander for the Allied Powers, *Reports of General MacArthur*, 2, pt. 2, 608–11, 619–21, 623n48.

15. *Hondo kessen junbi (2) Kyūshū no bōei*, 278–83; Supreme Commander for the Allied Powers, *Reports of General MacArthur*, 2, pt. 2, 622.

16. CCS 417/11, Jan. 22, 1945, appendix A, Kyushu Terrain Estimate, 18–19; 381 POA 6–10–43, RG 218, box 686, sec. 11, NA.

17. *Hondo kessen junbi (2) Kyūshū no bōei*, 273–76.

18. Ibid., 294.

19. Ibid., 294–95; and Maj. Gen. Yoshitake Yasumasa, "Statement Concerning the Estimate of U.S. Army Plan of Invasion Against Southern Kyushu During the Period from April 1945 to August 1945 and Changes in the Operational Plans and Preparations of the 57 Army" (CMH), 5.

20. *Hondo kessen junbi (2) Kyūshū no bōei*, 294–96, 298–300, 458–59.

21. Ibid., 444. Contemporaneous plans at IGHQ reflected four reinforcing divisions. The story of the effort to secure a portion of the Thirty-sixth Army is covered in Maj. Gen. Sanada Jōichirō, "Statement on the Operational Preparations for the Defense of Kyushu" (doc. 58513, CMH); Col. Sugita Ichiji, "Statement Concerning Homeland Defense in 1945" (CMH). The chief of the Imperial Army's intelligence section, Lt. Gen. Arisue Seizō, commented after the war that the reason why Imperial General Headquarters deferred a decision to dispatch "the decisive battle forces in the Kanto Area to the Kyushu Area" was lack of sound intelligence. Statement of Lt. Gen. Arisue, doc. no. 61660, CMH.

22. *Hondo kessen junbi (2) Kyūshū no bōei*, 565–75.

23. Richard B. Frank, *Downfall: The End of the Imperial Japanese Empire* (New York: Random House, 1999), 204–11.

24. Statement of Lt. Col. Ōta Kiyoshi, staff officer in charge of transportation and line of communications, Sixteenth Area Army, 1–2, CMH. By way of comparison, a staff officer at Imperial General Headquarters reported that the First General Army possessed somewhat less than 50 percent of the provisions it was calculated to require, and that this total was far better than the levels of accumulated arms, ammunition, and fuel. Statement of Lt. Col. Iwakoshi Shinroku, doc. no. 62800, CMH.

25. Statement of Lt. Col. Ōta Kiyoshi, staff officer in charge of transportation and

line of communications, Sixteenth Area Army, 2–3, CMH. For a further discussion of postwar evidence on Japanese logistics, see Frank, *Downfall*, 176–77.

26. Robert Ross Smith, *Triumph in the Philippines* (Washington, D.C.: Government Printing Office), 694, appendix H-2.

27. Thomas M. Huber, *Japan's Battle of Okinawa, April–June 1945*, Leavenworth Papers, no. 18 (Leavenworth, Kans.: Combat Studies Institute, U.S. Army Command and General Staff College, 1990), 13; George Feifer, *Tennozan: The Battle of Okinawa and the Atomic Bomb* (New York: Ticknor & Fields, 1992), 532–33; Frank, *Downfall*, 71–72.

28. *Hondo kessen junbi (2) Kyūshū no bōei*, 406–9, 414–15.

29. Ibid., 410–13.

30. Thomas R. H. Havens, *Valley of Darkness: The Japanese People and World War Two* (1978; Lanham, Md.: University Press of America, 1986), 188–90; statement of Lt. Gen. Yoshizumi Masao, former chief of the army's Bureau of Military Affairs, Imperial General Headquarters, Dec. 22, 1949, doc. no. 61388, 3, CMH; W. F. Craven and J. L. Cate, eds., *The Army Air Forces in World War II*, vol. 5: *The Pacific: Matterhorn to Nagasaki, June 1944 to August 1945* (repr., Washington, D.C.: Office of the Chief of Air Force History, 1983), 696.

31. The Japanese Plan for the Defense of Kyushu, 1, 39 (July 21, 1945), Marine Corps History Center [hereafter MCHC]. Other important assessments include: (1) Report by British Combined Observers (Pacific), "Report of Operation OLYMPIC and Japanese Countermeasures," Apr. 4, 1946, CAB 106, No. 97, Public Record Office, Kew, London; Report of Reconnaissance Southern Kyushu, IX Corps Zone of Operation, Dec. 3–5, 1945, RG 407, entry 427, WWII Operations Reports, IX Corps 209-2.0, NA; and (3) File: Intelligence Specialist School and Information, Edmund J. Winslett Papers, U.S. Army Military History Institute [hereafter USAMHI].

32. Frank, *Downfall*, 190–95, discusses the assumptions behind these figures. In Pacific island battles, Japanese units were normally annihilated. It is assumed that since the United States aimed only to secure the southern third of Kyūshū, a substantial portion of the defenders would have been pushed back rather than killed. The Japanese civilian casualties represent a very conservative estimated fatality rate of 10 percent among the civilian population in the three prefectures the U.S. military intended to seize, not including deaths resulting from the ongoing campaign of bombing and blockade. U.S. loss estimates assumed that the campaign would require only ninety days (a very optimistic assumption) and that casualties would have only matched the total generated by the most conservative formula contemplated by the JCS in April 1945. This should not be regarded as a rebuttal of the figures used by Secretary of War Henry Stimson or President Truman after the war. They were referring to losses in the event there was no organized capitulation of Japan's armed forces, some five million strong, not just losses in the initial invasion of Japan.

33. Ibid., 134.

34. American battle casualties were not spread evenly across all branches, but were overwhelmingly concentrated in the infantry. For the war as a whole, in the U.S. Army, the infantry accounted for 80 percent of fatalities in ground units. Statistical and Accounting Branch, Office of the Adjutant General, *Army Battle Casualties and Nonbattle Deaths in World War II, Final Report, 7 December 1941–31 December 1946*,

5, gives totals from which the percentage of infantry casualties is extracted. The same data show artillery sustained 5.2 percent and engineers 4.2 percent of all battle deaths for the war among ground branches. The assumption that 92,500 overall casualties results in a doubling of losses in the assault divisions is derived by multiplying this number by 80 percent to approximate the 74,239 casualties Olympic divisions had already sustained. Frank, *Downfall*, 122.

35. Marshall to MacArthur and MacArthur to Marshall, June 19, 1945, RG 4, USAFPAC Correspondence WD, folder 4, MacArthur Archives.

36. "Statement on the Crucial Battle of the Homeland," Maj. Gen. Sanada Jōichirō, chief of the Operations Bureau, Imperial General Headquarters, Army Section, Statements of Japanese officials on World War II, General Headquarters, Far East Command, Military Intelligence Section, Historical Division, CMH.

37. Statement of Maj. Gen. Amano Masakazu, June 10, 1950, doc. no. 59617. See also statement Dec. 29, 1949, doc. no. 54480, CMH.

38. Statement of Lt. Gen. Arisue Seizō, doc. no. 52506. In the same vein, Lt. Gen. Kawabe, deputy chief of the General Staff, spoke of how he did not expect Ketsu Gō to result in victory, but after his personal inspection in late June of Kyūshū, he was confident of inflicting "staggering losses" on the attackers. Statement of Kawabe, June 18, 1949, doc. no. 50569, 3, CMH.

39. Attitudes among the Big Six on the decisive battle in the homeland: statement of former admiral Toyoda Soemu, former chief, Naval General Staff, Aug. 29, 1949, doc. no. 61340, 3; interrogation of Premier Baron Suzuki, Admiral IJN (Ret.), Strategic Bombing Survey Interrogation No. 531, Dec. 26, 1945, 308, CMH; statements of Lt. Gen. Yoshizumi Masao, former chief of the army's Bureau of Military Affairs, Imperial General Headquarters, Dec. 22, 1949, doc. no. 54484, 4, doc. no. 54485, 2, 3, doc. no. 61338, 3, CMH; statement of Col. Hayashi Saburō, doc. no. 54482, 3, CMH. A mass of statements attest to Anami's confidence in the prospects for Ketsu Gō. In addition to the quoted statements from Gen. Yoshizumi and Col. Hayashi, Hayashi said in another interview: "I think War [Army] Minister Anami's ideas of continuing the war was that he wanted to make peace after dealing a heavy blow to the enemy" (doc. 61436, 5, CMH). Col. Matsutani Makoto said: "It seems to me that General Anami had hopes of concluding peace in early August on fairly advantageous terms after at least inflicting a blow in Japan proper upon the enemy" (statement, Jan. 13, 1950, doc. no. 54227, 2, CMH). Maj. Gen. Nagai Yatsuji, chief of the Army Ministry's Bureau of Military Affairs, commented that Anami believed strongly in the idea that the tide of war could be turned to some degree in Japan's favor by a decisive battle on the homeland. Apparently, he thought that in this way, an "Honorable peace could be concluded" (statement of Dec. 27, 1949, doc. no. 54228, 2, CMH). In the mildest of these statements, Col. Arao Okikatsu, also an important staff officer at the Army Ministry, said: "War Minister Anami was confident of victory to some extent (at least lessen the conditions in the Potsdam Proclamation)" (statement of Dec. 27, 1949, doc. no. 54226, 2, CMH).

40. The estimate that the initial Japanese capability was to garrison Kyūshū with a total of six divisions, with only three in southern part of the island, is mentioned repeatedly in planning documents from at least mid 1944 on and reiterated in "Downfall: Strategic Plans for Operations in the Japanese Archipelago" (author's copy). A copy of the Downfall plan may be found in OPD 350.05, sec. 1, RG 165, NA. MacArthur's

projection of ultimate Japanese capabilities is from the same Downfall plan. General Marshall's estimate before Truman of ultimate Japanese strength of eight to ten divisions and 350,000 men is found in "Minutes of Meeting Held at White House on Monday, 18 June 1945 at 1530" (xerox 1567, George C. Marshall Library). These minutes make no mention of Japanese air capabilities.

41. Joint Intelligence Committee, "Japanese Reaction to an Assault on the Sendai Plain," J.I.C. 218/10, 10 August 1945" (final revision, Aug. 20, 1945). The total for Kyūshū includes the Tsushima Fortress, which fell under the Fifty-sixth Army. Geographic file 1942–45, CCS 381 Honshu (7–19–44), sec. 4, RG 218, box 90, NA.

42. SRS-486, July 19, 1945; SRS-507, Aug. 9, 1945, RG 457, NA.

43. SRMD-008, 266, July 16, 1945, 2; 297, Aug. 23, 1945, 297, RG 457, NA.

44. U.S. Strategic Bombing Survey, Military Analysis Division, report no. 62, *Japanese Air Power* (Washington, D.C.: Government Printing Office, 1946), 24–25, 70. For a discussion of the various numbers offered concerning Japanese air strength in the homeland, see Frank, *Downfall,* 182–83 and notes.

45. "History of the Special Distribution Branch Military Intelligence Service, WDGS, Part 3, Section 7," SHR-132, RG 457, NA. When writing *Downfall*, I was very cautious on the subject of the delivery of Ultra/Magic materials to Truman at Potsdam. Subsequently, however, I located this document, which describes the actual distribution system for the top level summaries. It establishes that both the "Magic" Diplomatic Summary and the "Magic" Far East Summary were delivered daily by locked pouch officer courier to the president. As noted in *Downfall*, 240–41, the White House Map Room files show that the officer courier system was in place for the conference, with a three-day delay between publication of the daily summaries and physical delivery to Potsdam. When the intercepts apparently showed the emperor's intervention in the effort to secure Soviet mediation, a jury-rigged system was established by July 17 to provide same-day delivery through Marshall and King to Leahy. It is not clear whether both the diplomatic and the military summary were on same-day delivery. At worst, the evidence shows that the "Magic" Far East Summary reached Truman three days after the publication date, and it may well have been delivered the same day. We do not know definitively what Truman saw of this material. It has been taken for granted for decades that Truman was seeing the diplomatic intercepts, though this assumption is based entirely on the inference that since other members of his administration, notably Byrnes and Forrestal, reported seeing the intercepts then or later, Truman must have seen them. In my view, now that we know what was actually distributed, one cannot arbitrarily pick and chose what intercepts one prefers to believe Truman saw or learned about. Consistency requires that either you believe that he saw or learned about nothing or that he saw or learned about everything. The implications of even a brief summary of the facts about the Japanese buildup on Kyūshū are clear. Moreover, I think Truman's "Potsdam" diary entry for July 25 contains the powerful inference that Marshall and Truman discussed the radio intelligence revelations about Kyūshū. See *Downfall*, 243–44.

46. Magic Far East Summary, July 27, 1945, SRS 494, NA-1, RG 457, NA.

47. General Headquarters, U.S. Army Forces Pacific, Military Intelligence Section, General Staff, "Amendment No. 1 to G-2 Estimate of the Enemy Situation with Respect to Kyushu," July 29, 1945, 1, Gen. John J. Tolson Papers, USAMHI (copy in RG 4, box 22, MacArthur Archive).

48. SRMD-008, 238; June 4, 2; SRMD-008, 247; June 18, 2; SRMD-008, 257–58; July 2, 2–3, all in RG 457, NA.

49. CINCPAC ADVAN to COMINCH 030209, August 1945, CINCPAC Command Summary, 3503, Naval History Center [hereafter NHC].

50. Joint War Plans Committee, J.W.P.C. 397, August 4, 1945 (with attached copy of "Defensive Preparations in Japan," Joint Intelligence Committee), RG 218, NA.

51. Ibid.

52. Joint Staff Planners on August 8: Joint Staff Planners, Minutes of 213th Meeting, Aug. 8, 1945, xerox 1540, pt. 9, George C. Marshall Papers, George C. Marshall Library.

53. OPD (WAR) [Marshall] to MACARTHUR WAR 45369; CINCAFPAC [MacArthur] to WARCOS [Marshall] C 31897, CINCPAC Command Summary, bk. 7, 3508–10. The exchange is also found in OPD top secret incoming msg, Jul. 28–Aug. 17, 1945, RG 165, box 39, NA.

54. Drea, *MacArthur's ULTRA*, 180–85, 229–30.

55. Diary of Henry S. Stimson, Dec. 27, 1944, Yale University Library. Along the same lines, in March, when Stimson contemplated MacArthur's fitness to command the final invasion of Japan, the secretary of war noted that despite MacArthur's success, his "unpleasant" personality had affronted "all the men of the Army and the Navy with whom he has to work," and his staff, infected by his personality, were a "source of danger to harmony in what ought to be a most harmonious operation." Stimson Diary, Mar. 30, 1945.

56. Memorandum for the Joint Chiefs of Staff, Subject: Campaign Against Japan, Apr. 30, 1945, 381 POA (6–10–43), sec. 12, RG 218, box 169, NA.

57. COMINCH and CNO to CINCPAC ADV HQ 092205, August 45 (headed "KING TO NIMITZ EYES ONLY") and attached copies of CINCAFPAC to WARCOS C 31897 and OPD (WAR) to MACARTHUR WAR 45369, CINCPAC Command Summary, bk. 7, 3508–10, NHC. This section of the Command Summary contains closely held or "EYES ONLY" traffic. The daily narrative in the Command Summary is silent on this exchange. The conclusion that Nimitz never replied to King is based upon an exhaustive search of voluminous message files, including those dealing with secret flag officer communications, with the invaluable assistance of the staff of the Naval History Center.

58. Maj. Gen. Clayton Bissell, memorandum for the Chief of Staff, Subject: Estimate of the Japanese Situation for the Next 30 Days, Aug. 12, 1945, RG 165, entry 422, box 12, executive no. 2, item no. 11, NA. Bissell's pessimism almost certainly stemmed from intercepts on August 11 disclosing that Japan's foreign minister conceded that the imperial army and navy had not agreed to the peace proposal dispatched the day before, and from a very belligerent message from Imperial General Headquarters in Tokyo that appeared to portend noncompliance with any surrender. These are discussed further below.

59. Maj. Gen. John E. Hull and Col. L. E. Seeman, telephone conversation, Aug. 13, 1945, 13:25, verifax 2691, George C. Marshall Papers, George C. Marshall Library.

60. Robert Butow, *Japan's Decision to Surrender* (Stanford: Stanford University Press, 1954), vi.

61. Ibid., 36–38.

62. Statement by former foreign minister Tōgō, May 17, 1949, 32–33, CMH; statements of former admiral Toyoda Soemu, Dec. 1, 1949, doc. no. 57670, 3–4, 6,

and doc. no. 61340, 8–10, CMH; transcript, International Military Tribunal for the Far East [hereafter IMTFE], Tōgō 35787, Library of Congress; Butow, *Japan's Decision to Surrender*, 161.

63. Bōeichō Bōei Kenshūjo Senshi Shitsu, *Senshi Sōsho*, no. 82, *Daihon'ei Rikugunbu*, 10 (Tokyo: Asagumo shinbunsha, 1975), 492–93, 504 [hereafter *Daihon'ei Rikugunbu*, 10]; Asada Sadao, "The Shock of the Atomic Bomb and Japan's Decision to Surrender—A Reconsideration," *Pacific Historical Review* 64, no. 4 (November 1998): 492–93, 504. *Daihon'ei Rikugunbu*, 10, notes that a pair of staff officers in the Army Ministry's Bureau of Military Affairs drafted a very similar program featuring the declaration of martial law as its centerpiece. This illuminates the mind-set at imperial General Headquarters. For explicit acknowledgment that martial law was targeted to stop the "peace faction," see statement of Lt. Col. Ida Masataka, May 23, 1950, doc. no. 62348, CMH. Ida was with the Military Affairs Section of the Bureau of Military Affairs. As to why martial law was not declared, Ida reported that he had urged that the plan be carried out as soon as possible, "but [I] was told to remain quiet, for a day or two would make little difference so long as the entire army would unite in their determination to carry out the plan. I was convinced that everyone thought that at the last resort, military administration would be established through the enforcement of martial law."

64. Hidenari Terasaki and Mariko Terasaki Miller, eds., *Shōwa Tennō dokuhaku-roku—Terasaki Hidenari, Goyōgakari nikki* (Tokyo: Bungei shunjū, 1990), 133–36.

65. See "Draft Plan for Controlling the Crisis Situation," in Koichi Kido, *The Diary of Marquis Kido, 1931–45: Selected Translations into English* (Frederick, Md.: University Publications of America, 1984), 435–36.

66. *Daihon'ei Rikugunbu*, 10437–38, and IMTFE Tōgō 35,787, Kido 31175–76.

67. Tsuyoshi Hasegawa, *Racing the Enemy* (Cambridge, Mass.: Belknap Press of Harvard University Press, 2005), 3–4, 205–14, 238–40.

68. Frank, *Downfall*, 295–96, 345–46. The concern of the emperor and his advisers over the collapse of domestic morale is a theme of Bix, *Hirohito and the Making of Modern Japan*, 488–91, 509–11, and is addressed by John Dower, "Sensational Rumors, Seditious Graffiti, and the Nightmares of the Thought Police," *Japan in War and Peace* (New York: New Press 1993), 101–54.

69. Memorandum of Vice Admiral Hoshina Zenshirō, doc. no. 53437, 1, CMH, and statement of Ikeda Sumihisa, Dec. 27, 1949, doc. no. 54483, CMH.

70. David Glantz, *Soviet Tactical and Operational Combat in Manchuria, 1945: August Storm* (London: Frank Cass, 2003), 33–34; *Daihon'ei Rikugunbu*, 10: 432. Hasegawa, *Racing the Enemy*, 199–200, 343–44n, argues that Tokyo did comprehend that the Soviet onslaught in Manchuria was an "all out invasion" on August 9, citing particularly the recollections of two staff officers. This argument confuses the question of whether the Kwantung Army reported that the attack was more than a border incursion incident with the issue of the actual scale of the attack. The Kwantung Army's report of an "all out invasion" correctly alerted Tokyo to the fact that this was no minor incident. But the official history of Imperial General Headquarters makes it clear that the Kwantung Army knew nothing of the Soviet attack from the west (with about 41 percent of all Soviet forces) on August 9, and that the reports of the numbers of Soviet units attacking along the border was a gross understatement. The actual reports on August 9 seem far more reliable than the recollections of the two staff officers.

71. Frank, *Downfall*, 278–81.

72. David Glantz, *The Soviet Strategic Offensive in Manchuria, 1945: August Storm* (London: Frank Cass, 2003), 110; *War in the East*, Strategy and Tactics Staff Study No. 1 (New York: Simulations Publications, 1977), 118.

73. David M. Glantz, "The Soviet Invasion of Japan," *Military History Quarterly* 7, no. 3 (Spring 1995): 96–97; id., *Soviet Strategic Offensive in Manchuria*, 280–310; Hasegawa, *Racing the Enemy*, 258–64, 271–72, 280–85, 288–89.

74. *Daihon'ei Rikugunbu*, 10: 491–92, 504–5.

75. Ibid., 506–7; Butow, *Japan's Decision to Surrender*, 207–8.

76. *Daihon'ei Rikugunbu*, 10: 514–15.

77. Butow, *Japan's Decision to Surrender*, 248.

78. Dower, *Embracing Defeat*, 290.

79. Statement of Baron Suzuki, Dec. 26, 1945, interrogation no. 531, 308, CMH.

80. SRH-090, 9–10, RG 457, NA.

81. SRH-203, Aug. 12–13, 1945, no. 121, RG 457, NA.

82. *Daihon'ei Rikugunbu*, 10: 466–67.

83. SRH-090, 20–22.

84. Ibid., 24–25; SRMD-007, Aug. 18, 1945.

85. Butow, *Japan's Decision to Surrender*, 223–24; William Craig, *The Fall of Japan* (New York: Dial Press 1967), 230–33, 255–56.

86. As quoted in Bix, *Hirohito and the Making of Modern Japan*, 530.

87. Ibid., 529–30. This is also an argument of Alperovitz. In my view, Bix's analysis addressing the August 17 rescript contains considerable ambiguity. He notes that the imperial rescript broadcast on August 15 made only indirect and vague reference to Germany's defeat and Soviet entry ("the general trends of the world have all turned against [Japan's] interest"). On the other hand, this rescript was explicit about the atomic bombs as a reason for ending the war. Bix adds, "Whether the emperor and his advisers ever really believed that, however, is unlikely." Bix then cites the imperial rescript of August 17 as indicating a "cause and effect" relationship between Soviet entry alone and the surrender, "conspicuously omitting any mention of the atomic bombs." Thus Bix appears to subscribe to the view that the August 17 rescript reflected the "real reason" for the surrender. But Bix then concludes his analysis in this segment of his work with the comment: "Dissembling until the end—and beyond—the emperor stated two different justifications for the delayed surrender. Both statements were probably true." This appears to mean that both the atomic bomb and Soviet intervention were reasons for the surrender. This section, however, stands in contrast to an earlier paragraph where Bix states firmly: "The twin psychological shocks of the first atomic bomb and Soviet entry into the war, coupled with Kido's and the emperor's concern over growing popular criticism of the throne and its occupant, and their almost paranoiac fear that, sooner or later, the people would react violently against their leaders if they allowed the war to go on much longer—these factors finally caused Hirohito to accept, in principle, the terms of the Potsdam Declaration" (511).

88. Louis Allen, *Burma: The Longest War, 1941–45* (1984; repr., London: Phoenix Press, 2000), 543–47.

89. SRH-090, 16–19.

90. This astute analysis was first offered by Edward Drea.

3. Hatano: The Atomic Bomb and the Soviet Entry into the War

1. Gunji Shigakukai ed., *Miyazaki Shūichi chūjō nisshi* (Tokyo: Kinseihsa, 2004), entry, July 27, 1945. The situation report drawn up by the Army General Staff right before the Soviet entry into the war (on August 3) ("Bei-Ei-'So' Santō Kaidan, Eikoku senkyo oyobi 'So' no tai-Nichi sakusen junbi shinchoku to ni tomonau jōsei kansatsu," Aug. 3, 1945, in *Henkan Shiryō* in the National Archives of Japan [Kokuritsu Kōbunsho Kan], I 3A-14/60–3) said: "[W]e will complete preliminary preparations for putting the operations into action by the end of August, and from the military point of view, there is the extremely high possibility of military action [by the Soviet Union] against Japan in the early fall this year."

2. "'So'-ren no tai-nichi saigo tsūchō no naiyō ni kansuru kenkyū," Aug. 7, 1945, Division of Military Affairs, in *Rengō-koku tono sesshō kankei jikō* in the archives of Bōeikenkyūjo Senshishishitsu [the National Institute for Defense Studies] in Tokyo.

3. Nishihara Masao, *Shūsen no keii*, 2 vols. (kept by Officer Nishihara Masao, Kōseishō Hikiage Engokyoku Shiryōshitsu [Office of the History in the Repatriation and War Victims' Relief Bureau of the Welfare Ministry]) in the possession of Hatano Sumio and Ken Kurihara, 1: 112–13.

4. A different document (cited in n. 2 above) states: "[W]e think it is worth considering peace through exploiting the Soviet Union while the two-million-man imperial forces deployed to the southern theater are in good condition."

5. Lieut. Col. Inoue Tadao, memorandum (in Bōeikenkyūjo Senshishishitsu), and Army Ministry Bureau of Military Affairs, "Kimitsu shūsen nisshi" (entry Aug. 9, 1945) owned by Bōeikenkyūjo Senshishishitsu, reprinted in Gunji Shigakukai, ed. *Sanbō honbu sensōshidō han: Kimitsu sensō nisshi,* vol. 2 (Tokyo: Kinseisha, 1998).

6. Nishihara, *Shūsen no keii*, 1: 114.

7. "Kawabe Torashirō Chinjutsuroku (Genshibakudan no Shutsugen)," Aug. 23, 1948, in GHQ Rekishika Chōshu Kiroku (hereafter cited as GHQ Interrogation Records).

8. Kido Nikki Kenkyūkai, ed., *Kido Kōichi nikki*, vol. 2 (Tokyo: Tōkyō Daigaku shuppankai, 1966) [hereafter cited as *Kido nikki*], Aug. 7, 1945.

9. "Tōgō Shigenori Chinjutsuroku (Taiheiyō Sensō no shūketsu no shijitsu ni kansuru moto Gaimu Daijin Tōgō-shi no chinjutsu)," May 17, 1949, in GHQ Interrogation Records.

10. "Chinjutsuroku" cited above claimed that the meeting was not convened because "that day was inconvenient for someone."

11. "Matsumoto Shun'ichi Shuki" (March 1946), owned by the Bōeikenkyūjo Senshishishitsu, reprinted in Gaimushō, ed., *Shūsen shiroku* (Tokyo: Shinbun gekkansha, 1952), 2: 570, 579, 618, and 654. All references to Gaimushō, ed., *Shūsen shiroku* in this chapter are to the 1952 edition.

12. Suzuki Kantarō, *Shūsen no hyōjō* (Tokyo: Rōdō bunkasha, 1946), 35.

13. *Kido Nikki*, vol. 2, Aug. 9, 1945.

14. Sakomizu Hisatsune, *Kikanjū ka no shushō kantei* (Tokyo: Kōbunsha, 1986), 255.

15. "Tōgō Shigenori chinjutsuroku"; Tōgō Shigenori, *Jidai no ichimen* (Tokyo: Hara shobō, 1985), 357–58.

16. Toyoda Soemu, *Saigo no teikoku kaigun* (Tokyo: Sekai no Nihon sha, 1950), 187–88.

17. "Toyoda Soemu chinjutsuroku (49 nen 8 gatsu 29 nichi no shitsumon ni taisuru kaitō)," Toyoda, *Saigo no teikoku kaigun*, 207–9; Shimomura Kainan [Hiroshi], *Shūsenki* (Tokyo: Kamakura bunko, 1948), 116–21.

18. Shimomura, *Shūsenki*, 121–24.

19. Sakomizu, *Kikanjū ka no shushō kantei*, 256–58.

20. "Kawabe Jichō nisshi," August 9 (in Bōeikenkyūjo Senshishishitsu). *Kawabe Torashirō Kaisōroku* (Tokyo: Jijitsūshinsha, 1979) reprinted his diary, but it contains some parts not corresponding to the original one.

21. *Kido nikki*, vol. 2, Aug. 9, 1945.

22. Itō Takashi and Watanabe Yukio, eds., *Shigemitsu Mamoru shuki* (Tokyo: Chūōkōronsha, 1986), 522–23.

23. Ibid., 519–20 .

24. *Shigemitsu Mamoru shuki*, 523; Hosokawa Morisada, *Hosokawa nikki* (1953; repr., Tokyo: Chūōkōronsha, 1979), 2: 140–41, Aug. 9, 1945.

25. *Kido nikki,* vol. 2, Aug. 9, 1945.

26. "Matsumoto Shun'ichi Shuki."

27. *Shigemitsu mamoru shuki*, 522–23

28. Ibid., 523–24; *Kido nikki*, vol. 2, entry Aug. 9, 1945.

29. Hosokawa, *Hosokawa nikki*, 2: 141–42.

30. For the debate on the emperor's "positive intervention" in the formulation of the "sacred decision" of August 9, see Chimoto Hideki, *Tennōsei no Shinryaku Sekinin to Sengo Sekinin* (Tokyo: Aoki Shoten, 1990), 100–101.

31. "Tōgō Shigenori chinjutsuroku"; Shimomura, *Shūsenki*, 125.

32. Kido Kōichi, "Sensō shūketsu e no doryoku," in Kido Nikki Kenkyūkai, ed., *Kido Kōichi kankei bunsho* (Tokyo: Tōkyō Daigaku shuppankai, 1966), 85.

33. Sakomizu, *Kikanjū ka no shushō kantei*, 259–60

34. Toyoda, *Saigo no teikoku kaigun*, 210–11.

35. Sakomizu, *Kikanjū ka no shushō kantei*, 255–56.

36. See Memorandum of Hoshina Zenshirō reprinted in his book, *Dai Tō-A Sensō hishi* (Tokyo: Hara shobō, 1985), 141–47, and also "Ikeda Sumihisa shuki," titled "8 gatsu 9 nichi Gozen Kaigi ni tsuite," Dec. 27, 1949, in Kurihara Ken and Hatano Sumio, eds., *Shūsen kōsaku no kiroku* (Tokyo: Kōdansha, 1986), 2: 392–400.

37. See "Ikeda Sumihisa Shuki," cited above, and also *Hiranuma Kiichirō chinjutsuroku (Shūsen ni kansuru kaisō)*, Dec. 16, 1949, in GHQ Interrogation Records.

38. Tajiri Akiyoshi, *Tajiri Akiyoshi kaisōroku* (Tokyo: Hara shobō, 1980), 132.

39. "Ikeda Sumihisa shuki."

40. "Kimitsu shūsen nisshi," entry Aug. 10, 1945; Nishihara, *Shūsen no keii*, 1: 139.

41. "Matsumoto Shun'ichi shuki."

42. Ibid.

43. Telegram from Minister Tōgō to ambassadors in Manchukuo, China, and Thailand, Aug. 11, 1945 (Gō, no. 659), Diplomatic Record Office in Tokyo (Gaimushō Gaikō Shiryōkan).

44. Shimomura, *Shūsenki*, 130.

45. Ibid., 131.

46. "Inaba Masao, Chinjutsuroku (Shūsen ji no Anami Rikushō no shinkyō)," Oct. 13, 1949, in GHQ Interrogation Records.

47. It is not yet clear whether Anami officially approved Lieut. Col. Inaba's draft, but inasmuch as Col. Oyadomari Chōsei of the Information Bureau and Lieut. Col. Takeshita of the army's Bureau of Military Affairs sought to force the announcement, Shimomura let it be made for fear that "going too far cornering the army minister might cause an unexpected event around him." See "Shimomura Hiroshi chinjutsuroku (Shūsen ji no kaisō)," Mar. 30, 1950, in GHQ Interrogation Records.

48. Hayashi Saburō, "Shūsen korono Anami-san," Sekai, August 1951.

49. Shimomura, Shūsenki, 129.

50. When Ministers Yasui and Sakurai pointed out about the necessity of "the unity between the government and the military" at the cabinet meeting on August 13, Suzuki replied: "the sacred decision [of August 10] made them united." See Shimomura, Shūsenki, 141.

51. "Kawabe Jichō nisshi," entry Aug. 9, 1945.

52. "Hoshina Zenshirō shuki."

53. "Kawabe Jichō nisshi," entry Aug. 10, 1945 (this part is different from that reprinted in Kawabe Torashirō kaisōroku).

54. Kawabe also noted his "honest feeling" that "the difficulty in continuing the war is what the Army General Staff in charge of operations is most aware of" ("Kawabe Jichō nisshi," entry Aug. 10, 1945).

55. "Ōta Saburō shuki," in Gaimushō, ed., Shūsen shiroku, 2: 618–19; Mori Moto-jirō, Aru shūsen kōsaku (Tokyo: Chūōkōronsha, 1980), 189–99; Nishihara, Shūsen no keii, 1: 143–44.

56. These telegrams are collected in Nishihara, Shūsen no keii, 1: 146–48.

57. Secret army telegram no. 61, Nishihara, Shūsen no keii, 1: 148–49. The contents were delivered orally to the First General Army and the Aviation General Army.

58. "Shūsen shori tōji no Arao-san no shinkyō o omou (Zadankai)," in Takayama Shinobu, ed., Arao Okikatsu-san o shinobu (privately printed, 1978), 54–55, 196.

59. Nishihara, Shūsen no keii, 1: 149–50.

60. "Yonai Kaishō chokuwa," Aug. 12, 1945, in Itō Takashi, ed., Takagi Sōkichi: Nikki to jōhō (Tokyo: Misuzu Shobō, 2000), 2: 927.

61. Tanaka Nobumasa, Dokyumento shōwa tennō 5, Haisen, vol. 2 (Tokyo: Ryokufū shuppan, 1988), 475–76.

62. Hosokawa, Hosokawa nikki, 2: 140, Aug. 9, 1945.

63. For recent historiography studying the influence of the atomic bombs on the policymaking before the end of the war, see Asada Sadao, "The Shock of the Atomic Bomb and Japan's Decision to Surrender—A Reconsideration," Pacific Historical Review 67, no. 4 (November 1998): 477–95.

4. Hasegawa: The Atomic Bombs and the Soviet Invasion

1. On the American debate about the use of the atomic bombs, see Barton J. Bernstein, "The Struggle over History: Defining the Hiroshima Narrative, in Judgment at the Smithsonian, ed. Philip Nobile (New York: Marlowe, 1995), 127–256.

2. Sadao Asada, "The Shock of the Atomic Bomb and Japan's Decision to Surrender—A Reconsideration," *Pacific Historical Review* 67, no. 4 (1998): 481.

3. See, e.g., the interesting exchange between Alperovitz/Messer and Bernstein in *International Security* 16 (1991–92). Neither Alperovitz/Messer nor Bernstein confronts the issue of the Soviet factor in inducing Japan to surrender. Gar Alperovitz in his *The Decision to Use the Atomic Bomb and the Architecture of an American Myth* (New York: Knopf, 1995) devotes more than 600 pages to the U.S. motivation for using the atomic bombs but does not directly address the question of whether the atomic bombings or the Soviet entry had the more decisive influence on Japan's decision to surrender.

4. Asada, "Shock," 479–83; its Japanese version, Asada Sadao, "Genbaku tōka no shōgeki to kōfuku no kettei," in Hosoya Chihiro et al., *Taiheiyō sensō no shūketsu* (Tokyo: Kashiwa shobō, 1997), 195–222; and Richard B. Frank, *Downfall: The End of the Imperial Japanese Empire* (New York: Random House, 1999), 271.

5. Asada, "Shock," 486.

6. Frank, *Downfall*, 271. Frank's source is Asada's article. Frank also cites Robert J. C. Butow, *Japan's Decision to Surrender* (Stanford: Stanford University Press, 1954), 152–53, but Butow has nothing to say about the August 7 cabinet meeting. Frank explains that Asada's source is Tōgō Shigenori, *Jidai no ichimen* (Tokyo: Kaizōsha, 1952; repr., Hara shobō, 1989), but Tōgō's memoirs are silent about the Potsdam Proclamation.

7. Tōgō, *Jidai no ichimen*, 355. In his notes written in September 1945, Tōgō referred to the cabinet meeting on August 7 without saying that he had proposed the acceptance of the Potsdam Proclamation. See "Tōgō gaisō kijutsu hikki 'Shūsen ni saishite' September 1945," in Gaimushō, ed., *Shūsen shiroku* (Tokyo: Hokuyōsha, 1977), 4: 60. Hereafter all references to Gaimushō, ed., *Shūsen shiroku* are to the 1977 edition.

8. Kurihara Ken and Hatano Sumio, eds., *Shūsen kōsaku no kiroku* (Tokyo: Kōdansha, 1986), 2: 355–56.

9. Sakomizu Hisatsune, *Kikanjū ka no shushō kantei* (Tokyo: Kōbunsha, 1964), 243–44. Sakomizu published another memoir in 1973, *Dainihon teikoku saigo no 4-kagetsu* (Tokyo: Orientosha, 1973), but he makes no reference to the August 7 cabinet meeting in the later book.

10. Kido Nikki Kenkyūkai, ed., *Kido Kōichi nikki* (Tokyo: Tōkyō Daigaku shuppankai, 1966), 2: 1222.

11. *Kido Kōichi nikki: Tōkyō saibanki* (Tokyo: Tōkyō Daigaku shuppankai, 1980), 421.

12. Asada, "Shock," 487.

13. Frank, *Downfall*, 272.

14. Tanaka Nobumasa, *Dokyumento shōwa tennō* 5, *Haisen*, vol. 2 (Tokyo: Ryokufū shuppan, 1988), 2: 460–61.

15. Quoted in Asada, "Shock," 488.

16. Ibid.

17. Frank, *Downfall*, 272.

18. Tōgō's statement comes from his memoirs, *Jidai no ichimen*, 355–56. Asada does not include the words in brackets in the Japanese version. See Asada, "Genbaku tōka," 199.

19.   During an interview with Ōi Atsushi for the military history project of Military Intelligence Section of the General Staff of the Supreme Commander for the Allied Powers (SCAP), Tōgō said that he suggested to the emperor on August 8 that Japan should accept the Potsdam terms. Continuing the question, Ōi tried to establish that Tōgō and the emperor had already decided to terminate the war on the terms stipulated in the Potsdam Proclamation before the Soviet entry into the war. Tōgō equivocated, saying that Soviet mediation would not be limited only to the clarification of the Potsdam terms. He was not sure whether the Kremlin would convey Japan's wishes to the Allied powers or would take the trouble to make an arrangement for Japan to hold direct negotiations with the United States and Britain. To this, Oi interjected by saying that whether they went through Moscow or by a direct route, the meaning was that the war would be terminated on the basis of the Potsdam Proclamation. Tōgō agreed, but without conviction. "Tōgō Shigenori chinjutsuroku," in Kurihara and Hatano, eds., *Shūsen kōsaku no kiroku*, 2: 357–58.

20.   Sakomizu, *Dainihon teikoku*, 185.

21.   Asada, "Shock," 489.

22.   Sakomizu, *Dainihon teikoku*, 185, 187.

23.   Sakomikzu, *Kikanjū ka no shūshō kantei*, 245–46.

24.   Hasegawa Saiji, "Hōkai no zenya," *Fujin kōron*, August 1947, in Gaimushō, ed., *Shūsen shiroku*, 5: 84.

25.   Asada and Frank also cite Suzuki's statement made in December 1945, which will be discussed later.

26.   Suzuki Hajime, ed., *Suzuki Kantarō jiden* (Tokyo: Jijitsūshinsha, 1969), 294–95.

27.   Sakomizu's 1964 memoirs also take this view. Sakomizu, *Kikanjū ka no shūshō kantei*, 255.

28.   Tōgō to Satō, telegram no. 993, 15:40, Tokyo, Aug. 7, 1945, in Gaimushō, ed., *Shūsen shiroku*, 4: 77.

29.   This was also confirmed by Sakomizu, who allegedly stated that Tōgō had made a statement at the cabinet meeting on August 7 in support of accepting the Potsdam Proclamation. Sakomizu, *Kikanjū ka no shūshō kantei*, 244–45.

30.   Information obtained by Harano Sumio.

31.   Asada, "Shock," 491–92. This term does not appear in the Japanese version. Asada, "Genbaku tōka," 201.

32.   Bōeichō Bōeikenshūjo Senshishitsu, *Senshi sōsho: Daihon'ei rikugunbu*, vol. 10: *Shōwa 20 nen 8 gatsu made* (Tokyo: Asagumo shinbunsha, 1975), 443.

33.   Asada, "Shock," 504.

34.   Frank, *Downfall*, 348.

35.   Bōeicho Bōeikenshūjo Senshishitsu, *Kantōgun*, vol. 2: *Kantokuen, Shūsenji no taiso sen* (Tokyo: Asagumo shinbunsha, 1974), 326.

36.   Ibid.

37.   Ibid., 328.

38.   Ibid., 330.

39.   Ibid., 332; Tanemura Suetaka, *Daihonei kimitsu nisshi* (Tokyo: Fuyō shobō, 1995), 295.

40.   "Soren no tainichi saigo tsūchō ni taishite torubeki sochi no kenkyū," in

Nishihara Masao [Kōseishō Hikiage Engokyoku Shiryōshitsu], *Shūsen no keii* (typescript, in possesion of Hatano Sumio and Kurihara Ken), 1: 104–8; Kurihara and Hatano, eds., *Shūsen kōsaku no kiroku*, 2: 363–64.

41. Bōeichō Bōeikenshūjo Senshishitsu, *Kantogun*, 2: 318.

42. Ibid.

43. Quoted in Bōeichō Bōeikenshūjo Senshishitsu, *Senshi sōsho: Daihonei rikugunbu*, 10: 427.

44. Bōeicho Bōeikenshūjo Senshishitsu, *Kantōgun*, vol. 2: 330.

45. Asada, "Shock," 504.

46. Kawabe Torashirō, "Jichō nisshi," vol. 2, quoted in Bōeichō Bōeikenshūjo Senshishitsu, *Senshi sōsho: Daihonei rikugunbu*, 10: 430; also Kurihara and Hatano, eds., *Shūsen kōsaku no kiroku*, 2: 364. The handwritten original is Kawabe Torashirō Sanbōjichō nisshi, Shōwa 20. 7.26–20.9.2, in Bōeikenkyūjo senshishitsu, chuō, sensō shidō jūyō kokusaku bunsho, 1206. Although *Daihonei rikugunbu* 10 occasionally alters the original when it quotes from Kawabe's diary, this part is accurately quoted. A slightly different version is given in Kawabe Torashirō, "Sanbō jichō no nisshi," in *Kawabe Torashirō Kaisōroku* (Tokyo: Manichi shinbunsha, 1979), 253.

47. Quoted in Bōeichō Bōeikenshūjo Senshishitsu, *Senshi sōsho: Daihonei rikugunbu*, 10: 420; Kawabe, "Jichō nisshi," 252.

48. Jichō nisshi, quoted in Bōeicho Bōeikenshūjo Senshishitsu, *Senshi sōsho: Daihonei rikugunbu*, 10: 440–41. This part is not included in Kawabe, "Jichō nissi," in *Kawabe Kaisōroku*, 254.

49. Jichō nisshi, quoted in Bōeichō Bōeikenshūjo Senshishitsu, *Senshi sōsho: Daihonei rikugunbu*, 10: 452, "Jichō nisshi" in *Kawabe Kaisōroku* is slightly different.

50. # 52608, Kawabe Torashirō, Nov. 21, 1949, 5–6, Historical Manuscript File, Center for Military History [hereafter CMH]. I thank Richard Frank for allowing me to use his collection from the Center for Military History.

51. Frank, *Downfall*, 346–67.

52. *Arisue kikanhō*, no. 333, Nov. 16, 1945, Rikugunshō, "Beikoku shireibu no 'Teikokusakusen oyobi shidō kankei shitsumon' ni taisuru kaitō," Bunko Yu, 395, Beoei Kenkyūjo, Senshishitsu.

53. # 59617, Maj. Gen. Amano Masakazu, Historical Manuscript File; also see Amano Masakazu Chinjutsusho, GHQ Senshika, vol. 6, Chuō Shūsen shori 228, Bōei Kenkyūjo Senshishitsu. The English translation of the Historical Manuscript File is modified in view of the original Japanese testimony in the Bōei Kenkyūjo.

54. # 54479, Ikeda Sumihisa, Historical Manuscript File, 4–5; also see Ikeda Sumihisa Chinjutsusho, GHQ Senshika, vol. 1, Chūō Shūsenshori 227, Bōei Kenkyūjo, Senshishitsu.

55. Hayashi Saburō Chinjutsusho (Dec. 23, 1949), vol. 6, GHQ Senshika, Chūō Shūsenshori 228, Bōei Kenkyūjo, Senshishitsu.

56. # 61340, Toyoda Soemu (Aug. 29, 1949), 7–8, CMH.

57. # 531, Suzuki Kantarō (Dec. 26, 1945), CMH.

58. Frank, *Downfall*, 347.

59. Frank's argument is questionable in his methodology here. If he discounts Kawabe's and Toyoda's testimonies as having been given years after the events in question, why should Suzuki's testimony, which was given several months after the end of

the war, be deemed more reliable? Frank's method of looking critically at testimonies made after the events is admirable, but he is inconsistent in this approach.

60. "Gikai tōben shiryō," Kokubō taikō kankei jūyōimanaka shorui tsuzuri, Riku-gunshō Gunjika, Rikugun Chūsa Shimanaka Shigero hokan, Chūō, Sensōshidō sonota 78, Bōeikenkyūjo Senshishitsu.

61. Ibid.

62. *Kantōgun*, 2: 280–81.

63. Ibid., 368–70.

64. Bōeichō Bōeikenshūjo Senshishitsu, *Senshi sōsho: Hokutō hōmen rikugun sakusen*, vol. 2: *Chishima, Karafuto, Hokkaidō no bōei* (Tokyo: Asagumo shinbunsha, 1971), 337.

65. Ibid., 342–45.

66. Frank, *Downfall*, 323.

67. For this, see Tsuyoshi Hasegawa, *Racing the Enemy: Stalin, Truman, and the Surrender of Japan* (Cambridge, Mass.: Belknap Press of Harvard University Press, 2005), chaps. 5 and 6.

68. Handō Toshikazu, *Nihon no ichiban nagai hi*, ed. Ōya Sōichi (Tokyo: Bungei shunjū, 1973), 36. Handō does not cite his source, but this popular book, though lacking citations, seems to be based on reliable sources.

69. Shigemitsu Mamoru, *Shōwa no dōran* (Tokyo: Chūkōronsha, 1952), 2: 286.

70. "Yonai Kaishō chokuwa," Aug. 12, 1945, in Itō, ed., *Takagi Sōkichi: Nikki to jōhō*, 2: 927; Yonai Mitsumasa, "Takagi oboegaki," quoted in Kurihara and Hatano, eds., *Shusen kōsaku no kiroku*, 2: 379.

71. Kido Nikki Kenkyūkai, ed., *Kido Kōichi nikki*, 2: 1225–27.

72. Ambassador Satō, who was usually very astute, made a grave error here in as-suming that Molotov's declaration of war effective midnight August 9 meant midnight Moscow time. Soviet tanks rolled into Manchuria at midnight Transbaikal time, 6 P.M. Moscow time, less than an hour after Molotov handed Satō the declaration of war, mag-nifying the sense of betrayal felt by the Japanese. See Hasegawa, *Racing the Enemy*, chap. 5.

73. Matsumoto Shun'ichi, "Shūsen oboegaki," in Gaimushō, ed., *Shūsen shiroku*, 4: 158–59.

74. *Shōwa Tennō dokuhakuroku* (Tokyo: Bungei shunjū, 1991), 120–21.

75. Asada, "Shock," 505, citing *Kido nikki: Tokyō saibanki*, 444. This does not appear in the Japanese original, Asada, "Genbaku tōka," 207–8.

76. Sakomizu, May 3, 1949, "Interrogations," quoted in Asada, "Shock," 505.

77. Quoted in Wada Haruki, "Nisso sensō," in Hara Teruyuki and Togawa Tsuguo, eds., *Kōza Surabu no sekai*, vol. 8: *Surabu to nihon* (Tokyo: Kōbundo, 1995), 119.

78. Sakomizu, *Kikanjū ka no shūshō kantei*, 246.

79. Hasegawa Saiji, "Hōkai no zenya," *Fujin kōron*, August 1947, quoted in *Shūsen shiroku*, 4: 84.

80. See n. 70 above.

81. Hosokawa Morisada, *Hosokawa Nikki* (1953; repr., Tokyo: Chūōkōronsha, 1979), 2: 415.

82. Asada, "Shock," 495.

83. Frank, *Downfall*, 345, based on Bōeichō Bōeikenshūjo Senshishitsu, *Senshi*

sōsho: *Daihonei rikugunbu*, 10: 449, which comes from Daihon'ei Rikugunbu Sensō Shidōhan, *Kimitsu sakusen nisshi*, 2: 756. Frank cites the emperor's statement as recreated by Butow, but Butow's record says nothing about the emperor's reference to the atomic bomb. Frank inserts in brackets "[At about this point, he also made specific reference to the greatly increased destructiveness of the atomic bomb]," supposedly from "the official Japanese military history series." Frank, *Downfall*, 295–96. Bōeichō Bōeikenshūjo Senshishitsu, *Daihonei rikugunbu*, vol. 10, on which Frank relies, takes this part from Takeshita's *Kimitsu sakusen nisshi*.

84. Asada's source is Sanbo Honbu, ed., *Haisen no kiroku*, 362, and Frank's source is Bōeichō Bōeikenshūjo Senshishitsu, *Daihonei rikugunbu*, 10: 449, but the original source of both is Takeshita's *Kimitsu sakusen nisshi*.

85. Gaimushō, ed., *Shūsen shiroku*, 4: 139, 142. In addition to the excerpts from Tōgō and Sakomizu, *Shūsen shiroku* also contains excerpts from Toyoda and Hoshina Zenshirō, who attended the imperial conference, and Kido and Shimomura, who did not. None of them mention anything about the emperor's reference to the atomic bomb.

86. Frank, *Downfall*, 345–46.

87. "Rikukaigunjin ni taisuru chokugo," in Hattori Takushirō, *Daitōa sensō zenshi* (1 vol. repr., Harashobō, 1965), 948, trans. based on Herbert P. Bix, *Hirohito and the Making of Modern Japan* (New York: HarperCollins, 2000), 530, with a slight modification.

88. Sakomizu was the author of the imperial rescript on the termination of the war. Sakomizu had been drafting the rescript since the first imperial conference on August 9–10. After the second imperial conference was over, he returned to the prime minister's residence to revise the draft in view of the emperor's statement at the imperial conference. Since he had to revise the draft to be presented to the cabinet under pressure of time, he asked his subordinate Kihara Michio to prepare the draft of the imperial rescript for the soldiers and sailors. Handō, *Nihon no ichiban nagai hi*, 45. Presumably, Sakomizu gave Kihara the basic ideas along which the rescript should be written. But it is not clear why only the atomic bomb, not Soviet entry into the war, was mentioned in the imperial rescript for the termination of the war, why Soviet entry into the war, but not the atomic bomb, was mentioned in the later rescript, or whether Kihara consulted any military leaders. It seems likely, however, that the draft was completed by August 15.

89. Frank, *Downfall*, 344.

90. "Naikaku kokuyu," in Matsutani Makoto, *Shūsen ni kansuru shiryō*, Matsutani shiryō, Shūsenji shiryō, Chūō, Shūsen shori 236, Bōei Kenkyūjo Senshishitsu.

91. "Taisho o haishite," in Matsutani Makoto, *Shūsen ni kansuru shiryō*, Matsutani shiryō, Shūsenji shiryō, Chūō, Shūsen shori 236, Bōei Kenkyūjo Senshishitsu.

92. This part of argument is taken partially from Hasegawa, *Racing the Enemy*, 294–98.

93. U.S. Strategic Bombing Survey, *Summary Report (Pacific War)* (Washington, D.C.: Government Printing Office, 1946), 26. See Alperovitz, *Decision to Use the Atomic Bomb*, 4, 321, 368–69, 464, 465.

94. Barton J. Bernstein, "Compelling Japan's Surrender Without the A-bomb, Soviet Entry, or Invasion: Reconsidering the US Bombing Survey's Early-Surrender Conclusion," *Journal of Strategic Studies* 18, no. 2 (June 1995): 101–48.

95. Ibid., 105, 127. Asada also agrees with Bernstein's conclusion on the assessment of the U.S. Strategic Bombing Survey. Asada, "Shock," 511.

96. Asada, "Shock," 510–11.

97. Bernstein, "Compelling Japan's Surrender," 129. Asada cites Bernstein's article, but only for the criticism of the U.S. Strategic Bombing Survey. He does not refer to Bernstein's important assertion that Japan would likely have surrendered before November after the Soviet intervention, without the use of the A-bomb, which directly contradicts Asada's assertion.

98. Asada, "Shock," 504.

99. Maj. Gen. John E. Hull and Col. L. E. Seeman, telephone conversation, Aug. 13, 1945, 13:25, OPD Executive File # 7, item 35a, folder # 1, telephone conversations, Aug. 6–25, 1945, RG 165, NA.

100. Kido Kōichi Kenkyūkai, ed., *Kido Kōichi nikki: Tokyō saibanki*, 444.

5. Holloway: Jockeying for Position

AUTHOR'S NOTE: I am grateful to Barton Bernstein, Lynn Eden, Tsuyoshi Hasegawa, Jonathan Haslam, and Norman Naimark for many helpful discussions and for comments on earlier drafts of this chapter.

1. The literature does deal with Soviet policy, but largely through American eyes, and often very briefly. See, e.g., Herbert Feis, *The Atomic Bomb and the End of World War II* (Princeton, N.J.: Princeton University Press, 1970); Gar Alperovitz, *Atomic Diplomacy: Hiroshima and Potsdam* (1965; rev. ed., New York: Penguin Books, 1985); Martin Sherwin, *A World Destroyed* (New York: Vintage Books, 1977).

2. For example, John Erickson's two volumes on *Stalin's War with Germany: The Road to Stalingrad* (London: Weidenfeld & Nicolson, 1975) and *The Road to Berlin* (London: Weidenfeld & Nicolson, 1983), widely regarded as the best books on the Soviet Union in World War II, do not deal with the war against Japan at all. Nor does Alexander Werth's classic *Russia at War, 1941–1945* (London: Pan Books, 1964). Similarly, Richard Overy's survey, *Russia's War* (New York: Penguin Books, 1997), devotes no more than a few pages to the Soviet war with Japan.

3. See, in particular, David M. Glantz, *The Soviet Strategic Offensive in Manchuria, 1945: August Storm* and *Soviet Operational and Tactical Combat in Manchuria, 1945: August Storm* (London: Frank Cass, 2003). Earlier, Glantz published two monographs, *August Storm: The Soviet 1945 Strategic Offensive in Manchuria* and *August Storm: Soviet Tactical and Operation Combat in Manchuria, 1945* (both Fort Leavenworth, Kans.: Combat Studies Institute, U.S. Army Command and General Staff College, 1983). See also Jacques Sapir, *La Mandchourie oubliée: Grandeur et démesure de l'art de la guerre soviétique* (Paris: Éditions du Rocher, 1996).

4. Tsuyoshi Hasegawa, *Racing the Enemy: Stalin, Truman, and the Surrender of Japan* (Cambridge, Mass.: Belknap Press of Harvard University Press, 2005). This paper was written before I read Hasegawa's book. I have revised it to take account of Hasegawa's research and to point to some differences in the interpretation of Soviet policy.

5. See, e.g., M. V. Zakharov, ed., *Finale: A Retrospective Review of Imperialist Japan's Defeat in 1945* (Moscow: Progress Publishers, 1972).

6. See, e.g., "Atomnye bombardirovki 1945" in *Voennyi Entsiklopedicheskii*

Slovar', 2nd ed. (Moscow: Voenizdat, 1986), 53; and V. Larionov et al., eds., *World War II: Decisive Battles of the Soviet Army* (Moscow: Progress Publishers, 1984), 469.

7. Especially notable in this connection is the work of Boris Slavinskii. See, e.g., his *Pakt o neitralitete mezhdu SSSR i Iaponiei: Diplomaticheskaia istoriia, 1941–1945 gg.* (Moscow: Novina, 1995) and *SSSR i Iaponiia—na puti k voine: diplomaticheskaia istoriia, 1937–1945 gg.* (Moscow: ZAO "Iaponiia segodnia," 1999). See also V. P. Safronov, *SSSR, SShA i Iaponskaia Agressiia na Dal'nem Vostoke i Tikhom Okeane. 1931–1945 gg.* (Moscow: Institut Rossiiskoi istorii RAN, 2001). For very helpful comments on new archival materials, particularly in relation to the study of Stalin, see Norman M. Naimark, "Cold War Studies and New Archival Materials on Stalin," *Russian Review* 61 (2002): 1–15.

8. For an insightful discussion of this issue, see Jonathan Haslam, "The Cold War as History," *Annual Review of Political Science, 2003*, 78–98. See also Melvin Leffler's review of John Gaddis's *We Now Know: Rethinking Cold War History* (Oxford: Oxford University Press, 1997), in "The Cold War: What Do 'We Now Know,'" *American Historical Review* 104 (1999): 501–24, and Leonid Gibianskii, "Sovetskie tseli v vostochnoi Evrope v kontse vtoroi mirovoi voiny i pervye poslevoennye gody," *Russian History/Histoire russe* 29 (2002), nos. 2–4 (Summer–Fall–Winter): 197–215.

9. When Soviet forces occupied Manchuria in August 1945, they turned over to the People's Liberation Army the Japanese arms and equipment that they had captured and helped to turn Manchuria into a revolutionary base for the Chinese Communist Party, even though the official policy of the USSR was that it would not interfere in the conflict in China. Some historians maintain that Stalin planned to do this all along; others argue that he did so only in response to American policy in China in the second half of 1945. See, for conflicting views, John W. Wheeler-Bennett and Anthony Nicholls, *The Semblance of Peace: The Political Settlement After the Second World War* (London: Macmillan, 1972), 359, and Chen Jian, *Mao's China and the Cold War* (Chapel Hill: University of North Carolina Press, 2001), 26–29. I realize that in entering the war against Japan, the Soviet Union had goals in China, but I do not attempt to deal fully with that issue here.

10. Norman M. Naimark, "Stalin and Europe in the Postwar Period, 1945–53: Issues and Problems," *Journal of Modern European History* 2 (2004): 53–56.

11. David Holloway, *Stalin and the Bomb: The Soviet Union and Atomic Energy, 1939–1956* (New Haven, Conn.: Yale University Press, 1994), 116–18, 122–33.

12. V. A. Zolotarev, ed., *Sovetsko-iaponskaia voina 1945 goda: Istoriia voenno-politicheskogo protivoborstva dvukh derzhav v 30–40e gody* published in the series *Russkii Arkhiv: Velikaia otechestvennaia* as volumes 7 (1) and 7 (2) (Moscow: Terra, 1997, 2000).

13. V. S. Miasnikov, ed., *Russko-kitaiskie otnosheniia v XX veke*, 4, bk. 1 (1937–1944) and bk. 2 (1945) (Moscow: Pamiatniki istoricheskoi mysli, 2000).

14. L. D. Riabev, ed., *Atomnyi proekt SSSR: Dokumenty i materialy* (various volumes and publishers).

15. See n. 103 below.

16. See Michael T. Florinsky, *Russia: A History and an Interpretation*, vol. 2 (New York: Macmillan, 1961), 977–79, 1262–68. I have stuck with the older names and older spellings for Chinese names because that is how they appear in contemporary documents.

17. Ibid., 1270–78.

18. I. V. Stalin, "Obrashchenie predsedatelia soveta narodnykh komissarov SSSR k sovetskomu narodu," in Zolotarev, ed., *Sovetsko-iaponskaia voina 1945 goda, Velikaia otechestvennaia*, 7 (2): 130.

19. Jonathan Haslam, *The Soviet Union and the Threat from the East, 1933–41* (London: Macmillan, 1992), 2, 24–30, 47–50, 80–81, 92–94; see also V. S. Miasnikov and A. M. Ledovskii, "Otnosheniia SSSR s Kitaem v period Iapono-Kitaiskoi Voiny (1937–1945)," in Miasnikov, ed., *Russko-kitaiskie otnosheniia*, 4, bk. 1: 8–9, 12; and Safronov, *SSSR, SShA,* 215–37.

20. Zolotarev, ed., *Sovetsko-iaponskaia voina, Velikaia otechestvennaia*, 7 (1): 18.

21. Haslam, *Soviet Union and the Threat*, 133–63.

22. Herbert P. Bix, *Hirohito and the Making of Modern Japan* (New York: HarperCollins, 2000), 397–98; Miasnikov and Ledovskii, "Otnosheniia SSSR," 15–16.

23. I. M. Maiskii, "O zhelatel'nykh osnovakh budushchego mira," *Istochnik*, 1995, no. 4 (17): 124–44.

24. Vladimir Pechatnov, *The Big Three After World War II: New Documents on Soviet Thinking About Post War Relations with the United States and Great Britain*, Cold War International History Project Working Paper No. 13 (Washington, D.C.: Woodrow Wilson International Center for Scholars, 1995).

25. Vladislav Zubok and Constantine Pleshakov, *Inside the Kremlin's Cold War* (Cambridge, Mass.: Harvard University Press, 1996), 28.

26. Maiskii, "O zhelatel'nykh," 124.

27. Ibid., 126, 127.

28. Ibid., 133.

29. Ibid., 133–34.

30. Ibid., 125.

31. Slavinskii, *SSSR i Iaponiia*, 338–41.

32. For a summary, see Slavinskii, *Pakt o neitralitete*, 239–44.

33. Jonathan Haslam, "Decision to War: Soviet Policy Towards Japan, 1944–1945" (paper given at the conference on Stalin and the Cold War, Yale University, September 1999), 7. Malik used "Russia" rather than "Soviet Union" here.

34. Slavinskii, *Pakt o neitralitete*, 239–44.

35. The full text of Lozovskii's memo can be found in B. N. Slavinskii, *Ialtinskaia konferetsiia i problema "severnykh territorii"* (Moscow: Novina, 1996), 74–78; quotations from 78, 85, 86.

36. Slavinskii, *Pakt o neitralitete*, 244.

37. Haslam, "Decision to War," 10–12. I do not pay much attention here to differences within the government and Party bureaucracies on issues such as these, interesting though they are. I have focused on Stalin because he seems so clearly to have dominated policy on the war against Japan.

38. Litvinov to the People's Commissariat of Foreign Affairs, Dec. 8, 1941, Molotov to Litvinov, Dec. 11, 1941, and Litvinov to the People's Commissariat of Foreign Affairs, Dec. 11, 1941, in *Sovetsko-amerikanskie otnosheniia vo vremia Velikoi Otechestvennoi voiny, 1941–1945: Dokumenty i materialy*, vol. 1: *1941–1943* (Moscow: Politizdat, 1984), 143–45; quotation from 144.

39. See the correspondence between Roosevelt and Stalin in December 1942 and January 1943, *Perepiska predsedatelia soveta ministrov SSSR s prezidentami SShA i*

premier-ministrami Velikobritaniia vo vremia Velikoi otechestvennoi voiny 1941–1945 gg., 2nd ed., vol. 2 (Moscow: Politizdat, 1986), 43–47. On American attitudes, see U.S. Department of Defense, *The Entry of the Soviet Union into the War Against Japan: Military Plans, 1941–1945* (Washington, D.C.: Government Printing Office, 1955), 9–16. See also Safronov, *SSSR, SShA,* 259–78.

40. Cordell Hull, *The Memoirs of Cordell Hull*, vol. 2 (New York: Macmillan, 1948), 1309.

41. W. Averell Harriman and Elie Abel, *Special Envoy to Churchill and Stalin, 1941–1946* (New York: Random House, 1975), 266; U.S. Department of State, *Conferences at Cairo and Teheran, 1943* (Washington, D.C.: Government Printing Office, 1961), 489.

42. S. M. Shtemenko, *General'nyi shtab v gody voiny* (Moscow: Voenizdat, 1981), 1: 400.

43. Harriman and Abel, *Special Envoy*, 363–64.

44. Ibid., 379–80.

45. A. A. Gromyko, *Pamiatnoe*, 2nd ed., vol. 1 (Moscow: Politizdat, 1990), 231.

46. The full text of the accord can be found in U.S. Department of State, *The Conferences at Malta and Yalta, 1945* (Washington, D.C.: Government Printing Office, 1955), 984; also in Zolotarev, ed., *Sovetsko-iaponskaia voina 1945 goda, Velikaia otechestvennaia,* 7 (1): 295–96.

47. Slavinskii, *SSSR i Iaponiia,* 365.

48. U.S. Department of Defense, *Entry of the Soviet Union,* 41.

49. Jonathan Haslam, "Soviet-Japanese Relations Since World War II," in Tsuyoshi Hasegawa, Jonathan Haslam, and Andrew C. Kuchins, eds., *Russia and Japan: An Unresolved Dilemma Between Distant Neighbors* (Berkeley: International and Area Studies, University of California at Berkeley, 1993), 6.

50. Hasegawa, *Racing the Enemy*, 19.

51. Glantz, *Soviet Strategic Offensive*, 60–64.

52. *Istoriia vtoroi mirovoi voiny, 1939–1945* [hereafter *IVMV*] (Moscow: Voenizdat, 1980), 11: 185–86. The Stavka was the highest Soviet strategic leadership body in the war. Headed by Stalin, it consisted of a small number of top military and political leaders. Stavka directives were signed by Stalin and the chief of the General Staff.

53. *IVMV,* 11: 183–84. This was in fact slightly below the 33–34 divisions the General Staff had estimated would be needed. See Glantz, *Soviet Strategic Offensive,* 6.

54. Shtemenko, *General'nyi shtab*, 1: 404.

55. Zakharov, ed., *Finale*, 54–55; Shtemenko, *General'nyi shtab*, 1: 404–5; S. P. Ivanov, "Iz opyta podgotovkii provedeniia Man'chzhurskoi operatsii 1945 goda," *Voennaia mysl'*, 1990, no. 8: 42–43.

56. The June 28 directive to the Maritime Group (the First Far Eastern Front) specified that it should take the northern Korean ports of Ranan, Seisin, and Rasin in order to prevent Japanese reinforcements arriving by way of them. See Zolotarev, ed., *Sovetsko-iaponskaia voina, Velikaia otechestvennaia,* 7 (1): 334.

57. See Shtemenko, *General'nyi shtab*, 1: 404–15; Glantz, *Soviet Strategic Offensive*, 140–50; on Hokkaidō, see Boris N. Slavinsky, "The Soviet Occupation of the Kurile Islands and the Plans for the Capture of Northern Hokkaido," *Japan Forum*, April 1993, 98.

58. According to one account, there was disagreement on the issue of Hokkaidō at the meeting on June 26 and 27 attended by Stalin, Molotov, Khrushchev, and N. A. Voznesenskii, the head of Gosplan, as well as Marshals G. K. Zhukov, R. Ia. Malinovskii, and K. A. Meretskov. During the discussion, Meretskov, commander of the Maritime Group, proposed that Soviet forces occupy Hokkaidō. The General Staff had apparently drawn up plans for such an operation. Khrushchev, according to this account, seconded Meretskov's proposal, but Molotov, Voznesenskii, and Zhukov opposed it. Molotov claimed that the Allies would regard the landing of forces on Hokkaidō as a serious breach of the Yalta Agreement. Stalin apparently did not express an opinion on the matter. See Slavinsky, "Soviet Occupation of the Kurile Islands," 97–98. There was a four-hour meeting in Stalin's office on the evening of the 26th, and extending into the 27th, with many of those listed in attendance, but neither Voznesenskii nor Meretskov are named in Stalin's visitors book. That does not prove they were not there, of course, and the account of disagreements over landing on Hokkaidō is plausible in view of what happened later, in August. For Stalin's visitors book for June 26, see *Istoricheskii arkhiv*, 1996, no. 4: 105.

59. The directives can be found in Zolotarev, ed., *Sovetsko-iaponskaia voina, Velikaia otechestvennaia*, 7 (1): 332–36

60. Glantz, *Soviet Strategic Offensive*, 339; Safronov, *SSSR, SShA*, 323.

61. A. M. Vasilevskii, *Delo vsei zhizni* (Moscow: Politizdat, 1974), 505.

62. Glantz, *Soviet Strategic Offensive,* 139–40.

63. The commander of the Transbaikal Front was Marshal R. Ia. Malinovskii, who had commanded the Second and Third Ukrainian Fronts and was to become minister of defense in 1957; Marshal K. A. Meretskov, who commanded the First Far Eastern Front, was a former chief of the General Staff; he had commanded fronts in Europe. Gen. M. A. Purkaev, commander of the Second Far Eastern Front, had commanded an army in the battle of Moscow and had held other senior commands before being posted to the Far East in 1943.

64. V. A. Zolotarev, ed., *Velikaia otechestvennaia voina, 1941–1945* (Moscow: Nauka, 1999), 3: 388.

65. On March 26, the Stavka had sent directives to the forces in the Far East to plan for a possible Japanese attack. Among the measures used to hide Soviet intentions were camouflage and concealment of various kinds, night movements of troops and matériel, assembly areas remote from the frontier, assumed names and junior-officer insignia for the senior commanders, and the banning of radio communication. See Glantz, *Soviet Strategic Offensive*, 42–43; S. P. Ivanov, ed., *Nachal'nyi period voiny* (Moscow: Voenizdat, 1974), 294.

66. The denunciation of the pact can be found in Zolotarev, ed., *Sovetsko-iaponskaia voina, Velikaia otechestvennaia*, 7 (1): 272.

67. Slavinskii, *SSSR i Iaponiia*, 367.

68. The GRU (Glavnoe Razvedyvatel'noe Upravlenie: Chief Intelligence Directorate of the People's Commissariat of Defense) *rezidentura* in Tokyo reported to Moscow on March 22 that one million people had been left homeless and several tens of thousands killed in that raid. See Zolotarev, ed., *Sovetsko-iaponskaia voina, Velikaia otechestvennaia*, 7 (1): 207–8.

69. Malik to the People's Commissariat of Foreign Affairs, Feb. 18, 1945, in "Za

kulisami tikhookeanskoi bitvy," *Vestnik ministerstva innostrannykh del SSSR*, 1990, no. 49: 45–46.

70. Zolotarev, ed., *Sovetsko-iaponskaia voina, Velikaia otechestvennaia*, 7 (1): 207.

71. Ibid., 208.

72. Ibid., 209.

73. Malik to Molotov, Apr. 21, 1945, in "Za kulisami," 46. The meeting did not take place.

74. Robert J. C. Butow, *Japan's Decision to Surrender* (Stanford: Stanford University Press, 1954), 88–92; Richard B. Frank, *Downfall: The End of the Imperial Japanese Empire* (New York: Penguin Books, 1999), 93–95.

75. Zolotarev, ed., *Sovetsko-iaponskaia voina, Velikaia otechestvennaia*, 7 (1): 213.

76. Ibid., 215. Yukiko Koshiro has written an interesting paper on Japanese views of the role the Soviet Union might play in counterbalancing American power after the war. Yukiko Koshiro, "Eurasian Eclipse: Japan's End Game in World War II," *American Historical Review* 109, no. 2 (April 2004): 417–44. I have not found in the Soviet materials I have looked at any receptivity at the end of the war to the idea that Soviet influence in Asia could be enhanced, and American hegemony prevented, by a Soviet-Japanese alliance of some kind.

77. Malik to the Foreign Affairs Commissariat on June 7, 28, and 30, in "Za kulisami," 46–52. The plan is set out in Malik's dispatch of June 30, ibid., 52.

78. Molotov to Malik, July 8, 1945, in "Za kulisami," 53.

79. Zolotarev, ed., *Sovetsko-iaponskaia voina, Velikaia otechestvennaia*, 7 (1): 216.

80. Slavinskii, *SSSR i Iaponiia*, 393–94.

81. Frank, *Downfall*, 225.

82. Hasegawa, *Racing the Enemy*, 125.

83. The minutes of Stalin's conversation with Hopkins, in *Sovetsko-amerikanskie otnosheniia*, 2: 406. See also Hopkins's own cable on the meeting, in Robert E. Sherwood, *Roosevelt and Hopkins: An Intimate History* (New York: Harper, 1950), 903–4.

84. Miasnikov, ed., *Russko-kitaiskie otnosheniia*, 4, bk. 2: 130. The Soviet minutes of these meetings correspond in general terms to English-language notes made by the Chinese delegation, but the Soviet minutes are much fuller. The Chinese notes record the above passage as follows: "*Stalin*: Germany was also disarmed. Even if destroy all war industry, light industry must be maintained. They can be switched into war industry. Present generation is hostile to Japan. Government change, they will forget about sufferings and will make concessions. *Soong*: You don't believe you can't [*sic*] disarm Germany? *Stalin*: No, I said that in a speech. Twenty, thirty years, Germany will get back to her feet. Now less possibility but in forty years she may get on her feet again if someone helps Germany." Victor Hoo Papers, box 2, file "Sino-Soviet Relations 1945–46," "Record of the Meeting Between T. Soong and Stalin on July 11, 1945," Hoover Institution Archive.

85. Minutes of a meeting between Stalin and Harriman, April 13, 1945, *Sovetsko-amerikanskie otnosheniia*, 2: 357–58.

86. *Sovetsko-amerikanskie otnosheniia*, 2: 406. The Tokyo *rezidentura* reported on April 20 that a basic aim of the Suzuki government was to find a way to conclude a truce with Britain; and on May 30, it reported that there were widespread rumors that the Suzuki government was conducting secret peace talks with the British. See Zolotarev, ed., *Sovetsko-iaponskaia voina, Velikaia otechestvennaia*, 7 (1): 211, 216.

87. *Biulleten' Biuro informatsii TsK VKP(b): Voprosy vneshnei politiki*, 1945, no. 13 (July 1): 1–6. Federal'noe arkhivnoe agentstvo Rossii (Rosarkhiv), Rossiiskii gosudarstvennyi arkhiv sotsial'no-politicheskoi istorii [Russian State Archive of Sociopolitical History, hereafter cited as RGASPI] f. 17, op. 128, t. 1, d. 50. Haslam finds evidence that in the summer of 1944, the Soviet Union had direct access, through intelligence sources, to Joseph Grew, who was then head of the Office for Far Eastern Affairs in the State Department. If that link continued into 1945, Moscow might have been informed of the discussions in Washington about the possibility of relaxing the surrender conditions. Haslam, "Decision to War," 10.

88. I have seen no evidence that Stalin ever discussed the possibility of leaving the emperor in place, which was the focus of much debate in Washington. But he did tell Hopkins: "The Japanese may offer to surrender and seek softer terms. While consideration of this has certain dangers as compared with [unconditional surrender] it nevertheless cannot be ruled out. Should the Allies depart from the announced policy of unconditional surrender and be prepared to accept a modified surrender, Stalin visualizes imposing our will through our occupying forces and thereby gaining substantially the same results as under [unconditional surrender]. In other words, it seemed to us that he proposes under this heading to agree to milder peace terms but once we get into Japan to give them the works." Sherwood, *Roosevelt and Hopkins*, 903–4.

89. Butow, *Japan's Decision to Surrender*, 128–29. No approach was made to the Soviet Union at the time. But if Moscow had pursued Hirota's overtures in June 1945, it might have been able to get very extensive concessions from Japan.

90. Sherwood, *Roosevelt and Hopkins*, 904. It was only in August that Truman definitively rejected the idea of occupation rights for the Soviet Union in Japan.

91. For analyses of the talks, see John W. Garver, *Chinese-Soviet Relations, 1937–1945: The Diplomacy of Chinese Nationalism* (Oxford: Oxford University Press, 1988), 214–22, 224–28; Odd Arne Westad, *Cold War and Revolution: Soviet-American Rivalry and the Origins of the Chinese Civil War 1944–1946* (New York: Columbia University Press, 1993), 36–56.

92. Miasnikov, ed., *Russko-kitaiskie otnosheniia*, 4, bk. 2: 74.

93. Ibid., 77.

94. Ibid., 111.

95. Ibid.

96. Ibid., 128.

97. Ibid., 134–37.

98. Antony Beevor, *The Fall of Berlin 1945* (New York: Viking Penguin, 2002), 138–39. Beevor claims that Stalin summoned Beria and leading nuclear scientists to his dacha in March 1942 to berate them for having neglected nuclear research, which then expanded "dramatically" over the next three years. There is no evidence that such a meeting took place, however, and the Soviet project had rather low priority until August 1945. It is implausible that it weighed heavily in Stalin's decision to take Berlin

first. The geopolitical reasons for his wanting to do so were sufficient and much more powerful than the nuclear factor seemed to him to be at the time. See Holloway, *Stalin and the Bomb*, 114–15.

99. The order can be found in L. D. Riabev, ed., *Atomnyi proekt SSSR*, vol. 1: *1938–1945*, pt. 1 (Moscow: Nauka, Fizmatlit, 1998), 269–70.

100. Merkulov to Beria, Feb. 28, 1945, ibid., pt. 2 (Moscow: MFTI, 2002), 235.

101. Ibid., 330. According to his confession to Michael Perrin, Klaus Fuchs had told the Soviet Union that the expected yield was ten kilotons. See Fuchs's confession in Robert Chadwell Williams, *Klaus Fuchs, Atom Spy* (Cambridge, Mass.: Harvard University Press, 1987), 191. In early March, a target date of July 4 was set for the test. There was considerable discussion in June about the date of the test; on June 30, July 16 was set as the earliest date. See "Scheduling the Trinity Test," J. R. Oppenheimer to All Group Leaders Concerned, June 14, 1945, and K. T. Bainbridge, *Trinity* (Los Alamos, N.M.: Los Alamos Scientific Laboratory, 1945; reissued in 1976 as LA-6300-H), both at www.lanl.gov/history/atomicbomb/trinity.shtml (accessed June 25, 2006).

102. Merkulov to Beria, July 10, 1945, in Riabev, ed., *Atomnyi proekt*, 1, pt. 2: 335.

103. Indirect confirmation is provided by the fact that the original of this memorandum was not found in Beria's papers. No search was done in Stalin's papers. Riabev, *Atomnyi proekt*, 1, pt. 2: 335–36. Klaus Fuchs was one of the sources of the information given to Beria. In June, he had told his contact Harry Gold when and where the test would take place, saying, however, that he was "dubious about the possibilities for any real and immediate utilization of atomic energy in the form of a weapon." See Gold's statements to the FBI in Williams, *Klaus Fuchs, Atom Spy*, 199.

104. *Sovetsko-amerikanskie otnosheniia*, 2: 404.

105. Shtemenko, *General'nyi shtab*, 1: 416.

106. Victor Hoo Papers, box 2, file "Sino-Soviet Relations, 1945–46," 24, Hoover Institution Archive; Miasnikov, ed., *Russko-kitaiskie otnosheniia*, 4, bk. 2: 113–14.

107. S. M. Shtemenko, "Iz istorii razgroma Kvantunskoi armii," *Voenno-istoricheskii zhurnal*, 1967, no. 4: 66, writes that in June the planned date of attack was August 20–25. In an article with the same title in *Voenno-istoricheskii zhurnal*, 1967, no. 5: 54, he writes that the planned date of attack was August 11 when Vasilevskii reported to Stalin on August 3 recommending that the attack begin on August 9–10. A. M. Vasilevskii, "Final," *Voenno-istoricheskii zhurnal*, 1967, no. 6: 85, writes that Stalin telephoned him on July 16 to ask him to advance the date of attack by ten days to August 1. The consistency between the accounts of Shtemenko and Vasilevskii, the two officers most directly involved in planning the war, is important and lends credence to the view that between July 16 and August 3, the planned date of August 11 for entry into the war remained unchanged. In his memoirs, published in 1974, Vasilevskii does not mention a specific date for entry into the war when writing about his conversation with Stalin on July 16 (Vasilevskii, *Delo vsei zhizni*, 513), but I do not see that as a reason for disregarding the evidence in the earlier article. At Potsdam, both Stalin and Chief of Staff General Aleksei Antonov told the Allies that the Soviet Union would enter the war by the middle of August or in the second half of August. This vagueness can perhaps be explained by the fact that Stalin had not yet given the order to attack on a particular date and by a belief on Stalin's part that entering the war a few days before

the Allies expected would give the Soviet Union a useful element of political surprise. Stalin would have been unlikely to tell the Allies that he was intending to enter the war on a date earlier than he had planned.

108. Vasilevskii, "Final," 85.

109. U.S. Department of State, *The Conference of Berlin* (Washington, D.C.: Government Printing Office, 1960), 2: 45; *Sovetskii Soiuz na mezhdunarodnykh konferentsiiakh perioda velikoi otechestvennoi voiny 1941–1945 gg.*, vol. 4: *Berlinskaia (potsdamskaia) konferentsiia* (Moscow: Politizdat, 1980) [hereafter *Berlinskaia konferentsiia*], 43.

110. U.S. Department of Defense, *Entry of the Soviet Union*, 92.

111. Vasilevskii, "Final," 86; id., *Delo vsei zhizni*, 513.

112. It is not clear from the newly released documents when Stalin was first informed that the Alamogordo test had taken place successfully. Sergo Beria, in his book about his father, *Moi otets—Lavrentii Beria* (Moscow: Sovremennik, 1994), 260, writes that Beria reported to Stalin on the test before Truman's remark about the bomb on July 24. This is certainly quite plausible. So too is Sergo Beria's description of Stalin's reaction to Truman's remark: he was dissatisfied and when he returned from the session, he asked Beria to prepare proposals for speeding up the Soviet work (261). Sergo Beria is not always a reliable source, however, and needs to be treated with great caution. For example, he reports that at Potsdam, Beria told Stalin that they had already obtained plutonium (260), even though the first production reactor did not go critical until 1948, and the first experimental reactor went critical only in December 1946. The first plutonium was separated only in 1946 from uranium irradiated in a cyclotron, although trace quantities had been obtained in October 1944. See Holloway, *Stalin and the Bomb*, 99. The earliest report on the test in the documentary collection on the atomic project is dated Oct. 19, 1945, when Merkulov sent Beria a detailed report on the test. Riabev, *Atomnyi proekt SSSR*, 1, pt. 2: 330.

113. Harry S. Truman, *Memoirs*, vol. 1: *1945, Year of Decisions* (1955; repr., New York: Signet Books, 1965), 458.

114. Ibid.

115. Anthony Eden, *The Reckoning: The Memoirs of Anthony Eden, Earl of Avon* (Boston: Houghton Mifflin, 1965), 635.

116. V. G. Trukhanovskii, *Angliiskoe iadernoe oruzhie* (Moscow: Mezhdunarodnye otnosheniia, 1985), 23.

117. G. K. Zhukov, *Vospominaniia i razmyshleniia*, 10th ed. (Moscow: Novosti, 1990), 3: 334; Feliks Chuev, *Sto sorok besed s Molotovym: Iz dnevnika F. Chueva* (Moscow: Terra, 1991), 81; Gromyko, *Pamiatnoe*, 2nd ed., 1: 276.

118. The new volumes of documents on the Soviet atomic project contain nothing to indicate what conclusions Stalin drew from the meeting at Potsdam. We know that the Soviet Union bugged Roosevelt's quarters at the Teheran and Yalta conferences (see Gary Kern, "How 'Uncle Joe' Bugged FDR," in *Studies in Intelligence* 47, no. 1 [2003]: 19–31), and it reportedly bugged Truman's quarters at Potsdam too (see Hasegawa, *Racing the Enemy*, 132, 331). What Stalin learned from this is not clear. He might have been given transcripts or summaries of Stimson's conversations with Truman about the bomb. Whether Stalin would have received any information about the plan to bomb Japan is unclear. There is no evidence that this intelligence-gathering exercise produced

any effect on Stalin's decisions at Potsdam. This is nevertheless an intriguing aspect of the history of the conference that remains largely unexplored. The reference to Britain is appropriate, because Britain was a junior partner in the Manhattan Project.

119. Shtemenko, *General'nyi shtab*, 1: 425.

120. Vasilevskii, "Final," 86.

121. Hasegawa, *Racing the Enemy*, 44.

122. Ibid., 155, 331–32.

123. U.S. Department of State, *Conference of Berlin*, 2: 45. The published Soviet minutes do not have this last clause about agreement being reached with China first. See *Berlinskaia (potsdamskaia) konferentsiia* (Moscow: Politizdat, 1980), 43; Robert H. Ferrell, ed., *Off the Record: The Private Papers of Harry S. Truman* (New York: Harper and Row, 1980), 53.

124. Barton J. Bernstein, "Truman at Potsdam: His Secret Diary," *Foreign Service Journal*, July–August 1980, 33.

125. Harry S. Truman, *Dear Bess: The Letters from Harry to Bess Truman, 1910–1959*, ed. Robert H. Ferrell (New York: Norton, 1983), 519.

126. U.S. Department of Defense, *Entry of the Soviet Union*, 92.

127. Ibid., 92–104. One of the issues the Chiefs of Staff agreed on was zones of naval and air operations, divided by a line that ran from the interior of Asia into Manchuria, down to Busui Tan (Cape Boltina) on the Korean coast, and then through the sea of Japan to a point in the La Pérouse Strait between Sakhalin and Hokkaidō. Soviet forces were to operate to the north of this line, American forces to the south. Part of southern Manchuria and most of the Korean peninsula, as well as the Japanese home islands, were in the American zone of operations.

128. U.S. Department of State, *Conference of Berlin*, 2: 87. Truman already knew about the Japanese approach to the Soviet Union from decrypted Japanese messages. For a discussion of what Truman actually knew, see Frank, *Downfall*, 240–51.

129. U.S. Department of State, *Conference of Berlin*, 2: 460; *Berlinskaia konferentsiia*, 222.

130. The phrase is from Herbert Feis, *The China Tangle: The American Effort in China from Pearl Harbor to the Marshall Mission* (Princeton, N.J.: Princeton University Press, 1953), 304.

131. Sherwood, *Roosevelt and Hopkins*, 902–3; *Sovetsko-amerikanskie otnosheniia*, 2: 405–6.

132. "Minutes of Meeting Held at the White House, 18 June 1945," in U.S. Department of State, *Conference of Berlin*, 1: 905, 909.

133. Richard G. Hewlett and Oscar E. Anderson Jr., *The New World: A History of the United States Atomic Energy Commission*, vol. 1: *1939–1946* (Berkeley: University of California Press, 1990), 389.

134. Bernstein, "Truman at Potsdam," 33; Ferrell, ed., *Off the Record*, 54.

135. Henry L. Stimson and McGeorge Bundy, *On Active Service in Peace and War* (New York: Harper & Brothers, 1948), 637. I do not deal here with the controversy about the role of the atomic bomb in U.S. policy in 1945. Barton Bernstein's chapters in this volume discuss the historiography in depth. On the assumptions underpinning Truman's policy, see Barton J. Bernstein, "Roosevelt, Truman, and the Atomic Bomb, 1941–1945: A Reinterpretation," *Political Science Quarterly* 89, no. 4 (1974–75): 23–69.

136. Diary of Henry L. Stimson, July 23, 1945, Yale University Library.

137. Great Britain, *Documents on British Policy Overseas*, ed. Rohan Butler et al., 1st ser. (London: Her Majesty's Stationery Office, 1984), 1: 573. Byrnes was probably referring to the message that Truman sent Chiang on July 23. Truman wrote: "I asked you to carry out the Yalta agreement but I had not asked that you make any concession in excess of the agreement. If you and Generalissimo Stalin differ as to the correct interpretation of the Yalta agreement, I hope you will arrange for Soong to return to Moscow and continue your efforts to reach complete understanding." U.S. Department of State, *Conference of Berlin*, 2: 1241. Truman was consistent in urging the Chinese to accept the Yalta agreement but not to make concessions beyond the agreement. The Soviet and Chinese sides disagreed on the interpretation of the agreement. There was, of course, an asymmetry here, because the Soviet Union was party to the agreement and China was not.

138. Feis, *Atomic Bomb*, 16–26.

139. The full text of the Potsdam Proclamation can be found in Butow, *Japan's Decision to Surrender*, 243–44.

140. *Sovetsko-amerikanskie otnosheniia*, 2: 407.

141. Feis, *Atomic Bomb*, 106.

142. Notes on a telephone conversation between V. Pavlov and Matthews, a member of the American delegation, in Miasnikov, ed., *Russko-kitaiskie otnosheniia*, 4, bk. 2: 146.

143. U.S. Department of State, *Conference of Berlin*, 2: 460; *Berlinskaia konferentsiia*, 222.

144. The full text is in Safronov, *SSSR, SShA*, 331–32. Safronov, who found and published the document, states that it was written late in the evening after Stalin and Molotov had learned of the Potsdam Proclamation (331). Hasegawa, without giving a source, writes that the Soviet delegation had brought the document with them to Potsdam. See Hasegawa, *Racing the Enemy*, 161.

145. Safronov, *SSSR, SShA*, 334.

146. Butow, *Japan's Decision to Surrender*, 145–47; Hasegawa, *Racing the Enemy*, 165–70.

147. Feis, *Atomic Bomb*, 110–11.

148. James V. Forrestal Papers, Diaries, 1944–1949, Seeley G. Mudd Manuscript Library, Princeton University, July 28, 1945.

149. Feis, *Atomic Bomb*, 111.

150. Still less was there any discussion about the possibility of modifying the terms in order to make it easier for Japan to surrender. It is true that Stalin, if he had been brought into such a discussion, would almost certainly have opposed any concessions to the Japanese.

151. The text of Vasilevskii's report is in Zolotarev, ed., *Sovetsko-iaponskaia voina, Velikaia otechestvennaia*, 7 (1): 337–38; Shtemenko's comment is in his "Iz istorii razgroma Kvantunskoi armii," *Voenno-istoricheskii zhurnal*, 1967, no. 5: 54.

152. The Stavka directive of August 7 is given in Zolotarev, ed., *Sovetsko-iaponskaia voina, Velikaia otechestvennaia*, 7 (1): 340–41.

153. On Molotov's meeting with Sato, see Safronov, *SSSR, SShA*, 336–37.

154. This deception had little practical effect, however, because the NKVD "held up" the coded telegram from the ambassador to Tokyo. See Slavinskii, *SSSR i Iaponiia*, 470.

155. See the Soviet government statement in *Sovetsko-amerikanskie otnosheniia*, 2: 478–79.

156. Cable from Kennan to Washington, D.C., Aug. 8, 1945, W. A. Harriman Papers, box 181, Library of Congress.

157. Hasegawa, *Racing the Enemy*, 186–87.

158. Svetlana Alliluyeva, *Twenty Letters to a Friend* (Harmondsworth, UK: Penguin Books, 1968), 164.

159. Even senior U.S. officials who were well informed about the bomb were un- sure after Hiroshima that Japan would surrender quickly. Secretary of the Navy James Forrestal wrote to Truman on August 8 recommending that Admiral Chester Nimitz take command of "final operations against Japan in the Pacific" (Forrestal Papers, cited n. 148 above). In other words, he did not anticipate a quick surrender by Japan. And Secretary of War Henry Stimson noted in his diary on August 10 that the Japanese provisional acceptance of the Potsdam Proclamation disrupted his planned vacation (Henry Lewis Stimson Diary and Papers, Yale University Library). My thanks to Barton Bernstein for these references.

160. Gen. Hata Hikosaburō's testimony, in Zolotarev, ed., *Sovetsko-iaponskaia voina, Velikaia otechestvennaia*, 7 (2): 321.

161. See, e.g., Sapir, *Mandchourie oubliée,* 175; Peter Vigor, *Soviet Blitzkrieg Theory* (New York: St. Martin's Press, 1983), 102–21.

162. G. F. Krivosheev, ed., *Grif sekretnosti sniat* (Moscow: Voenizdat, 1993), 222– 23. The Manchurian campaign involved 1.669 million Soviet troops and lasted from August 9 to September 2, 1945. In the Berlin operation, from 16 April until 8 May, 1.9 million Soviet troops took part and there were 350,000 casualties: 78,000 killed and 274,000 wounded (ibid., 219–20).

163. See Zolotarev, ed., *Sovetsko-iaponskaia voina, Velikaia otechestvennaia*, 7 (2): 121–23, on the numbers of Japanese casualties and prisoners, and ibid., 174–234, on the treatment of Japanese prisoners. See also E. L. Katasonova, *Iaponskie voenno- plennye v SSSR* (Moscow: Kraft, 2003).

164. For the text, see Butow, *Japan's Decision to Surrender*, 245.

165. Hasegawa, *Racing the Enemy*, 252–55.

166. Glantz, *Soviet Strategic Offensive*, 213.

167. Ibid., 182–307; B. N. Slavinskii, *Sovetskaia okkupatsiia kuril'skikh ostrovov (avgust–sentiabr' 1945 goda)* (Moscow: Lotos, 1993); V. P. Zimonin, *Poslednyi ochag vtoroi mirovoi voiny* (Moscow, 2002), 283–333.

168. This exchange of letters can be found in *Perepiska predsedatelia soveta min- istrov SSSR*, 2: 279–87; quotation from 285. Stalin uses "Russian" rather than "Soviet" in the original.

169. Stalin to Truman, August 22, 1945, *Perepiska predsedatelia soveta ministrov SSSR*, 2: 286–87.

170. Slavinsky, "Soviet Occupation of the Kurile Islands," 98.

171. On the cable to the Stavka, see V. P. Galitskii and V. P. Zimonin, "Desant na

284   Notes to Chapter 5

Khokkaido otmenit'," *Voenno-istoricheskii zhurnal*, 1994, no. 3: 7; for the order of August 18, see Zolotarev, ed., *Sovetsko-iaponskaia voina, Velikaia otechestvennaia*, 7 (2): 35–36.

172. Zolotarev, ed., *Sovetsko-iaponskaia voina, Velikaia otechestvennaia*, 7 (2): 39. According to Glantz, *Soviet Strategic Offensive*, 110, a Soviet rifle division had a nominal strength of 11,780 troops.

173. Galitskii and Zimonin, "Desant na Khokkaido," 7.

174. Ibid., 8.

175. This operational directive is given in Zolotarev, ed., *Sovetsko-iaponskaia voina, Velikaia otechestvennaia*, 7 (2): 42.

176. Galitskii and Zimonin, "Desant na Khokkaido," 9.

177. Zolotarev, ed., *Sovetsko-iaponskaia voina, Velikaia otechestvennaia*, 7 (2): 45.

178. Slavinskii, *Sovetskaia okkupatsiia*, 124. I have not touched in this paper on the controversial Kuril Islands/Northern Territories dispute. Here it is worth noting that the Yalta agreement did not define what was covered by the term "Kuril Islands." Stalin interpreted the term as broadly as possible.

179. Zimonin, *Poslednyi ochag*, 318–24.

180. Zolotarev, ed., *Sovetsko-iaponskaia voina, Velikaia otechestvennaia*, 7 (2): 261–62. Derevianko was also to raise the question of stationing Soviet troops in Tokyo with MacArthur.

181. Zolotarev, ed., *Sovetsko-iaponskaia voina, Velikaia otechestvennaia*, 7 (2): 263.

182. Galitskii and Zimonin, "Desant na Khokkaido," 9.

183. Bruce Cumings, *The Origins of the Korean War: Liberation and the Emergence of Separate Regimes, 1945–1947* (Princeton, N.J.: Princeton University Press, 1981), 118–22; Erik Van Ree, *Socialism in One Zone: Stalin's Policy in Korea, 1945–1947* (Oxford: Berg, 1989), 48–64.

184. Miasnikov, ed., *Russko-kitaiskie otnosheniia*, 4, bk. 2: 157.

185. Ibid., 159.

186. Memorandum of conversation between Harriman and Stalin, Aug. 8, 1945, W. A. Harriman Papers, box 181, Library of Congress.

187. In a memorandum of his conversation with Soong on July 12, 1945, Harriman wrote, "In the early discussions I urged [Soong] to be more realistic in the arrangements regarding the ports and the railroads and that he would have to make further concessions than he had been authorized to propose. In the last two talks I expressed the personal opinion that he should not make further concessions since he had now met any reasonable interpretation of the Yalta Agreement." W. A. Harriman Papers, box 181, Library of Congress.

188. Memorandum of conversation between Harriman and Stalin, Aug. 8, 1945.

189. Miasnikov, ed., *Russko-kitaiskie otnosheniia*, 4, bk. 2: 164.

190. Harriman to the president and the secretary of state, Aug. 11, 1945, W. A. Harriman Papers, box 181, Library of Congress. This point does not appear in either the Soviet minutes or the Chinese notes of the meeting.

191. For the texts of the agreements, see Miasnikov, ed., *Russko-kitaiskie otnosheniia*, 4, bk. 2: 187–98.

192. Minutes of a conversation between Molotov and Harriman on Aug. 14, 1945, in *Sovetsko-amerikanskie otnosheniia*, 2: 486.

193. See, e.g., Sergei N. Goncharov, John W. Lewis, and Xue Litai, *Uncertain Partners: Stalin, Mao, and the Korean War* (Stanford: Stanford University Press, 1993), 6; and Iu. M. Galenovich, *Rossiia—Kitai: shest' dogovorov* (Moscow: Muravei, 2003), 80–89, 136–75.

194. Stalin, "Obrashchenie," 130–31.

195. For a discussion of Stalin's conception of postwar international politics, see Holloway, *Stalin and the Bomb*, 150–53.

196. Stalin had written very bitter letters to Roosevelt on March 29 and April 3, 1945, about meetings in Switzerland of U.S. and British and officers with representatives of the German High Command. On April 3, he accused the Americans and the British of reaching agreement with Field Marshal Albert Kesselring, the German commander of the Western Front, "to open the front and allow Anglo-American forces to the east, while the Anglo-Americans have promised in return for this to lighten the terms of the armistice for the Germans." *Perepiska predsedatelia soveta ministrov SSSR*, 2: 219. Roosevelt rejected Stalin's version of events, but apparently without success. See the exchange of letters in *Perepiska predsedatelia soveta ministrov SSSR*, 2: 217–18.

197. Haslam, "Decision to War," 22.

198. For a discussion of that speech, see Holloway, *Stalin and the Bomb*, 150–51.

199. See nn. 135 and 159 above.

200. The decree is in L. D. Riabev, ed., *Atomnyi proekt SSSR: Dokumenty i materialy,* vol. 2: *Atomnaia bomba, 1945–1954*, bk. 1 (Moscow: Nauka, 1999), 11–13.

201. Riabev, ed., *Atomnyi proekt SSSR*, 1, pt. 2: 239.

202. Gromyko, *Pamiatnoe*, 2nd ed., 1: 276.

203. Zhukov, *Vospominaniia i razmyshleniia*, 10th ed., 3: 334. When Stalin told Molotov about Truman's remark that the United States had a bomb of unusual destructive force, Molotov responded, "They're trying to raise the price."

204. Anatolii Gromyko, *Andrei Gromyko: V labirintakh Kremlia* (Moscow: Avtor, 1997), 65.

205. This was in response to Secretary of State James Byrnes's proposal for a U.S.-Soviet Anti-German Pact. On the background, see Vladimir Pechatnov, "Soiuzniki nazhimaiiut na tebia dlia togo, chtoby slomit' u tebia voliu," *Istochnik* 38, no. 2 (1999): 74–75.

206. Minutes of conversations between Molotov and Byrnes, Sept. 22 and 27, 1945. RGASPI, f. 558, op. 11, d. 237, ll. 36–37, 38. Byrnes responded that Molotov could think what he liked, but those were the Allies' documents; to which Molotov in turn said that those documents were valid only for the period before the Japanese Army was disarmed (cf. n. 88 above). Some days before the first of these conversations, on September 16, the Tokyo *rezidentura* had sent a report to Moscow to say that the Japanese were hiding supplies of arms in the mountains and in distant regions; that demobilized troops were being given uniforms, boots, and cartridges to keep at home; that an underground network of officers would be created throughout the country; and that in the 1946 parliamentary elections, many young officers espousing revanchist ideas would be elected. The same report noted: "Japanese in private and semiofficial conversations openly declare that America is the victor, and that victor's rights do not extend

to anyone else. The same line is taken by the Americans." Zolotarev, ed., *Sovetsko-iaponskaia voina, Velikaia otechestvennaia*, 7 (1): 217–18.

207. Memoranda of conversations between Harriman and Stalin, Oct. 24 and 25, 1945, W. A. Harriman Papers, box 183, Library of Congress.

208. This comment was interpolated into the minutes by Edward Page, Harriman's interpreter and note taker. Memorandum of conversation between W. A. Harriman and Stalin, Oct. 25, 1945, 5–6, W. A. Harriman Papers, box 183, Library of Congress.

209. Ibid., 3.

210. Ibid., 4–5.

211. Hull, *Memoirs of Cordell Hull*, 1310.

212. Stalin to V. M. Molotov, G. M. Malenkov, L. P. Beria, and A. I. Mikoian, Dec. 9, 1945, in *Politburo TsK VKP(b) i sovet ministrov SSSR 1945–1953* (Moscow: Rosspen, 2002), 202.

213. Pechatnov, "Soiuzniki nazhimaiut," 70–85.

214. Stalin to Molotov et al., Nov. 4, 1945. RGASPI, f. 558, op. 11, d. 98, l. 41

215. Holloway, *Stalin and the Bomb*, 253–72.

216. V. M. Molotov, "Doklad V. M. Molotova na torzhestvennom zasedanii mos-kovskogo soveta 6-go noiabria 1945g.," *Pravda*, Nov. 7, 1945.

6. Hasegawa: The Soviet Factor in Ending the Pacific War

AUTHOR'S NOTE: Boris Slavinsky wrote a paper entitled "The End of the Pacific War Revisited" for the 2001 conference of the Center for Cold War Studies at the University of California, Santa Barbara. Unfortunately, Slavinsky died on April 23, 2002, and since he was unable to revise his paper for this volume, Tsuyoshi Hasegawa wrote this chapter, incorporating the ideas in Slavinsky's original paper into a synthesis with his own ideas. This chapter also draws on Tsuyoshi Hasegawa, *Racing the Enemy: Stalin, Truman, and the Surrender of Japan* (Cambridge, Mass.: Belknap Press of Harvard University Press, 2005), which benefited from Slavinsky's paper, as well as from his extensive research materials and monographs. The author regrets that he did not have the opportunity to discuss further numerous points of minor disagreements on facts and interpretations that he had with Slavinsky. Undoubtedly, had Slavinsky been alive to settle these disagreements, his chapter would have been a much improved version of this one. Needless to say, Hasegawa takes fully responsibility for the views expressed in this chapter.

1. For a more detailed discussion of Soviet operations in Manchuria, Korea, southern Sakhalin, and the Kurils, see Hasegawa, *Racing the Enemy*, chap. 7. Also see David Holloway's Chapter 5 in this volume.

2. Hosoya Chihiro, "Sangoku dōmei to nisso chūritsu jōyaku," *Taiheiyō sensō eno michi: Kaisen gaikōshi*, vol. 5: *Sangoku dōmei, nisso chūritsu jōyaku* (Tokyo: Asahi shinbunsha, 1987), 312. For the conclusion of the Neutrality Treaty, see B. N. Slavinskii, *Pakt o neitralitete mezhdu SSSR i Iaponiei: Diplomaticheskaia istoriia, 1941–1945 gg.* (Moscow: TOO Novina, 1995); George Alexander Lensen, *The Strange Neutrality: Soviet-Japanese Relations During the Second World War, 1941–1945* (Tallahassee, Fla.: Diplomatic Press, 1972).

3. Hasegawa, *Racing the Enemy*, 16; Hosoya, "Sangoku dōmei," 320.

4. Hasegawa, *Racing the Enemy*, 16–17; Hosoya, "Sangoku dōmei," 315–21.

5. N. M. Pegov, "Stalin on War with Japan, October 1941," *Soviet Studies in History* 24, no. 3 (1985–86): 33–36.

6. Hasegawa, *Racing the Enemy*, 17; V. A. Zolotarev, ed., *Sovetsko-iaponskaia voina 1945 goda: Istoriia voenno-politicheskogo protivoborstva dvukh derzhav v 30–40e gody*, *Velikaia otechestvennaia*, 7 (1) (Moscow: Terra, 1997), 193–94.

7. *Sovetsko-Amerikanskie otnosheniia vo vremia Velikoi otechestvennoi voiny, 1941–1945* (Moscow: Politizdat, 1984), 1: 144.

8. Hasegawa, *Racing the Enemy*, 19; O. A. Rzheshevskii, "Vizit A. Idena v Moskvu v dekabre 1941 g. i peregorova s I. V. Stalinym i V. M. Molotovym: Iz arkhiva prezidenta RF," *Novaia i noveishaia istoriia*, no. 3 (1994): 105, 118.

9. Hayashi Shigeru, "Taiso kōsaku no tenkai," Nihon Gaikō Gakkai, *Taiheiyō sensō shūketsu ron* (Tokyo: Tōkyō daigaku shuppankai, 1958), 189, 195–96.

10. Hasegawa, *Racing the Enemy*, 18–20.

11. Morishima Gorō, "Kunō suru chūso taishikan," in Morishima Yasuhiko, *Shōwa no dōran to Morishima Gorō no shōgai* (Tokyo: Ashi shobō, 1975), 61–73, 78–104.

12. Cordell Hull, *The Memoirs of Cordell Hull* (New York: Macmillan), 2: 1113, 1309–10; U.S. Department of Defense, *The Entry of the Soviet Union into the War Against Japan: Military Plans, 1941–1945* (Washington, D.C.: Government Printing Office, 1955); Charles E. Bohlen, *Witness to History, 1929–1969* (New York: Norton, 1973), 128; NHK Nisso purojekuto, *Korega soren no tainichi gaikō da: Hiroku, Hoppōryōdo* (Tokyo: NHK, 1991), 15–17; B. N. Slavinskii, *SSSR i Iaponia—na puti k voine: Diplomaticheskaia istoriia, 1937–1945 gg.* (Moscow: ZAO "Iaponia segodnia, 1999), 327–33; S. M. Shtemenko, *The Soviet General Staff at War, 1941–1945* (Moscow: Progress Publishers, 1981), 2: 405; id., "Iz istorii razgroma Kvantunskoi armii," *Voenno-istoricheskii zhurnal*, 1967, no. 4: 55.

13. Hasegawa, *Racing the Enemy*, 25; Bohlen, *Witness to History*, 195; U.S. Department of Defense, *Entry of the Soviet Union*, 24; memorandum, Jan. 12, 1945, Papers of George M. Elsey, Harry S. Truman Library, Independence, Mo.; Iokibe Makoto, *Beikoku no nihon senryō seisaku* (Tokyo: Chūōkōronsha, 1985), 2: 76–79. The only concession he did not include in the Yalta agreement was the trusteeship of Korea.

14. Aleksei Kirichenko, "Hakkutsu: KGB himitsu bunsho: Sutârin shūnen no tainichi sansen, sore wa shino tetsudōkara hajimatta," *This Is Yomiuri*, December 1992, 236–43.

15. Hasegawa, *Racing the Enemy*, 24.

16. Ibid., 26–27. See also David Holloway's Chapter 5 in this volume. For Maiskii's report, see document no. 5, "Zaniat'sia podgotovkoi," *Istochniki*, 1995, no. 4: 124–25, 133–34. For Malik's report, see Arkhiv vneshnei politici Rossiskoi Federatsii [hereafter AVP RF], fond 06. papka. 58, delo, 803a, listy. 204–58; Slavinskii, *Pakt o neitralitete*, 239–44; Yokote Shinji, "Dainiji taisenki no soren no tainich seisaku," Keiō Daigaku Hōgaku Kenkyūkai, *Hōgaku kenkyū* 71, no. 1 (1998): 216–18, 222–25; Jonathan Haslam, "Soren no tainichi gaikō to sansen," in Hosoya Chihiro et al., *Taiheiyō sensō no shūketsu* (Tokyo: Kashiwa shobō, 1997), 74–81.

17. Hasegawa, *Racing the Enemy*, 27; G. N. Sevost'ianov. "Iaponiia 1945 g. v otsenke sovetskikh diplomatov, novye arkhivnye materialy," *Novaia i noveishaia istoriia*,

1995, no. 6: 37; A. Vasilevskii, *Delo vsei zhizni* (Moscow: Izd-vo politicheskoi literatury, 1975), 552–53; Shtemenko, *Soviet General Staff at War*, 1: 406; id., "Iz istorii razgroma Kvantunskoi armii," *Voenno-istoricheskii zhurnal*, 1967, no. 4: 57.

18. Hasegawa, *Racing the Enemy*, 27–28; U.S. Department of Defense, *Entry of the Soviet Union*, 30–32.

19. Hasegawa, *Racing the Enemy*, 28–29.

20. Ibid., 29; "Taiso gaikō shisaku ni kansuru ken (an)," in Gaimushō, ed., *Shūsen shiroku* (Tokyo: Hokuyōsha, 1977), 1: 248–52 [hereafter all references to Gaimushō, ed., *Shūsen shiroku* refer to the 1977 edition].

21. Hasegawa, *Racing the Enemy*, 29; "Nisso gaikō kōshō kiroku (Gaimusho chōsho)," in Gaimushō, ed., *Shūsen shiroku* 1: 152–54; Morishima, "Kunō suru chūso taishikan," 180–84.

22. Hasegawa, *Racing the Enemy*, 31; Harriman to Roosevelt, Sept. 23, 1944, Moscow Files, Sept. 19–24, 1944, W. A. Harriman Papers, Library of Congress; U.S. Department of Defense, *Entry of the Soviet Union*, 34–35.

23. Hasegawa, *Racing the Enemy*, 31; Harriman to Roosevelt, "Eyes Only" cable, Oct. 15, 1944, and "Summary of Conclusions of the Meeting Held at the Kremlin, October 15, 1944," Moscow Files, Oct. 15–16 and 17–20, 1944, W. A. Harriman Papers, Library of Congress.

24. Hasegawa, *Racing the Enemy*, 31; "Conversation, the Far Eastern Theater," Oct. 15, 1944, Moscow Files, Oct. 15–16, 1944, W. A. Harriman Papers, Library of Congress.

25. "Interpretive Report on Developments in Soviet Policy Based on the Soviet Press for the Period, October 15–December 31, 1944," Moscow Files, Oct. 13, 1944, W. A. Harriman Papers, Library of Congress. As for Japan's reactions to Stalin's speech, see Itō Takashi, ed., *Takagi Sōkichi: Nikki to jōhō* (Tokyo: Misuzu shobō, 2000), 2: 781.

26. Hasegawa, *Racing the Enemy*, 32; U.S. Department of Defense, *Entry of the Soviet Union*, 39–41.

27. Hasegawa, *Racing the Enemy*, 32–33; "Conversation: MILEPOST," Dec. 14, 1944, and Harriman to the president, Dec. 15, 1944, Moscow Files, Dec. 8–14 and 15–20, 1944, W. A. Harriman Papers, Library of Congress.

28. Hasegawa, *Racing the Enemy*, 34–35; U.S. Department of State, *Conferences at Malta and Yalta*, 984.

29. A. A. Gromyko, *Pamiatnoe* (Moscow: Politizdat, 1988), 1: 189.

30. Hasegawa, *Racing the Enemy*, 33; AVP RF, f. 06, op. 7, pap. 55, d. 898, l. 102; Slavinskii, *Pakt o neitralitete*, 261–63; Sevost'ianov, "Iaponiia 1945 g.," 35–36.

31. Immediately after the renunciation of the pact, Molotov instructed Gromyko to inform the U.S. government of this action. See *Sovetsko-amerikanskie otnosheniia vo vremia Velikoi Otechestvennoi voiny, 1941–1945: Dokumenty i materialy* (Moscow: Politizdat, 1984), 2: 347–48.

32. Hasegawa, *Racing the Enemy*, 46–47; Slavinskii, *Pakt o neitralitete*, 265–67; "Priem Iaponskogo posla Sato," Apr. 5, 1945, Iz dnevnika V. I. Molotova, AVP RF, f. 06, op. 7, pap. 2, d. 30, ll. 32–34; also f. Sekretariat V. M. Molotova, op. 7, por. 28, pap. 2, l. 3. For English translation from the Japanese, see SRH-071, "Abrogation of the Soviet-Japanese Neutrality Pact: PSIS 400–8," Apr. 23, 1945, 8, Records of National Security

Agency/Central Security Service, Studies on Cryptograph, 1917–1972, box 23, RG 457, NA. SRH is a summary based on the Magic Intercepts. PSIS is a daily summary of the Magic Intercepts. Hereafter archival reference is omitted.

33. Hasegawa, *Racing the Enemy*, 47–48; Dnevnik Malika, Mar. 22. 1945, AVP RF, f. Molotova, op. 7, pap. 54, d. 891, ll. 201–2. This information was also buttressed by intelligence reports from the Tokyo *rezidentura*, documents 195, 312, and 313. Zolotarev, ed., *Sovetsko-iaponkaia voina 1945 goda, Velikaia otechestvennaia*, 7 (1): 207–8, 330–32.

34. For the more detailed discussion on these issues, see Hasegawa, *Racing the Enemy*, chaps. 2 and 3.

35. Memorandum of conversation, Apr. 23, 1945, Truman Papers, President's Secretary's Files, Harry S. Truman Library, Independence, Mo.; W. Averell Harriman and Elie Abel, *Special Envoy to Churchill and Stalin, 1941–1946* (New York: Random House, 1975); Harry S. Truman, *Memoirs*, vol. 1: *Year of Decisions* (Garden City, N.Y.: Doubleday, 1955), 82. For the Soviet reactions, see Gromyko, *Pamiatnoe*, 1: 212–13.

36. Hasegawa, *Racing the Enemy*, 66; Stalin to Truman, Apr. 24, 1945, quoted in Truman, *Memoirs*, 1: 85–86.

37. Hasegawa, *Racing the Enemy*, 74; George C. Herring Jr., *Aid to Russia, 1941–1946: Strategy, Diplomacy, the Origins of the Cold War* (New York: Columbia University Press, 1973), 205; Arnold A. Offner, *Another Such Victory: President Truman and the Cold War, 1945–1953* (Stanford: Stanford University Press, 2002), 44–46; Dale M. Hellegers, *We, the Japanese People: World War II and the Origins of the Japanese Constitution*, vol. 1: *Washington* (Stanford: Stanford University Press, 2001), 53–56.

38. Herring, *Aid to Russia*, 215.

39. For more details, see Hasegawa, *Racing the Enemy*, chaps. 2, 3, and 6. For the argument that Truman's decision was driven by domestic politics, see Barton J. Bernstein, "The Perils and Politics of Surrender," *Pacific Historical Review* 46 (November 1977): 5–6; Leon V. Sigal, *Fighting to a Finish: The Politics of War Termination in the United States and Japan, 1945* (Ithaca, N.Y.: Cornell University Press, 1988), 246, 250.

40. "Vybody," Dnevnik Malika, AVP RF, f. Molotova, op. 7, pap. 54, d. 891, l. 267.

41. Bōeichō Bōeikenshūjo Senshishitsu, Senshi sōsho, *Kantōgun*, vol. 2: *Kantokuen, Shūsenji no taiso sen* (Tokyo: Asagumo shinbunsha, 1974) [hereafter *Kantōgun* 2], 325.

42. Hasegawa, *Racing the Enemy*, 59–60; Tanemura Taisa, Gokuhi [Top Secret], "Kongo no tai'so' shisaku ni taisuru iken," Apr. 29, 1945, Bōei Kenkyūjo Senshishitsu; also Sanbō honbu shozō, *Haisen no kiroku* (Tokyo: Hara shobō, 1989), 343–52. For a shortened version, see Kurihara Ken and Hatano Sumio, eds., *Shūsen kōsaku no kiroku* (Tokyo: Kōdansha, 1986), 2: 61–66.

43. Hasegawa, *Racing the Enemy*, 60–61; Kawabe Torashirō, *Jichō nissi*, quoted in Kurihara and Hatano, eds., *Shūsen kōsaku no kiroku*, 2: 57.

44. For more details, see Hasegawa, *Racing the Enemy*, chap. 4.

45. Hasegawa, *Racing the Enemy*, 83. The best account of the Hopkins-Stalin talks is "Hopkins-Stalin Conference: Record of Conversations Between Harry L. Hopkins and Marshal Stalin in Moscow," May–6 June, 1945," Papers of Harry S. Truman, SMOF, Naval Aide to the President Files, 1945–53, box 12, Harry S. Truman Library, Independence, Mo. The Hopkins-Stalin conversations are also contained in U.S.

Department of State, *Conference of Berlin*, 1: 21–62, but this record is incomplete, deleting a portion of the fourth session and the entire fifth session. For the Russian version, see *Sovetsko-amerikanskie otnosheniia*, 2: 397–403, 404–11, docs. 258 and 260.

46. Hasegawa, *Racing the Enemy*, 83; doc. 260, *Sovetsko-amerikanskie otnosheniia*, 2: 406. The Soviet version better conveys Stalin's talk here than the American version, "Hopkins-Stalin Conference," third meeting, 3; U.S. Department of State, *Conference of Berlin*, 1: 43–44.

47. Hopkins to Truman, paraphrase of navy cable, May 30, 1945, "Hopkins-Stalin Conference."

48. Ibid.

49. Hasegawa, *Racing the Enemy*, 84.

50. "Hopkins-Stalin Conference," third meeting, 7; U.S. Department of State, *Conference of Berlin*, 1: 47; doc. 260, *Sovetsko-amerikanskie otnosheniia*, 2: 406.

51. Hasegawa, *Racing the Enemy*, 97; Grew's memorandum of conversation, June 12, 1945, Grew Papers, Houghton Library, Harvard University.

52. "Minutes of Meeting held at the White House on Monday, 18 June 1945 at 1530," Miscellaneous Historical Documents Collection, C. #736, Harry S. Truman Library, Independence, Mo.; U.S. Department of Defense, *Entry of the Soviet Union*, 78–79, 84, 85. On the casualty issue, see Douglas J. MacEachin, *The Final Months of the War with Japan: Signal Intelligence, U.S. Invasion Planning, and the A-Bomb Decision* (Washington, D.C.: Center for the Study of Intelligence, 1998), 11–14; Hellegers, *We, the Japanese People*, 1: 106–8.

53. For more details, see Hasegawa, *Racing the Enemy*, chap. 4.

54. For more details and archival references, see ibid.

55. Stimson "[Enclosure 2] Proclamation by the Heads of States," in U.S. Department of State, *Conference of Berlin*, 1: 894.

56. G. A. L[incoln], "Memorandum for General Hull, Subject: Timing of Proposed Demand for Japanese Surrender, 29 June 1945," ABC, Historical Draft Documents—JAP Surrender, 1945, RG 165, NA; also in Office of Secretary of War, Stimson Safe File, Japan (after Dec. 7, 1941), RG 107, NA. Also in Records of the U.S. Joint Chiefs of Staff, JCS Historic Office, Lilly Papers on Psychological Warfare, RG 218, NA.

57. John McCloy, "Memorandum for Colonel Stimson," June 19, 1945, ABC, Historical Draft Documents—JAP Surrender, 1945, RG 165, NA; Hasegawa, *Racing the Enemy*, 113.

58. Hirota Kōki Denki Kankōkai, ed., *Hirota Kōki* (Tokyo: Hirota Kōki Denki Kankōkai, 1966), 359.

59. For the Hirota-Malik negotiations, see Hasegawa, *Racing the Enemy*, chap. 4; Dnevnik Malika, AVP RF f. 0146, op. 29, papka 269, de. 4, ll, 261–93, 463–69; "Za kulisami tikhookeanskoi bitvy," *Vestnik ministerstva innostrannykh del SSSR*, 1990, no. 49 (October 15): 46–52.

60. "Za kulisami," 49.

61. Suzuki, Tōgō, and Yonai were generally considered to belong to the peace party, and Anami, Umezu, and Toyoda to the war party, although each group had disagreements on details, and Suzuki's position was ambiguous.

62. Hasegawa, *Racing the Enemy*, 106; Gaimushō, ed., *Shūsen shiroku*, 3: 109–17.

63. At this meeting the participants disagreed on whether Hokkaidō should be included in the operation. For this, see Holloway's Chapter 5 in this volume. Also see B. N. Slavinskii, *Sovetskaia okkupatsiia Kuril'skikh ostrovov (avgust–sentiabr' 1945 goda): Dokumental'noe issledovanie* (Moscow: TOO Lotos, 1993, 126–27); Slavinskii, *Pakt o neitralitete*, 305–6, *Izvestiia*, July 28, 1992. The record of this important meeting has not been made public.

64. Hasegawa, *Racing the Enemy*, 116; docs. 314, 315, and 316, Zolotarev, ed., *Sovetsko-iaponkaia voina 1945 goda, Velikaia otechestvennaia*, 7 (1): 332–36; directives 11112, 11113, and 11114, Papers of Dmitrii Antonovich Volkogonov, reel 4, Library of Congress. The precise date of attack is still clouded in mystery. Deputy Chief of Staff S. M. Shtemenko states in his memoirs that originally the date of attack was set for sometime between August 20 and 25. S. M. Shtemenko, *General'nyi shtab v gody voiny* (Moscow: Voenizdat, 1985), 1: 390; id., "Iz istorii razgroma Kvantunskoi armii," *Voenno-istoricheskii zhurnal*, 1967, no. 4: 66. In *Racing the Enemy* and in the previous version of this article, I took the position that the original date was set between August 20 and 25, since it corresponded to the date given by Antonov during the Potsdam Conference. But in view of Holloway's criticism and Shtemenko's second reference to the date as August 11 (Shtemenko, "Iz istorii razgroma Kvantunskoi armii," *Voenno-istoricheskii zhurnal*, 1967, no. 5: 54), I have changed my view here, accepting Holloway's date, August 11. Still, the question remains as to when exactly the original date of August 20–25 was changed to August 11.

65. Hasegawa, *Racing the Enemy*, 120–22. For the emperor's decision to send Konoe as his special envoy, see Gaimushō, ed., *Shūsen shiroku*, 3, 138–42, 147–49; Kido Kōichi Kenkyūkai, ed. *Kido Kōichi nikki* (Tokyo: Tōkyō Daigaku shuppankai, 1966), 2: 1215; Itō, ed., *Takagi Sōkichi: Nikki to Jōhō*, 2: 909; Kurihara and Hatano, eds., *Shūsen kōsaku no kiroku*, 2: 225–26; Tōgō Shigenori, *Jidai no ichimen*, 342–43. For the draft proposal for Konoe, see Itō, ed., *Takagi Sōkichi: Nikki to jōhō*, 2: 921–22.

66. Hasegawa, *Racing the Enemy*, 123–24; Magic Diplomatic Summary, #1205, July 13, 1945, #1207, July 15, 1945; SRH-084, 9–10; SRH-085, 7–8; Gaimushō, ed., *Shūsen shiroku*, 3: 167, 169–70; AVP RF, f. Molotova, op. 7, por. no. 889, papka 54, ll. 19, 20.

67. For a more detailed discussion on this issue, see Hasegawa, *Racing the Enemy*, chaps. 3 and 4.

68. Stalin told Hopkins on May 28 that "it would be obviously be impossible to conceal from the Japanese very much longer [than the first part of July] the movement of Soviet troops." "Hopkins-Stalin Conference," third meeting, May 28, 1945, 2.

69. Vasilevskii, *Delo vsei zhizni*, 570; id., "Final," 85. In "Final" (1967), Vasilevskii writes that Stalin had asked to move up the date by ten days to August 1 from the previously agreed date, but he does not specifically mention that Stalin requested to move the date of attack to August 1 in *Delo vsei zhizni* (1974). In *Racing the Enemy* and in the previous version of this paper, I still took the position that before the Potsdam Conference, the date of attack had been set for August 20–25. Holloway's criticism in Chapter 5 of this volume led me to revise my view on this.

70. See Odd Arne Westad, *Cold War and Revolution: Soviet-American Rivalry and the Origins of the Chinese Civil War, 1944–1946* (New York: Columbia University Press, 1993), 32, 35.

71. Davies diary, July 16, 1945, Papers of Joseph E. Davies, chronological file, co. no. 18, Library of Congress; see Hasegawa, *Racing the Enemy*, 136. The first news of the success of this test reached Stimson only on July 17.

72. "Bohlen Notes," U.S. Department of State, *Conference of Berlin*, 2: 1585. For a more detailed discussion, see Hasegawa, *Racing the Enemy*, 137–38.

73. *Berlinskaia (Potsdamskaia) konferentsiia rukovoditelei trekh soiuznykh derzhav—SSSR, SShA i Velikobritanii, 17 iulia–2 avgusta 1945 g.: Sbornik dokumentov* (Moscow: Izd-vo politicheskoi literatury, 1980) [hereafter *Berlinskaia konferentsiia*], 43.

74. "Bohlen Notes," in U.S. Department of State, *Conference of Berlin*, 2: 43–46.

75. Ibid., 1584; *Berlinskaia konferentsiia*, 43.

76. "He'll be in the Jap War on August 15th. Fini Japs when that comes about," Truman noted in his Potsdam diary on July 17, 1945. *Off the Record: The Private Papers of Harry S. Truman*, ed. Robert H. Ferrell (New York: Harper & Row, 1980), 53. His memoirs state: "There were many reasons for my going to Potsdam, but the most urgent, to my mind, was to get from Stalin a personal affirmation of Russia's entry into the war against Japan, a matter which our military chiefs were most anxious to clinch. This I was able to get from Stalin in the very first days of the conference." Truman, *Memoirs*, 1: 411. Orthodox historians take these passages to indicate that Truman did not harbor any hostility toward the Soviet Union. See David McCullough, *Truman* (New York: Simon & Schuster, 1992), 419; Frank, *Downfall*, 243. It is possible to argue that Truman's diary entry can be read as a statement of fact, not an endorsement. His memoirs imply his *reluctant* endorsement of Soviet entry into the war against Japan. He had to do it, because he was urged by the military leaders. See Hasegawa, *Racing the Enemy*, 138–39.

77. Truman, *Off the Record*, 53.

78. Truman, *Memoirs*, 1: 350.

79. "Bohlen Notes," in U.S. Department of State, *Conference of Berlin*, 2: 1586.

80. U.S. Department of State, *Conference of Berlin*, 2: 81.

81. "Bohlen Memorandum, March 28, 1960," in U.S. Department of State, *Conference of Berlin*, 2: 1587–88; Hasegawa, *Racing the Enemy*, 142.

82. For more details, see Chapter 5 in this volume and Hasegawa, *Racing the Enemy*, chap 4. See also Truman, *Memoirs*, 1: 416. The impressions of Byrnes, Leahy, and Churchill are recorded in "Truman-Stalin Conversation, Tuesday, July 24, 1945, 7:30 PM," in U.S. Department of State, *Conference of Berlin*, 2: 378–79. On July 24, prior to Truman's talk with Stalin during the recess, the U.S., British, and Soviet military leaders had a joint staff meeting, at which Chief of Staff Antonov revealed that the USSR "would be ready to commence operations in the last half of August." The actual date would, however, depend on the outcome of the negotiations with the Chinese. Tripartite Military Meeting, Tuesday, July 24, 1945, in U.S. Department of State, *Conference of Berlin*, 2: 345. During his meeting with Truman on July 17, Stalin said that the USSR would join the war by the middle of August. This seems to support Holloway's date of August 11, but Antonov's statement supports the date between August 20–25, as Shtemenko states.

83. Enclosure "A," Report by the Joint Strategic Survey Committee, Military Aspects of Unconditional Surrender Formula for Japan, Reference: JCS, 1275 series,

Records of the Office of the Secretary of War, Stimson safe file, RG 107 NA; H. A. Craig's memorandum for General Handy, July 13, 1945, Records of the Office of the Secretary of War, Stimson safe file, RG 107, NA. For more details, see Hasegawa, *Racing the Enemy*, chap. 4.

84. Henry Stimson Diary, July 17, 45, Sterling Library Manuscript Collection, Yale University.

85. Hasegawa, *Racing the Enemy*, 156.

86. For more details, see ibid., chap. 4.

87. AVP RF, f. 0639, op. 1, d. 77, l. 9. Also see Viacheslav P. Safronov, *SSSR, SShA i Iaponskaia agressia na Dal'nem vostoke i Tikhom Okeane, 1931–1945 gg.* (Moscow: Institut Rossiskoi istorii RAN, 2001), 331–32; Hasegawa, *Racing the Enemy*, 161. A full translation of this document is to be found in Chapter 5 in this volume.

88. Tenth Plenary Meeting, Saturday, July 28, 1945, Thompson Minutes, U.S. Department of State, *Conference of Berlin*, 2: 449–50; James Byrnes, *Speaking Frankly* (New York: Harper & Brothers, 1947), 207; Walter Brown Diary, July 26, 1945, James F. Byrnes Papers, Clemson University, Clemson, S.C. In the Soviet version of the Potsdam conference records, there was an interesting exchange between Byrnes and Molotov, in which Molotov accused Byrnes of erroneously stating the time of Molotov's first protest, which is omitted from the American collection of documents. Doc. 22, *Berlinskaia konferentsiia*, 218.

89. Truman, *Memoirs*, 1: 396.

90. "Truman-Molotov meeting, Sunday, July 29, 1945, Noon," in U.S. Department of State, *Conference of Berlin*, 2: 476; Byrnes, *Speaking Frankly*, 207; Hasegawa, *Racing the Enemy*, 163. Molotov's request for an Allied invitation to the Soviet government to join the war is entirely omitted from the Soviet version of the minutes of the Potsdam Conference. See *Berlinskaia konferentsiia*, 234–43.

91. Hasegawa, *Racing the Enemy*, 163; Byrnes, *Speaking Frankly*, 208. The Moscow Declaration provided that "for the purpose of maintaining international peace and security pending the re-establishment of law and order and the inauguration of a system of general security, they will consult with one another and as occasion requires with other members of the United Nations with a view to joint action on behalf of the community of Nations." It was a flimsy legal basis, a mere declaration of four powers, and whether it could override the existing treaty obligations was open to question. Moreover, if the United States accepted Soviet entry into the war as a necessary joint action, as the Moscow Declaration stipulated, it did not make sense to reject Stalin's request for an invitation and refer merely to the general principle only enunciated by the Moscow Declaration. Article 106 of the UN Charter provided that "in the event of a conflict between the obligations of the Members of the United Nations under the present Charter and their obligations under any other international agreement, their obligations under the present Charter shall prevail." This is also a questionable justification for Soviet entry into the war, since the UN Charter had not been ratified by any powers.

92. Truman, *Memoirs*, 1: 402–3.

93. Byrnes, *Speaking Frankly*, 208.

94. For a more detailed argument on this, see Hasegawa, *Racing the Enemy*, chap. 4; Naka Akira, *Mokusatsu* (Tokyo: NHK Books, 2000).

95. Truman, *Memoirs*, 1: 422. In two places, his memoirs state that the Japanese government did not reply to the Potsdam Proclamation, thus contradicting himself with this passage. See ibid., 396–97, 421.

96. Doc. 318, Zlotarev, ed., *Sovetsko-iaponkaia voina 1945 goda, Velikaia otechest-vennaia*, 7 (1): 336; Stalin/Antonov Order No. 11120, Volkogonov Papers, microfilm, reel 5, Library of Congress.

97. Doc. 319, Zlotarev, ed., *Sovetsko-iaponkaia voina 1945 goda, Velikaia otechest-vennaia*, 7 (1): 336–37; Stalin/Antonov's Order 11121, Volkogonov Papers, reel 4, Library of Congress.

98. Doc. 321, Zlotarev, ed., *Sovetsko-iaponkaia voina 1945 goda, Velikaia otechest-vennaia*, 7 (1): 337–38.

99. Ibid., 322; doc. 325, ibid., 341; Shtemenko, "Iz istorii razgroma Kvantunskoi armii," *Voenno-istoricheski zhurnal*, 1967 no. 5: 54. In view of Holloway's criticism of my view in *Racing the Enemy*, I revised the view of the date of attack given in *Racing the Enemy* and in the previous version of this paper. While Holloway believes that Vasilievskii's recommendation for the change in the date of attack was on his own initiative, I speculate that Vasilevskii's recommendation came in response to Stalin.

100. See the recently opened Stalin archive, Rossiiskii gosudarstvennyi arkhiv sotsial'no-politicheskoi istorii (Russian state archive of sociopolitical history) [hereafter cited as RGASPI], f. 558, op. 1, d. 416, ll. 66ob–67.

101. *Shōwashi no tennō* (Tokyo: Yomiuri shinbunsha, 1968), 5: 180–81.

102. Statement read by President Truman aboard the USS *Augusta*, Aug. 6, 1945, Papers of Harry S. Truman, President's Secretary's File, General File A-Ato, President's Secretary's File–General File, Atomic Bomb, Harry S. Truman Library, Independence, Mo.

103. *Pravda*, Aug. 7, 8, 1945.

104. RGASPI, f. 558, op. 1, d. 416, l. 65ob. Stalin's daughter Svetlana Alliluyeva notes: "The day I was out at his *dacha* he had the usual visitors. They told him that the Americans had dropped the first atom bomb over Japan. Everyone was busy with that, and my father paid hardly any attention to me." Svetlana Alliluyeva, *Twenty Letters to a Friend* (New York: Harper & Row, 1967), 188. Alliluyeva is vague about the date, however. Holloway notes in Chapter 5 in this volume that it is not clear whether she is referring to August 6 or August 7, and that visitors to Stalin's dacha were usually not recorded in his appointment book.

105. Hasegawa, *Racing the Enemy*, 186; memorandum of conversation between Harriman and Molotov, Aug. 7, 1945, W. A. Harriman Papers, Moscow files, 5–9 Aug. 45, Library of Congress.

106. For more detailed argument, see Chapter 4 in this volume.

107. Doc. 325, 326, 327, and 328, Zlotarev, ed., *Sovetsko-iaponkaia voina 1945 goda, Velikaia otechestvennaia*, 7 (1): 341–43.

108. Satō to Tōgō, telegram 1530, in Gaimushō, ed., *Shūsen shiroku*, 4: 77–78; Magic Diplomatic Summary, SRS 1753, Aug. 8, 1945.

109. For the detailed minutes of negotiations, see Hoo notes, Aug. 7, 1945, 44–46, Victor Hoo Papers, box 6, Hoover Institution Archive; doc. 693, *Russko-Kitaiskie otno-sheniia v XX veke*, 4 (2): 156–61.

110. This translation of the Soviet declaration of war is taken from a telegram from Harriman to the president and secretaries of state, war, and navy, Aug. 8, 1945, W. A. Harriman Papers, Moscow Files, Aug. 5–9, 1945, Library of Congress. For the Russian original, see *Izvestiia*, Aug. 9, 1945, doc. 694, *Russko-kitaiskie otnosheniia*, 4 (2): 161–62; "Ob ob"iavlenii voiny Iaponii SSSR," Iz dnevnika Molotova, AVP RF, fond Molotova, op. 7, por., no. 904, pap. 55, l. 2, l. 7. For a Japanese translation, see Gaimushō, ed., *Shūsen shiroku*, 4: 83.

111. Hasegawa, *Racing the Enemy*, 190; Iz dnevnika Molotova, ll. 5–6.

112. Truman, *Memoirs*, 2: 425; "Declaration of War on Japan by the Soviet Union," W. A. Harriman Papers, Moscow Files, Aug. 5–9, 1945, Library of Congress; Hasegawa, *Racing the Enemy*, 193.

113. "Declaration of War on Japan by the Soviet Union," W. A. Harriman Papers, Moscow Files, Aug. 5–9, 1945, Moscow Files, Library of Congress; Hasegawa, *Racing the Enemy*, 192–93.

114. Three hours after the Soviet tanks crossed the Manchurian border, and three hours before Truman's press conference, a B-29 Superfortress dubbed "Bock's Car" carrying the second atomic bomb, "Fat Man," took off from Tinian. Notwithstanding Slavinsky's paper "The End of the Pacific War Revisited" at the Center for Cold War conference at University of Santa Barbara in 2001, suggesting that Truman had ample time to recall "Bock's Car," it was technically impossible. Moreover, Acting Chief of Staff Handy's order to Gen. Carl Spaatz left the decision about dropping the second bomb to the discretion of the local commander. The effect of the Nagasaki bomb on Japan's decision was in any case negligible, as Chapter 4 in this volume argues.

115. For more details, see Hasegawa, *Racing the Enemy*, chap. 6.

116. Frank MacNaughton to Eleanor Welch, Aug. 10, 1945, Truman Papers, OF 197, Mis (1945–1946), box 685, Harry S. Truman Library, Independence, Mo., quoted in Hellegers, *We, the Japanese People*, 1: 151.

117. Diaries of James V. Forrestal, 1944–1949, Seeley G. Mudd Manuscript Library, Princeton University, Aug. 10, 1945; Henry A. Wallace, *The Price of Vision: The Diary of Henry A. Wallace, 1942–1946*, ed. John Morton Blum (Boston: Houghton Mifflin, 1973), 474.

7. Bernstein: Conclusion

AUTHOR'S NOTE: The acknowledgments to scholars and funding sources in Chapter 1 also apply here.

EPIGRAPHS: The first epigraph is from Harold Balfour to Foreign Office, dispatched 1:08 P.M., Aug. 14, 1945, and received 7:10 P.M., file 800/461, Public Record Office, Kew, London. Truman had met with Balfour and the duke of Windsor, from 11:45 to about 12:15 that day, according to the appointment book in the Harry S. Truman Library, Independence, Mo. The second epigraph is from Walter Brown, journal entries, Aug. 14, 1945, box 10, Brown Papers, Special Collections, Clemson University, Clemson, S.C. The paragraphing in the typescript is somewhat erratic, and this segment has been compressed here into one paragraph.

1. Graham Allison, *Essence of Decision: Explaining the Cuban Missile Crisis*

(Boston: Little, Brown, 1971); and Barton J. Bernstein, "Understanding Decisionmaking, U.S. Foreign Policy, and the Cuban Missile Crisis," *International Security* 25 (Summer 2000): 134–64.

2. For a symposium reconsidering Hirohito apparently partly triggered by Bix's book, see Takahashi Tetsuya, "The Emperor Showa Standing at Ground Zero: On the (Re)Configuration of National 'Memory' of the Japanese People," and R. Kersten. "Revisionism, Reaction, and the 'Symbol Emperor' in Post-War Japan," both in *Japan Forum* 15 (April 2003): 3–14 and 15–32. These issues are also treated in Noriko Kawamura, "War Memory and Peace: A Historian's Case Study of the Myths of Japan Surrender," in Yoichiro Murakami, Noriko Kawamura, and Shin Chiba, eds., *Toward a Peaceable Future: Redefining Peace, Security, and Kyosei from a Multidisciplinary Perspective* (Pullman: Washington State University Press, 2005), 217–27; Kawamura, "Emperor Hirohito and Japan's Decision to Go to War with the United States: Re-examined," *Diplomatic History* (forthcoming, 2007); and Kawamura, "The Myth of Emperor Hirohito's Role in Japan's Decision to Surrender" (unpublished paper, 2006), which seem to be returning to Butow's conceptions.

3. Some work mostly on the American side examines these issues primarily in the context of Olympic. See Richard B. Frank, *Downfall: The End of the Imperial Japanese Empire* (New York: Random House, 1999), esp. 28–31, 134–48, 164–213; Bernstein, "The Alarming Japanese Buildup on Southern Kyushu, Growing U.S. Fears, and Counterfactual Analysis: Would the Planned November 1945 Invasion of Southern Kyushu Have Occurred?" *Pacific Historical Review* 68 (November 1999); and Edward J. Drea, *In the Service of the Emperor: Essays on the Imperial Japanese Army* (Lincoln: University of Nebraska Press, 1998), 154–68. The issue of casualty estimates had become a controversial subject in the United States since about 1994–95, and see Bernstein, "Alarming Japanese Buildup," n. 4, for some pre-1999 literature on the issue. Maddox, *Weapons for Victory* (2004), xv–xvi provides a spirited anti-revisionist perspective while omitting the counter-literature since about 1998. Barton J. Bernstein, "Marshall, Leahy, and Casualty Issues—A Reply to Kort's Flawed Critique," *Passport: The Newsletter of the Society for Historians of American Foreign Relations* 34 (August 2004): 5–14, suggests how detail-filled this controversy can become.

4. Robert P. Newman, *Enola Gay and the Court of History* (New York: Peter Lang, 2004) dedication: "To Paul Tibbets[:] A great flier who dropped no atomic bomb in anger, deplores our overkill arsenal, and drives a Toyota." In phone interviews on November 29, 2004, Maddox and Drea were supportive of, whereas Frank was very uneasy about and opposed to, this dedication.

5. S. Woodburn Kirby et al., *The War Against Japan*, vol. 5: *The Surrender of Japan* (London: Her Majesty's Stationary Office, 1969), chap. 20 and pt. 3, provides some useful material on surrender issues and postwar matters. More significantly, see Louis Allen, *The End of the War in Asia* (London: Hart-Davis MacGibbon, 1976) on surrender problems, and id., *Burma: The Longest War, 1941–45* (New York: St. Martin's Press, 1984), 501–53.

6. See, e.g., John Whittier Treat, *Writing Ground Zero: Japanese Literature and the Atomic Bomb* (Chicago: University of Chicago Press, 1995); John Dower, "The Bombed: Hiroshima and Nagasaki in Japanese Memory," *Diplomatic History* (Spring 1995): 275–95; Yoshikuni Igarashi, *Bodies of Memory: Narratives of War in Japanese*

Culture, 1945–1970 (Princeton: Princeton University Press, 2000), chap. 1; Laura Hein and Mark Selden, eds., *Living with the Bomb: American and Japanese Cultural Conflicts in the Nuclear Age* (Armonk, N.Y.: M. E. Sharpe, 1997); and the often little-noticed works by Lawrence Wittner, including a brief summary of some of his work on Japan in his "Resisting Nuclear Terror: Japanese and American Antinuclear Movements Since 1945," in Mark Selden and Alvin So, eds., *War and State Terrorism: The United States, Japan, and the Asia-Pacific in the Long Twentieth Century* (New York: Rowman & Littlefield, 2004), 251–76; and Samuel Hideo Yamashita, ed., *Leaves from an Autumn of Emergencies: Selections from the Wartime Diaries of Ordinary Japanese* (Honolulu: University of Hawai'i Press, 2005).

7. Michael Gordin of Princeton University is publishing a book exploring the rise of these differences.

8. See Barton J. Bernstein, "Eclipsed by Hiroshima and Nagasaki: Early Thinking About Tactical Nuclear Weapons," *International Security* 15 (1991).

9. See Chapters 5 and 6 in this volume; Boris Slavinsky, "The Soviet Occupation of the Kurile Islands and the Plans for the Occupation of Northern Hokkaido," trans. Ljubica Erickson, *Japan Forum* 5 (April 1993), 95–114; and id., *The Japanese-Soviet Neutrality Pact: A Diplomatic History, 1941–1945*, trans. Geoffrey Jukes (New York: RoutledgeCurzon, 2005). For important background on USSR policy, see Jonathan Haslam, *The Soviet Union and the Threat from the East, 1933–41: Moscow, Tokyo, and the Prelude to the Pacific War* (Pittsburgh: University of Pittsburgh Press, 1992).

10. The literature on even loosely connecting the ending of World War II and the emerging Cold War in Asia is large, as is the literature on KMT-CCP issues, but much of it operates without sharply focusing on the related issue of Japan's surrender. Useful studies include, among others, Marc Gallichio, *The Cold War Begins in Asia: American East Asian Policy and the Fall of the Japanese Empire* (New York: Columbia University Press, 1988), 59–104; Bruce Cumings, *The Origins of the Korean War*, vol. 1: *Liberation and the Emergence of Separate Regimes* (Princeton, N.J.: Princeton University Press, 1982), 68–91; Chen Jian, *Mao's China and the Cold War* (Chapel Hill: University of North Carolina Press, 2001), 22–31; Dieter Heinzig, *The Soviet Union and Communist China, 1945–1950: The Road to an Alliance* (Armonk, N.Y.: M. E. Sharpe, 2004), 53–88; and Allen, *End of the War in Asia*.

11. T. S. Eliot, "Little Gidding," no. 4 of "Four Quartets," in Eliot, *The Complete Poems and Plays, 1909–1950* (New York: Harcourt, 1952), 145.

Bibliographical Note

Archives in the United States

There is no need to list archival materials in the United States dealing with the U.S. decision to drop the atomic bombs, inasmuch as there are excellent archival references in books by Martin J. Sherwin, Gar Alperovitz, and Robert Norris, and numerous articles by Barton Bernstein. As for U.S. archives dealing with Japan's surrender, Richard Frank provides an excellent guide in his book *Downfall*. Iokibe Makoto's book *Beikoku no senryō seisaku*, 2 vols., Dale Hellegers's book, *We, the Japanese People*, vol. 1, and my own book, *Racing the Enemy* provide a thorough archival guide to U.S. policy on Japan's surrender. As for U.S. policy toward the Soviet Union with regard to the Pacific War, *Racing the Enemy* provides a sufficient archival guide. I would like to draw special attention, however, to the importance of the W. A. Harriman Papers at the Library of Congress, and decoded Japanese diplomatic and military message traffic, which is a source of untempered authentic contemporary material.

As for recent monographs, see Select Bibliography.

TSUYOSHI HASEGAWA

Sources in Russian

Archives

There was a very narrow window of opportunity after the collapse of the Soviet Union when archives in the former Soviet Union became substantially open. But soon the Russian government began to tighten archival access. Boris Slavinsky is one of few Russian scholars who took advantage of that opportunity, making copies of newly released archival materials. Many of these materials are extensively used in his numerous works cited in the Select Bibliography.

The most important archives open to researchers, although with increasing difficulty, are the Foreign Ministry archives (Arkhiv vneshnei politiki Rossiskoi federatsii), of which Fond referentura po Iaponii, Fond Molotova, and Fond Lozovskogo are important. Of particular importance is Malik's diary (Dnevnik Malika), which Ambassador Malik periodically sent to Molotov, some of the entries in which are extensively, if not entirely, quoted in Slavinsky's works.

Another important archival depository is RGASPI (Rossiskii gosudarstvennyi arkhiv sotsial'no-politicheskoi istorii)—former Communist Party archives—which recently opened the Stalin fond. RGASPI also houses the GKO (State Defense Committee) archives. These archives have only recently become open to researchers.

Two crucial archives remain tightly closed. The most important archival collection, the Presidential Archive, is beyond the reach of ordinary researchers with the exception of a privileged few, who occasionally dish out tantalizing pieces of archival materials. Thus the process of decision making at the highest level on key issues is still shrouded in secrecy.

The second set of archival materials closed to researchers are the military archives. This makes Slavinsky's *Sovetskaia okkupatsiia Kuril'skikh ostrovov* extremely valuable, since he extensively uses and cites archival materials from the Central Naval Archive (Tsenrral'nyi voenno-morskoi arkhiv), which is now closed to researchers.

Three additional sets of archival materials should be mentioned. First, a Japanese newspaper, *Sankei shinbun*, obtained a collection of Soviet archives with regard to the First Far Eastern Front, which were translated into Japanese and given to Professor Hatano Shumio. These materials provide important information on Soviet military actions and Soviet negotiations with the Kwantung Army for a cease-fire after August 15, 1945. The second is the Papers of Dmitrii Antonovich Volkogonov, deposited at the Library of Congress. Although scattered all over without any coordination and bibliographical guide, the Volkogonov collection also contains valuable information on the Soviet Manchurian and the Kuril operations. The third is the report by A. R. Gnechko, commander of the Kamchatka Regional Defense, on the Kuril operation, deposited in the Sakhalin regional archive.

Published Sources

At the current stage of research, newly published sources provide a more important opportunity than archival materials for researchers to reexamine the Soviet role in Japan's surrender. Three sets of collections of documents are valuable. First, V. A. Zolotarev, ed., *Velikaia otechestvennaia*, vol. 7, books 1 and 2, contain not only military, but also political, diplomatic, and intelligence sources, many of which are from archives and published for the first time. Second is a two-volume set of documents on Sino-Soviet relations, V. S. Miasnikov, ed., *Russo-kitaiskie otnosheniia v XX veke*, vol. 4, books 1 and 2. The detailed minutes of the Sino-Soviet negotiations especially, as well as Soviet-American-Chinese diplomatic interactions, provide valuable information. Third, L. D. Riabev, ed., *Atomnyi proekt SSSR*, contains interesting information about the Soviet atomic bomb project.

Three additional sets of collections of sources that were published during the Soviet period but have not been extensively used by American scholars should be mentioned. First, *Sovetsko-amerikanskie otnosheniia vo Velikoi otechesevennoi voiny, 1941–1945*, published in 1984, contains valuable diplomatic documents on U.S.-Soviet relations during World War II. Second, *Berlinskaia (Potsdamskaia) konferentsiia* is the Soviet record of the Potsdam conference. A careful comparison between the Soviet record and the U.S. Department of State's *The Conference of Berlin*, 2 vols., in the Foreign Relations of the United States series, reveals different perceptions and motivations between the Soviet Union and the United States at the Potsdam Conference. Also to be consulted on the Potsdam Conference is *Documents on British Policy Overseas*, edited by Rohan Butler and M. E. Pelly, 1st ser., vol. 1 (1984). Third, *Perepiska predsedatelia Soveta ministrov SSSR s prezidentami SShA i prem'er-ministrami Velikobritanii vo vremia Velikoi otechestvennoi voiny* is a collection of correspondence between Stalin, on the one hand, and Churchill, Roosevelt, and Truman, on the other.

TSUYOSHI HASEGAWA

Sources in Japanese

Major Sources

Anyone attempting to document the Japanese role in terminating the Pacific War based on Japanese source materials needs to be aware of the fact that innumerable primary documents were destroyed. While important materials certainly survived, irretrievable damage to the historical record was perpetrated in 1945.

As a basic documentary source, Gaimushō, ed., *Shūsen shiroku*, published just after the conclusion of the Peace Treaty of 1951, contains not only the memoirs of Japan's main policymakers and records of the Tokyo war crimes trials, but also a number of manuscripts and memoranda written specifically for this volume by those leaders who are known as the "peace party." This volume has retained great value to researchers. Robert Butow's classical account *Japan's Decision to Surrender* (1954) makes full use of these materials. Long out of print, *Shūsen shiroku* was reprinted in a new format in six volumes (Hokuyōsha, 1978–79) with a historiographical essay by Hatano Sumio, followed by a bibliography listing more than 1,300 items.

In 1986, Kurihara Ken and Hatano Sumio thoroughly revised *Shūsen shiroku*, and the new edition was published as *Shūsen kōsaku no kiroku*. It contains materials not found in *Shūsen shiroku*, such as Foreign Ministry materials that were released after the publication of *Shūsen shiroku*; GHQ interrogation records; Rear Admiral Takagi Sōkichi's materials; the plan to dispatch Prince Konoe Fumimaro to the Soviet Union to seek mediation; and hitherto unpublished materials of the army and the Army General Staff relating to war plans.

There are numerous memoirs, diaries, and biographies of top leaders, but few contain reliable accounts: the rich diary of Kido Kōichi (*Kido Kōichi nikki*, 2 vols.), Lord Keeper of the Privy Seal; *Shūsen hishi*, and *Shūsenki,* by Shimomura Kainan [Hiroshi], director-general of the Information Bureau; Shūsen no hyōjō, by Prime Minister Suzuki Kantarō, and *Suzuki Kantarō jiden*, edited by Suzuki Hajime, one of Suzuki's sons; *Jidai no ichimen* (reprinted as *Togo Shigenori Gaikō Shuki*) by Foreign Minister Tōgō Shigenori; *Saigo no teikoku kaigun*, by Toyoda Soemu, chief of the Naval General Staff; *Higashikuni nikki*, by Higashikuni Naruhiko, who was prime minister after the Suzuki cabinet; *Kikanjū ka no shūshō kantei*, by Cabinet Secretary Sakomizu Hisatsune; *Shigemitsu Mamoru shuki*, and *Zoku Shigemitsu Mamoru shuki* (private manuscripts by

Shigemitsu Mamoru, the former foreign minister), edited by Itō Takashi and Watanabe Yukio; *Tajiri Aiyoshi kaisōroku*, memoirs of the deputy minister of the Greater East Asian Ministry); *Hosokawa nikki*, 2 vols., by Hosokawa Morisada, who was private secretary to Prince Konoe; and *Dai Tōa sensō hishi*, by Hoshina Zenshirō, chief of the Naval Affairs Bureau. Deputy chief of Army Staff Kawabe Torashirō's diary (Kawabe Jichō nisshi, deposited in the Bōei Kenkyūjo Senshishitsu) is reprinted in *Kawabe Torashirō kaisōroku*, but it contains some parts not corresponding to the original one.

The clandestine activities of the navy's "peace party" (headed by Navy Minister Yonai Mitsumasa) can be traced throughout the Takagi collection: *Takagi Sōkichi: nikki to jōhō*, which contains not only records dictated by Yonai himself and his memoranda but also the rich diary of Rear Admiral Takagi Sōkichi who secretly served under Navy Minister Yonai to bring about a speedy end to the war.

In 1967, the official documents at the highest levels of the Japanese military and government were collected and published as Sanbō Honbu, ed., *Haisen no kiroku*. This collection contains the official documents of the Supreme War Council and Imperial Conferences during the crucial years 1944–45. Appended to *Haisen no kiroku* is *Kimitsu sakusen nisshi*, the confidential diary of the Bureau of Military Affairs of the Army Ministry, the most staunch advocate of continued fighting. This diary gives detailed information on the plan for a coup d'état prepared among the army's middle-echelon officers to prevent Japan's surrender.

Of special interest are *Kimitsu sensō nisshi* and *Miyazaki Shūichi Chūjō nikki* (diary of Lt. Gen. Miyazaki Shūichi, chief of the Army Operational Division), both of which were edited and published by Gunji Shigakukai recently as important records from within the Army General Staff. *Kimitsu sensō nisshi* provides daily activities of the War Guidance Section of the Army General Staff from June 1, 1940, to August 1, 1945. Miyazaki was the head of the Operational Division of the Army General Staff at the time of Japan's surrender.

Important unpublished official records on the end of the war deposited at Bōei Kenkyūjo Senshishitsu are Kokubō taikō kankei jūyō shorui tsuzuri, 5 vols., Dai-tōa Sensō sensō shidō kankei tsuzuri (Shōwa nijū nen), and Rengōkoku tono sesshō kankei jikō, 5 vols. In addition to official records, Bōei Kenkyūjo Senshishitsu holds several thousand items in the form of personal papers: diaries, memoirs, and memoranda. Access to many of these unpublished personal manuscripts is restricted in accordance with the conditions specified by their authors or surviving relatives. No list of these papers has been published. The way to find out whose diaries or personal papers are deposited at the Bōei Kenkyūjo Senshishitsu Library is to check the footnotes of *Senshi sōsho* (war history series). Relating to the decision making on terminating the war, most of the important manuscript sources of interest are heavily utilized in the following volumes: vols. 75, 81, 82 (*Daihon'ei Rikugunbu*, nos. 8–10); vols. 51–52 (*Hondo Kessen*); vols. 45, 93 (*Daihon'ei Kaigunbu*, nos. 6–7); and vol. 73 (*Kantōgun no. 2*).

During the occupation, interviews with key Japanese civilians and military figures were conducted by General Headquarters, Far Eastern Command, Military Intelligence Section, Historical Division. These materials, translated by GHQ officials into English, were deposited in the Center for Military History in Washington, D.C. Most of the Japanese original versions (cited here as GHQ Interrogation records) in the Bōei Kenkyūjo Senshishitsu, were reprinted in Satō Motoei and Kurosawa Fumitaka, eds., *GHQ rekishika chinjutsu roku: Shūsen shiryō*.

Books and Monographs

The first academic research project on Japan's surrender was organized by Nihon Gaikō Gakkai, headed by Ueda Toshio. In 1958, *Taiheiyō Sensō shūketsu ron* was published as the fruit of joint work involving some twenty specialists in history, economy, and international law.

During the Pacific War, the "peace party" in Japan pinned their last hopes of ending the war on Soviet mediation. The gap between this unrealistic expectation and the actualities of international politics is expertly discussed in Hosoya Chihiro's essay in his book *Ryōtaisenkanki no Nihon Gaikō*. The first four volumes of the *Shōwashi no Tennō* series, which is the first systematic oral history project in Japan, undertaken by the staff of the *Yomiuri* newspaper, provide detailed information of great value relating to peace negotiations through the Soviet Union, the abortive plan to send Konoe on a special mission to Moscow, top leaders' responses to the Potsdam Declaration, the impacts of the A-bombs, and the Soviet entry into the war.

The political process of the end of the Pacific War was expertly treated as early as 1955 by Kurihara Ken in his pioneering work *Tennō: Shōwashi oboegaki*. It was followed by a series of noteworthy studies: Ishida Takeshi's *Hakyoku to heiwa*; Fujiwara Akira's work, *Taiheiyō Sensō shiron* (Aoki Shoten, 1982); Fujimura Michio's essay on Japan's surrender and the collapse of the military in *Shōwashi no gunbu to seiji*, edited by Miyake Masaki; three works on the role of the emperor in the process of the decision to surrender: Chimoto Hideki, *Tennōsei no shinryaku sekinin to sengo sekinin* (Aoki Shoten, 1990),Yamada Akira, *Shōwa Tennō no sensō shidō* (Shōwa Shuppan, 1990), and Tanaka Nobunao, *Dokyumento Shōwa Tennō,* vol. 5 (Ryokufū Shuppan, 1988).

One of the historical issues relating to Japan's surrender is whether the determining factor in its decision to accept the Potsdam Declaration was the dropping of the A-bombs or the Soviet entry into the war. The prevailing view among Japanese scholars is that the shock of the Soviet entry was a more potent factor. Asada Sadao challenges this prevailing view, however, in his essays in Hosoya Chihiro, Iriye Akira, Gotō Kan'ichi, and Hatano Sumio, eds., *Taiheiyō sensō no shūketsu* (1997) and in the *Pacific Historical Review* 67, no. 4 (1998).

SUMIO HATANO

Select Bibliography

Sources in English

Akira, Iriye. *Power and Culture*: *The Japanese-American War, 1941–1945*. Cambridge, Mass., Harvard University Press, 1981.

Allen, Louis. *Burma: The Longest War, 1941–45*. New York: St. Martin's Press, 1984. Reprint. London: Phoenix Press, 2000.

———. *The End of the War in Asia*. London: Hart-Davis MacGibbon, 1976.

Allen, Thomas, and Norman Polmar. *Code-Name Downfall: The Secret Plan to Invade Japan—and Why Truman Dropped the Bomb*. New York: Simon & Schuster, 1995.

Alliluyeva, Svetlana. *Twenty Letters to a Friend*. Harmondsworth, U.K.: Penguin Books, 1968.

Alperovitz, Gar. *Atomic Diplomacy: Hiroshima and Potsdam. The Use of the Atomic Bomb and the American Confrontation with Soviet Power*. New York: Vintage Books, 1965. Rev. ed. New York: Penguin Books, 1985.

———. "Beyond the Smithsonian Flap: Historians' New Consensus." *Washington Post*, October 16, 1995.

———. *Cold War Essays*. Garden City, N.Y.: Anchor Books, 1970.

Alperovitz, Gar, et al. *The Decision to Use the Atomic Bomb and the Architecture of an American Myth*. New York: Knopf, 1995.

———. *The Decision to Use the Atomic Bomb*. New York: Vintage Books, 1996.

Alperovitz, Gar, Robert L. Messer, and Barton J. Bernstein. "Marshall, Truman, and the Decision to Drop the Bomb." *International Security* 16 (Winter 1991–92).

Appleman, Roy, et al. *Okinawa: The Last Battle*. Washington, D.C.: Government Printing Office, 1948.

Asada, Sadao. "The Mushroom Cloud and National Psyches: Japanese and American Perceptions of the A-Bomb Decision, 1945–1995." *Journal of American-East Asian Relations* 4 (1995).

———. "The Shock of the Atomic Bomb and Japan's Decision to Surrender—A Reconsideration." *Pacific Historical Review* 67, no. 4 (1998).

Auer, James, and Richard Halloran. "Looking Back at the Bomb." *Parameters* 26 (Spring 1996).

Awaya, Kentaro. "Emperor Showa's Accountability for War." *Japan Quarterly* 39 (October–December 1991).

Baldwin, Hanson. *Great Mistakes of the War*. New York: Harper, 1950.

———. "Our Worst Blunders in the War." *Atlantic Monthly* 185 (February 1950).

Beer, Francis, and Thomas Mayer. "Why Wars End: Some Hypotheses." *Review of International Studies* 12 (1986).

Beevor, Antony. *The Fall of Berlin 1945*. New York: Viking Penguin, 2002.

Behr, Edward. *Hirohito: Behind the Myth*. New York: Villard, 1989.

Bergamini, David. *Japan's Imperial Conspiracy*. New York: Morrow, 1971.

Bergerud, Eric. "Dropping the Bomb." *Newsday,* August 6, 1995.

Bernstein, Barton J. "The Alarming Japanese Buildup on Southern Kyushu, Growing U.S. Fears, and Counterfactual Analysis: Would the Planned November 1945 Invasion of Southern Kyushu Have Occurred?" *Pacific Historical Review* 68 (November 1999).

———. "The Atomic Bomb and American Foreign Policy, 1941–1945: An Historiographical Controversy." *Peace & Change* 2 (Spring 1974).

———. "The Atomic Bombings Reconsidered." *Foreign Affairs* 74 (1995).

———. "Compelling Japan's Surrender Without the A-bomb, Soviet Entry, or Invasion: Reconsidering the US Bombing Survey's Early-Surrender Conclusion." *Journal of Strategic Studies* 18, no. 2 (June 1995).

———. "Doomsday II." *New York Times Magazine*, July 27, 1975.

———. "Eclipsed by Hiroshima and Nagasaki: Early Thinking About Tactical Nuclear Weapons." *International Security* 15 (1991).

———. "Ike and Hiroshima: Did He Oppose It?" *Journal of Strategic Studies* 10 (September 1987).

———. "The Perils and Politics of Surrender: Ending the War with Japan and Avoiding the Third Atomic Bomb." *Pacific Historical Review* 46 (1977).

———. "Roosevelt, Truman, and the Atomic Bomb, 1941–1945: A Reinterpretation." *Political Science Quarterly* 89, no. 4 (Winter 1974–75).

———. "The Struggle over History: Defining the Hiroshima Narrative." In *Judgment at the Smithsonian*, edited by Philip Nobile. New York: Marlowe, 1995.

———. "Truman and the A-bomb: Targeting Noncombatants, Using the Bomb, and His Defending the 'Decision.'" *Journal of Military History* 62 (July 1988).

———. "Truman at Potsdam: His Secret Diary." *Foreign Service Journal*, July–August 1980.

———. "Understanding the Atomic Bomb and the Japanese Surrender: Missed Opportunities, Little-Known Near Disasters, and Modern Memory." *Diplomatic History* 19 (Spring 1995).

———, ed. *The Atomic Bomb: The Critical Issues*. Boston: Little, Brown, 1976.

Bix, Herbert P. *Hirohito and the Making of Modern Japan*. New York: HarperCollins, 2000.

———. "Hirohito's War." *History Today* 12 (December 1991).

———. "Japan's Delayed Surrender: A Reinterpretation." *Diplomatic History* 19 (1995).

————. "Japan's Surrender Decision and the Monarchy: Staying the Course in an Unwinnable War." *Japan Focus* 2005. http://www.zmag.org/content/showarticle. cfm?SectionID=17&ItemID=8229.

————. "Japan Studies Old and New at the End of the Eighties." *Bulletin of Concerned Asian Scholars* 23 (April–June 1991).

————. "Rethinking 'Emperor System Fascism': Ruptures and Continuities in Modern Japanese History." *Bulletin of Concerned Asian Scholars* 14 (April–June 1982).

————. "The Showa Emperor's 'Monologue' and the Problem of War Responsibility." *Journal of Japanese Studies* 18 (Summer 1992).

Blackett, P. M. S. *Fear, War and the Bomb: Military and Political Consequences of Atomic Energy.* New York: Whittlesey House, 1949. Originally published in Britain under the title *Military and Political Consequences of Atomic Energy* (London: Turnstile Press, 1948).

Bohlen, Charles E. *Witness to History, 1929–1969.* New York: Norton, 1973.

Buruma, Ian. *Wages of Guilt: Memories of War in Germany and Japan.* New York: Farrar, Straus & Giroux, 1994.

————. "The War over the Bomb." *New York Review of Books*, September 21, 1995.

Butow, Robert J. C. *Japan's Decision to Surrender.* Stanford: Stanford University Press, 1954.

Byrnes, James. *All in One Lifetime.* New York: Harper & Brothers, 1953, 1958.

————. *Speaking Frankly.* New York: Harper & Brothers, 1947.

Chen Jian. *Mao's China and the Cold War.* Chapel Hill: University of North Carolina Press, 2001.

Committee for a National Discussion of Nuclear History and Current Policy. "Views of American Military Leaders on the Atomic Bombings of Japan." N.d. (1994–95).

Cook, Theodore, and Haruko T., eds. *Japan at War: An Oral History.* New York: New Press, 1992.

Coox, Alvin. "The Enola Gay and Japan's Struggle to Surrender." *Journal of East-Asian Relations* 4 (Summer 1991).

Craig, William. *The Fall of Japan.* New York: Dial Press, 1967.

Craven, W. F., and J. L. Cate, eds. *The Army Air Forces in World War II.* Vol. 5: *The Pacific: Matterhorn to Nagasaki, June 1944 to August 1945.* Reprint. Washington, D.C.: Office of the Chief of Air Force History, 1983.

Cumings, Bruce. *The Origins of the Korean War.* Vol. 1: *Liberation and the Emergence of Separate Regimes, 1945–1947.* Princeton, N.J.: Princeton University Press, 1982.

Dockrill, Saki. "Hirohito, the Emperor's Army and Pearl Harbor." *Review of International Studies* 18 (October 1992).

————, ed. *From Pearl Harbor to Hiroshima: The Second World War in Asia and the Pacific, 1941–45.* New York: St. Martin's Press, 1994.

Dower, John W. *Embracing Defeat: Japan in the Wake of World War II.* New York: Norton/New Press, 1999.

————. "Sensational Rumors, Seditious Graffiti, and the Nightmares of the Thought Police." In id., *Japan in War and Peace: Selected Essays.* New York: New Press, 1993.

————. "Three Narratives of Our Humanity." In Edward Linenthal and Tom Engelhard, eds., *History Wars: The Enola Gay and Other Battles for the American Past*. New York: Holt, 1996.

———. *War Without Mercy: Race and Power in the Pacific War*. New York: Pantheon Books, 1986.

Drea, Edward J. *In the Service of the Emperor: Essays on the Imperial Japanese Army*. Lincoln: University of Nebraska Press, 1998.

———. *MacArthur's ULTRA: Codebreaking and the War Against Japan, 1942–1945*. Lawrence: University Press of Kansas, 1992.

———. "Previews of Hell: The End of the War with Japan." *Military History Quarterly* 7 (1995): 79.

Eden, Anthony. *The Reckoning: The Memoirs of Anthony Eden, Earl of Avon*. Boston: Houghton Mifflin, 1965.

Erickson, John. *Stalin's War with Germany: The Road to Stalingrad*. London: Weidenfeld & Nicolson, 1975.

———. *The Road to Berlin*. London: Weidenfeld & Nicolson, 1983.

Fearon, James. "Counterfactuals and Hypothesis Testing in Political Science." *World Politics* 43 (January 1991).

Feifer, George. *Tennozan: The Battle of Okinawa and the Atomic Bomb*. New York: Ticknor & Fields, 1992.

Feis, Herbert. *The Atomic Bomb and the End of World War II*. Princeton, N.J.: Princeton University Press, 1966, 1970.

———. *The China Tangle: The American Effort in China from Pearl Harbor to the Marshall Mission*. Princeton, N.J.: Princeton University Press, 1953.

———. *Japan Subdued: The Atomic Bomb and the End of the War in the Pacific*. Princeton, N.J.: Princeton University Press, 1961.

Frank, Richard B. *Downfall: The End of the Imperial Japanese Empire*. New York: Random House, 1999.

Freedman, Lawrence. *The Evolution of Nuclear Strategy*. New York: St. Martin's Press, 1981.

———. "The Strategy of Hiroshima." *Journal of Strategic Studies* 1 (May 1978).

Freedman, Lawrence, and Saki Dockrill. "Hiroshima: A Strategy of Shock." In Saki Dockrill, ed., *From Pearl Harbor to Hiroshima: The Second World War in Asia and the Pacific, 1941–1945*. New York: St. Martin's Press, 1994.

Gallichio, Marc. "After Nagasaki: General Marshall's Plan for Tactical Nuclear Weapons in Japan." *Prologue* 23 (1991).

———. *The Cold War Begins in Asia: American East Asian Policy and the Fall of the Japanese Empire*. New York: Columbia University Press, 1988.

Garver, John W. *Chinese-Soviet Relations, 1937–1945: The Diplomacy of Chinese Nationalism*. Oxford: Oxford University Press, 1988.

Gayn, Mark. *Japan Diary*. 1948. New York: W. Sloan Associates, 1948; Rutland, Vt.: Tuttle, 1981.

Gentile, Gian. *How Effective Is Strategic Bombing? Lessons Learned from World War II to Kosovo*. New York: New York University Press, 2002.

Giangreco, D. M. "To Bomb or Not to Bomb." *Naval War College Review* 51 (Spring 1998).

Glantz, David M. *August Storm: The Soviet 1945 Strategic Offensive in Manchuria*. Fort Leavenworth, Kans.: Combat Studies Institute, U.S. Army Command and

General Staff College, 1983. Rev. ed. *The Soviet Strategic Offensive in Manchuria, 1945: August Storm.* Portland, Ore.: Frank Cass, 2003.

———. *August Storm: Soviet Tactical and Operational Combat in Manchuria, 1945.* Fort Leavenworth, Kans.: Combat Studies Institute, U.S. Army Command and General Staff College, 1983. Rev. ed. *Soviet Operational and Tactical Combat in Manchuria, 1945: August Storm.* Portland, Ore.: Frank Cass, 2003.

———. "The Soviet Invasion of Japan." *Military History Quarterly* 7, no. 3 (Spring 1995).

Gluck, Carol. "The People in History: Recent Trends in Japanese Historiography." *Journal of Asian Studies* 38 (November 1978).

Goemans, H. E. *War and Punishment: The Causes of War Termination and the First World War.* Princeton, N.J.: Princeton University Press, 2000.

Goncharov, Sergei N., John W. Lewis, and Xue Litai. *Uncertain Partners: Stalin, Mao, and the Korean War.* Stanford: Stanford University Press, 1993.

Graham, Thomas, ed. *American Public Opinion on NATO: Extended Deterrence, and Use of Nuclear Weapons: Future Fission?* CSIA Occasional Papers 4. Cambridge, Mass.: Center for Science and International Affairs, 1989.

Great Britain. *Documents on British Policy Overseas.* Edited by Rohan Butler and M. E. Pelly, assisted by H. J. Yasamee. 1st ser. Vol. 1. London: Her Majesty's Stationery Office, 1984.

———. Ministry of Defence (Navy). *War with Japan.* Vol. 1: *Background to the War.* London: Her Majesty's Stationery Office, 1995.

Grew, Joseph. *Turbulent Era: A Diplomatic Record of Forty Years, 1904–1945.* 2 vols. Boston: Houghton Mifflin, 1952.

Halloran, Richard. "The Useful Bomb." *Far Eastern Economic Review,* August 17, 1995.

Harriman, W. Averell, and Elie Abel. *Special Envoy to Churchill and Stalin, 1941–1946.* New York: Random House, 1975.

Hasegawa, Tsuyoshi. *Racing the Enemy: Stalin, Truman, and the Surrender of Japan.* Cambridge, Mass: Belknap Press of Harvard University Press, 2005.

Haslam, Jonathan. "The Cold War as History." *Annual Review of Political Science,* 2003.

———. "Decision to War: Soviet Policy Towards Japan, 1944–1945." Paper given at the conference on Stalin and the Cold War, Yale University, September 1999.

———. "Soviet-Japanese Relations Since World War II." In Tsuyoshi Hasegawa, Jonathan Haslam, and Andrew C. Kuchins, eds. *Russia and Japan: An Unresolved Dilemma Between Distant Neighbors.* Berkeley: International and Area Studies, University of California at Berkeley, 1993.

———. *The Soviet Union and the Threat from the East, 1933–41: Moscow, Tokyo, and the Prelude to the Pacific War.* Pittsburgh: University of Pittsburgh Press, 1992.

Hatano, Sumio. "Japanese Foreign Policy, 1931–1945: Historiography." In Sadao Asada, ed., *Japan and the World, 1853–1952.* New York: Columbia University Press, 1989.

Havens, Thomas R. H. *Valley of Darkness: The Japanese People and World War Two.* New York: Norton, 1978. Reprint. Lanham, Md.: University Press of America, 1986.

Heizig, Dieter. *The Soviet Union and Communist China, 1945–1950: The Road to an Alliance.* Armonk, N.Y.: M. E. Sharpe, 2004.

Hellegers, Dale M. *We, the Japanese People: World War II and the Origins of the Japanese Constitution.* 2 vols. Stanford: Stanford University Press, 2001.

Herring, George C., Jr. *Aid to Russia, 1941–1946: Strategy, Diplomacy, the Origins of the Cold War.* New York: Columbia University Press, 1973.

Hewlett, Richard G., and Oscar E. Anderson Jr. *The New World: A History of the United States Atomic Energy Commission.* Vol. 1: *1939–1946.* Berkeley: University of California Press, 1990.

Holloway, David. *Stalin and the Bomb: The Soviet Union and Atomic Energy, 1939–1956.* New Haven, Conn.: Yale University Press, 1994.

Hoyt, Edward. *Hirohito: The Emperor and the Man.* New York: Praeger, 1992.

Huber, Thomas M. *Japan's Battle of Okinawa, April–June 1945.* Leavenworth Papers, no. 18 Leavenworth, Kans.: Combat Studies Institute, U.S. Army Command and General Staff College, 1990.

Hull, Cordell. *The Memoirs of Cordell Hull.* Vol. 2. New York: Macmillan, 1948.

Iklé, Fred. *Every War Must End.* New York: Columbia University Press, 1971.

Irokawa, Daikichi. *The Age of Hirohito: In Search of Modern Japan.* Translated by Mikiso Hane and John Urda. New York: Free Press, 1995.

Kagan, Donald. "Why America Dropped the Bomb." *Commentary* 100 (September 1995).

Kase, Toshikazu. *Journey to the Missouri.* Edited by David Nelson Rowe. New Haven, Conn.: Yale University Press, 1950.

Kecskemeti, Paul. *Strategic Surrender: The Politics of Victory and Defeat.* Stanford: Stanford University Press, 1958.

Kern, Gary. "How 'Uncle Joe' Bugged FDR." *Studies in Intelligence* 47, no. 1 (2003).

Khrushchev, N. S. *Khrushchev Remembers: The Glasnost Tapes.* Translated and edited by Jerrold L. Schecter with Vyacheslav V. Luchkov. Boston: Little, Brown, 1990.

Kido, Koichi. *The Diary of Marquis Kido, 1931–45: Selected Translations into English,* Frederick, Md.: University Publications of America, 1984.

King, Michael. "Bombs Away." *National Review,* November 4, 1995.

Kirby, S. Woodburn, et al. *The War Against Japan.* Vol. 5: *The Surrender of Japan.* London: Her Majesty's Stationary Office, 1969.

Koshiro, Yukiko. "Eurasian Empire: Japan's End Game in World War II." *American Historical Review* 109 (April 2004).

———. "Japan's World and World War II." *Diplomatic History* 25 (Summer 2001).

Kristof, Nicholas D. "The Bomb: An Act That Haunts Japan and America." *New York Times,* August 6, 1995.

Kurita, Wataru. "Making Peace with Hirohito and a Militaristic Past." *Japan Quarterly* 36 (April–June 1989).

Large, Stephen. "Emperor Hirohito and Early Showa Japan." *Monumenta Nipponica* 46 (Autumn 1991).

———. *Emperor Hirohito and Showa Japan: A Political Biography.* New York: Routledge, 1992.

Lee, Bruce. *Marching Orders: The Untold Story of World War II.* New York: Crown, 1995.

Leffler, Melvyn P. "The Cold War: What Do 'We Now Know.'" *American Historical Review* 104 (1999): 501–24.

———. "Truman's Decision to Drop the Atomic Bomb." *IHJ Bulletin* [A Quarterly Publication of the International House of Japan] 15 (1995).

Lensen, George Alexander. *The Strange Neutrality: Soviet-Japanese Relations During the Second World War, 1941–1945.* Tallahassee, Fla.: Diplomatic Press, 1972.

Levine, Alan. *The Pacific War: Japan Versus the Allies.* Westport, Conn.: Praeger, 1995.

Liddel Hart, B. H. *The Revolution in Warfare.* London: Faber & Faber, 1946.

Lifton, Robert Jay, and Greg Mitchell. *Hiroshima in America: Fifty Years of Denial.* New York: G. P. Putnam's Sons, 1995.

MacEachin, Douglas J. *The Final Months of the War with Japan: Signal Intelligence, U.S. Invasion Planning, and the A-Bomb Decision.* Washington, D.C.: Center for the Study of Intelligence, 1998.

MacIsaac, David. *Strategic Bombing in World War II: The Story of the United States Strategic Bombing Survey.* New York: Garland, 1976.

Maddox, Robert J. *Weapons for Victory: The Hiroshima Decision Fifty Years Later.* Columbia: University of Missouri Press, 1995. Paperback reprint, 2004.

McCullough, David. *Truman.* New York: Simon & Schuster, 1992.

Miller, Edward S. *War Plan Orange: The U.S. Strategy to Defeat Japan, 1897–1945.* Annapolis, Md.: Naval Institute Press, 1991.

Mitchell, Christopher. "Ending Conflicts and Wars: Judgment, Rationality, and Entrapment." *International Social Science Journal* 43 (February 1991).

Mitchell, C. R., and Michael Nicholson. "Rational Models and the Ending of Wars." *Journal of Conflict Resolution* 27 (September 1983).

Morgan, Forrest. *Compellence and the Strategic Culture of Imperial Japan: Implications for Coercive Diplomacy in the Twenty-First Century.* Westport, Conn.: Praeger, 2003.

———. "Compellence and the Strategic Culture of Japan." Ph.D. diss., University of Maryland, 1998.

Morton, Louis. "The Decision to Use the Atomic Bomb." *Foreign Affairs* 35 (January 1957).

Moskin, J. Robert. *Mr. Truman's War.* New York: Random House, 1996.

Naimark, Norman M. "Cold War Studies and New Archival Materials on Stalin." *Russian Review* 61 (2002).

———. "Stalin and Europe in the Postwar Period, 1945–53: Issues and Problems." *Journal of Modern European History* 2 (2004).

Nakamura, Masanori. *The Japanese Monarchy: Ambassador Joseph Grew and the Making of the "Symbol Emperor System," 1931–1991.* Translated by Herbert P. Bix, Jonathan Baker-Bates, and Derek Bowen. Armonk, N.Y.: M. E. Sharpe, 1992.

Newman, Robert P. "Ending the War with Japan: Paul Nitze's 'Early Surrender' Counter Factual." *Pacific Historical Review* 64 (1995).

———. *Enola Gay and the Court of History.* New York: Peter Lang, 2004.

———. "Hiroshima and the Trashing of Henry Stimson." *New England Quarterly* 71 (March 1998).

———. *Truman and the Hiroshima Cult.* East Lansing: Michigan State University Press, 1995.

———. "What New Consensus?" *Washington Post,* November 30, 1994.

Offner, Arnold A. *Another Such Victory: President Truman and the Cold War, 1945–1953.* Stanford: Stanford University Press, 2002.

Overy, Richard. *Russia's War.* New York: Penguin Books, 1997.

Pape, Robert A. "The Air Force Strikes Back: A Reply to Barry Watts and John Warden." *Security Studies* 7 (Winter 1997–98).

———. *Bombing to Win: Air Power and Coercion in War.* Ithaca, N.Y.: Cornell University Press, 1996.

———. "Why Japan Surrendered." *International Security* 18 (Fall 1993).

Pearlman, Michael D. *Unconditional Surrender, Demobilization and the Atomic Bomb.* Fort Leavenworth, Kans.: Combat Studies Institute, U.S. Army Command and General Staff College, 1996.

Pechatnov, Vladimir. *The Big Three After World War II: New Documents on Soviet Thinking about Post-War Relations with the United States and Great Britain.* Cold War International History Project, Working Paper No. 13. Washington, D.C.: Woodrow Wilson International Center for Scholars, 1995.

Pegov, N. M. "Stalin on War with Japan, October 1941." *Soviet Studies in History* 24, no. 3 (1985–86).

Rees, David. *The Defeat of Japan.* Westport, Conn.: Praeger, 1997.

Sayle, Murray. "Letter from Hiroshima: Did the Bomb End the War?" *New Yorker*, July 31, 1995.

Sheldon, Charles. "Japanese Aggression and the Emperor, 1931–1941, from Contemporary Diaries." *Modern Asian Studies* 12 (February 1976).

———. "Scapegoat or Instigator of Japanese Aggression: Inoue Kiyoshi's Case against the Emperor." *Modern Asian Studies* 12 (February 1978).

Sherry, Michael S. "Patriotic Orthodoxy and American Decline." In David T. Linenthal and Tom Engelhardt, eds., *History Wars: The Enola Gay and Other Battles for the American Past.* New York: Holt, 1996.

Sherwin, Martin J. "Hiroshima as Politics and History." *Journal of American History* 82 (December 1995).

———. "Hiroshima at Fifty: The Politics of History and Memory." *IHJ Bulletin* [A Quarterly Publication of the International House of Japan] 15 (1995).

———. *A World Destroyed: The Atomic Bomb and the Grand Alliance.* New York: Knopf, 1975.

Sherwood, Robert E. *Roosevelt and Hopkins: An Intimate History.* New York: Harper, 1950.

Shtemenko, S. M. *The Soviet General Staff at War, 1941–1945.* Moscow: Progress Publishers, 1981.

Sigal, Leon V. *Fighting to a Finish: The Politics of War Termination in the United States and Japan, 1945.* Ithaca, N.Y.: Cornell University Press, 1988.

Skates, John Ray. *The Invasion of Japan: Alternative to the Bomb.* Columbia: University of South Carolina Press, 1994.

Slavinsky, Boris N. "The Soviet Occupation of the Kurile Islands and the Plans for the Capture of Northern Hokkaido." *Japan Forum*, April 1993.

———. *The Japanese-Soviet Neutrality Pact: A Diplomatic History, 1941–1945.* Translated by Geoffrey Jukes. New York: RoutledgeCurzon, 2005.

Smith, Robert Ross. *Triumph in the Philippines.* Washington, D.C.: Government Printing Office, 1963.

Stimson, Henry L., and McGeorge Bundy. *On Active Service in Peace and War.* New York: Harper, 1948.

Supreme Commander for the Allied Powers. *Reports of General MacArthur, prepared by his General Staff.* Editor in chief, Charles A. Willoughby. Vol. 2: *Japanese Operations in the Southwest Pacific Area, Compiled from Japanese Demobilization Bureau Records.* Washington, D.C.: Government Printing Office, 1966.

Takaki, Ronald. *Hiroshima: Why America Dropped the Atomic Bomb.* Boston: Little, Brown, 1995.

Togo, Shigenori. *The Cause of Japan.* Translated and edited by Togo Fumihiko and B. B. Blakeney. New York: Simon & Schuster, 1956.

Truman, Harry S. *Dear Bess: The Letters from Harry to Bess Truman, 1910–1959.* Edited by Robert H. Ferrell. New York: Norton, 1983.

————. *Memoirs.* Vol. 1: *1945, Year of Decisions.* Garden City, N.Y.: Doubleday, 1955. Reprint, New York: Signet Books, 1965.

————. *Off the Record: The Private Papers of Harry S. Truman.* Edited by Robert H. Ferrell. New York: Harper & Row, 1980.

United States. Department of the Army. Office of the Adjutant General. Statistical and Accounting Branch. *Army Battle Casualties and Nonbattle Deaths in World War II, Final Report, 7 December 1941–31 December 1946.* Washington D.C.: Government Printing Office, n.d.

————. Department of the Army. Office of the Chief of Military History. *Air Defense of the Homeland.* Japanese Monograph No. 25. 1952.

————. Department of Defense. *The Entry of the Soviet Union into the War Against Japan: Military Plans, 1941–1945.* Washington, D.C.: Government Printing Office, 1955.

————. Department of State. *The Conferences at Malta and Yalta, 1945.* Foreign Relations of the United States. Washington, D.C.: Government Printing Office, 1955.

————. Department of State. *The Conference of Berlin (Potsdam).* Foreign Relations of the United States. 2 vols. Washington, D.C.: Government Printing Office, 1960.

————. Department of State. *Conferences at Cairo and Teheran, 1943.* Foreign Relations of the United States. Washington, D.C.: Government Printing Office, 1961.

————. Department of State. *Foreign Relations of the United States, 1945, VI, Europe.* Washington, D.C.: Government Printing Office, 1969.

————. Strategic Bombing Survey. *Japan's Struggle to End the War.* Washington, D.C.: Government Printing Office, 1946.

————. Strategic Bombing Survey. *Japanese Air Power.* Washington, D.C.: Government Printing Office, 1946.

————. Strategic Bombing Survey. *Summary Report (Pacific War).* From the Chairman's Office. Washington, D.C.: Government Printing Office, 1946.

————. Strategic Bombing Survey. *The Effects of Strategic Bombing on Japan's Wartime Economy.* Washington, D.C.: Government Printing Office, 1946.

————. Strategic Bombing Survey. *The Effects of Strategic Bombing on Japanese Morale.* Washington, D.C.: Government Printing Office, 1947.

————. Strategic Bombing Survey. *Effects of Air Attack on Osaka-Kobe-Kyoto.* Washington, D.C.: Government Printing Office, 1947.

————. Strategic Bombing Survey. *Effects of Air Attack on Urban Complex Tokyo-Kawasaki-Yokohama.* Washington, D.C.: Government Printing Office, 1947.

————. Strategic Bombing Survey. *The Effects of Air Attacks on the City of Nagoya.* Washington, D.C.: Government Printing Office, 1947.

————. Strategic Bombing Survey. *The Effects of Bombing on Health and Medical Services in Japan.* Washington, D.C.: Government Printing Office, 1947.

————. Strategic Bombing Survey. *The War Against Japanese Transportation, 1941–1945.* Washington, D.C.: Government Printing Office, 1947.

Van Ree, Erik. *Socialism in One Zone: Stalin's Policy in Korea, 1945–1947.* Oxford: Berg, 1989.

Vigor, Peter. *Soviet Blitzkrieg Theory.* New York: St. Martin's Press, 1983.

Villa, Brian, and John Bonnet. "Understanding Indignation: Gar Alperovitz, Robert Maddox, and the Decision to Use the Atomic Bomb." *Reviews in American History* 24 (September 1996).

Wainstock, Dennis. *The Decision to Drop the Atomic Bomb.* Westport, Conn.: Praeger, 1996.

Walker, J. Samuel. "The Decision to Use the Bomb: A Historiography Update." *Diplomatic History* 14 (Winter 1990).

————. "The Decision to Use the Bomb: A Historiographical Update." In Michael Hogan, ed., *Hiroshima in History and Memory.* New York: Cambridge University Press, 1996.

————. "History, Collective Memory, and the Decision to Use the Bomb." In Michael Hogan, ed., *Hiroshima in History and Memory,* 197–199. New York: Cambridge University Press, 1996.

————. *Prompt and Utter Destruction: Truman and the Use of Atomic Bombs Against Japan.* Chapel Hill: University of North Carolina Press, 1997.

————. "Recent Literature on Truman's Atomic Bomb Decision: A Search for Middle Ground." *Diplomatic History* 19 (April 2005).

Wallace, Henry A. *The Price of Vision: The Diary of Henry A. Wallace, 1942–1946.* Edited by John Morton Blum. Boston: Houghton Mifflin, 1973.

War in Asia and the Pacific. Vol. 12: *Defense of the Homeland and End of the War.* New York: Garland, 1980.

Watts, Barry. "Ignoring Reality: Problems of Theory and Evidence in Security Studies." *Security Studies* 7 (Winter 1997–98).

Werth, Alexander. *Russia at War, 1941–1945.* London: Pan Books, 1964.

Westad, Odd Arne. *Cold War and Revolution: Soviet-American Rivalry and the Origins of the Chinese Civil War, 1944–1946.* New York: Columbia University Press, 1993.

Wetzler, Peter. *Hirohito and War: Imperial Tradition and Military Decisionmaking in Prewar Japan.* Honolulu: University of Hawai'i Press, 1998.

Wheeler-Bennett, John W., and Anthony Nicholls. *The Semblance of Peace: The Political Settlement After the Second World War.* London: Macmillan, 1972.

Williams, Robert Chadwell. *Klaus Fuchs, Atom Spy.* Cambridge, Mass.: Harvard University Press, 1987.

Zakharov, M. V., ed. *Finale: A Retrospective Review of Imperialist Japan's Defeat in 1945.* Moscow: Progress Publishers, 1972.

Zeller, Thomas. *Unconditional Defeat: Japan, America, and the End of World War II.* Wilmington, Del.: Scholarly Resources, 2004.

Zubok, Vladislav, and Constantine Pleshakov. *Inside the Kremlin's Cold War.* Cambridge, Mass.: Harvard University Press, 1996.

Sources in Russian

"Atomnye bombardirovki 1945." In *Voennyi Entsiklopedicheskii Slovar'*. 2nd ed. Moscow: Voenizdat, 1986.

Beria, Sergo. *Moi otets—Lavrentii Beria*. Moscow: Sovremennik, 1994.

Biulleten' Biuro informatsii TsK VKP(b): Voprosy vneshnei politiki, 1945, no. 13 (July 1).

Chuev, Feliks. *Sto sorok besed s Molotovym: Iz dnevnika F. Chueva*. Moscow: Terra, 1991.

Galenovich, Iu. M. *Rossiia—Kitai: shest' dogovorov*. Moscow: Muravei, 2003.

Galitskii, V. P., and V. P. Zimonin. "Desant na Khokkaido otmenit'." *Voenno-istoricheskii zhurnal*, 1994, no. 3.

Gibianskii, Leonid. "Sovetskie tseli v vostochnoi Evrope v kontse vtoroi mirovoi voiny i pervye poslevoennye gody." *Russian History / Histoire russe* 29, nos. 2–4 (Summer–Fall–Winter), 2002.

Gromyko, A. A. *Pamiatnoe*. 2nd ed. 2 vols. Moscow: Politizdat, 1990.

Gromyko, Anatolii. *Andrei Gromyko: V labirintakh Kremlia*. Moscow: Avtor, 1997.

Istoriia vtoroi mirovoi voiny, 1939–1945. Vol. 11. Moscow: Voenizdat, 1980.

Ivanov, S. P. "Iz opyta podgotovkii provedeniia Man'chzhurskoi operatsii 1945 goda," *Voennaia mysl'*, 1990, no. 8.

———, ed. *Nachal'nyi period voiny*. Moscow: Voenizdat, 1974.

Katasonova, E. L. *Iaponskie voennoplennye v SSSR*. Moscow: Kraft, 2003.

Krivosheev, G. F., ed. *Grif sekretnosti sniat*. Moscow: Voenizdat, 1993.

Maiskii, I. M. "O zhatel'nykh osnovakh budushchego mira." *Istochnik* 1995, no. 4 (17).

Miasnikov, V. S., ed. *Russko-kitaiskie otnosheniia v XX veke*. Vol. 4, bk. 1 (1937–1944) and bk. 2 (1945). Moscow: Pamiatniki istoricheskoi mysli, 2000.

Molotov, V. M. "Doklad V. M. Molotova na torzhestvennom zasedanii moskovskogo soveta 6-go noiabria 1945g." *Pravda*, November 7, 1945.

Pechatnov, Vladimir. "Soiuzniki nazhimaiiut na tebia dlia togo, chtoby slomit' u tebia voliu." *Istochnik* 38 (1999) no. 2.

Perepiska predsedatelia soveta ministrov SSSR s prezidentami SShA i premier-ministrami Velikobritanii vo vremia Velikoi otechestvennoi voiny 1941–1945 gg. Vol. 2. 2nd ed., Moscow: Politizdat, 1986.

Politburo TsK VKP(b) i sovet ministrov SSSR 1945–1953. Moscow: Rosspen, 2002.

Riabev, L. D., ed. *Atomnyi proekt SSSR*. Vol. 1, *1938–1945*. Part 1, Moscow: Nauka, Fizmatlit, 1998. Part 2, Moscow: MFTI, 2002.

———. *Atomnyi proekt SSSR: Dokumenty i materialy*. Vol. 2: *Atomnaia bomba, 1945–1954*, bk. 1. Moscow: Nauka, 1999.

Rzheshevskii, O. A. "Vizit A. Idena v Moskvu v dekabre 1941 g. i peregorova s I. V. Stalinym i V. M. Molotovym: Iz arkhiva prezidenta RF." *Novaia i noveishaia istoriia*, 1994, no. 3.

Safronov, Viacheslav P. *SSSR, SShA i Iaponskaia agressiia na Dal'nem vostoke i Tikhom Okeane. 1931–1945 gg*. Moscow: Institut Rossiiskoi istorii RAN, 2001.

Sevost'ianov, G. N. "Iaponiia 1945 g. v otsenke sovetskikh diplomatov, novye arkhivnye materialy." *Novaia i noveishaia istoriia*, 1995, no. 6.

Shtemenko, S. M. "Iz istorii razgroma Kvantunskoi armii." *Voenno-istoricheskii zhurnal*, 1967, nos. 4 and 5.

――――. *General'nyi shtab v gody voiny*. 2 vols. Moscow: Voenizdat, 1985.

Slavinskii, B. N. *Ialtinskaia konferentsiia i problema "severnykh territorii."* Moscow: Novina, 1996.

――――. *Pakt o neitralitete mezhdu SSSR i Iaponiei: Diplomaticheskaia istoriia, 1941–1945 gg.* Moscow: TOO Novina, 1995.

――――. *Sovetskaia okkupatsiia Kuril'skikh ostrovov (avgust–sentiabr' 1945 goda)*. Moscow: Lotos, 1993.

――――. *SSSR i Iaponiia—na puti k voine: Diplomaticheskaia istoriia, 1937–1945 gg.* Moscow: ZAO "Iaponiia segodnia," 1999.

Sovetskii Soiuz na mezhdunarodnykh konferentsiiakh perioda velikoi otechestvennoi voiny, 1941–1945 gg. Vol. 4: *Berlinskaia (Potsdamskaia) konferentsiia rukovoditelei trekh soiuznykh derzhav—SSSR, SShA i Velikobritanii, 17 iulia–2 avgusta 1945 g.: Sbornik dokumentov*. Moscow: Izd-vo puliticheskoi literatury, 1980.

Sovetsko-amerikanskie otnosheniia vo vremia Velikoi Otechestvennoi voiny, 1941–1945: Dokumenty i materialy. 2 vols. Moscow: Politizdat, 1984.

Trukhanovskii, V. G. *Angliiskoe iadernoe oruzhie*. Moscow: Mezhdunarodnye otnosheniia, 1985.

Vasilevskii, A. *Delo vsei zhizni*. Moscow: Politizdat, 1974.

――――. "Final." *Voenno-istoricheskii zhurnal* 1967, no. 6.

Zhukov, G. K., *Vospominaniia i razmyshleniia*. Vol. 3. Moscow: Novosti, 1990.

"Za kulisami tikhookeanskoi bitvy." *Vestnik ministerstva innostrannykh del SSSR*, 1990, no. 49.

"Zaniat'sia podgotovkoi," *Istochniki*, 1995, no. 4.

Zimonin, V. P. *Poslednyi ochag vtoroi mirovoi* voiny. Moscow, 2002.

Zolotarev, V. A., ed. *Sovetsko-iaponskaia voina 1945 goda: Istoriia voenno-politicheskogo protivoborstva dvukh derzhav v 30–40e gody. Russkii Arkhiv: Velikaia otechestvennaia*, vols. 7 (1) and (2). Moscow: Terra, 1997, 2000.

――――. *Velikaia otechestvennaia voina, 1941–1945*. Vol. 3. Moscow: Nauka, 1999.

Sources in Japanese

Arai Shin'ichi. *Dainiji sekai taisen*. Tokyo: Tōkyō Daigaigaku shuppankai, 1973.

――――. *Genbaku tōka e no michi*. Tokyo: Tōkyō Daigaku shuppankai, 1985.

Arisue Seizō. *Shūsen hishi: Arisue kikanchō no shuki*. Tokyo: Fuyō shobō, 1976.

Asada Sadao. "Genbaku tōka no shōgeki to kōhuku no kettei." In Hosoya Chihiro, Irie Akira, Gotō Kan'ichi, and Hatano Sumio, eds., *Taiheiyō sensō no shūketsu*. Tokyo: Kashiwa shobō, 1997.

Awaya Kentarō, ed. *Kido Kōichi jinmon chōsho*. Tokyo: Ōtsuski shoten, 1987.

Bōeichō Bōeikenshūjo Senshishitsu. *Senshi sōsho: Daihonei rikugunbu*. Vol. 10: *Shōwa 20 nen 8 gatsu made*. Tokyo: Asagumo shinbunsha, 1975.

――――. *Senshi sōsho: Hokutō hōmen rikugun sakusen*. Vol. 2: *Chishima, Karafuto, Hokkaidō no bōei*. Tokyo: Asagumo shinbunsha, 1971.

――――. *Senshi sōsho: Hondo kessen junbi*. Vol. 2: *Kyūshū no bōei*, Tokyo: Asagumo shinbunsha, 1972.

————. *Senshi sōsho: Hondo bōkū sakusen.* Tokyo: Asagumo shinbunsha, 1968.

————. *Senshi sōsho: Kantōgun.* Vol. 2: *Kantokuen, Shūsenji no taiso sen.* Tokyo: Asagumo shinbunsha, 1974.

Butow, Robert J. C. *Shūshen gaishi: Mujōken kōfuku made no keii.* Translated by Ōi Atsushi. Tokyo: Jiji tsūshinsha, 1958.

Chimoto Hideki. *Tennōsei no shinryaku sekinin to sengo sekinin.* Tokyo: Aoki Shoten, 1990.

Fujita Hisanori. *Jijūchō no kaisō.* Tokyo: Kōdansha, 1960. Reprinted in 1987 by Chūōkōronsha.

Gaimushō, ed. *Gaikō shiryō: Nisso gaikō kōshō kiroku no bu.* Tokyo: Gaimushō, 1946.

————. *Shūsen shiroku.* 2 vols. Tokyo: Shinbun gekkansha, 1952.

————. *Shūsen shiroku.* 6 vols. Tokyo: Hokuyōsha, 1977.

Gunji Shigakukai, ed. *Sanbō honbu sensōshidō han: Kimitsu sensō nisshi.* 2 vols. Tokyo: Kinseisha, 1999.

————. *Miyazaki Shūichi chūjō nisshi.* Tokyo: Kinseisha, 2004.

Handō Toshikazu. *Nihon no ichiban nagai hi.* Edited by Ōya Sōichi. Tokyo: Bungei shunjū, 1973.

Haslam, Jonathan. "Soren no tainichi gaikō to sansen." In Hosoya Chihiro et al., *Taiheiyō sensō no shūketsu.* Tokyo: Kashiwa shobō, 1997.

Hata Ikuhiko. *Shōwa tennō itsutsu no ketsudan.* Tokyo: Bungei shunjū, 1994.

Hatano Sumio. "'Kokutai goji' to Potsudamu sengen." *Gaikō jihō,* no. 1320 (1995).

————. "Mujōken kōfuku to nihon." *Keiō Daigaku Hōgaku Kenkyūkai, Hōgaku kenkyū* 73, no. 1 (2000).

Hattori Takushirō. *Daitōa sensō zenshi.* 8 vols. Tokyo: Masu shobō, 1953–56; one vol. reprint, Tokyo: Hara shobō, 1965.

Hayashi Shigeru. "Taiso kōsaku no tenkai." In Nihon Gaikō Gakkai, *Taiheiyō sensō shūketsu ron.* Tokyo: Tōkyō Daigaku shuppankai, 1958.

Hayashi Shigeru, ed. *Nihon shūsenshi.* 3 vols. Tokyo: Yomiuri shinbunsha, 1962.

Higashikuni Naruhiko. *Higashikuni nikki.* Tokyo: Tokuma shoten, 1968.

Hirota Kōki Denki Kankōkai, ed., *Hirota Kōki.* Tokyo: Hirota Kōki Denki Kankōkai, 1966.

Hoshina Zenshirō. *Taiheiyō sensō hishi.* Tokyo: Hara shobō, 1975.

Hosokawa Morisada. *Jōhō tennō ni tassezu: Hosokawa nikki.* 2 vols. Tokyo: Dōkōsha Isobe shobō, 1953. Reprinted as *Hosokawa nikki.* Tokyo: Chūōkōronsha, 1979.

Hosoya Chihiro. *Ryōtaisenkanki no Nihon gaikō.* Tokyo: Iwanami shoten, 1988.

————. "Sangoku dōmei to nisso chūritsu jōyaku." In Rekishigaku Kenkyūkai, *Taiheiyō sensō eno michi: Kaisen gaikōshi,* vol. 5: *Sangoku dōmei, nisso chūritsu jōyaku.* Tokyo: Asahi shinbunsha, 1987.

Hosoya Chihiro, Irie Akira, Gōtō Ken'ichi, and Hatano Sumio, eds. *Taiheiyō sensō no shūketsu.* Tokyo: Kashiwa shobō, 1997.

Ikeda Sumihisa. *Nihon no magarikado.* Tokyo: Chishiro shuppan, 1968.

Iokibe Makoto. *Beikoku no nihon senryō seisaku.* 2 vols. Tokyo: Chūōkōronsha, 1985.

Ishida Takeshi. *Hakyoku to Heiwa.* Tōkyō Daigaku shuppankai, 1968.

Itō Takashi, ed. *Takagi Sōkichi: nikki to jōhō.* 2 vols. Tokyo: Misuzu shobō, 2000.

Itō Takashi and Watanabe Yukio, eds. *Shigemitsu mamoru shuki.* Tokyo: Chūōkōronsha, 1986.

——. *Zoku Shigemitsu mamoru shuki.* Tokyo: Chūōkōronsha, 1988.

Kawabe Torashirō. *Kawabe Torashirō kaikoroku.* Tokyo: Jiji tsūshinsha, 1979.

——. "Sanbōjichō no nisshi." In *Kawabe Torashirō Kaisōroku.* Tokyo: Manichi shinbunsha, 1979.

Kido Kōichi Kenkyūkai, ed. *Kido Kōichi nikki.* 2 vols. Tokyo: Tōkyō Daigaku shuppankai, 1966.

——. *Kido Kōichi kankei bunsho.* Tokyo: Tōkyō Daigaku shppankai, 1966.

——. *Kido Kōichi nikki: Tōkyō saibanki.* Tokyo: Tōkyō Daigaku shuppankai, 1980.

Kirichenko, Aleksei. "Hakkutsu: KGB himitsu bunsho: Sutârin shūnen no tainichi sansen, sore wa shino tetsudōkara hajimatta." *This Is Yomiuri,* December 1992.

Kōketsu Atsushi. *Nihon kaigun no shūsen kōsaku.* Tokyo: Chūōkōronsha, 1996.

Kurihara Ken. *Tennō: shōwashi oboegaki.* Tokyo: Yūshindō, 1956.

Kurihara Ken, and Hatano Sumio, eds. *Shūsen kōsaku no kiroku.* 2 vols. Tokyo: Kōdansha, 1986.

Matsutani Makoto. *Daitōa Sensō shūshū no shinsō.* Tokyo: Fuyō shobō, 1980.

Miyake Masaki et al., eds. *Shōwashi no gunbu to seiji.* Vol. 4. Tokyo: Daiichi hōki, 1983.

Morishima, Gorō. "Kunō suru chūso taishikan." In Morishima Yasuhiko, *Shōwa no dōran to Morishima Gorō no shōgai.* Tokyo: Ashi shobō, 1975.

Naiseishi Kenkyūkai and Nihon Kindai Shiryō Kenkyūkai, eds. *Ōkura Kinmochi nikki.* Tokyo, 1971.

Naka Akira. *Mokusatsu.* 2 vols. Tokyo: NHK Books, 2000.

NHK Nisso purojekuto. *Korega soren no tainichi gaikō da: hiroku, Hoppōryōdo.* Tokyo: NHK, 1991.

Nihon Gaikō Gakkai, ed. *Taiheiyō sensō shūketsu ron.* Tokyo: Tōkyō Daigaku shuppankai, 1958.

Nishihara Masao [Kōseishō Hikiage Engokyoku Shiryōshitsu]. *Shūsen no keii.* 2 vols. Typewritten manuscript in possession of Hatano Sumio and Kurihara Ken, n.d.

Nishijima Ariatsu. *Genbaku wa naze tōka saretaka: Nihon kōfuku o meguru senryaku to gaikō.* Tokyo: Aoki shoten, 1985.

Okabe Nagaakira. *Aru jijū no kaisōroku.* Tokyo: Asahi sonorama, 1990.

Ōki Misao. *Ōki nikki.* Tokyo: Asahi shinbunsha, 1969.

Rekishigaku Kenkyūkai. *Taiheiyō sensōshi: Taiheiyō sensō.* 6 vols. Tokyo: Aoki shoten, 1973.

Sakomizu Hisatsune. *Dainihon teikoku saigo no 4-kagetsu.* Tokyo: Oriento shobō, 1973.

——. *Kikanjū ka no shūshō kantei.* Tokyo: Kōbunsha, 1964.

——. *Kōfukuji no shinsō.* Tokyo: Jiyū kokuminsha, February 1946.

——. *Shūsen no shinsō.* Tokyo: privately printed, n.d. [1955?].

Sanbō Honbu shozō, ed. *Haisen no kiroku.* Tokyo: Hara shobō, 1989.

Satō Motoei and Kurosawa Fumitaka, eds. *GHQ Rekishika Chinjutsu Roku: Shūsen shiryō.* 2 vols. Tokyo: Hara shobō, 1999.

Satō Naotake. *Kaiko hachijū-nen.* Tokyo: Jiji tsūshinsha, 1964.

Shigemitsu Mamoru. *Shōwa no dōran.* 2 vols. Tokyo: Chūōkōronsha, 1952.

Shimomura Kainan (Hiroshi). *Shūsenki.* Tokyo: Kamakura bunko, 1948.

——. *Shūsen hishi.* Tokyo: Kōdansha, 1950.

Suzuki Hajime, ed. *Suzuki Kantarō Jiden.* Tokyo: Jiji tsūshinsha, 1968.

Suzuki Kantarō. *Shūsen no hyōjō.* Tokyo: Rōdō bunkasha, 1946.

Tajiri Akiyoshi. *Tajiri Akiyoshi kaisōroku.* Tokyo: Hara shobō, 1980.

Takagi Sōkichi. *Shūsen Oboegaki.* Tokyo: Kōbundō, 1948.

———. *Takagi kaigun shōshō oboegaki.* Tokyo: Mainichi shinbunsha, 1979.

Takagi Sōkichi and Sanematsu Yuzuru, eds. *Kaigun taishō Yonai Mitsumasa oboegaki.* Tokyo: Kōjinsha, 1978.

Takamatsunomiya Nobuhito. *Takamatsunomiya nikki.* Vol. 8. Tokyo: Chūōkōronsha, 1997.

Takayama Shinobu, ed. *Arao Okikatsu-san o shinobu.* Privately printed, 1978.

Tanaka Nobumasa. *Dokyumento shōwa tennō 5, Haisen.* Vol. 2. Tokyo: Ryokufū shuppan, 1988.

Tanemura Suketaka. *Daihon'ei kimitsu nisshi.* Tokyo: Fuyō shobō, 1995.

Terasaki Hidenari and Miller, Mariko Terasaki, eds. *Shōwa Tennō dokuhakuroku—Terasaki Hidenari, Goyōgakari nikki.* Tokyo: Bungei shunjū, 1990.

Tōgō Shigehiko. *Sofu Tōgō Shigenori no shōgai.* Tokyo: Bungei shunjū, 1993.

Tōgō Shigenori. *Jidai no ichimen.* Tokyo: Kaizōsha, 1952. Reprinted as *Tōgō shigenori gaikōshuki: Jidai no ichimen.* Tokyo: Hara shobō, 1989.

Tominaga Kengo, ed. *Gendaishi shiryō.* Vol. 39: *Taiheiyō sensō,* pt. 5. Tokyo: Misuzu shobō, 1975.

Tomita Kenji. *Haisen Nihon no uchigawa.* Tokyo: Kokon shoin, 1962.

Tōyama Shigeki, Imai Seiichi, and Fujiwara Akira. *Shōwashi.* Rev. ed. Tokyo: Iwanami shoten, 1959.

Toyoda Soemu. *Saigo no teikoku kaigun.* Tokyo: Sekai no nihonsha, 1950.

Wada Haruki. "Nisso sensō." In Hara Teruyuki and Togawa Tsuguo, eds., *Kōza Surabu no sekai,* vol. 8: *Surabu to nihon.* Tokyo: Kōbundō, 1995.

Yamada Akira. *Shōwa Tennō no sensō shidō.* Tokyo: Shōwa shuppan, 1990.

Yamada Akira and Kōketsu Atsushi. *Ososugita seidan: Shōwa Tennō no sensō shidō to sensō sekinin.* Tokyo, 1991.

Yokote Shinji. "Dainiji taisenki no soren no tainich seisaku." Keiō Daigaku Hōgaku Kenkyūkai. *Hōgaku kenkyū* 71, no. 1 (1998).

Yomiuri shinbunsha, ed. *Shōwashi no Tennō.* 30 vols. Tokyo: Yomiuri shinbunsha, 1968.

Yoshida Yutaka. *Shōwa tennō no shūsenshi.* Tokyo: Iwanami shoten, 1992.

Index

In this index an "f" after a number indicates a separate reference on the next page, and an "ff" indicates separate references on the next two pages. A continuous discussion over two or more pages is indicated by a span of page numbers, e.g., "57–59."

Stanford Nuclear Age Series

General Editor, Martin Sherwin

The End of the Pacific War: Reappraisals. Edited by Tsuyoshi Hasegawa. 2007.

Eisenhower, Science Advice, and the Nuclear Test-Ban Debate, 1945–1963. Benjamin P. Greene. 2006.

A World Destroyed: Hiroshima and Its Legacies, 3rd edition. Martin Sherwin. 2003

Averting 'The Final Failure': John F. Kennedy and the Secret Cuban Missile Crisis Meetings. Sheldon M. Stern. 2003.

The Struggle Against the Bomb, volume 3: *Toward Nuclear Abolition, A History of the World Nuclear Disarmament Movement, 1971–Present.* Lawrence S. Wittner. 2003.

Another Such Victory: President Truman and the Cold War, 1945–1953. Arnold A. Offner. 2002.

Einstein and Soviet Ideology. Alexander Vucinich. 2001.

Cardinal Choices: Presidential Science Advising from the Atomic Bomb to SDI. Revised and expanded edition. Gregg Herken. 2000.

'The Fate of the Earth' and 'The Abolition.' Jonathan Schell. With a new introduction by the author. 2000.

The Struggle Against the Bomb, volume 2: *Resisting the Bomb, A History of the World Nuclear Disarmament Movement, 1954–1970.* Lawrence S. Wittner. 1997.

James B. Conant: Harvard to Hiroshima and the Making of the Nuclear Age. James G. Hershberg. 1993.

The Struggle Against the Bomb, volume 1: *One World or None, A History of the World Nuclear Disarmament Movement Through 1953.* Lawrence S. Wittner. 1993.

A Preponderance of Power: National Security, the Truman Administration, and the Cold War. Melvyn P. Leffler. 1992.

The Wizards of Armageddon. Fred Kaplan. New foreword by Martin J. Sherwin. 1983. Reissued 1991.

Robert Oppenheimer: Letters and Recollections. Edited by Alice Kimball Smith and Charles Weiner. New foreword by Martin J. Sherwin. 1980. Reissued 1995.

The Advisors: Oppenheimer, Teller, and the Superbomb. By Herbert F. York. With a new Preface and Epilogue. Historical essay by Hans A. Bethe. 1976. Reissued 1989.

The Voice of the Dolphins and Other Stories. Leo Szilard. 1961. Reissued 1991.

Atomic Energy for Military Purposes. Henry D. Smith. Preface by Philip Morrison. 1945. New foreword 1989.